Hanging without a Rope

EDITORS

Sherry B. Ortner, Nicholas B. Dirks, Geoff Eley

PRINCETON STUDIES IN
CULTURE / POWER / HISTORY

Hanging without a Rope

NARRATIVE EXPERIENCE IN COLONIAL

AND POSTCOLONIAL KAROLAND

Mary Margaret Steedly

PRINCETON UNIVERSITY PRESS

PRINCETON, NEW JERSEY

Library of Congress Cataloging-in-Publication Data

Steedly, Mary Margaret, 1946–
Hanging without a rope : narrative experience in colonial and
postcolonial Karoland / Mary Margaret Steedly.
p.   cm. — (Princeton studies in culture/power/history)
Includes bibliographical references and index.

ISBN 0-691-09461-6 (cloth : acid-free paper)
ISBN 0-691-00045-X (pbk. : acid-free paper)
1. Karo-Batak (Indonesian people)   2. Karo-Batak (Indonesian
people)—Religion.   3. Karo-Batak (Indonesian people)—Folklore.
I. Title.   II. Series.
DS632.K3S74   1993
305.8'009598'1—dc20   93-3779 CIP

This book has been composed in Adobe Sabon and Adobe Optima

Princeton University Press books are printed on acid-free paper
and meet the guidelines for permanence and durability of the
Committee on Production Guidelines for Book Longevity of
the Council on Library Resources

Printed in the United States of America

1   3   5   7   9   10   8   6   4   2

1   3   5   7   9   10   8   6   4   2
(pbk.)

For my mother, Margaret Steedly Hemingway

and my brother, John Wesley Steedly

Contents

Illustrations

Acknowledgments

STORYTELLING is easy to start but hard to finish. So thanks are due first to the family members, friends, and colleagues whose persistent inquiries ("Is it done yet?") finally convinced me that, completeness being in any event unattainable, there is much to be said for simply being done. I single out in particular Michael Herzfeld and Ken George, with gratitude for their enthusiasm and impatience.

It is perhaps in the processes of writing and revision that one begins to recognize the amount of intellectual indebtedness that underwrites any authorial voice. Among those teachers whose thought and exemplary guidance have shaped my work, here and elsewhere, are: James Peacock, who introduced me to anthropology and to the textures of Indonesian city life; Daniel Patterson, whose meticulous scholarship taught me to attend carefully to the song and the story in the text; Sherry Ortner, who showed me the necessity of attending to gender in every detail of social analysis; Christopher Davis, who demonstrated how ethically charged the mutually imbricated practices of writing, teaching, and ethnographic fieldwork were, and what, at its best, anthropology could aspire to; and especially Michael Taussig, whose influence should be recognized throughout this present work.

I was first drawn to anthropology by the essays of Clifford Geertz; as an anthropologist of Indonesian societies I owe him a special debt. Directly and indirectly his writings have profoundly shaped studies of the region, including this one. Nicholas Dirks started me thinking about the relation between history and anthropology; Susan Harding, Lou Roberts, and Joan Scott showed me how important feminist theory could be in intersecting those disciplines.

Other friends and teachers who have contributed, directly or indirectly, to this project include Lawrence Cohen, Lindsay French, Ken George, Byron Good, Laurie Hart, Rita Kipp, Arthur Kleinman, Jennifer Krier, Terry O'Nell, John Pemberton, Elliott Shore, Patsy Spyer, Katie Stewart, Anna Tsing, and Debbie Tooker, whose helpful comments helped straighten out a particularly troublesome chapter. Masri Singarimbun, whose own exemplary ethnographic study guided me through the practical intricacies of Karo kinship, kindly read and commented on an earlier version of this work. Philip Yampolsky has helped in a multitude of ways, from guiding me around Medan's public transportation system, to counting the number of leaves in a betel packet (see chapter 6), to providing ethnomusicological advice, instant spell-check, and a close critical reading of portions of the manuscript.

My colleagues at Harvard have been consistently supportive of this project. Many of my students there have also (though not necessarily by choice) read sections of this work. Their comments, not to mention the inspiration and challenge that I have gained from them, have been of immense value to me. In particular, I gratefully acknowledge here the contributions of the students in my seminar on "Gender and Subjectivity" to the theoretical argument presented in chapter 1 of this book. Rebecca Grow has helped in many ways with the details of manuscript preparation, including careful copyediting and proofreading. Alexandra Guisinger and Bart Ryan assisted in the preparation of the book's index.

Princeton University Press editor Mary Murrell has facilitated the book's completion in a number of ways, not least being her encouragement through an overlong process of revision. Series editors Sherry Ortner and Nicholas Dirks have been enthusiastic and supportive guides from the beginning of this project. James Boon and an anonymous reader carefully reviewed an earlier version of this text for the Press; much more of their invaluable criticisms and comments have been incorporated into the present work than they may recognize. I also thank Maria denBoer for her meticulous and nonintrusive copyediting.

The fieldwork on which this book is based was carried out in North Sumatra, Indonesia, between February 1983 and December 1985. This research was supported by grants from the Fulbright-Hays Doctoral Research Abroad Program, the Social Science Research Council and American Council of Learned Societies, and the Rackham Graduate School of the University of Michigan. It was conducted under the auspices of the Lembaga Ilmu Pengetahuan Indonesia (LIPI, the Indonesian Institute of Science) and was sponsored locally by the Universitas Sumatera Utara. I would like to express my appreciation to all these institutions for their generous support.

In Indonesia, my first thanks must go to the faculty and students of the Department of Anthropology and the Faculty of Letters at USU; and to Patricia Sharpe, formerly of the U.S. Consulate in Medan, who did much to make the initial part of my stay there comfortable and easy. My deepest appreciation goes to my adopted parents, Bapa Petrus Sitepu and Nandé Petrus beru Ginting; to my adopted brother and sisters, Petrus, Nova, Cicik, and Linsi; and to all my Karo relatives who so generously accepted me as their sister, daughter, granddaughter, niece, or cousin. I also thank my Karo neighbors in Padang Bulan, who welcomed me into their community, and the many Karo families I visited in Medan and in Taneh Karo, whose generosity and consideration never failed. I am especially grateful to the members of the group I have called the Arisan of "Simpang

Meriah" (a pseudonym), who invited me to their rituals and talked with me about their experiences. In Berastagi, Pa Ngajar Bana Purba introduced me to the former organizers of Persadan Merga Si Lima and helped arrange a meeting with them; Belat Ginting provided the photograph of Merga Si Lima's first annual procession from his personal collection. For their hospitality, I thank Bapa and Nandé Juara in Medan (also Ipin, Alex, and Nelson); Bapa and Nandé Ernalem (also Hanna, Dalan, Amin, and Apen) in Berastagi; Bapa and Nandé Dixon, also in Berastagi; Bapa and Nandé Perulihen, and Bapa and Nandé Surya in Beganding and Pertomas; Bapa Sanggup and Nandé Perdamén in Tiga Nderket.

Rizaldi Siagian, Endo Suanda, and Philip Yampolsky of the Ethnomusicology Department of USU assisted, at various times, in recording Karo musical performances; the photograph of a Karo betel-seller's stall was taken for this book by Endo Suanda. Along with Rita Kipp and Susan Rodgers, they all offered helpful advice, friendship, and assistance during my time in North Sumatra.

My friends and fellow anthropology students of the "Si Baso Group"— Boni Tarigan, Aman Saragih, Rolexon Napitupulu, Astina br. Sebayang, and Ernalem br. Bangun—all participated in this research project, and I gratefully acknowledge their contributions. Juara Rimantha Ginting, who accompanied me throughout this research, deserves special thanks for his assistance, comments, and criticism. His own thesis (Drs. Anthropology, USU), "Pandangan tentang Gangguan Jiwa dan Penanggulangannya secara Tradisional pada Masyarakat Karo" ("Traditional Perceptions of Mental Illness and Therapy in Karo Society"), derives in part from our work together.

Bapa Surya Ginting of Pertomas and the late Bapa Sanggup Peranginangin of Tiga Nderket talked to me at length about Karo culture and, in their very different ways, exemplified to me the best of that culture. It has been both a pleasure and a privilege to know them and to learn from them.

Finally, a word of special appreciation to my mother, Margaret Steedly Hemingway, and my brother, John Wesley Steedly, to whom this book is dedicated, with much love, for their patience and support.

Some Notes on Language, Translation, and Orthography

IN SUMATRA the language issue is exceptionally complex. In this book I distinguish wherever possible between bahasa Indonesia, the contemporary national language of Indonesia, and the indigenous Malay language of the east coast of Sumatra, of which the national language is a (significantly modified) dialect. A simplified version of Malay was also the colonial lingua franca of the Netherlands East Indies. Thus by "Malay" I mean either the indigenous Sumatran dialect or the colonial lingua franca; likewise by "Indonesian" I mean either the present-day formal language of education, the media, and public speeches, or the specifically nationalist terminology introduced into the language during the revolution (what Benedict Anderson has called "revolutionary Malay"). A further difficulty is posed by local variations in dialect Indonesian, which I reference as "Malay/Indonesian." For example, in standard Indonesian the kin term *kakak* means "elder sibling (regardless of sex)." In North Sumatra, however, *kakak* refers specifically to a *female* elder sibling. (Curiously, the Karo cognate *kaka* means "elder sibling of either sex," as in standard Indonesian.)

The Karo language is one of a group of related though more or less mutually unintelligible languages categorized as "Batak." Karo is closer to Malay than are the other Batak languages, but these two languages are mutually unintelligible as well. They do share a basic syntactic structure as well as a number of etymological cognates (which do not necessarily coincide semantically). In such cases, or when the linguistic context of a statement is otherwise unclear, parenthetical notations indicate the language used, such as *keramat* (K.) or *keramat* (M./Arabic).

In the Karo language, but not in Indonesian/Malay, I distinguish between the mid-central vowel "e" (as in unemphatic English "the") and the mid-front "é" (as in English "play"). Otherwise I follow the new Indonesian orthography (*ejaan baru*) in Karo as well as Indonesian/Malay. Except in the case of proper names or in quoted material that follows the older orthographic conventions, I use the new orthography in all these languages. Thus, for example, I follow the original Dutch text in writing a Karo woman's name "Amei Kata Mehoeli" but elsewhere render that name as "Amé Kata Mehuli." Likewise, the provincial capital of the Karo highland district, spelled "Kabandjahe" according to the old orthography on the regional map (p. 46) is given elsewhere in the current spelling "Kabanjahé."

Karo sometimes say that their language sounds like Italian; in any event, the trilled "r" is relatively more pronounced, and syllabic stress more marked, than in standard Indonesian or Sumatran Malay, which pronunciation it otherwise resembles. In these languages light stress is usually placed on a word's penultimate syllable, unless it contains the mid-central vowel "e", in which case emphasis shifts to the final syllable. "C" is pronounced "ch" as in English "church."

Punctuation and division in transcribed speech are always approximate. Paragraphing in extended quotations is intended to increase the readability of the text's English translation, rather than to indicate anything about the form of the original narrative. An exception to this may be noted in the long story told by the man I call "Selam Ginting" in chapter 4. Here the speaker (as may be noted in my translation) in a sense made his own paragraph breaks by inserting appropriate audience responses of *ué* (K., "yes") into his narration—something like an encouraging "uh-huh" in English.

Karo etiquette prohibits one from speaking the personal name of one's elder, especially in the case of a kinsperson. Thus Karo use a system of teknonyms. After the birth of a couple's first child (whether male or female), the father and mother are known respectively as Bapa X and Nandé (or Amé) X. After the birth of their first grandchild they would be referred to by that child's name as Nini (grandparent) Y. However, Karo are more properly addressed by the relevant kinship term. The reader should keep in mind that Karo kin terms are rather broadly applied, and politeness prohibits asking whether, for example, a particular "bapa" referred to is the speaker's actual father, a father's brother, or a distant clanmate.

Kinship terms are given in the standard anthropological abbreviations, as follows:

B = brother	M = mother
D = daughter	S = son
F = father	W = wife
H = husband	Z = sister

In combination, terms should be read sequentially; for example, MBD = mother's brother's daughter. Kin terms in the text are given in rough equivalent translation with the kinship designation(s) in parentheses. Thus: uncle (*bapa nguda*, younger FB); auntie (*bibi*, HM, FZ, or MZ). Where specific relatives are intended I have indicated those.

All translations are my own. A glossary of foreign terms and phrases follows the notes.

Hanging without a Rope

Prologue

"THESE *nini*s of ours, the ones from the mountain," Nandé Randal said, using the polite term of address, nini (grandparent), for the spirits, "they care for traders. But for farmers, not at all." She was speaking from experience. Nandé Randal had been a spirit medium and curer for more than forty years and, until recently, a vegetable trader, first in the market town of Berastagi in the Karo highlands and then, after the end of the Indonesian Revolution in 1950, in the huge Central Market in the city of Medan, the sprawling, dusty capital of the province of North Sumatra. With the help of the spirits, she and her husband had done well enough financially to invest in a fleet of minibuses. But their children had squandered their money, and finally the buses had to be sold off. Now they were scraping by, without the spirits' help, on a ragged little farm just outside the city.

A slender, delicate-looking woman in her early sixties, dressed for work in patched trousers far too big for her but with her head neatly turbaned in a bright blue checked sarong, Nandé Randal was weeding her peanut patch when my co-worker Juara Ginting and I arrived for a visit. She greeted us cheerily and took a break from her work. Not far away, in a snarl of purposeful movement, the ordinary agitations of the city continued.

To get to Nandé Randal's farm, you take one of the multitude of bright yellow minibuses—known locally as sudakos—traveling noisily southward with klaxons blaring and rock-and-roll blasting from tinny speakers, along the congested road cutting through Padang Bulan, the city's Karo district. Built in the early years of Dutch colonial consolidation to link the urban administrative center of Medan with the newly conquered Karo highlands, the road has always been called the Berastagi highway, but it is now formally named Jalan Kapitan Pattimura, after a Moluccan hero of the anticolonial struggle; in the years following the Bandung Conference of nonaligned nations in 1956, it was known for a time as Jalan Patrice Lumumba. A major transport artery, it is usually packed with the ubiquitous sudakos and with larger buses painted to resemble (or so I imagined) some wild cross between a garish Chinese dragon and a Kwakiutl mask. Packs of schoolchildren, whose neat uniforms and well-shined shoes quickly grey with the dust and soot of passing vehicles, dawdle along the roadside and stray into traffic lanes. Traffic is slowed further by pushcart peddlers, bicycle-riding traders heading to the several markets along the road, and the occasional plodding buffalo-drawn cart.

Between these slip sedate Vespa-riding couples and young daredevil mo-
torcyclists racing against time and fate, darting around slower vehicles,
pedestrians, and the larger of the numerous potholes that lace the road.
Buses jerk to frequent, sudden stops, picking up or disgorging passengers,
accompanied by shrieks and complaints from the jolted riders within and
by the conductor's shouts, rapid and rhythmic as an auctioneer's chant,
announcing the vehicle's route and destination. At markets and major
intersections the road is often blocked by sudakos double- and triple-
parked, each hoping to take on a full load of passengers before being
forced to continue on its way. There too the road is narrowed by peddlers
who have set up temporary shop on its dusty shoulder, which otherwise
serves as a passing lane: noodle- and cake-vendors with their bicycle
carts; fruit and vegetable sellers—many of them wearing *tudung*, the distinctive flat, pillow-shaped turban of coarse dark-red cloth worn by Karo
women—squatting behind small piles of produce; itinerant cobblers,
tinkers, eyeglass-repairers, and hawkers of cigarettes, candy, and cheap
household miscellany.

Past the markets the traffic thins and the sudakos pick up speed, ca-
reening down the road and around one another in a race for the next
waiting fare, past scattered shops, houses and tiny rice fields, churches
and mosques, schools and medical clinics. Tall coconut palms, darkly
fringed against the sky, conjure up imaginary oases of shade against what
Karo, waxing nostalgic for their chilly mountain homeland, describe in
song as the "unsurpassed swelter" of the lowlands.

If you followed the road farther, it would twist through steep forested
inclines and across fertile plateaus, past the tall volcano Mount Sibayak
with its broken cone buried in the clouds; then, just beyond the mountain
and about an hour after your departure from Medan, another short,
sharp incline would take you onto the broad plateau that is the Karo
homeland, *Taneh Karo Si Malem*, the cool lands of Karo, and into the
busy market and tourist town of Berastagi. But to reach Nandé Randal's
farm, you only go to the outskirts of Medan, then change buses, paying
a second fare for the short distance to the Chinese graveyard on the edge
of the town of Pancur Batu. Behind the graveyard is a long, untended
footpath, and at the end of that path and through an overgrown hedge is
the one-room field hut where Nandé Randal and her husband live. If you
come by motorcycle, she warned us (as we in fact had that day, riding,
bouncing, and pushing the bike along the narrow, brushy path), be sure
not to leave it unwatched along the road, for it will surely be vandalized
or stolen.

There was a crudely painted sign over the single window of their tiny
shack: Thieves keep out. Steal at your own risk. And in the center of this
sign, arranged around a skull and crossbones, were several protective

symbols Nandé Randal had learned from Nini Raja Umang, the king of the supernatural wild men who inhabit the rugged slopes of Mount Sibayak. Years ago, she had "meditated" for seven months with the umang-king, she said. He showed her the special herbs that grew only on the mountaintop, and taught her how to protect herself from spirit-attack and sorcery, from the *kaba-kaba* wind that could blow away a whole offering table, from leprosy ("that was the one disease that really scared me"), from tall ghosts and tiny ones. He had written the magical signs out for her, so that she could memorize them, and she still had the white cloth on which the symbols had been inscribed. But neither the verbal warning to trespassers nor the symbols of the umang-king seem to have been very effective against the local predators, human or animal: on our first visit to her farm, Nandé Randal told us we'd have to eat duck for dinner, because all her chickens had been stolen. By our second visit, a few months later, the ducks were gone too, also stolen.

"There was a time," she said, speaking of her early years as a spirit medium back in the 1930s, "when I was just, really very popular. If it couldn't be treated, I'd treat it, cured! It was the same for madmen, the same for whatever. I'd sing, the ninis would come down, they were cured right off." These days, though, Nandé Randal didn't work much as a curer. "I don't have the wind for it anymore," she explained. Few people dared to come out to her farm. They were afraid of the graveyard and also of the local toughs who would sometimes bother strangers and would surely appropriate any motorcycles parked unattended along the road. But every Saturday she would go into the city, to her old house in the neighborhood of Simpang Meriah where her eldest son now lived with his family, and sometimes she would treat patients there. And every month she attended the *kerja nini*, the "grandparents' ceremony" for the spirits of Mount Sibayak, sponsored by the Arisan of Simpang Meriah.

It was through the Arisan's kerja nini ceremonies that I first met Nandé Randal. A kind of revolving credit association, the Arisan provided financial and participatory support for the ritual activities of its members, most of whom were small-scale market traders and produce brokers, as Nandé Randal had been before her luck went bad. At the time I was attending their ceremonies in 1984 and 1985, the Arisan had an active membership of about twenty-five families, each of whom was expected to contribute a small amount of money and rice every month to the group's treasury, which could then be drawn upon to defray the costs of ritual sponsorship. All were expected to take part in one another's ceremonies, helping out with the necessary work, "flattering" the spirits called down to bestow their blessings on the participants, or acting as spirit-carriers (*peninggeren*, "perch"), vehicles through whom the spirits could enjoy the entertainments provided for them and speak with those who had assembled to honor them. This participatory support was essential, since many members' Christian or Muslim relatives and neighbors refused to take part in these "heathen" ceremonies or to perform the work that would, in the past, have been the responsibility of the sponsor's kin.

The Arisan was established about two decades ago, as a branch of a Karo cultural/religious organization known as Persadan Merga Si Lima, the Association of the Five Clans. Dedicated to the preservation of Karo custom and the protection of the interests of those Karo who, in official terms, "did not yet have a religion"—that is, who still followed the old religion of spirit veneration, which they now called *Agama Pemena*, the "first" or "original" religion—Merga Si Lima had flourished in the troubled period following the alleged Communist coup attempt of 1965 (Gestapu, the "September 30th Movement") and the subsequent establishment of Suharto's New Order government. At that time, tensions were high between followers of Agama Pemena and their Christian neighbors. "Every week we got together, we had a little orchestra," Nandé Randal said. "The neighbors threw bricks in the windows at us. We were hit! 'Kill the drummer,' they said. 'Slit the musicians' throats, so there's no more Merga Si Lima.' Traitors, they called us. That's how bad it was. We were afraid to go out alone at night." Rumors spread that members of Merga Si Lima would be sent to jail for four years.

By the mid-1970s Merga Si Lima was largely moribund, fractured by internal political disputes and rivalries, and the Arisan was one of its few remaining active chapters. But in 1979, as part of a continuing effort to provide legitimacy to the religious beliefs of its members, the Arisan was reconstituted as a "Hindu" study group under the auspices of the Karo branch of the Bali-based national organization Parisada Hindu Dharma, promoters of a rationalized form of the Hindu religion and prime movers in the successful effort (in 1962) to have Balinese Hinduism officially recognized by the state as an approved religion. For a while there were meetings every Saturday night, and a local Tamil man—the provincial branch of Parisada Hindu Dharma was, at the time, controlled primarily by temple groups from Medan's large Tamil community—came to teach them about their religion. Nandé Randal didn't remember his name, and she didn't recall much of this instruction in Hinduism either, except that they were supposed to pray at the beginning of each meal.

A few times they had all gone, in their best clothes, to ceremonies at the new Hindu temple built in the Balinese style and serving mainly the local expatriate Balinese community of high-level civil servants and military personnel. But soon their teacher stopped coming and so, it seems, did invitations to the new temple. At the provincial level, a power struggle was being played out between Tamil and Balinese temple groups, and

Parisada Hindu Dharma was also busy absorbing Chinese Buddhists into its already rather miscellaneous ranks; at the branch level there was, as seems often to be the case in Karo organizations, some serious dispute going on over leadership positions and the distribution (or rather, nondistribution) of funds; and within the Arisan itself the marital problems of several of the group's male leaders led to their declining involvement in organizational matters. But Parisada Hindu Dharma's Karo followers had already received what they really needed: the official legitimacy provided by their own Book—a slim paperbound volume entitled *Upadeça: Concerning the Teachings of the Hindu Religion (Karo Language)*,[1] which, though she couldn't read it, Nandé Randal kept in case of trouble—and the name of a religion, "Hindu Karo," to put on their identification cards. "Once you've acknowledged this [i.e., Hinduism]," she explained, "they don't dare open their mouths. Here's the book, here, we'd say. Otherwise, back then, *iih*, that's why—whatever they did, give them that book."

Nandé Randal was the most senior of the spirit mediums who formed the group's core. They all deferred to her in matters of ritual protocol, but few took her seriously as a ritual participant anymore. These days she usually sat on the sidelines in her baggy old jacket and pink knitted turban, looking quietly out of place among the other participants, whose more fashionable, expensive attire was a conspicuous (and perhaps wishful) demonstration of the spirits' favor. The other Arisan members said that the spirits had deserted Nandé Randal: perhaps because she was too old, for the spirits preferred to perch on agile, attractive young people; or perhaps, as another Arisan member suggested, because she had offended the Muslim spirits around her lowland farm by raising pigs there. Nandé Randal herself said publicly that her rheumatism kept her from taking part more actively, and privately that she simply wasn't interested because the others didn't perform the ceremonies correctly (though it was not, she added primly, her place to tell them so). Still, she was always there, gossiping cheerfully and chewing betel with her friends, or, when things weren't going right, showing the others the proper way to make the offerings or to call the spirits. Other times she simply dozed in a corner through the noisy nightlong whirl of spirits coming and going: while rowdy stogie-smoking umangs hopped and hooted about amid peals of high-pitched laughter; while vain, silly girl-spirits flirted outrageously with the musicians, to their wives' dismay; while machete-waving war chiefs enthusiastically attacked unseen foes or displayed their skill in the martial arts; while European spirits danced disco-style to Malay pop tunes and sober Muslim spirits made their inevitable complaints about the pervasive odor of pig.

A few days before our visit, though, Nandé Randal had officiated at the kerja nini sponsored by another of the Arisan's senior mediums.[2] The ceremony was held in the sponsoring family's coffeeshop—one of the many such small, dusty shops on the edge of the Berastagi road where Karo men idle over tea, chess, and conversation—which was closed for the occasion and filled to the brim for the two days of the ceremony with dancers, musicians, children, and miscellaneous spectators, some bored, others curious, and not a few hopeful of some incidental boon from the spirits. For most of the audience, the event was a repetition of familiar experience. Gossip flowed steadily through the crowd, and the spirits' presence generated only sporadic interest among the onlookers.

But Nandé Randal's skillful performance drew an enthusiastic, if intermittent, response. This was the only time I ever saw her take an active part in one of the Arisan's ceremonies, and her elegant and often quite strenuous dancing must have served as a dramatic rebuttal to speculations that she was past her prime as a spirit medium. Later she told us that the considerable exertions of the two-day event had not only not tired her out, but had actually eased her bothersome rheumatism. The ninis from the mountain had brought their medicines, she said, and treated her while she danced.

Nandé Randal laughed at the photographs I had taken at the kerja, justifiably proud of her graceful appearance and the correctness of form evident even in the still pictures of her dancing. In one of these pictures she dances alone, stepping high, chin jutting and cigarette clamped in her lips, her head and waist wrapped in twined cloths—the plain white cotton of the spirits and the red-and-gold embroidered shawls worn ceremonially by Karo men. As the audience, unseen beyond the edges of the photograph, watches attentively, she performs the tari tongkat, the dance of the magic staff.

The tari tongkat was once the prerogative of the male guru, a trained practitioner of the magical arts, for whom the tongkat—a long staff carved from the wood of the spirit-infested tenggolan tree to represent the Karo version of the Malay "spectral huntsman" with his seven hounds— was a powerful supernatural weapon as well as a mark of ritual status. Today such staffs are, except for crude replicas aimed at the local tourist market, more likely to be found in European museums than in Karoland, and the male gurus, once figures of considerable power and authority, have mostly been consigned to the legendary world of a long-vanished past. But here in a roadside coffeeshop one of them makes a joyful momentary comeback as Nandé Randal moves through the complex figures of the guru's dance, guided by the spirit perched on her shoulder. Instead of the elaborately carved tongkat, she carries, with delicately back-curved fingers, a broom.

Nandé Randal performs the dance of the magic staff.

> A Klee painting named "Angelus Novus" shows an angel look-
>
> ing as though he is about to move away from something he is
>
> fixedly contemplating. His eyes are staring, his mouth is open,
>
> his wings are spread. This is how one pictures the angel of
>
> history. His face is turned toward the past.
>
> —WALTER BENJAMIN, "Theses on the Philosophy of History"

Like Walter Benjamin's angel of history, Karo envision the past as stretching out in front of them while they are moved into a future that lies unseen behind their backs. To the detached and melancholy angel, history seems "one single catastrophe which keeps piling wreckage upon wreckage at his feet" as he is propelled helplessly into the future by the storm of progress (Benjamin 1969c:257). But to people like Nandé Randal, who live in that storm, the horizon of this landscape of cumulative disaster is marked by an imagined Golden Age enshrined and perfected in memory. This memorialized past, forever distant from an experienced present in which things continually fall apart, is the home of the spirits. The cohabitation of humans and spirits—of the living and the dead— allows a momentary bridging of the borders between past and present, between experience and imagination. Yet the bridge is a fragile one, no stronger than memory or, perhaps, hope.

One of the spirits that Nandé Randal carried was her *kaka tua*, her elder brother, who had been killed during the post-Gestapu reprisals of the late 1960s at the instigation of a kinsman envious of the family's extensive landholdings. "That's one that I carry," she said. "But even he doesn't come anymore, my child. When we had good fortune, you see, he came too. Our ninis from the mountain came, and he came too. The good fortune decreased, he didn't come anymore. We're amazed, aren't we?" When she asked the spirits why this had happened, their response was that such was her fate: this was what her soul had requested from life and that there could be no increase beyond one's allotted destiny. "That's really true, I thought. Ah, true," she said. "If you think about it, well, isn't it really that way?"

In a classic Karo metaphor of unrequited love, the hapless lover is portrayed as suspended motionless,

> like a seagull in the noonday sky:
> you might say that it's hanging there

but there's no rope to be seen;
or you might say that it's been placed there
but no path can be seen.

Hanging without a rope: The phrase, which conveys the sheer incomprehensibility of an unsupported and seemingly inescapable situation, was often used by Karo who, like Nandé Randal, felt themselves trapped between a past that was no longer tenable and a present to which they were, at best, only marginally relevant. Isolated on the sidelines of a game with rules unclear, they might invoke their vision of the past, call up the spirits who embody that past for them, and find a temporary refuge in the spirits' consolations. But for Nandé Randal the fugitive comfort offered by the spirits, who care for traders but not for farmers, is small indeed. It is not, for all that, unworthy of consideration.

As past events are, in the Karo phrase, "left ahead," they may come to be seen as revelatory markers of destiny foreordained, of fatal choices made by the soul before birth "in order to become human": a confirmation of history's post facto inevitability. This historical inevitability is, however, always open-ended, for events and experiences continue to acquire new (and always mutable) significance in relation to a continually changing present situation. It is this openness, the constant possibility of interpretive revision, of rewriting "history" (or "fate"), which the spirits offer to those whom they follow, and which, at the same time, is the spirits' own fate. When Nandé Randal performs the tari tongkat, dancing gloriously in the shabby coffeeshop at the edge of the Berastagi road, is she not also revising the history of the old gurus as she wields her broom, the new magic staff of the disenchanted world? And can we not also take that broom, and use it—as Benjamin (ibid.) suggests—to "brush history against the grain"?

CHAPTER

One

Narrative Experience

> And you are born at the same time with a lot of other people,
>
> all mixed up with them, like trying to, having to, move your
>
> arms and legs with strings only the same strings are hitched
>
> to all the other arms and legs and the others all trying and
>
> they dont know why either except that the strings are all in
>
> one another's way like five or six people all trying to make a
>
> rug on the same loom only each one wants to weave his own
>
> pattern into the rug; and it cant matter, you know that, or
>
> the Ones that set up the loom would have arranged things a
>
> little better, and yet it must matter because
>
> you keep on trying . . .
>
> —WILLIAM FAULKNER, *Absalom, Absalom!*

GETTING TO KNOW THE BATAKS

On February 28, 1916, "Henk," a young clerk on one of the European plantation enterprises of East Sumatra and my pseudonymous predecessor in Karoland, took leave of his dreary office-stool and desk to seek, as he put it, more congenial companions among the wild folk of the forested interior. "I'm going to get to know the Bataks," he announced enthusiastically, "for surely the 'uncivilized savages' will be more agreeable to me than the European 'civilized savages.' . . . To become, with Natural Man, a man of nature!" With his Malay manservant, Henk settled in the Karo village of "Batu Gandjang" somewhere in the piedmont zone of Upper Deli and Serdang.

This savage Eden of Henk's imagination—"life under God's free heavens, in God's free nature; life without care and without all the discontents of civilization"—turned out, as such things usually do, to be neither all that Edenic nor even especially savage. What Henk discovered in Karoland was not the "golden freedom" he had hoped to enjoy, but rather a way of life no less socially constrained than the one he had left behind. Having begun, like many ethnographers, with the romantic dream of "becoming" one of the natives (though within limits, for he could not refrain from using knife and fork in the name of sanitary dining), Henk ended with what Clifford Geertz (1973c:13) has described as anthropology's more modest aim—of conversing with them.

Portions of Henk's diary, addressed to his friend "Karel," first appeared anonymously in the Medan *Kerkblad*. ("Be assured that I will keep you posted of my adventures," Henk wrote to his friend, "perhaps I can tempt you to share my destiny.") The full story, entitled *Een Jaar onder de Karo-Bataks*, was published in 1919 under the name of its author, missionary J. H. Neumann. As an anonymous text Henk's diary had to stand on its own literary merits, but once the identity of its author was known Neumann could cite his experience as proof of the authenticity of fictional Henk's adventures in Karoland. "I have lived with them for nineteen years," Neumann wrote of his time in the Karo mission field, "seen the old and the new times, and all their advantages and disadvantages, come and go, and have shared all of it insofar as this is possible for a European" (Neumann 1949:5). A sympathetic, engaging portrait of everyday life in a Karo village, Neumann's ethnographic novel is today, as the linguist and scholar of Batak literature P. Voorhoeve wrote of it in 1949, "still unsurpassed as a description of Karo-Batak folklife."[1]

Nothing else in Neumann's extensive ethnographic, linguistic, and religious writings approaches the narrative intimacy of this fictional diary.[2] The reader who follows in imagination young Henk's efforts to "get to know the Bataks" is gradually led to a complex, unromantic appreciation of the Karo social world, and of the practical and spiritual challenges faced by those who, like Neumann (and Henk), would share "all of it, insofar as this is possible for a European." The measure of Henk's growth during his year in Karoland is the touch of light self-mockery—as close as Neumann comes to an ironic critique of his naive young narrator—with which, at the end, Henk gives away as farewell presents to the village children "all the little pen-knives and beads that in my innocence I had brought along to trade with the 'savages' " (ibid.:115).

But *Een Jaar* is more than a Calvinist missionary's ethnographic *bildungsroman*; it is also the platform for Neumann's liberal-humanist message of social equality and moral individualism. Through Henk's experiences and in Henk's words, Neumann argues for an appreciation of individual particularities woven into the fabric of cultural life, and for a recognition of the core of common humanity lying beneath the ground of cultural difference. The diary's closing image of the "blessed Christ of

Thorwaldsen, and at his feet this folk too" (ibid.) is no wishful allegory of religious salvation; it is a Christian vision of moral equivalence among human societies.[3]

What makes Neumann's novel seem so remarkable today is neither its humanist message nor the accuracy of its ethnographic detail. Its uniqueness lies rather in the way that its double perspectives—the wide angle of the Christian moralist and the experiential close-up of the ethnographic diarist; the missionary *roman á clef* and the young clerk's Rousseauean fantasy—continually entangle and disrupt one another in the retelling of Henk's experiences. This is nowhere more evident than in the diary entry of "April 17, 1916," in which Henk describes the funeral seance (K., *perumah bégu*, "calling home the ghosts") he attended the night of April 15, in company with a group of fellow Karo villagers. "I am more convinced than ever of one thing," Henk confidently begins his account. "If one seeks 'the human' among these people, then one will perceive that the human surprisingly resembles 'us' humans quite a lot" (ibid.:40). Yet for Henk the seance is an unsettling encounter with absolute Otherness, in the person of the *guru si baso*—the possessed female medium through whom the spirits of the dead communicate with the living. All of Henk's certainties are shaken by this uncanny figure, and despite his bright (and ironically retrospective) avowal of faith in the universal human "us," he is left wondering if getting to know the Bataks is possible after all.

Whether they are set in the formal arenas of ritual performance or in the casual spaces of everyday life, stories of spirit-encounters raise with particular urgency questions of belief, agency, and authenticity—questions that lie at the heart of ethnographic experience and its representation. What to believe? Do others believe? Do I? Is this experience (of mine, of others) "real"? How to evaluate the evidence of unseen experience, or of experience shared yet incomprehensible? This uncertainty is by no means unique to the ethnographic encounter, nor does it emerge only in the face of the apparently uncanny. It may—indeed should—be present in any narrative encounter: yours, reader, with the book before you; mine with the stories I heard in Karoland and the ones I have read; and no doubt in the encounters of my Karo friends, colleagues, and teachers with what I have made of their experiences and my own.

This book records my efforts to build a kind of history around stories of encounters with spirits. Its locale is the greater area of Karo settlement in North Sumatra, a zone shaped by movements of people and goods—and of desire and ambition and hope—along the negotiable pathways of a political landscape. Animated by memories, stories, names of places and things, by strange nameless objects with stories yet unknown, by signs of passage and signs of arrest, the historical space of Karo habitation opens up many narrative possibilities, only a few of which I have traced here. Images of a road and a mountain are reference points in my peculiar mapping of this terrain. Around these relatively fixed sites lie the mutable and heterogeneous conversational thickets that I call "narrative experience"—a tricky space where lives are told and stories lived. A history made in these thickets demands an engaged, dialogical reading.

This is where spirits come in. Stories of spirits, situated outside the ordinary routines of social life yet with profound everyday effects, make visible the transparent conventions of narrative performance and of ethnographic evidence. In the circumscribed arenas of ritual enactment or on the wild borderlands of a familiar social world, encounters with spirits confront official standards of plausibility and good sense; truth here must come to terms with strangeness, strangeness with the regulative disciplines of narration.

This is not simply a matter of Western scientific rationality at its epistemic limits; Karo too are troubled, for reasons of their own, by the edgy double agency of spirit/medium. In 1902 Neumann told this story of Karo uncertainty, which he would later rewrite as the coda to Henk's encounter with the spirits of the dead:

> At Rumah Pil-pil, a village about an hour from [the mission station at] Si Bolangit, a perumah bégu was held for someone who was thought to be long dead. The bégu [spirit] readily entered the guru and said he was the desired person. But a few days later the man whom they thought was already dead returned, in the living flesh, to Rumah Pil-pil.—This is quite a wild case, but, the Batak reckons, *you can never know what is at the bottom of it.* (Neumann 1902a:35; emphasis added)[4]

As Henk was to discover, spirits provoke a way of reading narrative experience against the grain of credibility: as uncertain, duplicitous, always open to revision, *bottomless.* Following Henk's experience along what he calls the "border between two worlds," my intention is not to get to the bottom of it, but rather to provoke this mode of critical reading, against the grain.

ON THE BORDER

The perumah bégu of Henk's account was held in one of the old-style eight-family houses—four open apartments, two shared hearths, on either side of a raised central aisle—still scattered throughout the highlands today. Many of these "traditional houses" (I., *rumah adat*), as they are now called, were burned in the 1947 evacuation of Karoland, and few of those remaining are inhabited, but their high shaggy black roofs, pitched upward in a steep angular rush, still dramatically mark the skyline of some highland villages. In Henk's time cheap tin oil-lamps ("a giant step on the path of civilization," as Henk put it) and smoky cooking-fires provided the only illumination in these houses, and inadequate ventilation made even a short visit inside a test of endurance for European visitors. This was especially so on ceremonial occasions such as the seance—an all-night affair at once religious ritual and public entertainment—when the unpartitioned, cavernous interior would be so packed with guests that only the narrow aisle was free for movement and for the dancing of the guru si baso.

Unlike perumah bégu ceremonies held today, in which the medium usually does not dance and performs without musical accompaniment, Karo funeral seances of Henk's time featured the "great" five-piece orchestra or *gendang mbelin*, composed of an oboe (*seruné*), two small drums (*gendang*), and two gongs, one large and the other small.[5] Many Westerners find the music of the gendang orchestra discordant and shrill; to Henk the "flutes" [*sic*] seemed to shriek hysterically and the gongs bray and shake the house as the three mediums—fearsome old "viragos" (D., *feeksen*), he called them—began to dance, slowly at first and then with increasingly wild and rapid movements, finally falling, entranced, into the waiting arms of their female interrogators (K., *pertami-tami*, "flatterers"). As the entranced mediums conveyed to the assembled crowd the words of the spirits, Henk, caught up in the thrill of the uncanny, experienced what he took to be his longed-for moment of sympathetic union with the primitive Other:

> The dim lighting, the women with hair hanging loose, haggard expressions, vacant eyes, lying half naked in others' arms, the loud and wild weeping and lamentations—all this shocked me and I sat devoutly looking on with the others. If I was skeptically disposed to go away, gradually I came under the influence of the whole. It was uncanny, terrifying. (Neumann 1949:45)

Beneath Henk's "shock" the reader senses the pleasure of antipodal reconciliation—of becoming, as he had wished, a "man of nature" through the (temporary) immersion of rational European self in the flow of savage, pagan emotion. But more shocks are to come. Henk's hesitant dip into this Sumatran heart of (quasi-) darkness is immediately, and ironically, cut short by his discovery that the rapt attention constituting his passage into Otherness is not, in fact, shared by his fellow spectators. As Henk's comfortably familiar category-image of Natural Man gives way, the forces of absolute Otherness reassert themselves with a vengeance. In a series of increasingly frantic interrogative sorties, Henk rebuilds the

Guru si baso dances in the center aisle of a Karo house, Kabanjahé, c. 1910.

crumbling barrier of Same and Different that separates Civilized "Us" from Primitive "Them"—by dissolving for *them* the border between life and death:

> When I glanced around I was totally astonished, instead of a devout audience, I discovered the greatest possible indifference among the men, even among the women. A couple of men had stretched out calmly and slept, others lit a new cigarette and chatted with each other as if the whole thing was none of their business. . . . Did it not concern them that something so uncanny was taking place? Or are they accustomed to it and live so much on the border between two worlds that it is something that, to them, speaks for itself? Elsewhere it is certainly no ordinary event if one crosses the border between the living and the dead! Or does this border not exist in their thought? Do the dead and the living animate each other? (Ibid.:45–46)

But even the music seems to mock these efforts—

> Against my will my eyes returned to that spectral scene. The music laughed
> scornfully; my head thudded from the oppressive atmosphere and the noise
> of the gong; the flute, the weeping and mourning made me frantic; the
> half-deranged witches made a hideous impression. . . . I must have air, and
> coolness. (Ibid.:46)

—and so Henk finally retreats to the clear world of nature brightly illu-
mined, to God in His free heavens, and to the rational order of clock-
time.

> The moon shone brightly in the clear heavens; delicate little clouds floated
> here and there, the village common was illuminated white. Here it was cool,
> here all was clear and pure. Here God ruled! All breathed peace, but there all
> around in the forest, there the mystery lurked, and in that house there was
> found the bridge from the present into the future. I looked at my watch. It
> was one o'clock. (Ibid.)

Authors and their narrators—even ethnographic ones—are, like spirits,
notoriously duplicitous. In the very intimacy—the *immediacy*—of Henk's
vivid, troubled account, the narrative voice seems to detach itself from the
retold fictional event, and the reader begins to wonder: Whose story is
being told here?

AUTHORS AND NARRATORS

> A text consists of multiple writings, proceeding from several
>
> cultures and entering into dialogue, into parody, into contesta-
>
> tion; but there is a site where this multiplicity is collected, and
>
> this site is not the author, as has hitherto been claimed, but
>
> the reader. . . . the unity of a text is not in its origin
>
> but in its destination.
>
> —ROLAND BARTHES, "The Death of the Author"

Contemporary literary criticism, as Roland Barthes has noted, has generally broken with interpretive methods in which "*explanation* of the
work is . . . sought in the person of its producer, as if, through the more
or less transparent allegory of fiction, it was always, ultimately, the voice
of one and the same person, the *author*, which was transmitting his 'con-

fidences' " (Barthes 1986a:50). By a curious twist, recent ethnographic criticism, in rejecting conventional representations of "objectivity" that divorced the authorial person from the authored text, has tended to revalorize the explanatory fiction of authorial presence. New strategies of "ethnographic authority" (Clifford 1988) extend the illusion of narrative closure by more or less unselfconsciously resituating the iconic author within the body of the text. Focused upon the relational experience of fieldwork (the "ethnographic encounter"), the new ethnography rarely addresses the problematic relation of experience and representation. A transparent reproduction of the ethnographer's subjective experience becomes if not the rule then at least the ideal of "correct" ethnographic representation. The effect of this self-privileging stance is to efface—often, ironically, in the name of poststructuralism or dialogism or postmodern antisubjectivism—all subjects except for the author/narrator.[6]

Ethnographic plausibility has long been built on the illusion of experiential verisimilitude—the textual production of what Clifford Geertz (1988) has called "Being There." Like Neumann's introductory "I-have-seen-it-all" proclamation in *Een Jaar*, inscriptions of authorial presence within ethnographic texts aim for a direct identification of the fieldwork experience with its narrative representation, of the "I" who has seen it all with the I whom the reader encounters in the text. Yet as Barthes (1986a:61–62) properly warns, "the *I* that writes the text is never anything but a paper *I*":

> It is not that the Author cannot "return" in the Text, in his text; but he does so, one might say, as a guest; if he is a novelist he inscribes himself there as one of his characters, drawn as a figure in the carpet; his inscription is no longer privileged, paternal, alethic, but ludic: he becomes, one can say, a paper author; his life is no longer the origin of his fables, but a fable concurrent with his life.

Whether in the first-person confessional mode of the speaker written into the text, or the third-person omniscient of the detached and invisible author, the figure of the storyteller—the narrator-who-writes—operates in the text as an organizing trope for author and audience alike, shaping the narrative to the familiar frame of the experiencing subject.[7] Experientially based truth-claims intensify what de Man (1983:17) has called "the fallacy of unmediated expression," while at the same time confirming the authenticity of the individual as the *source* of narrative. The reader should recognize the factitiousness of such claims, wherever they occur.

"When experience is taken as the origin of knowledge," Joan Scott (1991:777) warns, "the vision of the individual subject . . . becomes the bedrock of evidence on which explanation is built." This evidential experience—of the ethnographer in the field or of the storyteller/witness retold—is not something that should put an end to interrogation but rather something that itself requires interrogation. The self-as-subject is continually produced and dispersed in experience; experience is generated and distributed in social practice; and the subject of experience is engendered in narrative. The point is to recognize the constructedness of even those experiences that seem most deeply "natural," most physically self-evident—and to include ourselves, all the way, in that recognition, even as we write (or read) ourselves into experience.[8]

FIGURING OUT THE FIGURE IN THE CARPET

What I want is for you to feel, around the story, a saturation

of other stories that I could tell and maybe will tell or who

knows may already have told on some other occasion,

a space full of stories that perhaps is simply my lifetime, where

you can move in all directions, as in space, always finding

stories that cannot be told until other stories are told first, and

so, setting out from any moment or place, you encounter

always the same density of material to be told. . . . it is not

impossible that the person who follows my story may feel

himself a bit cheated . . . but it is not impossible that this is the

very effect I aimed at when I started narrating, or let's say it's

a trick of the narrative art that I am trying to employ, a rule of

discretion that consists in maintaining my position slightly

below the narrative possibilities at my disposal.

—ITALO CALVINO, *If on a winter's night a traveler*

Much of the "fieldwork experience" consists in listening to other people's stories and learning to tell stories to others. Ethnographic writing is a process of translating this narrative practice into another kind of story-telling, for another kind of audience. Bringing these narrative fields together is the function of the author; appreciating their irreconcilable differences—figuring out the figures in the carpet—is the province of the reader.

Tellers of stories and the audiences to whom stories are addressed—interchangeable but not always equal partners in the narrative dialogue that Kathleen Stewart (1992:411) calls the "exchange of stories"—need to attend carefully to the poetics of form and to the limits of poetic license. This does not mean an analytic formalism but an active, repetitive engagement with the practical uses of formal narrative conventions. "An *exchange* of stories," Stewart writes,

> requires a knowledge of cultural genres and narrative poetics and a body of intertextual references to other stories and types of stories that only come from repeated instances of listening in order to retell. It is not a superficial attention to form that rushes to discover the cause or explanation but an immersion in form in which the elements that produce meaning become known in the act of using them, manipulating them, and repositioning them in another version. (Ibid.)

In order to engage in an exchange of stories, Stewart (ibid.) argues, "[t]he storyteller has to be placed *inside the story and yet also outside it*, constructing it." Yet I would suggest that this "doubled, haunting epistemology of speaking from within the object spoken of" is less a matter of authorial intention than of readerly attention. The ethnographic storyteller in the text is, like Neumann's "Henk," *already* there and yet not there, *always* the author and someone else: a paper diarist, an uncertain figure woven amid others, more or less vividly, in the narrative carpet.[9]

Despite (or perhaps because of) the separation of author Neumann from his fictional narrator Henk, the reader is continually tempted to find in Henk's account a *truer* expression of Neumann's personal experience—his feelings, impressions, reactions—than could be articulated through the equally constructed personae of "Missionary" and "Ethnographer" within which he elsewhere writes. But claims to narrative authenticity are precisely what I wish *not* to instantiate here. My concern throughout this book will be the precarious, creative, disruptive tension between experience and representation, and not the erasure of one by the other.

To quote another paper diarist, Italo Calvino's reader-obsessed novelist/narrator Silas Flannery, writing "always means hiding something in such a way that it then is discovered" (Calvino 1981:193). Reading Henk's perhaps apocryphal story of the seance I discover what might be a plausible record of the feelings and impressions of Neumann the missionary-author; I also find images borrowed from earlier ethnography: Baron von Brenner's (1894) breathless account of the possession ritual he attended in 1888 in the village of Pengambotan, on the Karo border;

missionary Joustra's (1896) brief report of a perumah bégu seance he witnessed in 1895; Neumann's (1902a) anecdote of the "wild case" of the Rumah Pilpil seance. These in turn borrow and activate conventional *topoi* of madness, duplicity, and feminine danger that can be traced as far back in European literature as the *Bacchae* of Euripides. I do not know if Neumann himself ever attended a funeral seance (or read the *Bacchae*), but as the invisible guest in Henk's narrative machinery, he continually writes himself and his history—a narrative experience not his alone—into the story.

It seems to me (and here I am perhaps putting a bit of my own history into the story, my southern background as well as the cold New England winter in which I write) that, of anyone, William Faulkner has most compellingly conveyed a sense of the dense, heterogeneous entangling of lives, stories, and desires that I mean by narrative experience. Set against the backdrop of a "horrible and bloody mischancing of human affairs" (Faulkner 1986:125 [repr. 1936]) retrospectively turned to deadly redemptive mythology, Faulkner's intertwined stories of Yoknapatawpha County are enacted in a landscape seething with memories. Memories saturate the common air; they are inscribed on the land in names-become-places: Frenchman's Bend, Sutpen's Hundred, Varner's store, Jefferson. These are white men's names, it is important to note, because the stories that marked and transmitted property in Faulkner's Mississippi would have been stories of white men, even though others lived and breathed there too.

But memory is never private property and experience is never a simple matter in this overinhabited terrain; voices are always multiple, fragmented, interrupted, possessed by the memories of other people's experiences. The transfer and transcription of historical experience—in names, monuments, genealogies; in collective fantasy and in the regulated social intercourse of everyday life; in law, property, and desire; in stories inhaled with the common air of a shared place or time—is the movement through which subjectivity is produced. "He was a barracks filled with stubborn backward-looking ghosts," Faulkner writes of Quentin Compson in *Absalom, Absalom!* "His childhood was full of them; his very body was an empty hall echoing with sonorous defeated names; he was not a being, an entity, he was a commonwealth" (ibid.:9).

In one remarkable passage, the thread of Faulkner's narrative moves from Quentin, waiting to accompany Miss Rosa Coldfield to Sutpen's Hundred on a wistaria-drenched summer evening in 1909 and listening to his father's story of Thomas Sutpen's rise and fall—a story Quentin would retell five months later in his frigid Harvard sitting-room, reminded by a letter carrying the scent of wistaria and cigar smoke and his father's news of Miss Rosa's death—back to the June morning in 1833 when Thomas Sutpen first rode into the town of Jefferson. It was a story Quentin

> mostly . . . already knew since he had been born in and still breathed the same air in which the church bells had rung on that Sunday morning in 1833 . . . when the other men sitting with their feet on the railing of the Holston House gallery looked up, and there the stranger was . . . already halfway across the square when they saw him. (Ibid.:34–35)

Even smoothed by my summation and truncated by my ellipses, the entangled lines of identity and genealogy, of experience and mythology—those complex designs Faulkner's characters struggle to weave and unweave, across time and against one another—show through the text's accumulation of interhabiting voices and memories. Behind them may lie, concealed, Quentin's unspoken desire for his sister (itself perhaps figured by the ghostly mythic postbellum reconstruction of the Old South), tracing its own figure of incest, miscegenation, and fratricide into the story of the Sutpen children. And beyond all these, "a space full of stories . . . something like a forest that extends in all directions and is so thick that it doesn't allow light to pass" (Calvino 1981:109).[10]

Stories, including our ethnographic ones, may be as much "about" other stories as they are about events, real or imagined. This intertextuality should no more elide the possibility of experience than the "eventness" of experience should obscure its narrative production. Experience is both generated and shaped by tropes and conventions, by the borrowed plots, moods, rhythms, and images of other stories and other people's words. The histories of other people's experiences saturate the various worlds in which we live; and it is with regard to the limits of the narratable that we build our lives and our stories.

As Joan Scott (1991:777) argues, questions of language, history, and social practice need to be raised rather than erased by the evidence of experience; but questions of experience must also be raised by the practices of storytelling. To accentuate the literariness of ethnographic representation is not to diminish anthropology's claims to what could be called "literalness." The ethnographic insistence on referring to a particular social world outside the text—on there being a "there" there—as well as on the ethnographer's having spent a certain amount of time in that world, should protect against a too-easy slide into endless textual self-referentiality. Something—call it event, experience, encounter—is, after all, being represented, and however intertextually, or even inauthentically, that representation is accomplished, it is worthwhile simply for whatever trace there may be of an ephemeral social moment (or even, as in the radically uninhabited pages of Lévi-Strauss's *Mythologiques,* for the evocative absence of such traces) lying in the "space full of stories" beyond the boundaries of the text. For me, as an ethnographic rather than a literary reader, Faulkner's novels point neither to a truth prior to narrative, nor to a reality within it, but rather, through the painfully conveyed, endlessly storied, grating complexity of lives lived in company with memories, to a way of thinking about experience.

THE SUBJECT OF EXPERIENCE

Nor can experience be allowed simply to appear as endlessly

plural and unchallengeable, as if self-evident, readily available

when we look 'inside' ourselves, and only one's own, or only

one's group's. . . . Just as nature is one of culture's most

startling and non-innocent products, so is experience one of

the least innocent, least self-evident aspects of historical,

embodied movement.

—DONNA HARAWAY, "Reading Buchi Emecheta"

The reading of fiction, as Donna Haraway (1991b:113) suggests, can be a productive means of remembering, reinterpreting, or reinventing experience. Attending to someone else's stories, whether as reader or as listener, can extend one's personal understanding to include another's experience, or (in a less utopian vein) to recognize the possibility of other kinds of experience: it can lead to a reconsideration of the meanings of one's own life. Such fictive encounters are of course not unproblematic, for we cannot simply step into other lives, fictional or not. They can, however, offer some insight into the processes by which experience is narratively produced and enmeshed in the practices of everyday social discourse. That is why I have shaped this chapter around a series of narrative encounters of the self-evidently fictional kind: Henk's experiences in Karoland and Quentin Compson's in Yoknapatawpha County; my experience as a displaced southerner in Cambridge, Massachusetts, reading of Quentin's earlier displacement there, and as an out-of-place anthropological traveler following Henk's imaginary trail through a very real Karoland of seventy years earlier; my efforts to reshape those encounters in ways meaningful to a hypothetical future reader "experienced" in the canonical discourses of a certain anthropology. Rather than taking experience for the raw material of narrative production, or narrative for the verbal replication or deformation of "lived experience," what I want you to see is the mutual shaping of each to the other, by means of the subject.

The question of experience has in recent years been profoundly and insistently raised by the work of feminist scholars. "Experience" has provided the common ground for mutual recognition, support, and political mobilization among women, as well as the oppositional ground upon which women's oppression has been identified, theorized, and resisted.[11] Writing or reading "as a woman" or "as a feminist" has been both the source of powerful insights in feminist scholarship and the hypothetical aim of feminist social practice.[12] At the same time, however, critiques from those on the movement's various margins—American women of color, right-to-life feminists, male sympathizers, gay and lesbian activists, among others—as well as from post- or anticolonial writers and Western theorists of race and class have argued against experience-based assumptions of unitary identity as both exclusionary and mystifying.[13] Oppression is neither encountered nor enacted in the same way by all women, they insist, and victimization is no less ideological, and no more "natural," than any other social product. Posited as the basis for an empowering difference between men and women, experience has become the site of ever more elaborately demarcated differences among women, and too often the epistemological horizon of feminist discourse.

By raising the issue of experience, feminism thus inevitably stands on the brink of fracture; it also necessarily operates in a moment of deferral. The hypothetical experience of "reading as a woman," as Jonathan Culler (1982:63) notes, "provides leverage for displacing or undoing the system of concepts or procedures of male criticism, but 'experience' always has this divided, duplicitous character: it has always already occurred and yet is still to be produced—an indispensible point of reference, yet never simply there." Women's experience, in other words, is both the generating force and the imagined object of feminist praxis; engendered within a preexisting interpretive matrix, it both exceeds and subversively falls short of the possibilities of that which produced it.

It is this divided, troublesome notion of experience that I wish to employ here: neither the beginning nor the end of analysis, but that which is at once most necessary and most in need of examination. The trick, as Gayatri Spivak (1989a:129) notes in regard to the equally important and problematic place of essentialism in feminist thought, is to recognize its risks and its necessity, to acknowledge "the unavoidable usefulness of something that is very dangerous." This risky necessity defines my approach to the subject of experience.

Commonsense definitions of "experience" have relied on the prior existence of an experiencing subject. This is the case whether experience is defined as the sensory encoding of data from an external, impinging event-world; as the internal shaping of that data to the mold of a unique emotional and interpretive landscape; or as the cumulative development of expertise through training, observation, or repetitive participation in events. In each of these senses, experience appears to be something that "happens to" the individual subject, or that the subject uniquely or collectively "has." In contrast, Teresa de Lauretis (1984:159) understands experience as

> a *process* by which, for all social beings, subjectivity is constructed. Through that process one places oneself or is placed in social reality, and so perceives and comprehends as subjective (referring to, even originating in, oneself) those relations—material, economic, and interpersonal—which are in fact social and, in a larger perspective, historical.

Subjectivity, de Lauretis argues, is an effect of experience, which she defines as one's personal engagement in the practices of social signification; it is thus "an ongoing construction, not a fixed point of departure or arrival from which one then interacts with the world."

This formulation creatively reworks the Althusserian notion of the constitution of the subject in ideology. According to Althusser, ideology works by bringing "concrete individuals" to recognize themselves as subjects—that is, at once self-identified autonomous actors and self-acknowledged subordinates to a Master Subject (God, the State, Society, Natural Law, etc.). By imposing "obviousnesses as obviousnesses" (Althusser 1971:172), ideology

> "recruits" subjects among the individuals (it recruits them all), or "transforms" the individuals into subjects (it transforms them all) by that very precise operation which I have called *interpellation* or hailing, and which can be imagined along the lines of the most commonplace everyday police (or other) hailing: "Hey, you there!" (Ibid.:174)

Since every individual is born into an existing ideological field, he is in fact "always-already" interpellated as a subject; there is, for the subject, no point outside of ideology.

I use the masculine pronoun above intentionally. While Althusser fleetingly refers to the sexual identification of the infant-subject as either male or female, the seemingly indiscriminate operation of subject-recruitment carries a decidedly masculine message. For the concrete *female* individual, such "hailing" involves a certain degree of misrecognition. I like to think of it not as the ungendered *Hé, vous, là-bas!* of Althusser's Gallic policeman,[14] but rather parodically as the universal Indonesian street greeting to foreign strangers (of either sex): *Allo Mister!* To which my response must be, ambiguously: "It's not (quite) me!"—reversing the direction, while taking the point, of *not-quite/not-white*, Homi Bhabha's (1984:132) phrasing of the mimic misrecognition of colonial subjects. Ideology, in short, may indeed "recruit them all," but it does not recruit them all *in the same way*.

Extending the process of subject-production into the "natural" experiential territory of men and women, into the messy interstices of social life, the warm spaces where bodies meet one another and the hollows where they do not, de Lauretis introduces the problem of the differing subject—a subject that is, as she elsewhere (de Lauretis 1986:9) remarks, "not divided in, but rather at odds with, language." For de Lauretis, the constitution of female subjectivity begins in the concrete embodiment of difference in sexuality. "The stakes," she writes, "for women, are rooted in the body—which is not to say that the body escapes representation, but quite the contrary" (ibid.:12). While I have been at pains here to indicate the significance of gendered experience within the heterogeneous fields of social meaning, I do not wish to restrict the play of differences to this one arena. Nor do I wish to close down the possibility of affinities that traverse the gender gap. Men as well as women may be "good subjects"; as Althusser (1971:181) puts it, they may "work all right 'all by themselves' "; but they may also be "experienced" as partial subjects at odds with language, or as double agents who, like Quentin Compson, encounter in themselves a commonwealth of too much subjectivity.

If the subject is always "inside" ideology/experience, it does not follow that ideology or experience is always and everywhere the same, or that the "good subject" is a simple, unitary replica of an imaginary Original Subject. Nor is agency merely the phantasmic delusion of a linguistically or performatively determined subjectivity. It is as much through a continual "differing-from" as through a perpetual "same-as" that ideology operates. Conflicts and contradictions coexist even in relatively unified discursive systems, more so among the various fields of discourse in which the subject is historically positioned (Joan Scott 1991:793). Ideology thus constitutes a maze of ambiguity in which subjects may "work by themselves" in unexpected and perhaps unintended ways—though always with the risk of being hailed as "bad subjects" and perhaps provoking "the intervention of one of the detachments of the (repressive) State apparatus" (Althusser 1971:181).

This invocation of an authoritarian "bottom line" of physical or institutional force (which is, of course, not only available to the State) begins

to suggest the limits of narrative possibility in any context. The politics of
narrative experience defines not only the expressive resources for subject-
production and the relative access of various persons to those resources,
but also the public (and private) recognition or nonrecognition accorded
to their varied efforts. The last word in representation (in its political and
discursive senses) is exclusion. Here let me return, briefly, to *Absalom,
Absalom!*

THE SOCIAL PRODUCTION OF EPHEMERALITY

In *Absalom, Absalom!* narrative, "like genealogy, is a matter of patro-
nymics," writes Peter Brooks (1984:302). Dispersed and multiply mediated, narrative experience in Faulkner's novel has no source and no authoritative center, but it does have a limit, and that is the limit of the
Father's name.[15] Two tales, the Sutpen blood-tragedy hinged on the un-
written word of acknowledged paternity—"*I am your father; burn this*"
(Faulkner 1986:408)—and the Compson memory-tragedy of paternity
inescapably embodied in the spoken word—"*I am listening to it all over
again I shall have to never listen to anything else but this again forever,*"
Quentin reflects as his friend Shreve picks up the narrative thread
Quentin's father had spun, "*so apparently not only a man never outlives
his father but not even his friends and acquaintances do*" (ibid.:345–
46)—simultaneously overwrite the multiple, necessary, and always
ephemeral traces of women's presence, just as the names of propertied
men overwrite the presence of unnamed others—not-male, not-white, or
simply "not-*us*"—in the landscape of memory.[16]
      When Judith Sutpen gives a scrap of her own history, a letter conveying
the marriage proposal that has become the sign of her own failed genealogy, to Quentin's grandmother, it is "[b]ecause you make so little impression, you see":

> And so maybe if you could go to someone, the stranger the better, and give
> them something—a scrap of paper—something, anything, it not to mean
> anything in itself and them not even to read it or keep it, not even bother to
> throw it away or destroy it, at least it would be something just because it
> would have happened, be remembered even if only from passing from one
> hand to another, one mind to another, and it would be at least a scratch,
> something, something that might make a mark on something that *was* once
> for the reason that it can die someday. . . (Ibid.: 158)

Like Judith's letter, narratives of descent and filiation can pass through
the lives of women "without date or salutation or signature" (ibid.). This
is not to say that "women's experience" (or any other) is situated some-

where outside of discourse, in a free zone of unconstrained *jouissance* that escapes the coarse nets of patriarchal narrative. It is instead to stress what I would call the social production of ephemerality.

"The event is not what happens," Allen Feldman (1991:14) has written in a recent ethnography of violence in Northern Ireland: *"The event is that which can be narrated."* Incorporating material enactment as well as verbal representation into his definition of narrative, the circularity of Feldman's proposition seems particularly appropriate for an analysis of the cyclical production and reproduction of sectarian violence between the oppositional communities of Belfast. But the question of narratability raised here begs a series of further questions. These can best be approached by following Feldman's reading of Renato Rosaldo's (1986) study of Ilongot hunting stories. "These stories Ilongot men tell themselves," Rosaldo writes,

> reflect what actually happened and define the kinds of experiences they seek out in future hunts . . . in this respect the story informs the experience of hunting at least as much as the reverse. . . . *Ilongot huntsmen experience themselves as the main characters of their own stories* when responding [in a hunt] to the challenge with speed and imagination. (R. Rosaldo 1986:134; cited in Feldman 1991:14–15 [ellipses in Feldman; emphasis mine])

Issues of material effect aside, this is a good enough account of the narrative reproduction of masculine agency, in which Ilongot actors "perform a mimesis of hunting as they hunt" (Feldman 1991:15). One is nevertheless compelled to ask: What happens to those persons (old men, incompetent or unlucky hunters) whose enacted stories don't turn out as narratively planned, who are unable to respond "with speed and imagination" to the challenges of the hunt?[17] What happens to the ones who never get to appear as the "main characters of their own stories"? What does it mean to say that a non-narratable event is, in effect, a nonevent?

There are two significant problems here. The first has to do with the poetics of storytelling practice, the second with its politics. Narrative enactment involves more than the repetition of formal elements in an unchanging pattern; it also involves the "expressive deformation of a conventional form within negotiable limits" (Herzfeld 1991:81; cf. Stewart 1992). A good story is one that surprises its audience, transgressing or temporarily exceeding the givenness of its form. This deformation may be as slight as the insertion of particular persons' names into a standard and thus predictable plot, or it may involve a full parodic deconstruction of narrative convention. This does not exempt creative agency from the ideological conditions of its own production, for it is precisely through this continual negotiation of "experience" and "representation" in narrative that subjectivity is produced.

While the poetics of storytelling practice thus engages in a perpetual practice of differing, its politics attempts both to limit the possibilities of difference and to cover the tracks of its own exclusionary operations. Conventions of narrative expression, emplotment, and plausibility not only construct events (in Feldman's sense) but also construct the *exclusion* of events from the field of narrative possibility. Rosaldo (1986:134) makes this point, albeit parenthetically, in the paragraph preceding that quoted above, in which he notes that the experience of hunting becomes narratable when it reenacts what could be called a hunting plot: "(unlike gardening, which never does)." It hardly needs stating that gardening is what Ilongot women do.

"Pound me rice for I am going off," say the male heroes to their sisters, wives, or mothers at the beginning of Ilongot stories (M. Rosaldo 1980:111). Narrative emplotment then tracks their movement through space, away from and back to the stable and thus non-narratable residential center imaged in women's domestic activity. The "uneventful" round of female domesticity (R. Rosaldo [1980:176] describes it as "[s]itting by the hearth, gathering firewood, fetching water, pounding rice, hoeing, planting, weeding, harvesting") from which narrative actors depart and to which they return is the stuff of gossip, not of stories.[18] The ephemerality of Ilongot women's experience is not a "natural" feature of their repetitive daily routine but rather a social effect of narrative forms shaped to the (equally repetitive) dimensions of masculine prowess.

These recognitions of narrative poetics and politics need to be drawn into the ethnographic exploration of storytelling practices; but no less should they be drawn out of the practice of ethnographic storytelling. Thus I should remind you that, like any narrative, the one I have constructed here is selective: it chooses from among varied materials and from many possibilities of meaning-making. My particular purpose is to convey as well as I can some of the concrete details of Karo imaginative experience—or at least of the imaginative experience of some people, some of whom are Karo—as it was told (to me, to others) at certain specific historical moments. Some of the stories I recount here came from Karo men and women I knew; others were transmitted by the ghosts, nature spirits, and legendary figures who speak through Karo mediums. Some were written (or written down) by Karo scholars and journalists, colonial administrators, German explorers, Calvinist missionaries, Malay aristocrats, Japanese soldiers, Indonesian nationalists, national bureaucrats, Karo political "players," and an American botanist, among others.

I have chosen to attend to stories situated *on the edge of exclusion*, on the borderlands of narrative plausibility—though not, for that reason, outside of ideology. By privileging these stories, others perhaps more central to the contemporary politics of Karo narrative experience have in turn been marginalized or excluded. The quite successful Karo middle class, the congregation of the Christian Gereja Batak Karo Protestan (GBKP), the educated urban professionals who are engaged in an ongoing formulation of their own authoritative version of "Karo Culture" in a national political arena, are not my focus here.

My attention to what Donna Haraway calls "subjugated standpoints" (1988:584) is intended neither to romanticize nor to appropriate "the vision of the less powerful while claiming to see from their positions." By moving (slightly) against the grain of official discursive practices I hope to make explicit the necessary exclusions by means of which all narratives— including these edgy ethnographic stories of spirits and spirit mediums— are engendered. This is not an attempt to create a "truer story" of Karo experience or a better account of Karo social reality; it is only a different path through the bottomless complexities of Karo narrative experience, and our own.

PROBLEMS OF BELIEF

When recently Pa Sepit disappeared, having fled to the

highlands on account of gambling debts and theft, his wife

thought that he was dead. He was gone more than a year. They

decided to call his spirit to the house. . . . Now, the spirit came

to the house, said he was hungry, etc., etc. The medium ate

tasty chicken and rice, got a dollar, a new mat and two yards

of white cloth as payment, and—two nights later we heard that

a policeman had picked him up and he was still alive. No, tuan,

I don't believe it anymore, not a whit.

—J. H. NEUMANN, *Een Jaar onder de Karo-Bataks*

I offer these comments on experience and subjectivity as a readers' guide to this book, a way of alerting my non-hypothetical readers to the complicated process of reading (from) others' experience. The way stories are told, the evaluation of storytelling practice, the narrative symbiosis of

storyteller and audience, the events that make or do not make a compelling story, the kinds of experience that "count" narratively and otherwise, the stories that serve as models for living and the stories that renego-
tiate the social terrain: these are the perspectives from which I regard the
subject of Karo experience. They all depend on an understanding of narrative production as an endlessly complicated process of negotiation
through difference toward the subject.

I did not bring these concerns to Karoland with me. Nor, for that matter, did I discover them there, ready-made—although now, looking back
on my time in Karoland, they seem to emerge almost visibly from that
remembered landscape. Rather, it was through the struggle to construct
for readers (including, of course, myself) a plausible story of Karo historical experience that they came to me. It is nearly impossible for me now
to distinguish the two moments, of event and of interpretation, which are
joined in my retelling. Their mutually authenticating synthesis creates *for
me* as author a kind of narrative plausibility that entraps me in the allegorical field of my own making.

If the dimensions of that well-measured literary field are by now familiar to you, those of the Karo field in which I lived from 1983 to 1985 are
no doubt less so. It is this latter social space to which I want to introduce
you here, in the same necessarily incomplete and frankly partisan way I
have come to know it. Keeping in mind the necessary duplicities of the
paper "I," the reader may step into that space by considering with me the
problem of belief.

Nearly seventy years after Henk's startling encounter with Otherness, I
found myself similarly face to face with the uncanny in Padang Bulan, the
Karo district of Medan. I was living there in a prosaic lower-middle-class
neighborhood just behind the campus of the University of North Sumatra
(USU). My research focused less on this neighborhood, however, than on
the loose networks of urban and rural spirit mediums who are the primary officiants and participants in the possession rituals that today form
the experiential core of Agama Pemena, the "original religion" of Karo
spirit veneration.

My mostly Christian neighbors considered it entirely proper that an
American student would come to learn about Karo culture, but they
found this interest in gurus and curing rituals somewhat puzzling. Folk
curers of all sorts were a familiar part of the urban scene—Darma, a
young law student who lived down the street, was probably the most
popular Karo guru in the city, and most of my neighbors would from time
to time have recourse (though perhaps surreptitiously) to one folk practi-

tioner or another—but in my neighbors' view their work was not an entirely proper topic of research, especially for an unmarried woman like myself. Anthropologists, they explained, are supposed to study kinship.

Furthermore (I was frequently informed), the city was the wrong place for my research. If I really wanted to learn about Karo curing practices I should look up some old sage in an isolated highland village, who might still retain the wisdom of the past. True, there were the famous Karo bonesetters who advertised their profession from storefront offices on Jalan Pattimura; there were the market booths where you could buy medicinal oils, powders, roots, and teas, along with colognes and ready-made packets of flower petals to be used as spirit-offerings; there was Darma, whose "office hours" were signaled to his neighbors by the queue of patients waiting in the street outside his house; and once there was even an enterprising guru who rigged up a loudspeaker on a rented trishaw and rode through the neighborhood blasting Karo pop music and touting the universal virtues of his curing oil. Less visible but still sufficiently known or rumored were the many spirit mediums and herbalists who went about their work more discreetly out of the public eye. Popular wisdom held that these city gurus were all decadent, imposters, fakes. People spoke of mediums whose powers were "made" through sorcery or derived from blood-thirsty demons known as *bégu ganjang* ("tall ghosts"); others warned me of poisons, love potions, and sometimes outright fraud. "You see a medium who has nice clothes and a good house," explained my musician friend Pa Paham, "and you're not so well off yourself. So you think, I can do that too. A lot of these people are just copy-cats. They don't know anything, their spirit-guides may be worthless, they just imitate others so they can make money too."

As Pa Paham's comments suggest, the most frequent complaint against the city gurus was that they were all *komersil*. Darma, for one, cheerfully admitted the truth of this accusation. "It's the size of the bank balance," he told me one day, "that shows how good a curer is. That's how you measure success." Darma demonstrated his success in other ways, too, like the disco-style gold chains he wore around his neck, and his expensive watch and fashionable clothes. "You have to know when to be commercial and when not to be," he added. "A regular person may just bring me a pack of cigarettes, but if someone has done well financially on account of my help I don't hestitate to ask for a percentage. The point is, if you're going to ask, don't do it halfway."[19]

For Darma this strategy had paid off socially as well as financially. His critical neighbors generally granted him a respectful tolerance they rarely extended to other folk practitioners. Still, he wasn't present when, not long after I moved into the neighborhood, I had my first direct encounter with the spirits. Some people later said it was because the family involved suspected him of ensorcelling Suci, the afflicted girl; Darma claimed that they were just too cheap to pay his fees. As was usually the case, the matter was left unresolved.

Suci was a village girl who was staying with my Christian next-door neighbors. It was a common arrangement for rural students to board with their urban kin, earning their keep by helping with the housework and babysitting. Sometimes the line between family ties and servitude was drawn a little fine, though, and Suci grumbled about the family's strictness to anyone who would listen. Local gossips had much to say about her unhappy situation, either deploring the excessive household demands made on her or else complaining of the girl's slatternly behavior.

One afternoon my friends and I heard a dramatic, prolonged shrieking coming from the house next door. We dashed over to see what was happening, and found what seemed like most of the neighborhood (conspicuously excepting Darma who was, he later explained, politely waiting to be called in) packed nonchalantly into the narrow hallway where Suci was writhing on the floor, cursing violently. For the next few hours we women held her down so she wouldn't hurt herself or anyone else, and tried to calm her as she hurled insults at us, Allah, and the prophets. It's a Muslim jin, someone said. She's just gone crazy from frustration and overwork, another onlooker confided. More likely love magic, someone else commented knowingly.

Feeling for the first time like a real ethnographer, I took mental notes on the event unfolding before me. I pictured myself stepping into a scene from The Exorcist; only now the uncanny moment was dissonantly embodied in the material chill of the concrete floor, the hard contact with struggling flesh, the familiar voices and faces of neighbors-turned-spectators. Here it was at last, I thought, my own version of the initiatory moment made famous by Clifford Geertz's "Deep Play": caught up in the drama of unexpected events (there, a police raid), the anthropologist gains access to the deeper social life of the community!

Experiencing yourself as the main character in your own story can be extremely gratifying, but it requires a certain cooperation from the story's plot. In this case the moment passed; Suci was sent off in the night to a doctor or a guru (I never learned which), and that, as far as I could tell, was that. The encounter didn't open any of my neighbors' doors, which in any event hadn't actually been shut before. But it did show me how events could be erased from public scrutiny after the fact, and it gave me a new angle from which to approach the problem of belief.[20]

Both before and after the incident people regularly asked me if I believed in spirits. My usual reply was some unconvincing platitude about cultural relativism and local truths: Anthropologists, I would say, study different ways of understanding the world; surely many people believe in a world inhabited by spirits. This noncommittal response seemed like good ethnographic practice but personal bad faith; the answer I should have given, I thought, was the more honest (if somewhat impolite, in Karo terms) "No, I don't believe that spirits exist."

In any event, my interrogator would almost always surprise me by insisting strongly, "Well, I don't believe in them," and then paradoxically (as it seemed to me then) going on to tell stories of neighbors or kin who had been plagued by troublesome spirits or ensorcelled by wicked gurus. The first of these apparently contradictory statements was, I assumed, a kind of formal disclaimer, in line with the official position of the Karo Protestant Church or with local assumptions of what a Westerner would want to hear. In other words, it was the polite Karo equivalent of my own disingenuous nonreply. Having properly denied the existential reality of spirits, my interrogator could then go on to explore in a practical way the troublesome, marvelous things that spirits and gurus do in the world.

While politeness and social conformity (on both sides) may have contributed to these small discursive misrecognitions, I have come to realize that what I had taken for a logical contradiction was primarily a mistake in translation. The Indonesian word *percaya* (and the equivalent Karo term *tek*) translates ambiguously as "believe" or "believe in." Asking whether I percaya/tek the spirits might mean "Do you believe in spirits?" but it could also mean "Do you *believe* spirits?" Do you *trust* them? Many Karo Christians believe in spirits and gurus, but whether they trust them is another matter altogether. Non-Christians, including spirit mediums, are even less likely to trust uncritically the actions and pronouncements of the spirits. In this sense, my uncertain answer, given for all the wrong reasons, was in fact the right reply to questions about the spirit world: Who knows? Who *ever* knows?

The simple faith that Henk had expected to encounter at the seance (and which he rediscovered for himself in the clear moonlight of God's rule) was a far cry from the complex blend of casual acceptance, skeptical disregard, and occasional awe with which Karo, in his time as in mine, confront the world of the spirits. Questions of belief in the existential sense are hardly at issue here; or at least they are hardly of interest. What is interesting to Karo, and what came to interest me very much as well, was the question of plausibility, of how one goes about making sense of something you can never get to the bottom of.

If my neighbors were less than enthusiastic about my project, the mediums themselves seemed delighted to have an anthropologist of their own. By the time I began to get acquainted with them, I was moderately comfortable speaking the Karo language and had been adopted into a Karo family. This gave me a position from which to reckon my kin relations with others and thus a means of determining appropriate terms of address to use in conversation. My participation in the discourse of kinship gave the mediums a playful way to incorporate my anomalous presence into their social world. They were, in any event, used to dealing with anomalous beings, human and spirit, and less concerned than my neighbors had been with living up to standards of middle-class respectability. "Oh, here's Beru Karo again," they would greet me, laughing, when I showed up with my tape recorder and camera. "Beru Karo," woman of the Karo-Karo clan, was their joking reference to my adoptive family, made funnier because it was also the form of address used for the frivolous sister-spirits who were among the favorites of the pantheon; they also addressed me, more familiarly, as "Si Mary," or *anakku*, "my child." (By way of contrast, my neighbors, from children to grandparents, consistently referred to me as "*kak* [M./I., *kakak*, elder sister] Mary.")

My first formal meetings with Karo curers came through a somewhat unsystematic survey conducted with the help of a group of university students, some Karo and others not, who had befriended me. Focusing primarily on the Padang Bulan area, we sought out as many mediums and other Karo folk practitioners as we could find. My co-worker Juara Ginting, an anthropology student at USU, was at the same time collecting materials for his thesis on Karo concepts of mental illness and folk therapies (Ginting 1986). Having grown up in Padang Bulan, he was personally acquainted with some of the first mediums we met; others were pointed out to us by their neighbors or by local shopkeepers and coffee-shop habitués. News of our activities spread ahead of us, and after a while mediums began referring us to their colleagues (or, contrariwise, warning us of their competitors). Because of the disreputable and thus slightly subterranean nature of urban mediumship there is no way of knowing how complete our survey was, but we identified and spoke to a total of nearly eighty Karo curers in Padang Bulan and elsewhere in Karoland.

Because we thought that my presence at a first meeting might be intimidating, initial contacts with mediums were made by my student helpers. If the medium agreed to a second visit I would come along with the original interviewers, stepping into a situation in which some degree of familiarity had already been established. This contributed significantly to the relaxed atmosphere of these meetings and, I think, to the welcome that I received from the curers.

Except for a few of the mediums I knew best, I rarely visited them alone. This was in part a concession to public standards of respectability, which demanded that unmarried women not travel about by themselves, but it was also a matter of local conventions of conviviality. Speaking privately with a medium suggested a professional consultation rather than a social visit and thus significantly inhibited conversation between us; it also cast me rather more as an "interviewer" and my host more as an "informant" than I found socially comfortable.[21] In contrast, for a group of students to drop in and swap stories with their elders was an event not far out of the ordinary, and having an attentive young audience (and the supply of cigarettes, betel, and snacks we provided) allowed our host to become the central figure in a lively evening's entertainment. At the same time, the explicitly public nature of these performances conferred on us all a necessary regard for the proper limits of narrative intimacy, which I have tried to respect in my re-presentation of their stories.

I have tried to stay as close as possible to what seems to me to have been the teller's intention in each case. Except where noted my retellings follow the transcript of recorded conversations; my translations aim to capture some of the feeling, if not the artfulness, of Karo narrative performance. Even so, readers should not mistake these representations of others' speech for the actual presence of other voices in this text, any more than they should regard the stories themselves as unmediated and disinterested accounts of "real" experience. Like any other stories of personal experience, these were public performances of remembered events, shaped by the narrative politics and poetics of previous tellings and retellings, and told (now) with an eye to the particular audience at hand. In all cases, my tellers appear pseudonymously, as does the spirit of the man I call "Setia Aron Ginting"; except for "Simpang Meriah" and the village of "Kuta Kepultaken," actual place names are used throughout. Since what I share with you here is mostly open knowledge within the Karo community, this imposed anonymity is intended not so much to ensure the privacy of my kind hosts as to avoid their being held accountable for any mistakes or misunderstandings that I may have unwittingly perpetrated in retelling their stories.

Although we approached these meetings with a standard set of questions about curing and spirit mediumship, these were in most cases quickly diverted into the flow of conversation. The talk consistently outplayed our expectations, guiding us to matters we should have been thinking about but hadn't considered and demanding that we all take part in the evening's exchange of stories. We talked about school, my friends joked about love charms, I told about life in America, and our hosts playfully offered to fix me up with their sons or nephews. Once I was offered a teaching charm—to make my students pay attention in class. (Unfortunately I passed it up.) We all talked about the weather, soccer scores, and vegetable prices, about local characters and mutual acquaintances. And the curers told us about their lives, their encounters with the spirits, and their feeling of being out of place—of hanging without a rope, as they sometimes put it—in a time officially designated as Indonesia's Age of Development. I had intended to study the mediums' curing practices, but in the end it was this sense of out-of-placeness that defined my project.

From our conversations I came to be on especially friendly terms with three groups of curers, two centered in Medan's Padang Bulan area and the third (no longer active) around the highland town of Berastagi. The first Medan group was the organized network of spirit mediums and ritual participants I have called the "Arisan of Simpang Meriah" and who sometimes call themselves the *persadan perkeramat deleng Sibayak*, the association of devotees of the spirits of Mount Sibayak. Much of my knowledge of Karo ritual performance comes from my attendance at their monthly kerja nini ceremonies to honor the mountain spirits. At these events I danced and ate with the spirits, provided the umangs with their preferred cigars, served tea to the musicians and guests, took photographs and notes, helped out in the kitchen, and did duty from time to time as the butt of spirit jokes. To my dismay, I became a favorite partner of the European spirits, who enjoyed the chance to "disco" and make lewd remarks in fractured foreigners' Malay, and who generously shared their expensive European food—apples and cake—with me.

Not everyone was so open. A few Arisan members, I later learned, suspected that I was going to make a fortune by publishing their secrets, or by setting up shop as a medium in America. (Not familiar at the time with New Age "channeling," I denied this latter suspicion by insisting that Americans did not go in for communicating with spirits.) While I had no such intentions, their concern is nonetheless valid, and it is one reason I have decided not to write here of the practice of curing or the rules of ritual performance.

The second group was less formally constituted, consisting of a number of male curers in Medan and the Karo highlands who occasionally worked together or consulted with one another. More mobile and on the whole better educated than their female counterparts, they tended to identify themselves with the "learned" characteristics of the wandering male guru rather dramatically described by Neumann (1910:2) as the "walking encyclopedia of his people." The gurus that I knew fell short of this ideal, as they well recognized. Some took this as a fact of the modern age in which they lived, but others saw it as a failure of their own training, whether because of (in one case) an adolescent unwillingness to take seriously a grandfather's guidance or (in another) a father's unwillingness to pass on to his son the core of his knowledge.

In colonial ethnographies and Karo folktales a sharp gender-based distinction is drawn between the trained male guru and the inspired female medium. In practice, however, this distinction is significantly blurred.[22] Mediums, inspired by the spirits of great gurus of the past, perform as ritual leaders and tap into the guru's wisdom; conversely, the gurus I knew augmented their always-incomplete training with the spirit-inspired (and so always hypothetically complete) skills of mediumship. Although Karo spoke of this confusion of ritual roles as an effect of tradition's decline, I do not think it is entirely a modern phenomenon. In the world of the spirits, categories are always open to alteration and history is always under revision.

The processes and possibilities of historical revision were most complexly articulated in the stories of the third group, an older generation associated, directly or indirectly, with Pa Kantur Purba, a famous local guru, chess master, village chief, and sometime counterfeiter in the highland village of Rumah Berastagi in the 1930s and 1940s. Pa Kantur, who was better known by the honorific title "Sibayak Berastagi," deftly ascended the precarious scaffolding of colonial statecraft, local lineage rivalry, and charismatic prestige-building that framed the political world of colonial Karoland. He was also reputed to be the first curer who "carried" for himself the regional tutelary spirits of Mount Sibayak's triple peak. Many of the people he cured were given their own spirit-guides from among the lesser spirits of the mountain's slopes, and after his death some began to claim for themselves the high spirits once associated with him.

In the 1960s a revitalization movement known as Persadan Merga Si Lima, the Association of the Five Clans, formed around several of Pa Kantur's former patients (K., *tinambaren*) who were practicing as spirit mediums in the market town of Berastagi. Focused on the spirits of Mount Sibayak (and especially my "namesakes," the frivolous Beru Karos), this organization flourished for nearly a decade, and subsequently formed the institutional basis for the contemporary Hindu Karo movement. Through the auspices of these organizations, the mountain spirits have now become "democratized" (as one devotee put it) as universal benefactors, without regard to kin affiliation, place of origin, or even ethnic identity among their supplicants.

The Arisan of Simpang Meriah was one of the few local branches of Persadan Merga Si Lima that remained active in the 1980s. In this sense and more directly as well the Arisan was descended from Sibayak Berastagi's curing practice, for Nandé Randal, the senior medium who brought many of them into the arts of mediumship, was one of his tinambaren and, for a time, his ritual assistant. Through Nandé Randal I met several of Sibayak Berastagi's other patient/helpers. I also discussed the Persadan Merga Si Lima movement with many of the original participants in Berastagi and in Medan, as well as with some of their Christian (and non-Christian) opponents, several members of the Purba lineages of Rumah Berastagi, and, on one memorable occasion, the mountain spirits themselves. What emerged from these conversations was a discordant collection of fragmentary recollections, debatable (and disputed) claims, and probably ad hoc explanations—all of which, I should add, the spirits did nothing to clarify.

I also spent a good deal of time with some of the musicians, professional and amateur, who played regularly at secular and religious ceremonies around Karoland. Unlike the curers, who tended to approach ritual enactment pragmatically and improvisationally, most of the musicians I knew were carefully attentive to the formal aspects of ritual performance. They were often quite critical of the mediums' skills and most particularly of their lack of ritual knowledge. In the musicians' view, spiritual efficacy was created by the replication of an authoritative pattern of words and acts, and a good ritual was one that adhered precisely to the prescriptive regulations of custom: the proper sequence of songs, the correct offerings, respect shown to spirits and to performers, the right words spoken in the appropriate order. From the curers' perspective, on the other hand, a good ritual was one that had a good effect—"effect" being rather broadly defined to include impressing and entertaining the audience as well as curing the patient. Like a good story, an effective ceremony exceeded, rather than conformed to, the rules of ritual order; that excess was the sign, for good or ill, of supernatural participation.

Such perspectival differences, sighted along lines of (among other things) gender, generation, profession, social standing, religion, and perhaps personal inclination, inflect the discursive field in which the out-of-placeness of Karo spirit mediums resides. Instead of reducing this contentious mixture to a monolithic, progressive narrative of gain and loss, of "change" and "continuity," I want to propose a history that is not about change and, conversely, an anthropology that is not about continuity. What I propose instead is a careful investigation of the concrete historical effects of incising certain imaginary figures of continuity and change across a living social world.

Over the past century Karoland has been the scene of colonial conquest, Christian conversion, commercial agricultural development, Japanese military occupation, political mobilization, national revolution, mass urban migration, waves of military and paramilitary violence, and, since the establishment of New Order rule in 1966, the persistent technological and rhetorical intrusions of state-sponsored modernization and military-bureaucratic regimentation. Through all this, Karo have held fast to what they describe as their distinctive *adat*. This Malay term, which has now come into common use to replace its Karo synonym *bicara*, was appropriated by the Dutch during the colonial period to refer to indigenous systems of customary law; as Neumann (1902b:66–67) noted, it had at that time the wider connotation of those spiritual and social bonds, encompassing obligation and habit, form and feeling, which constitute the Karo social world. The land and its supernatural inhabitants and guardians, human communities, kinsmen and -women, the living and the dead: all of these were joined and regulated through the flexibly pervasive, relatively pragmatic system of the bicara. More narrowly defined today as the universally accepted (and thus secular) rules of proper behavior between (living) kin, adat forms the basis for a contemporary Karo social identity imagined as historically continuous, culturally homogeneous, and ethnically discrete.

The ideological and practical importance of adat in Karo life and social imagination is undeniable. But to speak of adat as the unchanging basis of Karo communal identity is to obscure the external conditions and internal contests of the community's historical self-imagining. Such claims to continuity leave unexamined the process whereby the reproduction of adat has depended on its circumscription as kinship and thus on the exclusion or marginalization of those aspects of Karo historical identity—and of those members of the Karo community—deemed inappropriate to its modern secular form. It is this process of exclusion that constitutes "curing" for the ethnographer as a discrete analytical category and for my progressive Christian neighbors as at once a residual category of "superstition" persisting irrelevantly in the contemporary Age of Development, and a modern category of "commercialism" decked out (as Marx might have said) in the time-honored disguise of tradition: the spirits of the past invoked to serve the interests of the present.[23] Hence my neighbors' insistence that anthropologists should study kinship, not curing.

It is not simply that curing and spirit mediumship have been defined out of adat—though that is certainly the case—but in a rather more complex way that historical continuity has been invested in the repetition of formal regulative patterns rather than in the fortuitous, interruptive conjuncture of human agency with the persistent capriciousness of the spirits. Stories of spirit-encounters do not comprise a counter-tradition opposing this official discourse of adat-as-kinship. Instead they register, through an insistent, subversive differing—from normative representations of social reality as well as from one another—the displacement of mediumship as social practice. That displacement is the ground-point of my account of Karo narrative experience.

As Carolyn Steedman (1986:6) has pointed out, "the stories that people tell themselves in order to explain how they got to the place they currently inhabit—are often in deep and ambiguous conflict with the official interpretative devices of a culture." My reading of Karo narrative experience turns on this distinction, which will be set out in greater detail in chapter 4. In brief, it consists in the opposed tendencies *within ideology* toward, on the one hand, the totalizing pronouncements of "official discourse" and, on the other, the partial, "unofficial" status assumed by stories of personal experience. These stories, and particularly their lapses, disruptions, and distortions of narrative "good sense," consistently stake their subversive claims on the evidence of experience. As I have argued above, such claims should not be construed as unproblematic guarantees of narrative authenticity. Neither can these unofficial stories be understood as reflecting some access to a truth outside of ideology. They can, however, shed a little light on the murky political operations through which official standards of the "good" and the "true," of constancy and ephemerality, are established and maintained.

The chapters that follow are written in a historical vein that attempts to dislodge the categories of continuity and change that have so often served to motivate and to resolve the moral dramas we imagine, as well as those we enact. This means attending to the stories people tell about their lives, not as reservoirs of information about "what happened" at a particular moment, but rather as interested efforts to map a pathway across the shifting landscape of historical memory. The stories I tell are intended to be mutually illuminating; angles of approach, as well as focal instances, vary. As a preliminary sketch of the social terrain the reader is being asked to traverse, I offer in chapter 2 a brief historical description of some aspects of Karo kinship, religion, and political life.

Chapter 3, centered in the highland market town of Berastagi, is a more detailed examination of the political and economic effects of colonial rule in Karoland. The first section of this book to be written, it began as an attempt to answer what seemed to be a simple question of classification: Should Karo society be described as "tribal" or "peasant"? That question remains unanswered, and the chapter has developed instead into an exploration of the social meaning of markets and money in colonial Karoland—matters that were, though in a rather different sense, still of profound concern to my Karo neighbors and friends, and which they addressed through their critiques of the commercialism of contemporary mediumship.

Chapter 4 focuses on the politics of the supernatural. Here I consider some of the narrative strategies through which the spirits of Mount Sibayak were simultaneously represented and contained in the European literature of colonial Karoland. The processes of narrative incorporation and exclusion, and the tensions and complicities between officializing discursive strategies and unofficial subversive effects, are among the issues addressed here. As elsewhere in this book, my intention is not so much to expose the duplicities and failures of colonial narration (a task already engaged by others) as to open up unexpected ways of reading colonial and, by extension, contemporary ethnographic texts—beyond the figures in the carpet, and against the grain.

The end of chapter 4 begins a turn to Karo narrative, which continues in chapter 5 with a series of stories that constellate around Lau Debuk-Debuk, the hot springs at Mount Sibayak's base. Tracking the multiple intersections there of a popular legend, a song, and a social movement, I explore Lau Debuk-Debuk as a field of narrative possibilities, a "space full of stories," in Calvino's (1981:109) phrase, "where you can move in all directions . . . always finding stories that cannot be told until other stories are told first." In this setting, any search for origins is confounded by the perpetual mutability of the historical/ethnographic object.

In chapter 6, a set of stories about becoming a medium raises the ethnographic problem of women's subjectivity. Set in the commercial agricultural zone surrounding the Berastagi market, these stories look back on the last years of Dutch colonial rule, the first years of a marriage, and the mountainside adventure that changed a woman's life. Taking up the possibility of narration "at odds with language," I suggest that a revision in anthropological readership is needed as a first step toward the production of a thoroughly gendered ethnographic practice.

Drawing from conversations with one of Karoland's great raconteurs, the extraordinary man I call Pak Tua, I offer in chapter 7 another possible mapping of this terrain of commerce and wonder. Pak Tua's trickster-like narrative escapades were the inspiration for what I here call the "fugitive's eye view." Like these sly tales of strategic duplicity, the fugitive's view does not constitute a challenge to official order; rather, it operates subversively alongside and within more organized forms of compliance and resistance—which are, to be sure, both dependent upon and antagonistic to its disruptive presence.

I opened this chapter with the story of Henk's unexpected experiences at a Karo funeral seance. Through this fictional device I have tried to make visible some of the narrative assumptions that ground the writing of ethnography. In chapter 8 I close my textual circle with the story of a seance that I attended in 1985. Here the unexpected ground of narration is political, not literary. Casting historical memory—the memory, literally, of a moment of danger—across the border between the living and the dead, the seance reveals some of the life-and-death choices that have enabled the crossing of another violent divide, the one separating Indonesia's Old and New Order political regimes. Which should remind us all, finally, of what the stakes of storytelling may actually be for those whose lives are the subject of the ethnographer's stories.

Two

The Karo Social World

THE KARO are one of the linguistically and culturally related peoples of the North Sumatran interior—the others are Mandailing, Angkola, Toba, Simelungun, and Pakpak—generically classed as "Batak," a name that seems to have been initially used to distinguish pagan highlanders from the Muslim Malays of the coastal lowlands.[1] These clan-based, agrarian societies of the central Bukit Barisan mountain range are all characterized by a kinship-based social configuration ordered around patrilineal descent reckoning and preferential matrilateral cross-cousin marriage. Local languages are more or less mutually unintelligible, and there are significant differences in custom and social organization among these groups.

Karoland proper, the northernmost of the Batak homelands, stretches from the northern shore of Lake Toba through the Bukit Barisan mountain range to the southern border of Aceh. To the east, early Karo settlement extended through the piedmont (*dusun*) region into the coastal strip nominally controlled by the petty Malay sultanates of Deli, Serdang, and Langkat.[2] Administratively, Karoland today is divided among several regencies (*kabupaten*) within the Province of North Sumatra: Kabupaten Karo (the highland plateau), and the interior portions of Kabupatens Langkat and Deli-Serdang.

With an altitude of about 1,300 meters above sea level, the Karo plateau is cool and relatively dry. Two active volcanos, Mount Sibayak and Mount Sinabung, are located on its borders. Although the soils of the rest of the Batak highlands are relatively poor, volcanic eruptions have produced an extremely fertile topsoil in the Karo region; the land is, however, difficult to irrigate because of its permeability (Scholz 1983:79–80). Prior to the introduction of commercial agriculture in the early twentieth century dry-field rice was the principal crop throughout the region, with a small amount of wet rice grown seasonally along the riverbanks.[3] Today the Karo highlands are one of Indonesia's major vegetable- and fruit-producing regions.

In the early 1950s, after the conclusion of the Indonesian revolution, many highland Karo began to migrate to the coastal lowlands in search of available farmland.[4] These migrants took over large portions of the formerly European-owned tobacco estates on the outskirts of the city of Medan. Karo settlement in the 1950s was centered on the Padang Bulan Estate on Medan's southwest margin, an area still known as the Karo district of the city. As the city grew, rural Padang Bulan was absorbed into the metropole, and Karo who had moved to the lowlands in search of new agricultural land found themselves, willy nilly, city dwellers.

Most rural Karo are involved in mixed agricultural production, growing cash crops as well as rice for family consumption. Urban Karo fall roughly into three occupational groups. First are the petty entrepreneurs: traders and produce brokers, shopkeepers, and *toké motor*—owners of commercial transport vehicles. The second group is composed of better-educated Karo, who tend to gravitate to the professions: law, medicine, or education, rather than to business or office work. The third group, rather a residual category, is made up of young men who have neither the education (or, in some cases, the necessary connections) to enter a profession nor the capital to go into entrepreneurial activity. They may work as bus drivers or conductors, but more frequently spend their time idling in the coffeeshops, or else enter the quasi-underworld of the *preman* (from the Dutch *vrij man*, "freeman, civilian")—casual day laborers and petty criminals who serve as informal "security" guards in the markets and bus stations. Aside from these young men, most urban Karo men and women are involved in some sort of economic activity. Small-scale trade is mostly in women's hands, and whatever economic endeavors they, or their husbands, engage in, most women also maintain some farmland for growing the family's rice.

Travel throughout the region is relatively easy. Buses regularly cover the short distance—about a two-hour trip—between Medan and Kabanjahé, the district capital and market center of the Karo plateau. Main roads are paved and mostly well maintained; side roads often are not, however, and especially in the rainy season some remote villages can only be reached on foot, by buffalo cart, or (for the daring) by motorcycle. Upstream and downstream, travel is constant: traders carrying goods to sell, students going to a village harvest dance or coming home to see their family, grandparents off to visit their children in the city, city dwellers on their way to a ceremony in the highlands.

Although the 1908 opening of the Medan–Kabanjahé highway facilitated the flow of goods and people between highlands and lowlands, Karo mobility is not altogether an effect of improved transport conditions. It was already well established, if less secure, before the coming of European planters to the Sumatra east coast in the mid-nineteenth century. Traders and wandering gurus criss-crossed the Sumatran interior; young men sought to improve their fates through service among lowland

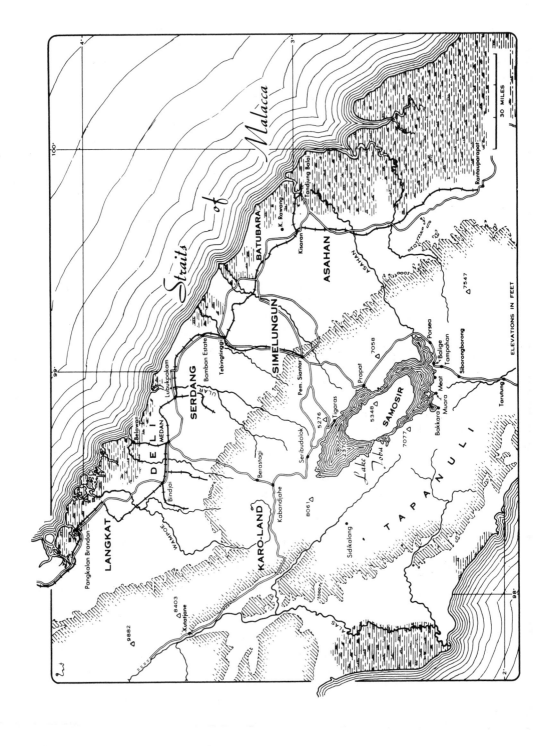

ELEVATIONS IN FEET

30 MILES

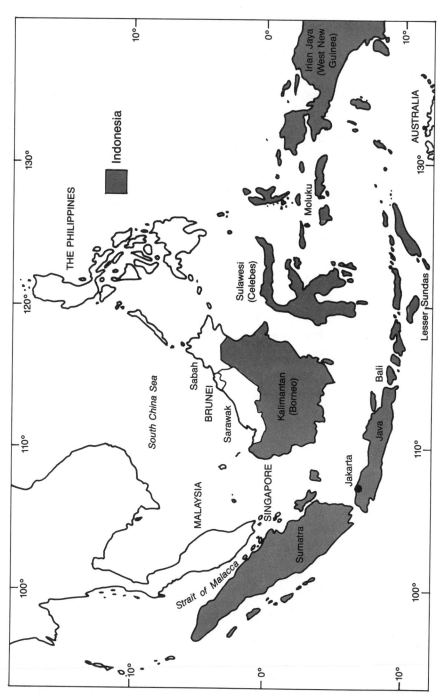

Above, map of Indonesia; *opposite page*, North Sumatra Province (formerly colonial residencies of East Sumatra and Tapanuli).

Malays; and when peace prevailed regional markets served as meeting places for men and women from sometimes distant highland villages. Clan dispersal and the expansiveness of Karo kinship calculations spun webs of relatedness across the whole area of Karo settlement—indeed beyond it, through conventional equivalences between Karo clans and those of other Batak groups, as well as through clan affiliations attributed to lowland Malays on the basis of putative Karo descent.[5] Marriage might move a young man or woman into a community of relative strangers; ceremonial participation followed the lines of distant marriages and prompted regular intercourse between communities so joined. It is thus not surprising that themes of travel predominate in the Karo laments (*bilang-bilang*), folktales, myths, and clan histories collected in the early years of colonial rule; nor that (as my Karo friends joked) while Toba Batak pop songs today are all about education and mothers, Karo songs are still mostly about leaving home.

Kinship

According to anthropologist Masri Singarimbun, who is himself Karo, "an understanding of the Karo system of social relations between kin and relatives by marriage is the necessary starting point for an understanding of most other aspects of Karo culture and society" (Singarimbun 1975: xv–xvi). Kin ties are almost infinitely expansive, at least in a notional sense, and provide the primary idiom for the articulation of social relations. For Karo, virtually every social relationship, even a chance encounter between strangers at the market, is conducted according to the principles of kinship. Upon meeting, two previously unacquainted Karo will establish a kin relation (actual or fictive) to one another through the process of mutual interrogation known as *ertutur*. Each in turn asks for the other's paternal (*merga* for men, *beru* for women) and maternal (*bebere*) clan and subclan affiliations, home village, and, in the case of a married woman, her husband's clan (*jé*). By tracing known, and often quite distant, relationships with agnatic and affinal kin, Karo can usually discover by at least one route (and usually several) a kin connection with any other person. Once determined, this presumptive tie defines the relative status of each, the particular terms of address used in their conversation, and the degree of deference or familiarity appropriate to their interaction.[6]

Karo society is composed of five major exogamous patrilineal clans (merga), each segmented into a number of subclans that are, in turn, divided into local lineages and lineage segments. Clans and subclans are dispersed and do not act as corporate groups, and there is no order of rank among either clans or subclans. While Karo mergas are commonly described in the ethnographic literature as "descent groups," it would be more appropriate, as Singarimbun (1975:72) notes, to describe them as "aggregates of named groups [i.e., subclans]," for there is no assumption that all clan members (or indeed subclan members) are descended from a single apical ancestor. Nevertheless, clanmates are bound together by ties of equality and mutual support, and consider one another as classificatory *senina* (same-sex sibling) or *turang* (opposite-sex sibling). The rule of clan exogamy is strictly observed, since marriage between turangs (even if they are of different subclans) is considered to be incestuous.[7]

Links between individual men and between groups (family units and local lineage segments) are established and maintained through the giving and receiving of women in marriage. Marriages between *impal*, or matrilateral cross-cousins (MBD-FZS), are a cultural ideal, but comprise only a small percentage of actual marriages (Singarimbun 1975:158).[8] However, all marriages are treated as if they were between actual cross-cousins. Thus, for example, the terms *mama* and *mami*—narrowly defined as mother's brother and mother's brother's wife, respectively—are used by a man to refer to his wife's parents, whether or not they are his relatives by birth.

Through marriage, asymmetrical relations are established between superior wife-giving groups (*kalimbubu*) and their subordinate wife-receivers (*anak beru*).[9] The kalimbubu–anak beru relationship is marked not only by a status differential, but also by numerous reciprocal rights and obligations between the two. The anak beru are expected to perform the necessary labor at rituals sponsored by their kalimbubu, to speak on their kalimbubu's behalf in public negotations, to offer advice and economic assistance when necessary, and to provide a variety of everyday services for the kalimbubu. Good health, prosperity, and especially procreative potential are dependent upon the continued benevolence and blessings of the kalimbubu, the "visible god" (*dibata niidah*) of their anak beru. The relation between wife-givers and wife-receivers is thus, despite its status asymmetry, one of mutual dependence. While the good will of the kalimbubu is necessary for the anak beru's well-being, little can be accomplished by the kalimbubu without the services of their anak beru.

A well-organized ritual is an indicator of kin-group solidarity and a significant marker of social status. Kin relations are symbolically acted out in all aspects of ritual, from the group dances that open the ceremony and the seating arrangements that mark kin-group roles and statuses, to the transfer of objects that serve as representations of the ties between kin. The presence of members of the various kin groups of the ritual's sponsor is essential, and each group has a specific role to play in the ritual. In practical terms, the most significant role is that of the anak beru, who perform all the necessary labor, cook and serve the food, distribute gifts to the guests, and serve as mediators in ritual negotiations. Without the labor provided by the anak beru, the sponsorship of a successful ritual is impossible. The kalimbubu (by birth and by marriage) of the sponsor must also attend the ritual to bestow their blessings and to legitimize the proceedings. The sponsor's own family and clanmates should likewise be present as a sign of group solidarity. Should any of these kin groups not be represented, the sponsor may expect serious spiritual as well as social repercussions.[10]

In a world Karo often describe as *modéren*, as Rita Kipp (1976:265) has noted, "the foundation of Karo life, the kinship system, remains firmly intact."[11] This claim is not simply an artifact of anthropological imagining; Karo tend to see the matter in much the same way, and to say so (repeatedly) in ritual oratory as well as in their conversations with outsiders. And as they say, "adat"—by which term Karo today mean the rules that govern proper behavior between kin and the acts that accord with those rules—does indeed provide coherence to contemporary Karo social life.

But the rhetorical *reproduction* of Karo adat as a transhistorical social object should not be mistaken for its *continuation* as a timeless structure of human social relations independent of actual human agency. This is an important distinction in any case, but given the practical mutability of Karo social arrangements, it is especially significant here. The diversity and instability of Karo political institutions, their engagement with Malay and European expansionist states, Calvinist missionary programs, and colonial entrepreneurial agendas, as well as their implication in the increasingly intrusive social and religious policies of the contemporary Indonesian state, necessitate a recognition of Karo adat as the outcome of quite complex historical processes of social negotiation.[12]

Colonial Cross-Purposes: Planters, Missionaries, and Administrators

Before the establishment of colonial rule in Sumatra, coastal populations and hinterlands communities throughout the region coexisted in an intricate social symbiosis. Unlike Southeast Asian agrarian kingdoms or European territorial states, the power of local rulers was directed mostly toward nonsubject populations. In a social-economic formation consistently (mis-)recognized by Europeans as "piracy" or "banditry," trade-based coastal principalities depended less on controlling land or people than on mediating the movement of goods along international distributive routes. Cultural as well as political boundaries were subtly articulated, flexibly adaptable, and often relatively indeterminate.[13]

These nuances of identity, alliance, and authority were largely invisible to the region's early European visitors, who inscribed instead rigidly antipodal and geographically determined "countertypes" (Boon 1990:30) across the Sumatran landscape: relatively civilized lowland Muslims, pagan savages in the interior highlands. Thus Admiral Beaulieu in 1622 wrote of the Bataks: "[t]he inland people are independent, and speak a language different from the Malayan. Are idolaters, and eat human flesh; never ransom prisoners, but eat them with pepper and salt. Have no religion, but some polity" (cited in Marsden 1966:390–91). Subsequent European observers continued to stress the cultural, religious, and even racial differences between Bataks and Malays, placing particular emphasis on the highlanders' anthropophagy (for which, it should be noted, there is no first-hand evidence).[14] Considerably less attention was paid to the political autonomy that Beaulieu described.

Although eastern Sumatra had by the early nineteenth century become extensively involved in European trade networks and peripherally linked to the competitive empire-building strategies of Britain and Holland, it was not until 1863 that there was a significant European presence in the region. In that year Jacobus Nienhuys, acting for the Dutch investment consortium of Pieter van den Arend, visited the east coast and established the first tobacco plantation there, on land leased from the Malay sultan of Deli. By 1888 there were 148 European agricultural enterprises in the region (Pelzer 1978:52), and the "Dollar Land of Deli," as the lowland *cultuurgebied* (plantation zone) was known, was becoming a primary revenue source for the colonial empire of the Netherlands East Indies, into which it had by that time been incorporated as the *Residentie van Sumatra's Oostkust.*

Contra the planters' mythologizing of Deli before their arrival as an "untrodden" and virtually uninhabited "primeval forest," the European plantation zone was located in a well-populated area of mixed Malay and Karo settlement (Volker 1928:7; cf. Stoler 1985:25). John Anderson, who visited the east coast in 1823 as an agent for the British East India Company's Penang office, estimated the Malay population of Deli at seven thousand, with "very numerous" Karo settlements inland from the narrow coastal strip of Malay habitation.[15] These lowland Karo traded, intermarried, and formed transitory political alliances with their Malay neighbors, in some cases strategically converting to Islam. But they were not politically subordinate to the Malay sultans; their primary extralocal allegiances were with their "upstream" kin in the highlands.[16]

It was thus an "unfortunate accident," as missionary Joustra later complained, that Karo settlements in Upper Deli were, in the early years of Dutch rule, administratively incorporated into the territory controlled by the sultan of Deli. Such an arrangement had no basis in law or custom,

Joustra argued, but was the result of the false claims of the sultan, "who, to put it bluntly, had our government badly hornswoggled [*bij den neus gehad heeft*]," and who asserted, "with a magisterial gesture, 'that all the land up to yonder blue mountains' was his possession" (Joustra 1905:364–65). "Empty" land that Karo villages considered to be their own was ceded by the sultan to European plantation enterprises in 1871 for the development of tobacco estates. Karo responded to this intrusion by attacking and burning the new tobacco plantations on their land.[17] The "Batak War" of 1872 was put down militarily by the Dutch and a territorially based administrative hierarchy—the "autonomous" native government (D., *inlandsche zelfbestuur*)—was formed, headed by the sultan, who ruled his new Karo subjects through Islamicized Karo intermediaries.[18]

As a result of its investigations into the causes of this unrest, the Netherlands Indies government came to acknowledge the validity of Karo grievances, and required that Karo rulers and village heads be compensated for lands alienated to the plantation companies. Terms more favorable to local communities were established for future agrarian concessions. Nevertheless, Karo continued sporadically into the 1890s to burn down tobacco barns and raid plantations.

In 1888, dissatisfied with the increasingly restrictive government interventions and eager to end the incendiary violence, the Deli Planters' Association tried another tack. J. T. Cremer, an influential Deli planter turned politician, offered to finance a mission post among the Karo communities of the upper plantation zone.[19] "Let us try to bring them civilization," he wrote in a circular soliciting funds for the project, "which is the consequence of Christian principles, to win their respect for Europeans in the Indies, and thereby to bind them to our rule" (cited in Rita S. Kipp 1990:45). Despite some misgivings about this ethically dubious source of funds, the liberal-Calvinist Dutch Missionary Society (Nederlandsch Zendelinggenootschap, NZG) accepted the offer in 1890. For the next forty years the small Karo mission community was subsidized by the plantations—a "providential boon" according to the mission's supporters but to its critics the "Faustian bargain that forever compromised the mission's hope of success" (ibid.:38).

It is an anthropologist's retrospective temptation to cast European colonialism as a monolithic force whose various components operated in a functionally integrated, not to say single-minded, manner. Such a perspective, as Stoler (1985, 1989b, 1992) has shown, does no justice to the complexities of the East Sumatran situation. Class-based conflicts of interests divided the European plantation community; doctrinal, tactical, and personal differences strained relations in the mission community; shifting Dutch political agendas arranged and rearranged colonial administrative structures. The three major wings of the colonial "establish-ment"—planters, government administrators, and, later, missionaries—were seriously at odds over the aims, policies, and principles of colonial rule. Metropolitan directives—from company executives in Amsterdam, government officials in Batavia and the Hague, or the NZG board in Rotterdam—were sometimes disregarded or circumvented by their local executors. Ethnic partisanships as well as racial and religious antipathies ran through the apparatus of colonial administration: C. J. Westenberg, the influential first Controleur for Batak Affairs, was a keen supporter of Karo interests against the Muslim-dominated native government and at times against the mission (Rita S. Kipp 1990:49–50, 89); many of his colleagues displayed a relatively lenient attitude toward the ambitions of their Muslim Malay allies (Joustra 1902a:61; Neumann 1902b:67). And the notoriously corrupt lifestyle, hierarchical pretensions, and frontier vi-olence of colonial Deli put it beyond the pale of "respectable" European society (Stoler 1989a).

From the colonized side, the East Sumatran political picture is no less complicated. The resentments and complicities that had found expression in the Batak War of 1872 continued for decades to disrupt the *rust en orde* (D., "peace and order") of the plantation zone. Malay political and religious expansionism, supported by the government as a means of uni-fying native political administration, created new animosities between and within local communities—local tensions that were further exacer-bated by the ongoing colonial war with Aceh, Deli's powerful Islamic neighbor to the north. The introduction of large numbers of Chinese, Indian, and, later, Javanese estate workers further complicated the ethnic geography of the plantation zone. Among Karo, long-standing conflicts and new ambitions were stimulated by the colonial distribution of gifts—guns, opium, and, later, mission schools—to cooperative local leaders.[20] Lineage and intervillage rivalries, a familiar feature of the Karo political scene, intensified in the decade prior to annexation. An especially violent dispute within the Purba lineage of the large highland village of Ka-banjahé threatened to draw the highlands into the Acehnese war. Dutch mediation led to a reconciliation between the village's two rivalrous headmen, but this in turn led other highland leaders to fear the growing influence and ambition of the Kabanjahé headmen.

H. C. Kruijt, the first missionary to the Karo, arrived on this conten-tious scene in April 1890. Two years later, disillusioned by colonial *real-politik* and dismayed by Karo mores, he departed from the mission field; his successor, Jan Wijngaarden, baptized the first six converts shortly be-fore his death in 1893. By the turn of the century the mission staff had grown to four European missionaries and their families, and about the same number of native (non-Karo) Christian teacher-evangelists.

Pressed by their backers for quick results but hindered by the dusun's rugged terrain and the obstructions of the Islamic native government, the missionaries lobbied the government for permission to open a highland post. Informally, colonial officials encouraged this ambition. What they did not reveal, however, was that a secret government policy denied the missionaries entry to the Karo plateau without the explicit invitation and safeguard of local Karo rulers (Rita S. Kipp 1990:86–87).

The invitation (but not, as it turned out, the safeguard) came in 1902. The now-reconciled headmen of Kabanjahé, Pa Pelita and Pa Mbelgah, suggested the establishment of a mission post and school in their village. Against government advice and amid rumors of continuing unrest in the region, the missionaries accepted the offer. This move, interpreted quite correctly by rival Karo leaders as a sign of the growing friendship between Kabanjahé and the Dutch, ignited an already explosive political situation. An alliance of hostile Karo leaders attacked Kabanjahé and carried off the lumber that was to have been used to build missionary Guillaume's house (Guillaume 1903).

For two years following the attack on Kabanjahé the colonial government negotiated with opposition leaders over punitive fines to cover the damages to the new mission post. Local recalcitrance resulted first in a government salt blockade, then in two military expeditions through the highlands. In the first of these, a sequel to Overste van Daalen's bloody Gayo campaign, twenty Karo were killed in two skirmishes; the second expedition, intended primarily to "show the colors," left fifteen Karo dead and put an end to organized armed resistance in the highlands.[21] C. J. Westenberg, who accompanied the second expedition as titular assistant resident of the newly established *Afdeling Simelungun- en Karo-landen*, personally pledged to the defeated leaders that no land would be alienated either by sale or by gift to outsiders. In 1907 five local rulers, hand-picked by the colonial authorities to represent the highland Karo, signed the *Korte Verklaring* ("Short Declaration"), formally ceding final authority in the region to the Dutch (Schadee 1920; Westenberg 1904a).

HISTORICAL TRADITIONS, COLONIAL POLITICS

Within Sumatra's East Coast Residency, colonial policy was one of indirect rule. Local government remained tacitly in the hands of the indigenous population, but under the supervision of colonial administrators. The success of this approach in the plantation zone, where local monarchies served as convenient intermediaries to the local population, encouraged the Dutch to apply the same principle in the Karo highlands. There, however, circumstances were quite different.

Each highland village was considered the "property" of its founding lineage (*bangsa taneh*), who collectively controlled the distribution of use rights to the village's open land. Such groups did not comprise a local aristocracy; even within their home village the authority of the bangsa taneh was quite circumscribed. The basic social and political unit was the *kesain* (village ward), and centralized political institutions were only minimally developed. Villages were composed of from one to ten autonomous kesains, each headed by a *pengulu* (chief), who was usually a member of the founding lineage. Larger political units above the kesain were virtually nonexistent, and cooperation between the chiefs seems to have been limited to the settling of those rare disputes that did not fall within the regulatory domain of kin groups.

Even within the kesain, the authority of the pengulu was weak and his rights—to village labor, market fees, and the like—difficult to enforce. This situation had worked to Dutch advantage in the years before they were, as Controleur W. Middendorp (1929a:46) put it, "entrusted with the historical task of governing the Karo lands." Joustra commented:

> The democratic spirit of the Karo-Bataks, whereby the chiefs in many ways are dependent upon the goodwill of their subordinates, and furthermore the always very great numbers of claimants and pretenders [to office], have been the cause that much emphasis could never be laid on the right [of the chiefs] and their incomes were small. The obligations (particularly the duty of hospitality) were, on the other hand, sometimes burdensome. Hence most chiefs attempted devious ways of "starching up" their cash—by conniving or secretly taking part in thievery, by encouraging the urge to gamble, by bribery, etc. Others let their "friendship" to the "*Kumpeni*" be bought with rifles, munitions and not least with balls of opium. (Joustra 1910:197)

Once the Dutch were in control, however, the autonomy and relative weakness of the chiefs—a "proof of the aversion to authority which the Karo possess in such high degree"—became an administrative liability, and steps were taken to end the "lack of discipline in this region" (van Rhijn 1936:37).

From the first, the colonial administration endeavored to "put an end to this multiplicity of rulers" (ibid.:38) and to establish a hierarchical system of authority. The Dutch thus turned to the *urung*, a cluster of villages acknowledging descent from a common parent village (*perbapan*), but with little else in the way of formal or administrative ties. The colonial administration transformed the urungs from genealogical groupings into "what they had never been i.e. purely administrative units as links between the European administration and the administration of the many villages which thereby lost their old sovereignty" (Middendorp 1929a:55). The foremost pengulu of the perbapan village was named as the regional ruler, with the new title of *raja urung*. Above the urung, a still larger political unit was created, the *landschap*, which was headed by a *zelfbestuurer* ("autonomous ruler") with the title of *sibayak*. Finally, above the indigenous rulers of the five landschaps stood the apparatus of colonial government, headed by a Dutch controleur.

The geographical division of the region into urungs and landschaps was a Dutch innovation, but there was some precedent for the office of sibayak (if less so for that of raja urung). The term "sibayak" was a general honoric title bestowed, in some areas, upon all adult males of the bangsa taneh. In other areas the term was used instead of pengulu to designate the kesain chief. According to Karo clan histories, the Acehnese had, centuries before, selected the four most powerful Karo pengulus, to whom they gave the title of sibayak, collectively designating them as the *raja berempat* ("the four kings"). The titles may never have had more than honorific significance; in any event, by the time of the highlands' annexation they had been largely forgotten. Westenberg, the architect of Karo political reorganization, resurrected this nominal tetrarchy to serve as the top level of local administration. Since the original four "kingdoms" did not cover the entire administrative area of *Onderafdeling Karolanden*, a fifth sibayak was chosen. It was these five sibayaks—their authority in fact a Dutch fiction—who acknowledged Dutch sovereignty over the Karo by signing the Korte Verklaring in 1907.[22]

In selecting raja urungs and sibayaks, the Dutch were initially forced by practical considerations to acknowledge in many cases joint claimants for each office. Basing right to rule on longevity, the decision was made to assign the office permanently to its surviving claimant and, subsequently, to his descendants in the eldest male line. Within a generation, a hereditary ruling aristocracy with a formal line of succession to political office had been created.[23]

For purposes of efficient colonial administration the Dutch thus created political offices and established a hierarchy of authority where none had previously existed. Local rulers, from the sibayak down to the kesain chief, were bound into a system of ascending power relations in which maintaining one's position was primarily dependent upon support from above. Under the circumstances, it was not simply that rulers no longer found it necessary to consider the interests of the people they ruled, but rather that they were forced by political expediency not to do so, at least insofar as those interests were in conflict with the interests of their superiors within the colonial administration.

This political arrangement, typical of colonial systems of indirect rule, had the advantage of appearing to maintain—or, even better, to perfect—a "traditional" precolonial order.[24] After decades of political unrest, the Dutch colonial ideal of rust en orde was achieved through the "governmentalization" (Foucault 1982:793) of local forms of social organization. Codified as a set of (hypothetically) binding juridical and administrative rules (*adatrecht*) and adapted to the rational exigencies of a bureaucratic hierarchy, Karo "adat" formed the basis of colonial rule in the highlands (Westenberg 1914).

Even at first hand, this selective replication of Karo social forms allowed different interpretations. Joustra mildly noted that while annexation might have occasioned some slight "modification in the manner of government" in the highlands, the "actual government institutions [were] not as a result impaired" (Joustra 1910:193). Controleur Middendorp's assessment was less upbeat: "Although we tried as much as possible to apply ourselves to existing conditions," he stated bluntly, "we brought and had to bring a totally different administrative system. The old one collapsed" (Middendorp 1929a:56).

ADAT AND RELIGION IN COLONIAL KAROLAND

One of the effects of the colonial reorganization of Karo political life was a significant decline in collective religious activity. As in many small-scale societies of island Southeast Asia, the domains of religion and politics in precolonial Karoland were largely coterminous. Tutelary spirits and their shrines formed focal sites in the shifting networks of a kin-based distributive politics. Alliances were made and unmade through the ritual commemoration of specific events of personal or supernatural significance (births, deaths, village foundings) cooperatively uniting living humans, their ancestors, and the autochthonous spirits of the land. Colonial rule replaced these supernatural underpinnings of local authority with a bureaucratically maintained rust en orde. "Just as in the newly-organized Karo society the sovereignty of the village-states was undermined," Middendorp (1929a:33) commented, in a particularly apt political analogy, "so also was the sovereignty of the countless spirits undercut."

Karo religion focused on the veneration of family and lineage spirits known as *bégu*—or, more politely, as *nini*, grandparents. These remained attached by ties of duty and affection to their living kin and, if sufficiently honored, protected their descendants from misfortune. Periodic offering rituals were held to ensure the continuing good will of the spirits, and in situations of crisis such as epidemic, drought, or war, or in cases of individual illness or adversity, special ceremonies were held to ask for the help of the spirits. Community and household rituals were led by a male guru formally trained in the healing and magical arts, or a female spirit medium (*guru si baso*), through whom the spirits made their wishes and requirements known.

Ritual practice was primarily directed toward social ends, focusing on the genealogical perpetuation of patrilineal descent groups within the network of asymmetrical relations established by such groups through marriage. The spirits of a man's immediate genealogical ancestors (*bégu jabu*), both male and female, served as guardians of his household.[25] The most important of the bégu jabu was the *bégu sintua*, the "household founder"—one of the husband's deceased parents, or, if these were still alive, his grandparents. Spirits of more remote ancestors played a lesser role and were rarely remembered past the third generation. There was also a special class of family spirits, the *dibata*, who might, because of their greater powers, be remembered and propitiated for a longer time. Foremost among the dibata were *si maté sada wari*, those who died by violence or accident "in a single day." These spirits, sometimes known as *nini galuh*, "grandparent-banana," were given a special shrine behind the house, a small fenced garden in which medicinal herbs, red hibiscus flowers (*bunga-bunga*), and a particular sort of banana tree (*galuh si tabar*) were planted. Aborted or miscarried fetuses, children who died before their teeth appeared (*bicara guru*), women who died in childbirth, and sometimes young girls who died before marriage (*tungkup*), were also included among the family dibatas, as were the bégus of persons of special status, such as master craftsmen (*pandé*), gurus, musicians, and local rulers.

Larger social units—lineage segments, villages, and village wards—also had their own protective spirits.[26] Again, the most important of these were the ancestral founders. The chief of these were the bégu sintua, representative of the founding lineage, and the *pengulu kubur* (the "founder" of the graveyard, i.e., the first person who died in the village) and his wife. Every village and kesain also had a number of shrines, known collectively as the *bahuta-huta*, where unique spirit guardians resided. These might include autochthonous spirit-owners of the village territory, with whom the village founders had established a political or marital alliance, but more often they were of human origin.[27] Often the village guardians also included a *pengulubalang*, a stone image located near the territorial border, whose spirit-inhabitant would call out a warning if enemies approached.

In the same way that the bégu jabu were attached to a family through the male household head as living representative of their descent group, the bahuta-huta were linked to the total community through the local bangsa taneh, descendants of the village founders. The political authority of the ruling lineage was based upon this relation to the spirits, whose continued benevolence was essential to the collective and individual well-being of all community members. Rituals honoring the village spirits were organized and led by the pengulu, as primary representative of the ruling lineage. Ceremonial expenses were shared equally by village residents and all were expected to take part in the proceedings, their particular role being determined by their kinship relation to the local bangsa taneh.

To European observers, the colonial disenchantment of this world seemed a perfectly reasonable outcome of the *Pax Neerlandica* and the extension of rational scientific knowledge, which rendered unnecessary such magical efforts to control the social and natural environment. Writing of the dusun Karo during the early years of Dutch control, Westenberg remarked that the pengulubalang village guardians had

> with rapid strides sunk in esteem during recent years, a natural result of the increase of our influence, and of the improvement of safety associated with this. . . . For a kota [village], which has nothing to fear of enemies, there is little use for a pengulubalang, and so these images which are present almost everywhere in the Dusun are neglected. (Westenberg 1891:237)

Middendorp, who served as controleur of Onderafdeling Karolanden during the critical period of agricultural development from 1914 to 1919, noted a growing indifference to the spirits of the land and the harvest, which he attributed to the rational example of government agronomy programs: "The more the Karo see demonstration-experiments of how seed-selection, tillage, and the use of organic and artificial fertilizers on their scant fields means an increase in yield, the less they worship their old spirits" (Middendorp 1922:461).

"The land lies open on all sides," missionary Bodaan reported enthusiastically in 1914:

> In each place, especially where the missionary lives, one finds some Christians and, though they are few in number, the whole heathen population observes that handful of Christians. . . . [I]f the Christians do what is Christian, and in sorrow and gladness seek their refuge in God, and endeavor to leave behind such occasions as the above-mentioned feasts of the heathen guru, then also the heathens do as the Christian does. They frequently see that nothing terrible happens to the Christians who lay aside the old customs. And . . . then the heathen also dares it, but . . . *ach*, poor things, where shall they go now, they now have nothing. The old is as good as finished. Above all in places where some Christians live, the heathens now at most give a heathen feast to ensure good health only once a year, while a few years ago the rule was to do so once a month. So heathenism dies here, because it can give nothing more that satisfies. (Bodaan 1915:117; first ellipsis added)

Bodaan's announcement of the "death of heathenism" was somewhat premature. Rice harvests were poor throughout the Karo highlands in 1914 (Talens 1915:131), and may well have been in Upper Serdang, where Bodaan was stationed. In such times of hardship, public ceremonial activities would quite naturally decrease in size and frequency, even without the moral example of the Christian community. In other respects as well 1914 was hardly a representative moment, for in that year the Dutch were being drawn into the Great War in Europe; as a result colonial social welfare programs were restricted and capitation taxes on the local population tripled. Bad weather, economic pressures, and the vague news that reached Karoland of war in Europe may all have contributed to the reduction in community ritual that Bodaan witnessed, just as these were blamed for the sudden drop in school attendance and the "virtual standstill" in conversions and baptisms that occurred throughout Karoland in that year (Bodaan 1915:119; Neumann 1915:108–9; Talens 1915: 128–29). Still, it is clear that the presence of Karo Christians was also a significant factor in the decline in collective ritual, though perhaps not for the reason Bodaan suggested. Christians were exempted from prescribed contributions to community ritual by colonial law, and the mission forbade their active participation in any ceremonies not in accord with the Christian faith. Since ritual efficacy depended on the involvement of the whole community, the refusal of only a few villagers to take part rendered the undertaking futile (Neumann 1902b:65; Vuurmans 1930:342–43).

Although they recognized the mission's losses as much as its gains as an expression of God's will, the continuing slow rate of conversions engendered a "sense of failure [that] persistently plagued the missionaries" throughout the field's history (Rita S. Kipp 1990:223). While Karo were eager for secular education, the religious instruction offered by the mission had little appeal, and in 1920 the mission schools were permanently closed due to low attendance. Counting the two hundred residents of the mission-run leper colony, there were in 1922 no more than five hundred Karo Christians in the highlands (Middendorp 1922:462); in 1942, after more than fifty years of mission work, only about five thousand men, women, and children—less than 3 percent of the Karo population—had converted to Christianity (Pedersen 1970:188).

THE NEW RELIGION

In 1915, according to the account of a young Toba Batak observer, "there suddenly arose a religion in Sisugasuga-Barus" in western Tapanuli (Lumban Tobing and Gobée 1919:389). Begun by a guru "who appeared on his own and had not studied anywhere," the movement centered on the supernatural figure of the twelfth and last holder of the title of Si Singamangaraja, a Toba Batak ruler from the Bakkara region who was killed in an encounter with the Dutch in 1907 but was widely believed to be immortal.[28] Apparently inspired by increased taxation and corvée labor requirements and by rumors of Dutch involvement in the Great War in Europe, the movement was said to focus on opposition to the European interlopers in the region.

> The purpose of that religion, the guru said, was: To oppose and expel all the white-eyes [Europeans] from the land, the Administrator and the Preacher, and they would not pay taxes or perform corvée labor any longer. Whoever did not want [to join] must be killed, even close kin, if they did not accept the religion. So everyone was afraid and whoever had no opportunity to run away had to accept [it] otherwise they would be killed. (Ibid.)

After a Dutch official was killed while attempting to disperse a Perhudamdam assembly, the movement was put down in Tapanuli by Dutch troops,[29] but it later reemerged in the East Coast Residency, reaching the Karo area by late November 1917. With "a bewildering speed" it spread throughout Karoland until "almost every mind was set ablaze" by the millennial hopes that it inspired (van den Berg 1920:23).

Some Karo, missionary van den Berg (ibid.) reported, thought God and Queen Wilhelmina were at war because of the imposition of taxes upon the Bataks. According to another Karo account, the new religion was begun by Si Singamangaraja XII himself. Captured and thrown into the sea by the Dutch, the Toba leader met with God and told Him of the Bataks' plight. Out of pity, God gave him a religion especially for the Bataks, through which they might gain the power to oppose the Dutch. It was also said that the "new religion" (*agama mbaru*) was given to the Bataks so that they might be spared from the impending apocalypse of flood and a rain of stones, in which all others would perish. Once the world had been cleansed of unbelievers—the *kapir* (heathens) and the *piske* (Christians)—a golden age would begin in which Si Singamangaraja would be reunited with his followers (ibid.:24).

In a similarly anticolonial vein, one of Neumann's Karo converts offered the following interpretation of a passage[30] from Christ's Sermon on the Mount:

> A Christian, whom I consider to be a member of the movement on account of his saying that this [i.e., Perhudamdam] is now the true "agama", explained Matt. 5:10–12 in this way, that the Bataks were exploited and persecuted. The Kompani had planned it so shrewdly, that they would, through the Controleur, make men's lives difficult, but through the Pendeta [preacher] would win their trust. [The Bataks] had already prayed for a long time for God's help, and the Great European War was the answer to his prayer. Namely: as God's punishment on the white race. (Neumann 1918:185)

That Biblical exegesis could figure in the anticolonial discourse of the agama mbaru is not surprising. One of the most striking aspects of the Perhudamdam movement was its appropriation of Christian discourse. The themes of divine retribution and apocalypse, salvation by faith, the community of believers, conversion by baptism, the communion meal in which the new religion is "eaten" (*ipan agama mbaru enda*) by the faithful, and the active role of God—who was significantly addressed in Perhudamdam prayers by the name given to the Christian Deity, *Tuhan Dibata*—all figured significantly in the movement's rhetoric and its rituals. Neumann (ibid.:188) noted a strong similarity between Perhudamdam's moral code and that of Christianity and Islam, and he also suggested that perhaps the image of the apocalypse was taken from the New Testament. These were not simply rhetorical borrowings tacked onto a prior framework of indigenous religious belief: the Gospel message, reworked in local terms, permeated the entire discourse of the new religion.

Still, to the missionaries Perhudamdam was "a revival of the old national religion of the Bataks." These few "borrowed elements" from Christianity might add to the movement's general appeal, they argued, but the new religion nonetheless remained "Batak through and through" (ibid.: 185, 188). It was an expression of "heathen conservatism" and "resistance to the spirit of the West, of which government and mission were the carriers," a call to return to "genuine Batak ways" (Joustra 1918a:163).

Although the anticolonial component of the agama mbaru is evident, both in its political critique of colonial exploitation and in its cultural and religious efforts to constitute a collective "Batak" identity vis-à-vis Christian Europeans, the Perhudamdam movement was essentially antagonistic to local custom. Thus, for example, Neumann noted that initiates who "ate" the new religion became "different people," and for them the bonds of the new community of the faithful superseded even the bonds and obligations of kinship (ibid.:185–86). It was the injustice of the colonial regime, rather than its disruption of the "old ways" that Karo proposed as the reason for divine retribution against the Dutch.[31] The old ways, and the kapir ancestors, were all to be swept away—along with the Dutch—as a prelude to the postdiluvian golden age of the new religion.

What the Perhudamdam movement, at least in its Karo manifestation, proposed was not a return to the old ways but a new, religiously based pan-Batak community. Instead of the multitude of localized ancestral and territorial spirits that had been the focus of Karo religious action and of the bicara, the movement posed a universal spirit-pantheon headed by the messianic figure of Si Singamangaraja—a figure who was nearly as alien to most Karo as were the Hebrew prophets of the missionaries' Bible tales. Other spirits in the pantheon—legendary Toba heroes and mythical figures such as "Guru Mulajadi" or "Marimbulubosi," or such modern characters as the *jaksa* (magistrate), *oppas* (policeman, from the Dutch *oppasser*), or the imaginatively named *krani Dibata*, "God's clerk"— were hardly less outlandish. This same incorporative effacement of local cultural difference is apparent in the movement's multilingual prayers, which were composed of phrases in Malay, Toba, and Karo as well as garbled Arabic (van den Berg 1920).

In Tapanuli, where there was a sporadic tradition of syncretic religious movements, Perhudamdam's incorporation of familiar mythical heroes and mythologized political leaders provided a strong local grounding for the movement's intertwined political and spiritual messages. In Karoland, however, it never formed close ties either with particular local religious and cultural practice, or with the relations of secular and spiritual authority that these underlay. As a result, even without the repressive measures the government instituted in Tapanuli and in the Simelungun region, the new religion faded in Karoland as rapidly as it had spread. By the middle of 1918 the millennial excitement was beginning to ebb, and soon Karo began to acknowledge (to the missionaries, at least) that they had "acted foolishly at that time" (van den Berg 1920:22).[32]

POLITICS, RESISTANCE, AND REVOLUTION

Perhaps because the Karo plateau appeared to have little to offer for co-lonial exploitation—the land being unsuitable for plantation develop-ment and the population less amenable to proletarianization than the seemingly unlimited supply of imported Chinese and Javanese contract laborers—the highlands remained a relatively unimportant backwater throughout the colonial period. Westenberg's 1904 pledge that Karo land would remain in Karo hands was honored at least by European indiffer-ence. As long as Onderafdeling Karolanden was self-supporting and trou-ble-free, colonial intervention was minimal. Aside from Perhudamdam's short-lived millenarian excitement, there was little overt opposition (though perhaps little overt support either) to Dutch rule. Karo antago-nism seems to have focused primarily on local rulers who reaped the ben-efits of the Dutch presence in the name of their "traditional" prerogatives.

Yet there must have been a strong undercurrent of the anticolonial sentiment that had briefly found expression in the rhetoric of the Perhu-damdam movement. When Japanese troops invaded East Sumatra in March 1942, the colonial government capitulated almost immediately, and all foreign nationals were interned in prison camps. This sudden collapse of the colonial establishment seems to have ignited popular re-sentment against the Dutch regime. The Japanese were welcomed as liber-ators and greeted in Karoland with mass demonstrations of support, complete with displays of the red and white flag of the Indonesian nationalist movement (Surbakti 1977:9).

This enthusiasm was short-lived. Karo describe the three and a half years of Japanese occupation as a time of privation and humiliation. As the Greater East Asian War continued, Japanese economic demands, corvée labor requirements, and requisitions of foodstuffs increased. By 1945 cloth had been virtually unavailable to the local population for more than a year, and near-famine conditions prevailed throughout Sumatra (Reid 1979:124, 136).

On August 17, 1945, three days after the bombing of Hiroshima brought the war to a sudden end, Indonesia declared its independence, and Sukarno and Mohammed Hatta were chosen as president and vice-president of the new republic. When news of this declaration reached East Sumatra several weeks later, local nationalist leaders began to prepare for the expected Allied invasion. The principal initiative was taken by urban youth (I., *pemuda*), many of whom had received some paramilitary training under the Japanese. The pemuda formed loose groups, primarily along ethnic lines, and began to collect arms.[33] British troops landed in Sumatra on October 10 and, with Japanese authority rapidly ebbing and Allied authority not yet established, armed pemuda groups in Medan struggled with one another for control of various parts of the city.

Similar groups formed in the market towns of Kabanjahé and Berastagi in the Karo highlands, although there was initially less rivalry between these groups than in multiethnic Medan. The first major confrontation between Allied and nationalist forces in East Sumatra occurred in Berastagi, when Allied soldiers removed the Indonesian flag from the front of their local headquarters. An attack by pemuda followed, with several casualties on both sides. Allied troops subsequently withdrew from the town (Surbakti 1977:53–68).

If Karo were initially unified in their resistance to the Allied occupation, the various militia groups quickly fell into political and personal disputes, as they struggled not only to oppose the Dutch return but also to define the nation that they were creating. Despite recurrent feuding between militia groups, Karo played a major part in the independence struggle in East Sumatra. During the first stage of the conflict, virtually the entire population evacuated areas that fell under Dutch control; when the Dutch began their second "police action" after the refugees' voluntary repatriation in 1947, they "encountered the most sustained guerilla resistance in Karoland" of any part of East Sumatra (Reid 1979:255).[34]

Capitulating in December 1949 to international opinion and to persistent Indonesian military assault, the Netherlands recognized the sovereignty of a "Federal Indonesian Republic" composed of the Jogjakarta-based Republic of Indonesia and a number of autonomous states, including the Malay-dominated State of East Sumatra. The inclusion of Karoland in what was perceived as a "Dutch-created puppet state" (Surbakti 1979:381) seemed to many ardent Karo republicans a betrayal of their revolutionary sacrifices. Mass demonstrations in Kabanjahé and throughout the Karo area spearheaded local opposition to the "Federated States" plan, which soon collapsed. On August 17, 1950, the fifth anniversary of Indonesian independence, East Sumatra was finally incorporated into the newly unified Republic of Indonesia.[35]

The end of colonial rule brought profound changes in Karo political organization. The "social revolution" of 1946—peaceful in Karoland as it was not in other parts of East Sumatra—had overthrown the Dutch-supported hereditary aristocracy.[36] Office-holders were subsequently chosen through local elections, and in some cases village officials were not members of the local bangsa taneh. In the years between 1945 and Sukarno's 1966 fall from power, numerous political parties formed and struggled for a share of popular support. The dominant parties in the region were Sukarno's PNI (Partai Nationalis Indonesia) and the PKI (Partai Komunis Indonesia). Under the auspices of these two parties' peasant unions, many Karo migrated to the lowlands and took over portions of the former tobacco plantations on the outskirts of Medan.

In those politically charged years, antagonisms nourished by the internecine conflicts of the revolutionary period reappeared in the form of ethnic feuding, regional independence movements, religious antipathies, and party vendettas. In Karoland as elsewhere in Indonesia a pervasive undercurrent of threatened political violence accompanied a steadily worsening economic situation. In the highlands, this economic decline was somewhat mitigated by a prospering agricultural export business. But in 1963 Sukarno's military "Confrontation" with Malaysia brought on a trade boycott that left Karo growers and traders dependent on the weak and unstable local market. Despite the disastrous economic repercussions of *Konfrontasi* (from which the Karo export trade had never fully recovered), and notwithstanding the Church's ambiguously moderate political stance, Karo remained until 1965 strongly committed to the Sukarnoist left wing of the PNI and, mostly through its land redistribution and farm support programs, to the PKI.

During the same period the Protestant Church began to emerge as a significant Karo social institution. Doctrinal principles and mission paternalism, as well as the missionaries' perceived collaboration with the Dutch establishment, had been major factors in the Church's slow progress during the colonial period. The missionaries had required a long period of catechization and probation before allowing Karo converts to join the Church, and their moral surveillance of the Christian community was unremitting and generally pessimistic. With little confidence in Karo

Christians' spiritual comprehension or managerial capabilities, they retained personal control over the entire administrative and clerical apparatus of the mission. Education was intended less to impart practical skills to students than to serve as a platform for religious indoctrination, yet no Karo ministers were ordained.

In 1943, following the Japanese internment of the mission's European staff, a local synod established the Gereja Batak Karo Protestan as an independent church, and ended all formal ties with the Dutch Missionary Society. Nevertheless, the new church kept the liturgy and regulations set by the mission-dominated 1941 synod. Although the GBKP in its early years opposed Karo custom even more strenuously than the Dutch missionaries had done (in some cases refusing to admit women wearing the tudung headdress or other "traditional" attire to services), with church leadership finally in Karo hands conversions increased greatly. By 1963 church membership had reached 23,000, with 120 congregations holding weekly services (Pedersen 1970:188).

In the highly politicized climate of the early 1960s, the GBKP, like other religious organizations, became enmeshed in the escalating rivalry for power between the army and the Indonesian Communist party. Anti-Communist forces within the government began to look upon religious organizations as potential allies in their efforts to "withstand communist aggression" (Ukur and Cooley 1979:367). Between 1960 and 1965 the GBKP faced increasing criticism from the local Communist party, which charged that the Church "weakened the revolutionary struggle" (Team Penelitian GBKP 1976:14–15). At the same time, some congregations were rumored to have been "infiltrated" by members of the PKI and its affiliated organizations (Pedersen 1970:189). Responding to this perceived politicization of the body of the Church, the GBKP in its 75th Anniversary Jubilee of 1965 reaffirmed its political neutrality, stating explicitly that "the church is not a political party" (Ukur and Cooley 1979:367). At the same time the Church began to take a more accommodative stance regarding customary practices. The use of the traditional gendang orchestra, both in church and in secular settings, had received tacit approval at the Jubilee and was officially approved by the synod of 1966, with the qualification that the performance should not "contain belief" (GBKP 1976:124).[37]

In October 1965, following the alleged Communist coup attempt known as the September 30th Movement (Gerakan September Tigapuluh, or Gestapu), the PKI was outlawed and the moderate-left PNI "frozen" by the government. Brutal reprisals against suspected Communists and fellow-travelers were carried out by the army and hastily recruited civilian supporters. In the wake of this violence, in which as many as a million people may have been killed, the Sukarno government was supplanted by a military-dominated "New Order" regime headed by General Suharto, who has remained in power until the present. At the army's urging, the multiparty system was replaced by a single quasi-party organization of "functional groups" known as Golkar (*Golongan Karya*), in theory a "coalition of professional and community associations [stressing] their shared interests in national harmony" (McDonald 1980:90) and in fact a virtual instrument of military political interests.[38]

It was in the chaotic period following Gestapu that Karo began to turn to Christianity in great numbers. According to Ukur and Cooley of the Indonesian Council of Churches (DGI), because the "coup attempt" was "generally considered as an act of the atheistic class [*kaum atheis*], the government urged the people to choose one among the religions and beliefs that were officially acknowledged by the government" (Ukur and Cooley 1979:520). Not surprisingly, such "urging" was taken seriously.

On May 28, 1966, the Council of Churches opened an aggressive evangelical campaign in the Karo area; its first "evangelization team" was composed of some 1,500 Christians, led by the governor and the military commander of the province and accompanied by DGI representatives, preachers, brass bands, and choirs. Similar teams followed shortly thereafter, spreading an evangelical net that gathered converts at an impressive rate. At one meeting, attended by an estimated 20,000 people, there were 1,903 baptisms (Pedersen 1970:190–91). Altogether some 40,000 Karo were baptized during the two years of mass evangelization, and by 1971 GBKP membership had reached 94,000 (Team Penelitian GBKP 1976:67; cf. Schreiner 1972).

GBKP leaders attribute this sudden turn to Christianity to the people's realization that "adat and the political teachings they had followed were no longer enough to carry them into a bright future" (ibid.:16). This realization, however, seems to have been based less on spiritual than on practical political concerns. During the Karo campaign, some of the more enthusiastic evangelists announced publicly that those who were not members of a state-approved religion would be "dealt with" in unspecified but clearly unpleasant ways.[39] In other cases, police and army personnel demanded that villagers choose a religion, enrolling those who did so on publicly displayed lists (Pedersen 1970:192). While instances of coerced conversion may not have been widespread, rumors about them certainly were, and the presence of small armies of Christian evangelists led by military and government officials must have contributed greatly to the credibility of such rumors.

The anti-Communist evangelical campaigns of 1966–67 marked "the beginning of a new history" for the Karo Church (ibid.:14). Once stigmatized for its complicity with the colonial regime, the Church had now aligned itself with the national programs and policies of Suharto's New

Order government. In subsequent years the GBKP would play "a very important role in the Government's efforts to alter the outlook [I., *mental*] of the people and to achieve a stabilization of the situation" (Ukur and Cooley 1979:132). Along these lines the Church has actively supported a variety of local development projects, promoted a social ethos of economic progress, and come to the defense of Karo adat as a stabilizing force in these "modern times" (*jaman modéren*).

RELIGIOUS TOLERANCE

At the time of my fieldwork in the mid-1980s, approximately 47 percent of the population of the rural highlands was Christian—this divided between the Karo Protestant Church, the GBKP (35 percent), and the smaller and less influential Roman Catholic Church—and 17 percent was Muslim. Most of the rest (about 35 percent of the total population)[40] remained adherents of the old religion of spirit veneration, known among its followers—who were themselves labeled *perbégu*, "ghost-keepers," by disapproving Christians—as Agama Pemena, the "first" or "original" religion. Data on the religious affiliation of Karo outside the highlands were not available at that time; however, this same pattern of religious pluralism appeared to hold true, although in the piedmont, where Malay influence has been stronger, there were more Karo Muslims, and among urban Karo the numerical and cultural dominance of the GBKP was more pronounced.[41]

Contemporary Karo religious practice is shaped by its political context, specifically by the concepts of religion (*agama*) and of "tradition" (adat) formulated by the Indonesian state in its current interpretation of the *Pancasila*, the "five principles" of Indonesian nationhood. Set forth by Sukarno in 1945, the Pancasila is said to be a distillation of the essence of all the local traditions of the peoples of the Indonesian archipelago, and thus the irreducible core of Indonesian national identity—to which all the various local adats are ipso facto presumed to conform. The first principle of the Pancasila is "faith in the Supreme Deity." Various interpretations are offered for this rather vague statement, but a rough approximation of its practical implication is that all Indonesian citizens should be members of some officially sanctioned, monotheistic religion. This technically means that all Indonesians are free to belong to the religion of their choice, but the options as to what counts as a religion are somewhat limited: Islam, Protestantism, Catholicism, and—with a bit of stretching of the concept of monotheism—Hinduism and Buddhism. What rather pointedly do not fall under the rubric of "agama" are the various local systems of spirit veneration such as Agama Pemena—

though its adherents, in its very naming, would insist otherwise. With neither a "book," a "church," nor (more important) a bureaucratic organization through which they can be "guided" by the government, these latter are, in official terms, not religions at all, but rather are considered to be "sects" (aliran kepercayaan, "streams of belief").[42] Falling under the auspices of the Department of Education and Culture rather than the Department of Religion, they are (marginally) tolerated for their touristic appeal.[43]

For Christians in the predominantly Islamic nation, the interpretation of the first principle of the Pancasila as a guarantee of religious freedom is seen as essential to the continuing existence of the congregation. But for followers of Agama Pemena, officially considered as people who "do not yet have a religion," such a statement of religious tolerance is less reassuring. Although they consider the first principle a guarantee of their own religious freedom as well, in practice they experience significant political and social discrimination, and they are under considerable pressure to convert to one of the approved religions.

In this situation, many followers of Agama Pemena have affiliated with the provincial chapter of a pan-Indonesian Hindu reformist organization, Parisada Hindu Dharma.[44] This overtly political move is justified by reference to what is described as a lost Indic tradition in precolonial Karoland, proof of which is located in the presence of a number of Sanskrit loan-words in the Karo language and in some wildly speculative accounts of the Sumatran wanderings of Shivaite Tamil priests prior to the sixteenth century (cf. Brahma Putro 1981).[45] On the basis of this putative Indic connection, Agama Pemena in 1977 received official recognition as the Karo branch of the government-approved Hindu religion. This affiliation has provided a legitimacy to Agama Pemena that protects its adherents from the more extreme aspects of social and political discrimination. It has until recently, however, had little effect on Karo religious practice—which, it should be noted, bears little resemblance to the formal priestly Hinduisms of either Bali or India.[46] In the contemporary Karo context, "becoming Hindu" has meant little more than attending a few lectures sponsored by the Department of Religion on the monotheistic basis of Hinduism and the virtues of the Pancasila.

Unlike other Indonesian societies where religious conversion has followed lines of kinship, patronage, or other group identity, or where communities have fissioned along religious lines, Karo villages and urban neighborhoods—even families—are resolutely mixed in their religious affiliation. Karo attribute the religious tolerance of their community to the continuing strength of adat, which requires cooperation among kin, whatever their faith. But under these circumstances of religious pluralism, such an insistence on the foundational status of kinship in Karo society has conversely necessitated the excision of all elements of religious belief from adat's enactments.[47] This process of secularization has taken place largely under the aegis of the Karo Protestant Church, the demographically and culturally dominant institution of contemporary Karo social life.

Over the last two decades the Church has, through a series of seminars and publications, attempted to redefine adat in a way acceptable to all Karo, regardless of their religious affiliation. "A troublesome problem in this field," as the Church's "research team" has written,

> is the difficulty or perhaps the "impossibility"—of separating adat from ethnic religion [agama suku] or pagan beliefs [kepercayaan kafir]. That such a problem exists is understandable because formerly adat and religion were unified; both uniquely Karo, they emerged and developed in a unified and indivisible social-cultural-religious milieu. With the entrance of the Christian faith, this unity was broken, so now the Church must endeavor to separate elements of belief from elements of adat. (Team Penelitian GBKP 1976: 124)

The GBKP rejects as confusing and misleading the view of adat as a total way of life, and instead distinguishes between adat, local custom—for which the Karo term bicara is used—and "belief" (kiniteken). Although in practice the three elements of tradition may appear inseparable, the argument goes, a "correct" understanding of tradition requires that these elements be clearly demarcated. So, for example, a distinction is now drawn between the secular music performed by the gendang adat and the supernatural gendang mistik, which "if played at a funeral ritual can cause the dancers to be possessed by spirits," thus weakening the faith of Christians. To ensure that such "undesirable matters do not occur," a congregation may obtain its own gendang instruments, to be played at funerals by Christian musicians: "the form stays the same (here, the musical instruments of the Karo gendang) but the content and intention are changed from that which contains belief to that which is neutral [netral]" (GBKP 1976:124–25).

Adat, in the rationalized form promoted by the GBKP, is composed of those aspects of Karo custom that are considered universally binding, the "rules that must be followed by Karo everywhere" (Intisari Adat-Istiadat Karo n.d.:2). It is a legalistic, overarching system of rules of proper behavior between kin, divorced from social and supernatural contexts, and ritual practice is uniformly codified in a set of performative rules based on kin-role obligations. Bicara, local customs, are the decorative frills (jilé-jilé) of adat which, although not obligatory, may be followed in certain locales or by certain persons. And "belief" consists of those practices directly implicated in the old religion of spirit veneration.[48] One can still follow adat, while rejecting those aspects of custom or belief deemed irrelevant or unacceptable.

In their segmentation of tradition into adat, custom, and belief, Karo Christians have, in the name of inclusiveness, effectively defined the "pagans" out of adat and themselves at its heart. If belief is distinguished from adat, then adat rituals become, by definition, secular events. This means that only those rituals which can be secularized are now a part of adat. Weddings, funerals, and house openings are the key performances of the new "universal" adat, while rites of spirit propitiation, seances for the souls of the dead, and spirit possession ceremonies—all the ritual expressions of Agama Pemena—are no longer adat rituals at all, but rather rituals of "belief." Christians are no longer obliged by adat to participate in rituals of spirit worship sponsored by their kin, any more than they would require their non-Christian kin to attend Christian worship services. This is the essence of religious tolerance, as set forth in the first principle of the Pancasila. Yet Christian faith is an individual matter and rites of spirit propitiation are communal in nature, and this makes a significant difference in the believer's ability to carry out the precepts of faith. If one's Christian anak beru fail to provide the necessary labor, or if one's Christian kalimbubu refuse to bestow their blessing, how can a ritual—even a ritual of "belief"—be undertaken?

THE ADAT OF THE KERAMATS

As it exists today, Agama Pemena is essentially a privatized cult of healing and personal success centering on individual purification rites known as *erpangir* (K., "hairwashings") and on the kerja nini possession ceremonies. These are led by spirit mediums, usually women, whose skill and knowledge derive from the spirit-guides (*jinujung*) with whom they have established permanent reciprocal relationships. Community-based rites of spirit propitiation have almost entirely ceased to be performed. Even smaller family ceremonies which, like all Karo rituals, stress the participation of members of quite extended kin groups, may be difficult to sponsor as a result of religious differences among kin. Discreetly indoors, small rituals continue and many family shrines are maintained; outside in public view they may provoke suspicions of sorcery.

In the face of Christian disapproval, groups like the Arisan of Simpang Meriah form alternative support networks for their members. The organization's leaders help with the paperwork for members seeking government recognition as licensed folk practitioners. Members jointly own a large set of plates and glasses for use in ceremonies. They contribute financially to one another's rituals, and take care of the tasks—cooking and serving the food, preparing offerings, and the like—that should have been the duty of the sponsor's anak beru. Equally important, the Arisan's monthly ceremonies serve as a training ground for novices and as a quasi-

Hairwashing ceremony (*erpangir ku lau*) at Lau Debuk-Debuk, 1985.

public arena for reputation-building for more experienced mediums. This is important because curing can be a lucrative profession for a well-known medium, whose clientele—drawn by word-of-mouth reports of performative "keenness" as much as of successful cures—might extend not only to Karo Christians and Muslims but even to individuals from other ethnic groups.

The most popular spirits of the contemporary pantheon are the *keramat* spirits of Mount Sibayak. Some of these are more powerful than others, and some have special areas of expertise—the umangs, for example, know all the herbs used for making medicines, the flirtatious Beru Karos specialize in the magic of attraction and popularity, the war-chiefs (K., *puanglima*) attack and repel black magic. What distinguishes these spirits as a group, however, is their universal benevolence, their concern with bodily purity and pollution, and their lack of identifiable kin ties to particular human supplicants. Unlike the family spirits whose affections order the living world into preferential categories of kin and nonkin, the keramats, so it is said, make no distinctions between persons.

Unlike the complex symbolic and practical elaborations of kinship that structure secular adat rituals, kinship may be disregarded altogether in Arisan performances, or it may be reduced to a brief opening acknowledgment of the importance of kalimbubu, anak beru, and senina as the cornerstones of Karo adat. One medium explained that this was acceptable because "we follow the adat of the keramats, not the adat of humans." The keramats' "adat" of moral individualism, cleanliness, and material success not only outranks the protocol of kinship in Arisan rituals, it also works in many ways against the incorporation of family spirits into religious practice. Nandé Sila, for example, complained that her keramat jinujung punished her whenever she called down the spirit of her deceased father. His presence made her too sad and thus interfered with her obligation to patients, the keramat explained. Yet the keramats also invoke traditional values and insist on a formal adherence to the rules of respect and obligation among kin. Nandé Jarum, another of the Arisan mediums, told me that her initial spirit helpers had been two young maiden aunts who died of smallpox. According to "human" adat, they should be brought to the house first in any possession ritual as a sign of respect; they were, after all, her original bridge to the spirit world. Now Nandé Jarum claimed a high keramat as her jinujung, and the keramat refused to let the unclean aunts descend. Still, on one ritual occasion this keramat, speaking through Nandé Jarum, contradictorily berated the medium for *failing* to call down the aunts first and thus violating adat. Living up to the keramats' high standards was a constant struggle.

The Arisan mediums insisted on the absolute moral opposition between sorcery and their own keramat-inspired curing practices. Sorcery (often instigated by some close though unnamed affinal kinsperson) was indeed the near-universal diagnosis the Arisan mediums offered to their clients, and it was clearly what most expected to hear. Still, there were also rumors, both within and outside the group, that certain successful mediums were themselves trafficking in black magic. Mediums who were doing well in turn feared that their prosperity would make them the target of competitors' sorceries. Since those envious competitors were most often fellow Arisan members (or former members), the organization's monthly kerja nini rituals were the regular scene of sorcerous attack and counter-attack as well as the subject of constant speculation and innuendo.

Nandé Randal, the group's most senior medium, recalled one such kerja nini, when a prominent Arisan member caused twenty people to be simultaneously possessed by evil spirits. With the help of her spirit-guide Puanglima La Tergigih ["the unyielding warchief"], she and another medium did battle with them. Soon everyone was rolling on the floor, she said, and finally the performance ended in confusion when the ceremony's sponsor hit her head on the *keteng-keteng* (a large bamboo tube zither, one of the main instruments of the "small" three-piece gendang ensemble) and had to be taken to a doctor to stop the bleeding. "So that's how it is," Nandé Randal concluded. "If we're all talking about one another all the time, well, can't you expect them to *teré* [from English, "try"] one another, too?"

HISTORY IN THE AGE OF DEVELOPMENT

State-guided conflations of political and spiritual domains are nothing new in Karoland, where religion has long served as the cultural vanguard of intrusive state politics. In the nineteenth century and no doubt earlier, Islam mediated Malay and Acehnese political ambitions among the Karo, as well as Karo aspirations to the courtly prestige of the Muslim sultanates. The Dutch colonial government explicitly endeavored to delete the political component from Karo ritual practice (and vice versa), but also offered Christianity as an enticement to Karo-European political collaboration. Under Sukarno the religious basis of citizenship and the state was confirmed by the constitution and embodied in the first principle of the Pancasila. But never has the political project of religious intervention been so systematically undertaken or so successfully implemented as by Suharto's New Order, in which nonadherence to a world religion ("atheism") is equated with communism, and independent religious associations are seen as dangerous sites of potential political mobilization.

In fact, since Suharto's rise to power, bureaucratic interventions at every level of social life have become increasingly intrusive, while overt military violence has mostly been pushed to the nation's contested margins—most notably Irian Jaya and East Timor. There are nonetheless frequent less-than-subtle demonstrations—such as the "mysterious shootings" of urban recidivists in Java and Sumatra in the early 1980s—of the state's paradoxical need to visibly work to confirm what John Pemberton (n.d.:6) describes as that "distinctly New Order state of idealized absence in which nothing . . . appears to happen." As Pemberton (ibid.:7–8) argues, this "relatively enigmatic" form of cultural politics is "founded upon routine, *explicit* reference to 'traditional' values, 'ritual' behavior, 'cultural' heritage, and similar New Order expressions bearing an acute sense of social stability." A rhetorical legacy of Sukarnoist national "keywords" (van Langenberg 1986) such as Pancasila, *musyawarah dan mufakat* ("consultation and consensus"), and *gotong royong* ("mutual assistance") frames a contemporary political discourse in which adat is figured as the natural ground of state legitimacy, and *politik*—by which is meant not the centripetal politics of the state but the centrifugal forces of opposition and individual self-interest—is relentlessly and repetitively constructed as the sign of national inauthenticity and social danger.[49]

Pembangunan ("development"), the New Order's special mantra and its symbolic alternative to the uncontrolled and therefore destructive forces of *politik*, links the stability of "nothing happening" with the desirable national goal of economic progress. In the official rhetoric of the New Order, social stability is a prerequisite for orderly infrastructural transformation; the "directed" economic changes of pembangunan in turn promise to make national stability a future reality. Change guarantees continuity, in other words: progress makes nothing happen.

New Order history is thus not so much a matter of events as of memorials. Elections, anniversaries, monuments, museums, tombs, the monthly *tujuhbelasan* ("seventeenth") commemoration of Indonesia's August 17, 1945 declaration of independence—these endless spectacles and simulations of the Age of Development—are replicas of imaginary mileposts on the teleological Road to Order-Without-End. Earlier nationalist histories assembled a pantheon of recognized "national heroes" (I., *pahlawan nasional*), whose deeds were reconfigured as local manifestations of a grand national destiny and whose names were repeated on street signs throughout the new nation—as if, to paraphrase Nicholas Dirks (1990:25), "Indonesia" had been the Subject of archipelagic history all along. Today's histories are both "roomier" (as Anthony Reid [1979:298] puts it) and less single-minded than the "somewhat brittle" orthodoxies of previous generations, but local events are still similarly imbued with historicity only as particular instances of a generic national ideal.

As with Sukarno's identification of the Pancasila as the universal core of Indonesian "adat," this officializing absorption of local history involves a double erasure. On one hand, occurrences that do not follow the ordered route of national progress and unity are dismissed as unfortunate "incidents" or irrelevant aberrations—not really historical. On the other hand, events that can be brought into line with that generic trajectory thereby lose their local specificity, becoming in the process the material evidence of national history.

A Karo history could be written in this way. Although it has received little attention outside North Sumatra, the Karo role in Indonesian national history is, as I have tried to suggest above, not insignificant, and Karo are rightly proud of their part in the nation's emergence and growth. Yet it seems to me that even within such a narrative frame there is the possibility of another kind of history, one that travels neither with nor against the purposeful emplotments of official order but rather around them: an "unofficial" history whose authority is located in the dubious evidence of personal experience.

This elusive history, in which transgression rather than repetition is the sign of authenticity, is for me embodied in the ritual enactments of the Arisan of Simpang Meriah. The spirits' perpetual carping about their hosts' faults or inadequacies; the hints of black magic at work, even in those exercises intended to oppose it; the disruptive supernatural "gate-crashers" like the oafish flute-playing cowherd or the cranky grand-mother who threatened to kick her disrespectful grandsons in the pants if they didn't paint her grave monument nicely; the endless arguments between spirits and spectators over ritual protocol: such "unexpected" moments (which seemed virtually scripted into Arisan performances, so regularly did they occur) at once underscored the superhumanly high standards of the spirits and displayed the profound power of the forces they were up against. But beyond such familiarly Foucauldian resistance-effects, these surprising and apparently pointless lapses in ritual order offered something else, too: an opening into intrigue, an expanse of pos-sibility, a proliferation of stories—and an escape into the subversive power of strangeness. The chapters that follow are written in the some-what utopian spirit of those moments, when *something* might have been happening, after all.

Three

Markets and Money

We arrived [in Berastagi] on a Saturday forenoon. Again it was

market day! Thousands of Karo Bataks thronged the passar

[market], purchasing vegetables, spices, fruits, and cloths. . . .

[N]ever have I seen people more mercenary than those in the

Brastagi [*sic*] market. Everyone wanted from one to five

guilders to pose for his picture. An old villager, carrying a fine

staff with the typical Batak horse and rider carved on it and

with the top tufted with feathers, halted before my camera

while I exposed a film; but when I handed him a sufficient tip

he sniffed in derision and handed it to his little grandson who

accompanied him.

—W. ROBERT MOORE, "Among the Hill Tribes of Sumatra"

ONE OF the great trials endured by the Calvinist missionaries of the Nederlandsch Zendelinggenootschap in Karoland was the apparent mercenary streak in the character of the people among whom they were placed. "To be rich: How desirable in the eyes of every Batak," wrote missionary Wijngaarden (1893:400), with the wry eloquence of perpetually thwarted good intentions—for he seems to have been viewed by his Karo public as a fount of worldly, rather than spiritual, resources.[1]

The rich man can be permitted the luxury of 2, 3, 4 wives or as many as he wishes; can commit murder and manslaughter, since the punishments consist simply of money-fines; can be certain of comrades in battle; he can buy his friends with money, and whoever has the most money can count on the most friends. A Batak war is thus simply a question of money, the rixdollars [*f.* 2.50] decide. . . . How badly off is he who is not favored by fortune! If he has no well-to-do relatives, then he cannot marry; if he has committed a

punishable offense, then he is placed in stocks, and left there until friends or
family pay his fine.

As the missionaries saw it, the love of money was the root of most of the
evil in Karo society, and they consistently portrayed Karo men as (to
paraphrase Joustra's [1896:242] telling description) "practical materialists" driven entirely by egoism and self-interest, inhabiting a world in
which virtually every social relationship could be reduced to a strictly
economic transaction.

The payment distributed at marriage to the bride's kin was, the missionaries felt, prima facie evidence of this, for it demonstrated that Karo
women were nothing more than chattel, "bought with gold"—this being
a polite Karo term (*tukur mas*) for a married woman. "Time and again
the purchasing of women is spoken of," Joustra wrote. "From this it appears that her position is a subordinate one, that she is actually transferred to the man like a commodity, becoming his property in the full
sense of the word." Karo might try to "disguise" this unpalatable reality,
Joustra argued, by not demanding full payment prior to marriage and by
insisting that "she is no buffalo, which can be bought." Nevertheless, he
added, "she is actually nothing else, and it is more from a certain kind-
heartedness, or in some cases even perhaps due to a sort of love, that the
lot of the woman is generally not more difficult" (Joustra 1902b: 403).[2]

Steeped in the rational spirit of capitalism as much as in the moral
individualism of the Protestant ethic, the missionaries found incomprehensible (or at least implausible) the distinction Karo made when they
described a woman as "bought with gold" yet insisted that she was "no
buffalo, which can be bought."[3] While Joustra is not entirely incorrect in
viewing the latter statement as a mystification of the actual situation of
Karo women, his counter-claim that these women are in fact merely commodities contains a mystifying move of its own, which takes as natural
and universal the arithmetic logic of private ownership and of the marketplace.[4] What he, and the other missionaries, failed to recognize was the
qualitative difference between money used as a medium of social exchange and as a medium of market exchange. Taking the former to be a
pernicious extension of the latter, the missionaries fashioned of Karo society an imaginary portrait of Man without God, created in the reflected
image of the Universal Marketplace.

During the fifty years of mission pastorage, and forty of colonial rule,
the "materialistic" Karo took up little of the spiritual message of Christianity. But the spirit of the marketplace, which the missionaries had raised
in imagination at the heart of Karo society and then attempted to sup-
plant with the True Gospel, grew into something very like what they had
assumed it already was. The town of Berastagi, founded as a expatriate
hill resort in 1908, was the center of that growth—the busy hub of the

"An old villager carrying a fine staff . . . halted before my camera."

highland produce trade, and (we are told) a place where pictures did not
come cheap.

In a picture taken in that marketplace (Moore 1930:193) an "old villager," carrying the carved staff that marks him as a guru, poses for a
camera-wielding tourist. To conclude their brief encounter, the tourist
gives him a "sufficient tip." In a gesture that might be contemptuous, the
old man passes the money to the boy who accompanies him, gently correcting the too-direct movement of the exchange, and, at the same time,

reversing the direction of authority that flows through the transaction. Is the tip too small? Does he think that the rich foreigner is a cheapskate? The tourist thinks that the old man is greedy and, perhaps, that he overestimates the worth of his portrait, which, after all, cost him nothing to pose for.

This scene played out in the Berastagi market seems at first to be little more than the usual minor comedy of cross-cultural errors enacted by ingenuous tourists and disingenuous natives everywhere. On one side, a social transaction is taken for an economic one; on the other, a market exchange is (strategically) misread as a social encounter. Yet it is more than that. Congealed on film, in words and in gesture, this small engagement encapsulates the double and—as it seemed at the time—mutually beneficial misrecognition upon which the Berastagi market was built and prospered.

THE PRECOLONIAL MARKETPLACE

One significant omission from the missionaries' consideration of the "buying" and "selling" of Karo women as commodities is the intricate pattern of distribution of marriage payments. These are divided into three major parts: the *ulu emas* given to the groom's kalimbubu by birth; the *unjuken* distributed among the bride's agnates; and the *si mecur*, the "tiny ones," divided among a wide range of the bride's more distant agnatic and affinal kin (Singarimbun 1975:171–78). Each of these segments is then subdivided into a number of often minuscule amounts, which are distributed among all representatives of the particular kin category. The main portion of the payment, the unjuken, is not distributed according to any fixed rules, and indeed does not have to be divided at all, although in practice it is usually shared among the many actual and classificatory agnates of the bride (Rita S. Kipp 1976:186).[5]

The problem of distribution of the unjuken payment figures importantly in the account of the founding of Tiga Bembem, one of the major markets of precolonial Karoland. In this tale, which is contained in the clan history of Siwah-Sada Ginting,[6] the market is established as the result of a dispute among nine brothers of the Ginting clan living in the village of Gurubenua, concerning the distribution of their sister's marriage payment.

> The nine brothers wished to slaughter and eat a great pig which belonged to their mother. But there was no salt with which to eat it, so the youngest brother, Si Aji Dibata, was ordered to go to the lowlands to fetch the salt. He was a long time in returning, and when he finally arrived home, laden with salt, he found that his brothers had impatiently killed and eaten the pig in his

absence. Angered, Si Aji Dibata fought with his brothers. "Let our fields no longer border one another's, let us have no common boundaries. If we have common boundaries, I'll set sharpened bamboo stakes around my fields, you set sharpened stakes around your fields. Let us no longer work one another's fields," said Si Aji Dibata. Then they set stakes around the borders of their fields, because of the great pig.

Si Aji Dibata then demanded that the entire marriage payment of their only sister, Si Bembem, be given to him. The nine brothers again quarreled. "Do not fight, my dear brothers," said Si Bembem. "If you heed my words, you can avoid quarreling, all will win, all will receive a share. Play the drum and the *seruné* [oboe] in the hills near your village, and I will dance. Fill a great platter with rice, and sit you down together all nine. Where the orchestra is played, build a place for people from downstream and upstream to bring goods and trade; the nine of you receive the market taxes," said Si Beru Bembem. "Put a golden *sertali*-chain about my brow, and I shall carry the platter of rice upon my head as I dance, so that my brothers' hearts may be softened," said Si Bembem. The orchestra played, and she danced, stamping on the ground, until she sunk into the earth and disappeared. Her nine brothers wept and shrieked. Thus the market of Tiga Bembem was founded because of the message of Beru Ginting, Si Beru Bembem.[7]

The tale of Si Bembem's death, versions of which are also told of at least two other early markets in Karoland—Tiga Deraya in Urung Telu Kuru, and the market of Gunung Meriah in Kembaren—provided a supernatural sanction of the "peace of the market."[8] It gave the marketplace the sacrality which, for Karo, was associated with certain burial sites or other places where a human spirit, in death, was fused with the otherwise inanimate objects of the natural environment (cf. Neumann 1927b). This magical aura of the marketplace created the necessary preconditions of trust whereby—as Mauss (1967:79) wrote—"men, despite themselves, learnt to renounce what was theirs and made contracts to give and repay."

Beru Bembem's sacrifice for her brothers establishes autonomous, though interlocking, spheres for the enactment of kinship relations and market relations, in which each contributes to the maintenance of, yet remains apart from, the other. The image of the market contained in her message is one of idyllic peace and prosperity, a place where "all will receive a share," where disputes can be set aside and "boundaries of sharpened bamboo stakes" forgotten. A meeting-place for people from "downstream and upstream" to come and trade, the market will resolve problems of inequitable distribution of scarce resources and provide access to necessary, but locally unavailable, goods such as salt. Moreover, it will provide an appropriate arena—one outside of marriage alliance and kin relations—for the seeking of personal gain. And this market is to be situated outside of the social world defined by kinship and mutual obligations, in the hills beyond the village.[9]

The major markets in Karoland were in fact located outside of villages, usually near the border of a village-federation's territory, and at a place with access to at least one of the main trade routes stretching out of the highlands.[10] A market might thus serve not only the villages of the federation in which it was located, but also of neighboring territories as well, whose population might be hesitant to travel long distances through lands belonging to possibly hostile groups. Thus the Tiga Bembem market was located on the western margin of the region dominated by the most important of the subclans claiming descent from the nine brothers of Gurubenua, Ginting Suka. The area controlled by this group stretched to the Simelungun border in the east and southward to the shores of Lake Toba.[11] Lying along the main route through Karoland from the Alas region in southern Aceh, and with access to the lake-port of Tongging through which trade from the island of Samosir flowed, the Tiga Bembem market was the largest in the Karo highlands (Kruijt 1891:363), and served not only nearby villages but also drew traders from the Gunung-Gunung region in southern Karoland and Sukapiring in the north, from Tobaland, and from as far away as Alas, some nine days' distant (ibid.).

Other major markets were neither as large nor as cosmopolitan as Tiga Bembem, but they were similarly located to serve a wide area and to assure access to external trade centers. Thus, Tiga Deraya on the western edge of Urung Telu (III) Kuru might serve not only the villages of that urung but also the large independent villages of the adjacent Teran region. Since Urung III Kuru formed a long finger of land stretching from Tiga Deraya to the western slopes of Mount Sibayak, traders from that region were assured relatively safe passage through that territory up to the Sepuluh Dua (XII) Kuta pass leading down to the lowlands and to the territory under the authority of the Malayized Karo datuk of Sunggal, who claimed descent from the Surbakti subclan of Urung III Kuru.[12] Similarly, the market of Tiga Belawan was situated on the southern border of Urung Sukapiring, where the urungs of Barus Jahé, Suka, and XII Kuta converged, and near the Cingkam pass leading to Deli Tua, the capital of the sultanate of Deli, with whom the rulers of Sukapiring were allied by marriage.[13]

These markets served as the major distribution points for goods entering Karoland and, to a lesser extent, as collection points for export goods. The Sumatran interior had long been involved in extensive trade networks linking upland agriculturalists and gatherers of forest products with coastal trading settlements and ports.[14] The interior highlands were the source of a number of important goods for international trade: benzoin, the famous camphor of Barus, as well as other aromatic resins; gold, silver, and other minerals; beeswax, birds' nests, ivory, and other luxury items. How much of this was coming from Karoland is not clear, but archaeological evidence as well as oral tradition does indicate a long history of trade relations between Karo producers and the Malay sultanates of the east coast (Edwards McKinnon 1984; Micsic 1985; Milner et al. 1978). It is certain, however, that at least a portion of the gold traded in the ports of Bulu Cina and Deli came from western Karoland,[15] as did the sulfur (from Mount Sibayak) sold at Deli (J. Anderson 1971b:203; von Brenner 1894:154; Edwards McKinnon 1984:19–20). Moreover, situated as they were along the major routes joining the camphor- and benzoin-producing areas of the western interior with the east coast ports, the Karo may well have acted as middlemen in the trade in aromatic resins, as they later did in the case of horses from the Toba area (J. Anderson 1971b:250–51; Edwards McKinnon 1984:36; de Haan 1870:6).

The Karo markets were not only nodes in a coast-hinterland trade network in precious goods, but they were also centers of small-scale local barter for a wide range of products. De Haan, who observed these markets in 1870, describes the range of goods imported and exported at that time:

> From Deli is imported salt, dried fish, European linen, trinkets, earthenware, iron, ironware (pots), rifles, condiments, lead, flints, camphor (used as medicine, as a seasoning for meat dishes, and for the embalming of corpses). To Deli are exported horses, water buffalo, a few cows, goats, pigs, chickens, a little linen and thread. From the dusuns (lowlands) is imported cotton, betel, gambir, areca nut, tobacco, coconuts and other fruit, anau-sugar (which is not manufactured here, though the anau-palm is abundant), in exchange for linen, red cotton, betel-lime, and goats. From Teba-Teba [the Toba region] are imported horses (which are found there in great numbers and brought to this region young, when full-grown carried to Deli and there sold for high prices), gold from the island (of Samosir), fresh fish from the lake, Toba linen (of inferior quality, coarse and poorly worked), iron, gongs, rifles and camphor (both gotten in Barus [on the west coast]), sirih, sirih-lime and little metal ingots (of iron, copper and tin). (de Haan 1870:38)[16]

Large market purchases were made with dollars, and salt served as small change. The amount of salt equivalent to one dollar was variable, and rose and fell in accord with the price of salt in the lowland markets (ibid.).[17]

According to de Haan, there were two sorts of traders at the markets. First, there were petty traders, many of them women, who sold salt, rice, sirih, gambir, and other everyday items on a small scale. Second were "those, who brought horses and other livestock to Deli, and returning from there with all sorts of goods, went round to the kampongs selling them." This latter group was comprised entirely of men, and, as de Haan notes, some of them were professional traders who did not engage in agricultural activities (nor, more to the point, did their wives). As a rule, however, trade was "mostly a sideline and therefore little developed; one finds here neither shopkeepers nor middlemen" (ibid.).

These markets were also gambling centers. H. C. Kruijt, the first missionary to the Karo, visited the highland market of Tiga Belawan in 1891. As he describes the scene,

> [t]here, where the pasar [market] was held, a bare field stretched out, with only grass and young lalang growing on it. A number of little huts are set up in the early morning, where the man with his roulette waits for those who want to take a chance. Each of the gambling-dens are already filled with men and youths. They know how much the odds are against them; they see the double-guilders, half-guilders and dollars disappear; but they set them down again and again. . . . The gambling-masters seem to me to be well-to-do gentlemen. Their clothing is better taken care of, more Malayish. (Kruijt 1891:357)

By Kruijt's estimate, at Tiga Belawan more than half of the market's activity took place in these "gambling-dens," of which he counted twenty-one scattered around the market grounds. Each was filled with from eighteen to twenty-four men, and the number of gamblers increased as the day wore on (ibid.:357, 363).[18]

Market days were also regularly used by village leaders to conduct political negotiations and to adjudicate extravillage disputes.[19] These gatherings might involve only village or kesain (village ward) heads within a cluster of allied communities, or leaders from adjacent, but non-allied, villages served by the market. Given the lack of effective political institutions above the village, or even the kesain level, the market-day forum provided virtually the only formal check upon the intervillage and inter-urung warfare endemic to the highlands prior to the Dutch conquest of the region.[20]

The pengulu of the village upon whose land the market was held was responsible for guaranteeing the peace of the market. For this, he received the right to collect a fee of one dollar from each gambling-house and one-tenth of all goods brought to the market, this amount then being divided with his anak beru and *senina* in a 4–3–2 ratio (Kruijt 1891:357; Middendorp 1929a:60). But, like many of the customary "rights" of local rulers, this seems to have been honored mostly in the breach; as Middendorp writes, such claims were "seldom taken advantage of as otherwise nobody came" (ibid.).

PERIPHERAL MARKETS AND CONSTRAINTS ON TRADE

Although trade and markets in precolonial Karoland provided support for a variety of social, political, and economic institutions, and served as an arena for personal ambition and enterprise, they were, to use Bohannan and Dalton's term, "peripheral" to the economic organization of Karo society, which was, instead, based on subsistence agriculture. In societies where such peripheral markets occur, "from the viewpoint of the entire economy, market sales are not the dominant source of material livelihood" (Bohannan and Dalton 1962:7), being, rather, a source of supplementary income for traders to make specific purchases or for "pin money." Likewise, for buyers the peripheral market is important as the only place to obtain certain special, but (as a rule) nonessential, items, and not as the source of subsistence goods. Were such markets to disappear, there might be some discomfort among consumers who had become used to obtaining certain goods there, but the economy would not be significantly disturbed (ibid.:8–9).

As Polanyi has argued, economic activity in what he describes as "precapitalist" societies does not constitute an autonomous sphere, around and through which social relations are ordered. Rather, in such societies,

> man's economy, as a rule, is submerged in his social relationships. He does not act so as to safeguard his individual interest in the possession of material goods; he acts so as to safeguard his social standing, his social claims, his social assets. He values material goods only in so far as they serve this end. Neither the process of production nor that of distribution is linked to specific economic interests attached to the possession of goods; but every single step in that process is geared to the number of social interests which eventually ensure that the required step be taken. These interests will be very different in a small hunting or fishing community from those in a vast despotic society, but in either case the economic system will be run on noneconomic motives. (Polanyi 1944:46)

Polanyi suggests that for such a system, in which the economy is embedded in social relations, to remain viable, it is necessary that market activities be restricted. Such restrictions on trade "arise from all points of the sociological compass: custom and law, religion and magic equally contribute to the result, which is to restrict acts of exchange in respect to persons and objects, time and occasion" (ibid.:61). This is the case in regard to barter, reciprocal exchange, and redistribution, but even more so with market exchange. In these systems, markets are everywhere "surrounded by a number of safeguards designed to protect the prevailing economic organization of society from interference on the part of market practices" (ibid.:61–62). The sacrality of the marketplace, ensured by ritual restrictions and ceremonial acts, not only guarantees the market peace and thus the market's continued functioning, but at the same time limits the spread and scope of markets. The precise nature of ritual limitations on trade in precolonial Karoland is not clear, but the tale of the market's supernatural origins suggests that such restrictions did exist. The subsidiary function of Karo markets as courts of justice and political meeting-places likewise tied them to specific locations, usually to villages considered the originary point of clan migration within an urung (perbapan).[21]

Long-distance trade might be limited by practical considerations as well, the most important of these being the difficulty of transportation. Agricultural crops (in precolonial Karoland, primarily rice) were often simply too bulky to be carried to market. A journey from the Karo highlands to the lowland trade centers in times before the introduction of motorized transport required six days' travel through rough, mountainous, and often hostile territory (J. Anderson 1971b). Pack animals were rarely used because of the rugged terrain (only one of the mountain routes, the Cingkam pass near Tiga Belawan, was safe for horses and livestock), and trade goods were thus generally limited to those that the trader could carry himself.

The general political instability of both highland and lowland regions was another constraining factor. Frequent hostilities between villages or allied village clusters kept traders from venturing far from the known routes defined by kinship and by political alliance. Moreover, large stretches of the piedmont (dusun) region lacked any sort of effective political control at all, and the presence of bandits and raiding parties was commonplace (cf. J. Anderson 1971b:49).

The most significant factor limiting the expansion of Karo trade and markets was, however, the nature of the social system itself. For Karo, all social interactions were (and indeed still are), in principle, interactions between kin. A person without kin in a community had neither guarantor nor protector, and so could neither trust nor be trusted. There was thus an impetus for traders either to move within networks of preexisting kin relations, or to establish (or discover) fictive or real kin links with persons in communities outside the sphere of known kinship relations. Even in the case of long-distance trade, Karo both followed existing kin networks and established such networks where they might not have previously existed. Trade by necessity moved along these established or establishable chains of kinship.[22]

At the same time, however, the kinship idiom, defined as it is by the assumed permanent bond of spiritual and material indebtedness of anak beru toward kalimbubu, and by the jural inferiority of anak beru to ka-

Karo salt-carrier, c. 1910.

limbubu, is clearly antithetical to the impersonal, transitory equality of market relations. Although the actual rights and duties implicit in kin relations become attenuated with genealogical distance, the basic principles of deference, respect, and obligation between kin, and the elaborate

rules of etiquette based on these principles do not (Singarimbun 1975:75–
76). Such rules and principles would have generated a tension in market
relations that, in turn, must have restricted to a great extent the expansion
of trade and markets.

A Taste for Hard Cash

If the story of the founding of Tiga Bembem poses the market as a means
of containing aggressive individual action and equalizing the distribution
of scarce resources, a different angle on the problem appears in the narrative of Sibayak Kuta Buluh, which suggests that, for enterprising individuals, economic activity could also provide a means of establishing or
maintaining political power, and of improving a problematic social situation. This story, which was transcribed in 1900 by missionary Joustra,[23]
is set not in the peripheral highland marketplace, but along the trade
routes linking Karoland to the the lowland Malay world.

Si Ajar Taki, the heir to the penguluship of the highland village of Kuta
Buluh, was deposed and sent into exile by his *bapa nguda*, his father's
younger brother. Learning that his uncle planned to have him murdered,
the young man traveled downstream to the court of the Malay sultan of
Deli. There he was placed in the sultan's quarters and exhibited to the
people: "Whoever wants to see the handsome Batak king, pay one dollar," said the *tengku* sultan of Deli to the people. One hundred people
looked, one hundred dollars. So because of his fine appearance Si Adjar
Taki became wealthy" (Joustra 1914:32). With the money, arms, and
soldiers supplied by the sultan of Deli, the young man returned to the
highlands, captured Kuta Buluh, killed his usurping uncle, and married
his faithful sweetheart.

The theme of seeking one's fortune in the lowlands is not unique to the
story of Si Ajar Taki, although the (probably parodic) strategy of self-
exhibition for profit is certainly unusual. Karo lovers' laments (*bilang-
bilang*) dwell with formulaic pathos on the plight of the spurned lover,
who complains of his lack of social standing, his rejection by anak beru
and senina, and often his massive gambling debts. Bidding farewell to his
uncaring sweetheart, who has added to his difficulties by her callous disregard for his feelings, he departs (in song, if not in deed) to search for
fame and fortune, and for new, more generous "mothers and fathers,"
downstream.[24]

Even before the establishment of European plantations made East Sumatra famous as the "Dollar Land of Deli," the lowlands were a source
of wealth for enterprising Karo men. In the early years of the nineteenth

century, Karo cultivators had become involved in the commercial production of pepper for export to the British Crown Colony of Penang.
Previously, most of the island's pepper trade had flowed through the west
and north coasts, or south through Siak, and the Sumatran east coast
appears to have been a relatively isolated backwater of little commercial
importance, over which the states of Aceh and Siak competed for sovereignty and alternately exercised political dominion (Pelzer 1978:1). But
with the establishment of a British colony directly across the Straits of
Malacca in 1786, the weak sultanates of Deli, Serdang, and Langkat were
in an ideal position to take advantage of this new market. The British, for
their part, were eager to encourage pepper production and trade in the
region.[25] In 1823 the British East India Company sent its agent, John
Anderson, on an exploratory mission to the Sumatran east coast to negotiate commercial contracts with the local Malay sultans and to study the
market potential for British imported goods (J. Anderson 1971a, 1971b).

At the time of Anderson's visit, the region was already in the midst of
a pepper boom. In the 1822–23 season over thirty thousand *pikul* (one
pikul = 61.76 kilograms) of pepper were exported to Penang from the
east coast ports of Deli, Bulu Cina, Langkat, and Serdang—a tenfold increase in production in less than a decade (J. Anderson 1971a:184). Most
of this pepper was grown by Karo cultivators (Ibid.:174), who came
down to the lowlands for the agricultural season and then returned to the
highlands after the crop was harvested (J. Anderson 1971b:61). These
men were not wage laborers, but rather farmed on a share basis.

> The Orang Kaya [a Malay aristocratic title] is the principal planter [in the
> Bulu Cina region of Langkat]. He advances to each Batta [*sic*] cultivator, on
> his arrival from the mountains, 160 gantons of paddy, and a sufficiency of
> salt for the year, and the necessary implements of husbandry, viz. a large
> hoe, a spade, a parang [a long knife], and a basket. This continues to be
> repeated for three years, when the Orang Kaya obtains two-thirds of the
> pepper, at the low price of nine dollars per bahar, and the other third at the
> selling price of the day to traders. The pangulus [*sic*] or superintendents get
> the profit of one-third being the difference between 9 dollars and 15. The
> vines bear after three years: the average produce of each tree is one ganton.
> (Ibid.:261)

During the period when pepper trade with Penang was flourishing,
competition among the petty sultanates for tax rights over pepper and
other goods caused an increase in warfare throughout the region, disrupt-
ing trade and travel between the coast and the highlands (ibid.:10).[26] But
this disorder also provided new sources of income for resourceful Karo
men. Some formed what Anderson describes as roving bands of indepen-

dent "banditti"; others hired themselves out as soldiers for the Malay sultans. Indeed, a large number of the fighting men that Anderson observed throughout the region were "Battas,"[27] and the proximity of these "wild savages, who feared neither God nor man," caused Anderson's party a good deal of sleeplessness—apparently much to the amusement of the "savages" themselves, who had enthusiastically fueled the Europeans' fears with wild tales of cannibalism (ibid.:69).[28]

Ever on the lookout for new commercial markets, Anderson felt that the desire for European goods was a major incentive for these "Batta" cultivators, traders, and soldiers of fortune to migrate to the lowlands. Thus, he describes a group of traders whom he met in Sunggal as follows:

They were of the tribe Karau Karau,[29] and were dressed entirely in blue cloth of coast manufacture, called murch and chelopan, of which such large quantities are annually imported by the Chooliahs [Tamils] into Pinang. Almost all the Battas whom I saw here dressed in these cloths; and some few had bajoos or jackets of European chintz or white cloth. Nothing but the want of means prevents them from all wearing European cloth, to which they have lately become very partial. The pepper plantations are thriving remarkably well in this quarter, and coming into bearing rapidly. Their produce will give these people increased means of purchasing their favourite dresses; and I have no doubt, from what I saw, and the evident partiality and growing taste for European chintzes, maddapollams, muslins, and handkerchiefs, and that the demand for these articles will soon be very great, and the sales extensive. (Ibid.:52)

However, these migrants to the lowlands appear to have been more concerned with getting money than with spending it on European chintzes. Despite his optimistic reports on the commercial prospects of the region, Anderson also notes that Karo are "extremely penurious and saving . . . they accumulate large sums, and make no show" (ibid.:268). They are, he remarks, "extremely avaricious [and] fond of amassing money, which makes them industrious, notwithstanding they are addicted to gambling, opium smoking and other vicious propensities" (ibid.:22).

To these "avaricious" Karo pepper-growers, not all dollars were the same, for their value lay not in their purchasing power but rather in the prestige they conveyed. Consequently, Karo cultivators demanded that payment for their crops be made only in the Spanish "Carolus" dollars. The high silver content of these coins made them ideal for melting down into jewelry, especially the huge double-coil *padung-padung* earrings worn by married women.[30] More important, only certain old Spanish dollars might be used for marriage payments.[31] And therein lay a problem for the British merchants of Penang. Anderson reports on the situation:

The greatest difficulty and discouragement to which the pepper trade has been subject, has arisen from the extreme aversion of the Batta cultivators to receive in payment any other than dollars of Carolus the 3rd and 4th, which have a remarkably large and full bust; the Ferdinands the 7th being all small and spare. This may appear a prejudice almost incredible; but such was the case, and the consequence was, that the favourite dollars seldom bore a less premium than 2 and 3 percent. and their scarcity had frequently been so great, as to render it impossible to purchase the cargoes of boats, which arrived from places where the objection existed to the small dollars, as the Ferdinands were called. The scarcity, of course, daily increased, for the Battas hoard up all the money they receive, either concealing the dollars or melting them and making them into ornaments, and *not a dollar left the country again.* (J. Anderson 1971a:188; emphasis added)

One of Anderson's tasks in East Sumatra was to convince Karo cultivators that all dollars were of equal worth. Although he signed treaties with several Karo leaders acknowledging the equivalent value of all dollars, and thus saved (at least temporarily) Penang's share in the pepper trade, this seems not to have lessened Karo enthusiasm for their favorite coins. Sixty years later, when Baron von Brenner (1894:21) was preparing for his "travels among the Sumatran cannibals," he faced the same difficulty: Spanish dollars were still the "sole accepted standard among the Bataks, who have a decided taste for hard cash."

This is a characteristic of that mountain-folk, that one must take into account and which, by the way, makes a journey through their land very expensive. The old Spanish dollars were from year to year rarer, and therefore increasingly difficult to obtain. . . . In Singapore only a few examples were to be located, so I had to inquire by telegraph to Manila, Hong Kong and Penang whether such were obtainable there. Finally, a stock arrived in Penang, which to be sure was far from covering my requirements, and with which I dared not find fault, and they [each] had to be paid for with 1.38 Mexican dollars.[32]

In the contentious and unstable political world of precolonial Karo-land, economic success was a major route to political power and social position. For the great majority of Karo men, who were neither of a ruling lineage nor trained in a professional craft, few legitimate means were available for obtaining the Spanish dollars necessary for a marriage payment (aside, that is, from claiming, like Aji Dibata, the entire amount of their sisters' marriage payment). Temporary or seasonal work in the lowlands offered a relatively easy way to improve that situation. For members of a ruling lineage, like Si Ajar Taki of Kuta Buluh, the accumulation of wealth was more than a means to gain a wife or to "buy" friends and supporters. It did—as Wijngaarden complained—permit a man the "luxury" of polygamous marriage, which in turn, by allowing him to establish separate households in several villages, gave him a voice in the political affairs of each community of residence. And it also gave him the means to sponsor rituals, to distribute favors, to invest in weapons, and to support a military bodyguard. But above all, economic success was the sign of a good fate, and of the *daulat*—the quality of sovereignty—that attached to a proper ruler.[33]

The Karo propensity for gambling must be seen in this same light, as a means of possible social and political advancement. As Wijngaarden (1894a:179–80) wrote, Karo gamblers "play not for the sake of playing, to pass the time or for recreation, but only in order to win money. There are not a few who go from place to place to try their luck. One day they are here, tomorrow there. They are sometimes away for months before returning home. On the whole," the missionary added, administering the coup de grace of the Protestant ethic, "such men think no more of working."

Given the possibilities for personal advancement that the gaming houses of Tiga Bembem and the other highland markets provided, it is hardly surprising that these establishments were, as Kruijt puts it, "chockfull of devotees of cardplaying" and other games of chance (Kruijt 1891:389). Nor is it surprising that Karo men were willing to risk the dangers of long-distance trade, or that they were eager to take advantage of the opportunities opened up by the pepper trade. But, while such efforts were directed primarily toward financial gain, money was less an instrument of trade than a form of social wealth. It might enter the Karo economic system in the form of profit or payment for crops, but it was then immediately transformed into hoarded wealth or a mark of status. It might be recirculated through gambling, but not, to any great extent, through the market. It entered Karoland through the market, and was then absorbed into the social system that stood apart from that market.[34]

For Karo, social production and reproduction were assured by kinship relations rather than by market activity. It was through kin ties (both real and fictive) that individuals obtained access to land, the primary means of production.[35] Marriage, obviously necessary for the physical reproduction of the family unit but also as the source of female agricultural and household labor, was likewise dependent on preexisting kin networks. Whether a marriage alliance established new kin ties, or reinforced prior ones, marriage negotiations and ceremonial validation could only occur through the mediation and agreement of anak beru, kalimbubu, and senina. It was the kalimbubu whose continuing benevolence spiritually ensured a family's reproductive and economic prosperity. Anak beru and senina were required as witnesses and guarantors in all legal transactions, and ritual sponsorship required the presence of anak beru to take care of the necessary labor. Social position, indeed individual survival, depended upon the maintenance of kin relationships and the performance of social obligations.

Valued as the currency for marriage payments, as a mark of social prestige, and as a means of parlaying that prestige into actual political power, money was ultimately no guarantee of social survival, which instead depended upon the maintenance of kin ties. And it was thus necessary to transform market gains into social gains for these to have any real value. This, as a result, restricted the availability of capital for market investment and trade, as well as the motivation to so utilize it. If the market provided a subsidiary means for filling in the chinks, as it were, in the system of social relations, market profits had nevertheless to be recontained within the social system for these gains to be of any real worth.

Nevertheless, it is likely that the expanded pepper market in the early years of the nineteenth century, and the increased trade opportunities that later developed when European tobacco plantations were established in the coastal area, led to an expansion of both local and long-distance trade in Karoland. But as long as the social system remained the primary guarantor of personal and communal well-being, and as long as market gains could continue to be transformed into social wealth, the effect of trade expansion on the economic and social systems was probably minimal. When, however, commercial vegetable farming was introduced into the highlands in 1914, its impact was both rapid and dramatic.

THE BERASTAGI MARKET

In 1913 Meint Joustra, who had retired from mission service and taken a post as archivist of the Bataksch Instituut in Leiden, returned to the Karo highlands after an absence of five years. In the report of his travels he comments enthusiastically on the "great transformations which have taken place there in recent years" (Joustra 1915:12), changes that would be apparent even to the casual visitor. Most such "day-trippers," he writes,

> see little more than a few European "villas" (finished and under construction) in the vicinity of Beras Tagi [sic], the buildings of the mission's teacher training school at Raya, and the government-emplacement and missionary residence at Kabanjahé. All the same, they recognize that they have seen something quite important. All this is, namely, neither more nor less than the

visible side of the real fact that the highlands have finally opened themselves for good to the influence of various Western culture-influences, which can be grouped under three headings: 1st, government; 2nd, the mission; 3rd, the European spirit of private enterprise. The three settlements named above may be considered as central points from which the powers called forth by the less immediately visible social, economic and intellectual (as well as ethical-religious) transformations emanate. (Ibid.:12–13)

The third of these influences—the "European spirit of private enterprise"—was the last to establish its presence directly in the highlands, an event Joustra fixes in 1908, with the building of the first of the European residences in the region that was to become the town of Berastagi.

The town is located at the point where the Medan–Kabanjahé highway first enters the highlands, and enjoys a stupendous view of Mount Sibayak. Looking back along this main road toward the lowlands in the early morning, before the volcano's sulfur-yellowed triple peaks are obscured by clouds, the road appears to emerge from the slopes of the mountain itself. As the steam from the volcano's crater slowly blends with the descending cloud-cover, one has the impression that the clouds are being produced somewhere within the mountain's interior. Enchanted by this prospect, European planters and civil servants of the plantation zone built their vacation villas there on the slopes of Gung Daling, a hill that features a sweeping panorama of the mountain and the ruggedly beautiful landscape beneath it. It is, one later tourist wrote,

> a glorious spot which boasts a first-rate hotel, the Grand Hotel Brastagi [*sic*]. Here the tourist can obtain everything he can wish for: cool, airy rooms, wide, beautiful terraces, glorious views, excellent food and trained service. Tennis courts and golf links adjoin the hotel which is on a magnificent situation opposite the crater of Sibayak, the rocks of which are greenish-yellow with the sulphur which is constantly emitted. (Hofman 1933:218)

In subsequent years, Berastagi would also become the commercial hub of the highland vegetable trade. For around this "glorious" hill resort a bustling trade entrepot (less picturesque surely but more significant to the local population) quickly grew up.

Just outside the present town of Berastagi, at the foot of Gung Daling, lies the original Karo settlement of Rumah Berastagi, from which the town took its name—the two being distinguished locally as simply "Rumah" for the earlier Karo village and "Tiga Berastagi" (the Berastagi market) for the newer commercial and resort center. Joustra in 1899 described the village of Rumah Berastagi as "well and spaciously built, and also tolerably regularly laid out. It was also tolerably clean and the 'kesain' [here, the village commons, an open area within the village] well cleaned of grass and weeds" (Joustra 1899b:129). Outside the village lay "splendid" well-tended wet-rice fields and a fine bath-place with a plentiful water supply. Altogether, the village, with its population of approximately 450 inhabitants,[36] showed all the signs of prosperity and made a "fine impression" (ibid.:128) on the missionary.

Rumah Berastagi and its outlying territories lay on the northern border of the urung-federation of XII Kuta, which was dominated by the Purba subclan of the perbapan village of Rumah Kabanjahé.[37] The village of Rumah Berastagi was divided into two wards (kesain), Rumah Gergeh and Rumah Mbelin, each under the control of a Purba lineage. According to local clan narratives, both these lineages had originated in Rumah Kabanjahé, from which they had separately migrated northward. In the course of these migrations, the two lineages had gained control of land and villages through the northern side of the urung, stretching up to the slopes of Mount Sibayak. Then, joining forces, the two lineages attacked and conquered Rumah Berastagi, expelling its ruling subclan, Ketaran, and establishing themselves as the new "founders" of the village.

As a result of these extensive land holdings and their strategic location—controlling both the sulfur of Mount Sibayak and the XII Kuta pass at Sibayak's foot—Rumah Berastagi and the village of Pecerén, which was jointly ruled with kesain Rumah Gergeh, thus constituted a secondary power center within Urung XII Kuta.[38] The Purbas of Rumah Berastagi and Pecerén were consequently entitled, as were the Rumah Kabanjahé Purbas, to use the title of sibayak as a mark of their special status within the urung. The Rumah Berastagi Purbas remained nominally subordinate to their kinsmen of Rumah Kabanjahé, but relations between the Purba lineages of the two villages appear to have been somewhat strained and competitive, particularly after the Kabanjahé Purbas became closely allied with the Dutch forces stationed at Bangun Purba (in Serdang) and with the missionaries residing at Bulu Hawar. Indeed, relations between the two were so hostile that Pa Jendahen Purba, the pengulu of Rumah Gergeh and Pecerén, was suspected of attempting to poison his Rumah Kabanjahé counterpart, Pa Pelita Purba, the great friend of the Dutch (Joustra 1899a:331).[39]

Before they had moved into Rumah Berastagi, the Rumah Gergeh Purbas had taken some land on the eastern side of Gung Daling from the Surbakti subclan. This land was relatively unproductive, however, and it was the inadequate water supply there, in contrast to the plentiful water of Rumah Berastagi, which encouraged the Purbas to take over that village. Thus, in 1908, when Joost von Vollenhoven, then chief administrative officer of the Deli Maatschappij, came to the highlands to acquire some land for a vacation home, the Rumah Gergeh Purbas were willing to negotiate a contract renting a portion of their Gung Daling land to the

Deli Mij., simultaneously making a profit on some of their less valuable land and establishing an alliance with Dutch plantation interests to counter the growing power of their rivals in Kabanjahé.

It was as a result of the building of this first villa that commercial agriculture entered the highlands. In the course of acquiring the land for his vacation estate, von Vollenhoven conducted discussions with the Purbas of Rumah Gergeh. Noticing broad expanses of unused land that seemed suitable for farming, he inquired why this land was not being used. The Purba men agreed that this would be a very good thing to do, but felt that they had not the skills or knowledge to do so. In this regard, they requested von Vollenhoven's assistance. Their request, as Joustra (1915:15) noted, "was not spoken to deaf ears. The *heer* v.V. [*sic*] promised to do his best and . . . placed himself in communication with the Bataksch Instituut, rightly assuming that such help lay entirely in the domain of this organization." By 1911 these plans had been implemented, and an agricultural expert, H. M. Botje, was dispatched from the Netherlands to serve in the capacity of agricultural advisor to the Karo, for a contracted trial period of three years.

The Gung Daling hillside was selected as the location for Botje's experimental garden, despite the unsuitability of climate and soil fertility, because the Deli Mij. offered both land and housing for Botje's use on their Gung Daling estate. A final, and determining, factor in this decision was the presence there of the Deli Mij.'s large stables, which would provide the necessary stock of manure for use in the gardens. Botje thus began his demonstration garden, assisted by a staff of twenty Karo laborers (ibid.:16).

Potatoes were chosen as the first crop to be tested.[40] Half of the available land was planted with potatoes, and the success of this first harvest encouraged Karo in other nearby areas to imitate Botje's agricultural methods.[41] Seed-potatoes were loaned to interested farmers, to be returned after harvest, and the remainder of the farmers' harvest was bought at the price of 70 cents per *blik* (approximately fifteen kilograms), or *f*. 3.50 per pikul. Joustra (ibid.:16) reports:

> This succeeded splendidly. First only a few persons, later whole villages, some lying hours distant from Beras Tagi, applied themselves to potato-farming. In June 1912 the first distribution of seeds had taken place; in June 1913, when I visited the highlands, I took walks through outstretched, splendid stands of potato-fields, which gave the impression such as one found in Holland. The yield was meanwhile so much increased, that Botje could not nearly place all of them as seed material.

At this point, with Botje's contract nearing expiration and the project a clear success, it was decided to give him a permanent position with the Bataksch Instituut. At the same time Botje was personally ceded a piece of land in the Kuta Gadung area (again, territory controlled by the Rumah Gergeh Purbas) near Rumah Berastagi.[42] The decision was reached to form a marketing cooperative, headed by three Karo men, with Botje as consultant. This cooperative was to handle not only the marketing of highland potatoes to (Chinese) agents in Medan who were connected to the markets in Singapore and Penang on the Malay Peninsula, but also to arrange for transport of the produce to Medan.

Thus far, the system of agricultural production introduced by the Dutch does not appear to differ substantially from the earlier pattern of pepper production by Karo for the lowland Malay entrepreneurs. There were, nonetheless, important differences. First, the highland potatoes entered directly into free market trade, not mediated, as the pepper trade had been, by the monopolistic control, and consequent relative price stability, established by the Malay sultans. Price fluctuations, and the relative inability of producers to affect prices, were further exacerbated by the bulky and perishable nature of the crop, which made the producers even more exposed to market forces. Finally, vegetable crops were produced within the highland region itself, rather than in the lowlands. In a short time, the profitable but uncertain commercial agricultural production began to encroach upon land previously used for subsistence rice production, especially in the environs of the town of Berastagi. The market was shifting from the periphery to the center of Karo life.

When the first commercial potato crop had been brought to market, the problems of the produce trade began to be apparent. An abnormally heavy rainfall made the roads impassible and stocks in the marketing cooperative's warehouses piled up, to the detriment of quality. In February 1914 the government came to the rescue, and provided for a truck to transport the potatoes to Medan. The problem seemed solved, when another difficulty arose: there was "unexpectedly and pretty well inexplicably . . . a formidable price-drop" (Joustra 1915:19), suspected to be the result of market manipulation by Chinese merchants. The stock of potatoes, now transported to Medan, could not be sold, and a large portion rotted in the warehouses. No longer able to guarantee the previously fixed price of eighty cents per blik (there had just been a ten cent per blik price increase), the cooperative was forced to buy potatoes from producers at the low market rate. As a result, the Karo farmers refused to deliver their produce. Suddenly, however, "in almost as inexplicable a fashion, the price recovered quickly, and the Chinese speculators who had been lying in wait, came to the fore and bought up the potatoes [in Medan] at very lucrative prices, even one guilder and higher" (ibid.). The producers, it should be noted, did not share in the profits that resulted from this speculation. The upshot of this initial disastrous introduction to capitalist market economics was not that the Karo turned away from commercial vegetable production, but rather that they lost faith in the cooperative and in Botje's guidance in marketing. Botje was relieved of his duties as marketing consultant, and he subsequently devoted all his energies to the new experimental garden at Kuta Gadung (ibid.:20). From that time, producers were left to their own devices in the marketing of their crops.

Many of the difficulties that have faced Karo vegetable producers up to the present can be seen here: uncertainty of transportation, inadequate storage facilities, mutual suspicion of producers and marketers, dramatic price fluctuations, and the (suspected) speculative practices of Chinese exporters and middlemen. These factors have created a fundamental instability in the production and marketing of vegetables, an instability exacerbated by crop seasonality and short harvest periods, as well as by the necessity of the immediate marketing of vegetable harvests. Vegetable crops were, and are, appealing to farmers because of the quick yields and immediate profits, unlike the case with tree crops (oranges and, more recently, cloves) which have prevailed in other parts of Karoland. Rice production, in contrast to vegetable-growing, has its own built-in safety net as well: the harvest can be stored from year to year in anticipation of an improved price, and if necessary can sustain a family through a poor market period. But the vegetables, when they are harvested, must either be sold immediately or left to rot. Market fluctuations, and the potential for "making a killing" in the market, have provided an incentive for the expansion of commercial vegetable production, but they have also increased the risks faced by producers and marketers alike. The farmers of the Berastagi region were "blessed" by the location of their land near enough to major transportation routes and market centers to allow them to take advantage of the opportunities of vegetable production, but this blessing turned into a disadvantage as they quickly became more and more dependent upon the unstable produce market.

Nonetheless, vegetable production had its rewards, and it was these rewards that encouraged the rapid expansion of commercial agriculture. Despite price fluctuations, variable weather conditions, and inadequate storage facilities, the demand for the highland potatoes was good. In 1915, 36,000 pikuls of potatoes passed through the government customs station at Tongkeh, and in 1916 the amount increased to 57,000 pikuls. In 1917 approximately 70,000 pikuls, with an estimated value of 350,000 guilders, were exported from the highlands, either for shipment to peninsular Malaya or for consumption in Medan and the coastal plantation region (Joustra 1918b:22). In 1916 over two million kilograms of potatoes were shipped abroad through the port of Belawan and in 1917 this figure had increased to nearly three and a half million. At the same time, vegetable production was diversifying. In mid-1916 cabbages were first planted; by the end of that year 2,800 heads of cabbage were exported. In 1917 this amount had increased almost tenfold (ibid.:23), and in 1918 exports of cabbage had reached 600,000 heads (Middendorp

1929a:64). Rice land was largely given over to the growing of potatoes and cabbages, and the region began to depend on other areas, notably Batu Karang and Payung, where the Dutch had subsidized the construction of irrigated fields, for its rice (Middendorp 1922:454).[43]

Commercial agriculture continued to expand throughout the 1920s and 1930s, though probably not at the previous rate. The continued growth of agricultural production was limited by an increasing scarcity of available land and labor. By the mid-1920s a number of villages in the prime vegetable-growing region around Berastagi had no more *taneh kosong* (literally, "empty land," a category including secondary forest and grasslands as well as unused fields) which could, with the permission of the pengulu, be opened and used for agricultural purposes by any village inhabitant (van Liere 1931:69).

Karo were in general unwilling to work as wage laborers, except in the traditional form of cooperative work groups (*aron*) composed of unmarried men and women who performed most of the harvest work in their families' fields on a rotating basis, for minimal payments or, more frequently, the promise of a dance festival (*guro-guro aron*) at the end of the harvest season.[44] Most of the heavy labor of opening and preparing fields (performed by men), as well as the daily chores of weeding and tending the crops (women's work), were the tasks of the family to whom those fields belonged. In this work Karo seem not to have to any extent utilized the labor of seasonal workers from other areas, either within or outside of Karoland. This may have been a result of colonial policy, which endeavored to limit migration between districts; Karo xenophobia probably played a part as well.[45] Consequently, the basic work unit remained the nuclear family, and agricultural expansion was restricted to the amount of land that could be worked by family units.[46]

Other factors also began to dim the success of commercial farming in the highlands. Potato cultivation began to decline in the early 1920s, as the potato vines were struck by blight, and efforts to develop a disease-resistant variety proved unsuccessful (ibid.:25; Meindersma 1938:15). By the mid-1920s Karo middlemen were losing control of the vegetable trade to their Chinese competitors. Although approximately two-thirds of the potato trade remained in Karo hands, the remainder of this important commodity, and most of the rest of the produce trade, was Chinese-dominated (Middendorp 1922:454). Transport between the highlands and the coast was still entirely controlled by Karo, although this too seemed threatened by the replacement of oxcarts by motorized vehicles (ibid.). And even though production must have been increasing or at least remained stable, it appears that real income was declining in the 1930s as the impact of the world depression began to be felt in Sumatra, and prices in the international market, in particular, dropped spectacularly.[47] Local markets were also increasingly circumscribed due to plantation unemployment and the shift of plantation workers from wage labor to subsistence agriculture, as well as declining income in the urban European and Chinese private sector (O'Malley 1977:134). At the same time, real income was affected by the institution of an emergency levy (*crisisheffing*) in 1932, a 50 percent tariff on imports, and increased corvée labor obligations (Holleman 1933:55; O'Malley 1977:139).[48]

Even given these constraints, the economic growth of Karoland was remarkable. In a brief period, the Karo had become the most successful commercial agriculturalists of the Residency's indigenous peoples. The distribution of commercial agriculture and its benefits were, however, uneven. The difficulty of transport on the highlands' limited road system meant that commercial agriculture was to a large extent restricted to the upper portion of the urungs XII Kuta and III Kuru (on the western side of Gung Daling) that had easy access to the Berastagi market and the highway to Medan, and, to a lesser extent, the few villages where irrigated rice fields had been constructed or orange groves planted.[49] The town of Berastagi itself, with its thriving market, drew people from all parts of the highlands, as well as Europeans and Chinese from the coastal region. As Middendorp (1922:455) noted,

> a trader, a hire-coachman, a blacksmith, not originating from Berastagi, will remain established in his home village, where his wife lives and his rice fields lie, but he also wishes to live in the environs of Berastagi, where in the village area by a cross-point of roads lies a well-attended market, where weekly hundreds of sacks of potatoes, hundreds of cabbages, much rice, fruit and other things are traded. Also foreigners (mostly Chinese) wish to build shops and warehouses. Europeans wish to build their villas in the cool climate.

As the center of commercial agricultural production and the site of the interregional produce market, the Berastagi region reaped the greatest economic benefits from that extraordinary growth. And no one had more to gain than the Purbas of Rumah Berastagi.

Land, according to Karo custom, belonged collectively to the founding (or ruling) lineage of a kesain. Use-rights to this land might be established by individuals, both of the ruling lineage and of other clans, based upon historical precedent: either through the opening of new *juma* (unirrigated fields) or gardens, through the planting of permanent tree crops, or through the working of previously opened fields for several generations. Such rights, once established, were permanent and heritable. However, should a landholder die without male heirs, or move to another village, his fields returned to the jurisdiction of the kesain, and were placed at the disposal of the pengulu, either for redistribution or for his own use. Pastureland, forest, and unused fields belonged to the kesain, and were likewise administered by the pengulu. The rights to forest products and minerals obtained within their jurisdiction also belonged to the kesain's ruling lineage (van Liere 1931:68–69). With a few exceptions, this system of land tenure remained intact under Dutch colonial government.[50]

Before the introduction of commercial agriculture, the ruling lineage's control over open land would not have been of much economic significance. Such land was less productive, or farther from the village, and thus less desirable. The main importance of open land lay in the possibility it presented to the bangsa taneh (and more specifically to the pengulu as chief representative of the ruling lineage) to create new anak beru relationships through its distribution, and in the guarantee of subsistence it provided should population increases strain the productive capacity of fields already in use. This open land took on a new value, however, when its potential for commercial vegetable-growing appeared. Open land became a village's most important resource, as its rapid disappearance in the main agricultural region of Berastagi indicates.[51] And as the value of open land increased, so did the importance, both politically and economically, of the pengulu's control over its allocation. The Purba lineages of Rumah Berastagi, strategically situated on the land immediately surrounding the town of Berastagi, were in an ideal position to take advantage of their customary right to this land, and of the new colonial legal and political institutions that supported that right.

With the growth of the market and resort town of Berastagi and the increasing incorporation of Karoland into the colonial economic system, other benefits accrued to the Purbas of Rumah Berastagi as well. Aside from their access to land for personal use, local rulers also profited from their rights to mineral and forest resources within their territory. For the Rumah Berastagi Purbas, this included not only lumber but also a share of the sulfur collected at the government station atop Mount Sibayak. They also received a portion of the rents from land concessions. Some land for vegetable production was being rented to Chinese farmers, usually for periods of from two to five years at a time (van Liere 1931:64). These "diligent folk," wrote Middendorp (1922:456), "are mostly in the service of the village head, who allows himself to be paid by them for his favor."

More important, especially in the Berastagi area, were land concessions for residential and commercial use. Ezerman (1926:32) describes the implications of this situation:

It now appears that in the kedai [shop] districts of the population centers such as Brastagi and Kaban Djahe—elsewhere there are virtually no foreign places of business—foreigners can in fact acquire no rights on the land. The Karo-Batak population do not alienate their rights, but if they give permission to place a building on their land, they draw, in so doing, an income.

In 1921 payments for such land were fixed at *f*. 2000 per *bouw* (one bouw = .71 hectare) as an initial fee (*present taneh*), with a fee (*hasil taneh*) of *f*. 100 per bouw paid annually thereafter.[52] Of this amount, the entire present taneh and 20 percent of the hasil taneh were given to the bangsa taneh and the local rulers, with the remaining 80 percent of the annual hasil taneh received by the government treasury (ibid.:31–32).[53] By 1929 there were 120 such concessions, mostly located in and around the town of Berastagi (van Liere 1931:65).

Van Liere (ibid.:30) reports on the results of the communal ownership of this land in terms of the commercial expansion of the towns:

> In Kaban djahe as well as in Brastagi practically all kedei's [*sic*] are the property of Bataks. Insofar as they do not use [these shops] themselves, they rent them to their compatriots or to Chinese. In 1929, 70 new kedei's all *by* and *for* Bataks, were built in Berastagi. This forced growth [*geforceered bouw*] was, however, also a result of the fact that the land used for kedei-building was communal property, on which kedei's could be built for a small compensation to the bangsa taneh of the kesains concerned. As a result, there was a race to build as many kedei's as possible.

As shopkeepers and as landlords, then, the Purbas profited from the growth of the new commercial center of Berastagi, and their eagerness to take advantage of the economic benefits of their position can be seen in the "race" to open shops in the town.

In part, an understanding of the commercial development of the Berastagi area must be set against a backdrop of the long-standing competitive relations between the Rumah Berastagi Purbas and their kinsmen of Rumah Kabanjahé. Since the Rumah Kabanjahé Purbas had improved their political position through alliances with the Dutch colonial government and with the missionary establishment, the Purbas of Rumah Berastagi countered by associating themselves with the third stream of Western influence, that is, with what Joustra (1915:13) described as "the European spirit of private enterprise," as embodied in the commercial interests of the plantation zone and the Bataksch Instituut. Yet this, in itself, provides no full explanation for the region's remarkable growth. The emergence of commercial agriculture in Karoland in general and Berastagi in particular must also be viewed in the larger context of Dutch colonial policy.

THE ETHICAL POLICY AND ITS IMPACT ON KAROLAND

By the close of the nineteenth century, Liberal policy in the Netherlands, which had stressed limited government intervention and the free play of private enterprise as the keys to opening up the resources of the East Indies, was generally considered a failure.[54] Home rule was a bureaucratic disaster, and the economic development of the colonies had brought prosperity neither to the local population nor to the Netherlands. As a response to the colonies' economic drain on Dutch resources, the obvious impoverishment of the indigenous population by extractive capitalist enterprise and governmental demands, and the threat of English intervention in the region, a new policy was formulated in the 1890s by Liberal, Socialist, and right-wing Clerical political figures.

The basic tenets of this new policy, which met with approval from all sides of the political spectrum, were concern for the welfare of the indigenous population; efficient colonial administration, expansion, and consolidation of control over the entire archipelago; and, as a subsequent development of the policy, government decentralization. Because this approach stressed the moral obligation of the Dutch to provide for the welfare of the people of the East Indies it was dubbed the "Ethical Policy." As Netherlands Privy Councillor Kielstra (1920, in Middendorp 1929a:44) described the mood that engendered this new policy, "the majority of our nation realized that in governing colonies we must not allow our desire for gain to get the upper hand, but must place our moral obligations in the foreground." In other words, colonial governments had an ethical responsibility to improve the lot of the governed, and not merely to enrich the treasury of Holland.

However, as Middendorp wryly noted, "these moral conceptions are related to the material possibilities, especially to those which the most powerful group regards as its primary interests." In this case, there was the realization that the East Indies was not simply the source of natural products for the markets of Europe, but might also (as John Anderson had pointed out nearly a century before) provide a market for European manufactured goods. Such a market was predicated upon the economic well-being of the local people, for an impoverished population had no means to purchase these goods. At the same time, the East Indies as a source of raw materials was becoming a losing proposition, and the colonies were proving to be a drain on the Dutch treasury. Thus it was from two fronts that the separation of home and colonial finances had appeal. By this means, the colonial government might become both more responsible and more responsive to the needs of its citizens; it would also in time cease to burden the economic resources of the Netherlands. In order to fit the colonies for "self-rule," however, a temporary increase in government expenditures was necessary; and, finally, in order to ensure the autonomy and tranquility of the region, and thus the safety of invested capital and the orderly flow of goods, the establishment of firm control over the entire archipelago was required. This "Ethical Policy" would ultimately lead not only to an improvement in the condition of the peoples of the East Indies but also to increased benefits for the Netherlands.

In many ways, Karoland was a classic example of the workings of the Ethical Policy. The Dutch conquest of the highlands occurred in 1904,

ostensibly as a result of local disturbances in the region and the consequent expulsion of missionary Guillaume from Kabanjahé.[55] But these
disturbances took place in the early years of the Ethical Policy, when an
expansionist mood in the Netherlands was particularly attuned to opportunities for extending colonial control over such peripheral areas as the
Karo highlands, and progress toward ending the Acehnese war in northern Sumatra had freed up both Dutch military forces and the financial
support necessary for further campaigns. The Korte Verklaring ("Short
Declaration") signed by Karo rulers after their defeat was largely designed with the principles of decentralization and increased local control
in mind. This declaration, rather than enumerating extensive rights and
obligations of local rulers within the colonial system, simply stated that
the rulers acknowledged their subordination to the colonial state, agreed
not to enter into relations with foreign governments, and assented to
comply with all regulations that the state prescribed.

Within the framework of the Short Declaration, the Ethical Policy retained the earlier principle, in direct as well as indirect rule, of governing
through local rulers and local institutions, insofar as this was possible.
The treaty, however, both strengthened the role of colonial administration in local affairs, and allowed for greater flexibility in adapting local
government to changing local circumstances. The general tendency of the
Ethical Policy to support greater governmental efficiency, at the same
time, strengthened the position of the indigenous rulers vis-à-vis the local
population. The results of this policy in Karoland were that the position
of the bangsa taneh, and particularly village and regional rulers, was
strengthened and reinforced by colonial legal and political institutions,
and they achieved a new importance in local government (Middendorp
1929a:56).

The protectionist tendency of the Ethical Policy, and its principle of
supporting the growth of local industry, can be clearly seen in the encouragement of commercial agriculture in Karoland, and indeed the success of
this endeavor might have been cited as a proof of the benefits of the Ethical course. It was not government, but private enterprise and private benevolent associations, in accord with the continuing Liberal influence in
Ethical policy, that provided the initial impetus for commercial agriculture; this development was subsequently supported by government regulation and government assistance. And, clearly, the results were economically beneficial to both government and people.

Lest the benevolent motives of the colonial government in Karoland be
overemphasized, it should be noted that it had little choice in the matter.
Because of Karo insistence on retaining their customary rights to the land
(verbally assented to by titular Assistant Resident Westenberg at the time
of the signing of the treaty[56] and honored in accord with the Ethical concern with the welfare of the local population), and Karo suspicion of any

attempt of outsiders to encroach upon these rights, there was virtually no foreign investment in the Karo highlands, and the colonial government was thus dependent upon the taxation of the local population in order to garner its revenues and support government services. Oderafdeling Karo-landen was, to paraphrase Martin Kilson's (1966:24) characterization of indirect rule in British Africa, an instance of colonialism-on-the-*very*-cheap. The only part of the East Coast Residency to be totally dependent upon the revenues of the indigenous population, it consequently had not only the lowest revenues but also the highest tax rate of any subdistrict in the Residency, and the government was as a result always seeking to increase local taxable incomes. The shifting of the place of the market from the periphery to the center of Karo society was thus seen not only as a beneficial move for the population, but also as an essential one for the maintenance of colonial government in the region.

WEALTH INTO CAPITAL

There is a critical difference between societies in which markets play a peripheral role in the economy and those in which the market is the central economic institution. In the former, social relations govern economic life, whereas in the latter economic life governs social relations. As Polanyi comments in regard to market-dominated societies,

> the control of the economic system by the market is of overwhelming consequence to the whole organization of society: it means no less than the running of society as an adjunct to the market. Instead of economy being embedded in social relations, social relations are embedded in the economic system. The vital importance of the economic factor to the existence of society precludes any other result. For once the economic system is organized in separate institutions, based on specific motives and conferring a special status, society must be shaped in such a manner as to allow that system to function according to its own laws. This is the meaning of the familiar assertion that a market economy can function only in a market society. (Polanyi 1944:57)

The emergence of market economy is not, Polanyi continues, a natural consequence of a presumed human propensity to seek economic gain, nor of the growth and spread of markets themselves. It is, instead, the outcome of "highly artificial stimulants administered to the body social" through the intervention of the state (ibid.). In colonial Karoland, these "artificial stimulants" to a large extent took the form of colonial fiscal and monetary policy, and government interventions that altered the role of money in Karo social life.

Karo participation in trade, and even in international trade, did not begin in the colonial period. However, this early trade had remained peripheral to the basic economic organization of Karo society due to a variety of practical and social constraints. The completion of a major highway in 1908 linking the highlands to coastal markets provided new opportunities for market production, with a resultant quantitative leap in market activity. But such a quantitative increase alone could not have produced the rapid and sustained economic transformation that Karo society underwent in the first decades of the twentieth century; nor could it have generated the social dislocations that began to appear during that period. More significant was the qualitative difference in the use of trade profits that came to the fore in the years following the establishment of Dutch colonial control over the Karo highlands, and in this the colonial government played an important role.

As Parry and Bloch (1989:21–22) have argued, there is in money neither an intrinsic, universal meaning nor an inherent (and thus inevitable) power of social transformation. In precolonial Karoland, money had an important but highly restricted place in social life. Its primary use was in certain social and ritual exchanges such as marriage payments, where silver coins—notably Spanish dollars—were given by the wife-receiving anak beru for distribution among the various classes of their kalimbubu. Other payments followed this same pattern, in which the giving of money was a mark of subordinate status and, conversely, its receipt a sign of superiority. Such a system encouraged the accumulation of wealth, primarily in the form of money or ornaments made from silver coins, but also in the form of livestock, rifles, or other valuable objects which, as purchases for which coins were the appropriate currency, served as an alternate representation of money. Wealth was a sign of daulat—the quality of sovereignty—given a tangible and permanent form.

Within societies based on subsistence production, such an accumulation of wealth is common, as Marx noted:

> Within the very earliest development of the circulation of commodities there is also developed the necessity, and the passionate desire, to hold fast the product of the first metamorphosis. This product is the transformed shape of the commodity, or its gold-chrysalis. Commodities are thus sold not for the purpose of buying others, but in order to replace their commodity-form by their money-form. From being the mere means of effecting the circulation of commodities, this change of form becomes the end and aim. The changed form of the commodity is thus prevented from functioning as its unconditionally alienable form, or as its merely transient money-form. The money becomes petrified into a hoard, and the seller becomes a hoarder of money. (Marx 1967:130–31)

According to Marx, the desire to hoard money arises from its dual nature: as imperishable metal, a physical form in which surplus production can be preserved indefinitely; and as the embodiment of pure exchange-value in the abstract, which permits it to be exchanged for any commodity (Marx 1970:129). The tendency to accumulate wealth was further encouraged in Karo society by the aura of daulat that attached itself to money and by the status differential that obtained between giver and receiver of money. Money was valued for its utility as a universal means of exchange but, at the same time, the very magnitude of this value made money the medium of very specific, social exchanges. This, in turn, curtailed to a great extent its use as a generalized means of exchange and enhanced its value as both a pure object of exchange and a means of specialized exchange. Theoretically, that is, anything might be exchanged for money, but its special value as the currency for particular sorts of exchanges ensured that it would not be used as such.

A second and related aspect of the meaning of money within Karo society was the denial that money was an abstract and universal measure of value, the worth of which was determined either by its relative metal-content or by legal definition. All dollars were not, for Karo, equally valuable, as Anderson and the pepper-merchants of Penang discovered to their dismay. The higher silver content of Spanish dollars did, to be sure, make them more desirable in Karo eyes, but not because of the intrinsic value of the silver in relation to other commodities. Rather, it was the functional utility of the relatively pure silver of the Spanish coins (that is, the softness of the metal) in jewelry-making that gave them special appeal. A coin's age, even the image imprinted on its face, reflected the daulat embodied in it, and made it more or less valuable. Money thus served less as a means of exchange than as a commodity desirable in its own right.

All of this was not in accord with the requirements of the Dutch colonial administration. As noted above, the governmental treasury of Onderafdeling Karolanden was entirely dependent upon the taxation of the local population. As a result it was necessary for the colonial government to encourage the expansion of local taxable income in order to defray its own expenses. But so long as money earned was immediately withdrawn from circulation rather than being reinvested in the market, the economic development of the highlands, and the expansion of the government's tax base, was impeded. Money had to be transformed from wealth into capital.

Colonial policy thus closed off the mechanisms that could have "decapitalized" the money flowing into the Karo highlands in the early twentieth century. The first, and most important, step in this direction was the standardization of currency. In 1908, immediately after colonial govern-

ment was established in the highlands, the use or possession of foreign
currency was forbidden and only Dutch coins were allowed to be passed
(Joustra 1910:312). This move, which asserted the equivalent exchange-
value of all coins while it withdrew from circulation precisely those coins
that had special value within the sphere of social exchange, in effect reduced all exchanges to the level of market transactions and extracted the
quality of daulat, which had served to confine money to the social sphere,
from coins.[57] It also had the subsidiary effect of ruining the silversmithing
industry by eliminating the source of silver for jewelry-making.

At the same time that the colonial administration was attempting to
standardize the currency, it was also endeavoring to rationalize the use of
currency. A variety of policies and programs of the government, the
Christian mission, and the Bataksch Instituut aimed at, or resulted in, a
decline in the social or prestige-oriented utilization of money. A legal limit
was, for example, placed on marriage payments, the size of which had
previously served as an indicator of the wife-giving group's prestige
(Lekkerkerker 1916:65).[58] Standards of ritual expenditure, including fees
charged by gurus and spirit mediums for their performances, were similarly fixed by law (Huender 1930:319). The practice of polygamy, another potential locus for the expansion of wealth as status, was, while not
abolished by the colonial government, definitely discouraged, and the
mission ruled that Christians might not take more than one wife. Likewise, the removal of Spanish dollars from circulation meant that the huge
silver padung-padung earrings that had been used as important markers
of status and wealth could no longer be produced.[59]

It has frequently been argued that taxation is an important means
whereby the domination of the market economy is extended.[60] In the
Karo case, the need for money to pay taxes to the colonial government
must have encouraged market activity and wage labor to some extent; but
the practical necessity of gaining an income to meet tax assessments was
probably less important than the social meaning of colonial tax practices.
It was largely cash income that was taxed, and not subsistence production, so that an increased income would result in increased taxation, and
not the other way round. In the case of capitation taxes, these were partially offset by the freedom from the obligation to pay prescribed fees to
local chiefs and to contribute financially to village ceremonial activities.
As a result, colonial taxation seems not to have been a substantial economic burden on the population.[61]

On the other hand, colonial tax policy did significantly disturb the
kinship basis of the system of social prestations that it replaced, and increased the power of local rulers vis-à-vis the population. Colonial taxation was extended universally,[62] eliminating kinship from consideration
as a factor in such payments. Customary fees had not only served as a

marker of particular kin relations (notably anak beru–kalimbubu); their direct payment had also reinforced the social rights and obligations embodied in these relations. The inability of local rulers to compel, by law or by force, the payment of fees had restrained them from abusing their positions, for if they abrogated their responsibilities their subjects might simply withhold payment. The rationalization of such fees in the form of taxation inserted the colonial state as mediator between kin groups, and between rulers and ruled. This generated a new element of coercion in payment demands and weakened the bonds of obligation that linked dominant and subordinate groups within Karo society while it strengthened the sense of pure domination of the state over all members of the population, ruler and ruled alike (Middendorp 1929a:61). Along the same line, the colonial government, acting at the request of the NZG missionaries, ruled that Christian Karo could be exempted from financial contribution to village or family rituals that could be classified as "pagan"—a very broad category indeed, including everything from curing rituals to the construction of funeral monuments.[63]

Aside from the local rulers, there were other persons whose socially important occupations—craftsmen (pandé), musicians (penggual), and ritual specialists and curers (the male guru and the female guru si baso)—entitled them to a variety of prescribed fees as acknowledgment of the daulat embodied in their professions. They, too, were affected by the colonial presence, if not by direct government intervention. In a variety of ways, the payment of customary fees for their services was discouraged or restricted, and the prestige of their positions was undercut. The silversmith's craft was, as noted above, largely destroyed by the introduction of Dutch currency, and the prestige and demand for the services of the master-builder (pandé tua) and blacksmith (pandé besi) were undermined by the establishment by the mission and the Bataksch Instituut of training schools for smiths and carpenters.[64] In a similar manner, the introduction of Western medicine by the missionaries brought about a decline in the importance of the guru's curing role, as Karo began increasingly to turn to the mission's clinics and, later, to the Bataksch Instituut's hospital in Kabanjahé for medical treatment.

Music played an important part in both secular and religious ceremonies, and the dances that it accompanied acted out kin relations and the qualities embodied in those relations (cf. Rita S. Kipp 1979). But because of its "heathen" associations, the gendang orchestra was strongly opposed by the mission. The government, for its part, outlawed the purely secular guro-guro aron.[65] For musicians, who had held an important position within the circle of custom, the declining significance of music in ceremonial life brought about a similar decline in social prestige and daulat.

The abolition of the guru-guro aron harvest dance was likewise a movement in the direction of fiscal rationality. While on one hand it contributed to the undermining of the musicians' prestige by eliminating what was perhaps the most significant social arena of musical performance, it also approached the situation from an opposite direction. The dance had been proper reward for the aron collective work groups, composed mostly of unmarried young people, at the end of the agricultural season, and its elimination thus encouraged a shift to the payment of (taxable) wages for agricultural labor.

It might appear that payments for the services of craftsmen, musicians, and curers were simply a step in the direction of wage labor and that the decline of these professions went counter to the trend of increasing market domination in Karo society. It might also seem that the replacement of traditional craftsmen by school-trained carpenters and blacksmiths, or gurus by doctors, would not produce a significant alteration in the relations embodied in payments for services. It is not, however, as simple as that. The positions of pandé, penggual, and guru were instituted and validated by custom, and restricted by birth or selection. They were special cases, designated respectfully (along with the pengulu) as *si erjabatan*, "those who have professions"; the payment of fees for their services was a mark of both their specialness and their social importance. It was not the principle of payment for services, but the social basis of such payments that was undermined by colonial interventions, which transformed them from social to purely economic transactions.

Aside from social exchange, display, and prestige, there was another important sphere in which money played a significant part: gambling. Dutch administrators, even more so the Christian missionaries, viewed such activities as an incitement to idleness and crime, a threat to "peace and order," if not absolutely depraved in themselves. Gambling, Wijngaarden (1894a:180) wrote,

> is not infrequently a source of misery and lawlessness. How often is not its outcome theft or, even worse, murder. A son ruins his parents. . . . The husband makes wife and children unfortunate; he gambles away everything that he has. He bets gold and good, his clothing, his great knife, his betel-pouch, the goods borrowed from his soedara [sibling]. . . . Wife and children can be pawned.

Gambling was thus quickly outlawed by the colonial government—though never eliminated, it seems, for even near the end of the colonial period the subdistrict controleur could remark that "combatting the evils of gambling is still a not unimportant part of the duties of the police force" (Lanting 1937:76) in Karoland, all the more so because gambling was seen as a root cause of violence, theft, and even grave-robbing (ibid.:77), in addition to contributing to general social unrest.

But it was not simply that gambling led to disturbances of colonial *rust en orde* (though it may also have done so); more than that, the gambling arena was a self-enclosed sphere of circulation, one that drained off income from reinvestment and thus hampered economic development. The importance of gambling as a male social activity (perhaps even as *the* male social activity par excellence) meant that large amounts of money might simply be absorbed into its distributive system—and not find its way out again, as it continued to circulate among gamblers. It was this quality, as much as the concern expressed by Wijngaarden that "such men think no more of working," which made gambling a threat to the new market economy, and the colonial administration's strongly oppositional stance must be viewed in the light of this threat.[66]

In sum, then, it appears that at virtually every point in Karo life where money played a social role, there was some sort of intervention on the part of the colonial establishment that served, intentionally or not, to limit that role. Outlawing gambling, removing the source of silver for the making of earrings, establishing trade schools, limiting the amount of marriage payments—all of these served the same purposes, which were to rationalize the use of currency and to free up money for market investment. With traditional avenues for the use of excess funds becoming increasingly closed, the marketplace was more and more the locus not only of the acquisition of wealth, but also for the display of wealth as status. That is, profits reinvested in trade, and most specifically in such highly visible tokens of market participation as shops and transport vehicles served in much the same way that earlier prestige items such as silver earrings and imported rifles had done. The description of the "race to build as many kedei's as possible" in Berastagi, even if this "forced growth" exceeded local demand, makes this point clearly.

The same process can be seen in the rapidity with which Karo men became involved in transport. In 1909 the first oxcart for long-distance transport had been introduced into the highlands; by 1918 there were a thousand Karo-owned carts, with a total value of *f*. 300,000, plying the roads between the highlands and the coast (Middendorp 1929a:63). In 1911 the first truck was used to transport highland produce; within a few years the Karo-run marketing cooperative was already planning to buy its own motor vehicles, and by the 1920s Karo-owned buses and trucks were serving villages some distance from the main commercial centers. To the present, the ownership of one or more commercial vehicles conveys a special distinction among Karo, and the status of a toké motor (transport entrepreneur) or even a bus-driver, may be greater than that of a high-level civil servant or a university instructor.[67]

It was in part because commercial activity could be cloaked in the forms of status display that Karo could so eagerly adopt the new economic system that had been offered to them. Nonetheless, there is a qualitative difference between profits transformed into pure objects of display such as silver earrings, and profits invested in a shop or truck that could, in turn, produce more profits. In the first case, the exchange of commodities reaches a dead-end in absolute and nonproductive consumption. In the second, there is an unceasing movement between money and commodities, the latter producing more money, which is in turn reinvested in profit-making commodities, and so on, in a nonstop, expansive spiral. The market is no longer external to society, but central. And money is no longer simply wealth, but also capital.

This new centrality of the market to economic life brought a restructuring of social relations in accord with market principles. As Marx noted, accumulated wealth provides a means of preserving surplus production in a permanent form, one that can be exchanged for necessities in case agricultural production is insufficient. Such wealth may be transformed into equally permanent social forms: prestige items signaling their owner's personal daulat; wives who expand or strengthen a man's kinship network; gifts and loans that generate ties of social reciprocity; the generous performance of customary duties to kin, which consolidate the ties of mutual obligation created at birth or through marriage.[68] When, however, wealth is no longer preserved in the form of valuable objects, or in such long-term social "investments" as brides, gifts, or ceremonies, the protective functions of wealth and social reciprocity no longer exist, and in the event of economic failure, subsistence is no longer assured. Investors become totally dependent upon the market and its vagaries for their continued existence. Social relations within such a market-dominated society are no longer mediated by bonds of kinship or communality, but rather by the circulation of commodities. Market relations, ephemeral and one-dimensional, could not offer the safeguards against temporary setback that were provided by the complex, permanent ties of kinship. Given the fundamental instability of the produce trade, this was a shaky basis indeed for social and individual survival. Under these circumstances, the continuing redistributive demands of kinship, which could lay claim to capital by turning it back into social wealth, threatened to undermine what fragile security the produce trade could offer.

The domination—even the economic domination—of Karo society by the market was, however, only partial. Production was oriented toward the marketplace, where the abstract equality of buyer and seller held sway and the calculated and egoistic seeking of profit was necessarily the primary mode of interaction. Yet access to land for commercial agricultural production was the originary point for the capital needed for market activity, as well as for the commodities offered for exchange—and access to land was governed not by the law of the market but by custom and kinship. And labor, when it went beyond the nuclear family, was organized through either cooperative village work-groups or through social relations of kinship. The production of commodities and the exchange of those same commodities thus operated under entirely different principles, even though the same persons might be involved in relations of production and in market relations.

Within the political system, the same juxtaposition of local and externally imposed institutions occurred, producing the same sort of antipathetic duality of social relations. Under the Dutch system of indirect rule, kinship-based village polities were incorporated (albeit in a modified form more in keeping with the exigencies of colonial government) into the new Dutch-controlled bureaucracy. Local rulers were bound into the colonial system by receipt of a salary and a percentage of taxes collected in their districts, as well as other significant favors (most notably advanced educational opportunities and exemption from corvée labor for members of their families). Their previously limited authority was both increased and reinforced by the power of the colonial state. Their positions now dependent upon Dutch support, local leaders were divided from their followers at the same time that they were coopted by the colonial government. The formerly minimal gap between rulers and ruled was widened by the increased economic and educational opportunities that accrued to local leaders, who, as their customary authority and prestige declined, were more than willing to take advantage of whatever they could legitimately lay claim to under the colonial system or could coerce or manipulate their European "supervisors" into granting, in order to bolster their sagging local status. Whether or not the continued existence of customary patterns of authority was more than a colonial fiction, the fact remains that the Karo (in most cases) perceived such a continuity, at least on the village and subvillage levels, while at the same time they were crucially aware of the real sources of power in the hands of the Dutch and their supporters. As a result, Karo resentment of the colonial regime tended to focus upon local rulers, who, in their eyes, not only cooperated with the Dutch but also abused their customary positions.

Middendorp, in 1922, saw the "penetrating money economy" and the related development of capital investment and debt as leading to "the creation of a proletariat and of a capitalist class" in Karoland (Middendorp 1922:458). This did not come about. Nor, during the relatively brief period of Dutch rule, did a true class system develop, although the foundations of one were laid. The disparity between the position of the ruling elite and the rest of the population in Karoland was never as great as in other areas of the East Coast Residency. Nevertheless, the contradiction between the new social order, with its emerging bureaucratic elite and market ethic, and the older, kin-based order that still governed social relations in daily life (not to mention the contradictions inherent in each), were significant. In practice the relative lack of differentiation between elite and *rayat* (common people) as well as the general economic success of the commercial agriculture venture tended to protect Karo from suffering the full impact of commodification and class formation, but on the ideological level these contradictions were both exceptionally acute and also widely experienced.

Unlike the case in the Malay sultanates and even the Simelungun Batak kingdoms, where a hereditary ruling aristocracy had been in power long before the coming of the Dutch, precolonial Karo society had had no elite class, and the power and privilege of local rulers and bangsa taneh were extremely limited. As a result, even minimal inequities were keenly felt by Karo, as might not have been the case within a society where status disparities were seen as more "natural." Further, in Karoland the influence of the market economy was not mediated by the ruling elite, nor, to any great extent, by an outside group (Dutch, Chinese, Mandailing, Toba), as was the case in the coastal plantation region. The Karo participated directly, if on a small scale, in the market, both as producers and sellers. Doubly dominated by the invisible forces of the market and the disguised hand of colonial power, Karo attempted occasionally to resist, but more often they tried to accommodate themselves to these new circumstances— looking toward the main chance and the sharp bet, gambling on whatever profits they could draw from the complex colonial transaction in which they were engaged.

PROFITS AND MISRECOGNITIONS

Representations and misrepresentations flourished around the colonial marketplace, and neither their aims nor their effects were entirely as they seemed. "Money is everything to the Batak," Wijngaarden wrote in his first published account of mission work in Karoland (Wijngaarden 1893:399).[69] A year later, however, he was complaining that the Karo, who suspected that some less benevolent motives lay behind the mission's efforts, held precisely the same view of the missionaries themselves. This was, to Wijngaarden, a further proof of the worldly nature of the Karo, for "[d]isinterestedness is so difficult for them to imagine" (Wijngaarden 1894a:169). But Karo suspicions were also, the missionary noted, a result of the particular circumstances in which they had become acquainted with European civilization: "They have learned to know this from only one side. The Europeans in Deli came to plant tobacco. To make money and go back to the mother-country is the usual course of things. Now the missionary comes. It is quite natural that the same intention is attributed to him" (ibid.:168–69).

Rumors abounded concerning the reasons for the missionaries' presence in Karoland. They were said to be inspecting the land with an eye to establishing new tobacco or coffee plantations. They were spies for the Kompeni. They wished to enslave the people, or to force them to serve as soldiers in the war with Aceh or as coolies on the plantations.[70] They received huge salaries for their labors, for why else would they travel so far to "live in the forest" with the Karo? They stood to make a "pretty penny" from their knowledge of Karo language and custom, and when they had thus made their fortunes they would leave, just as, it was said, missionary Kruijt had done (ibid.:168-70). It is, Wijngaarden (ibid.:168) wrote, "a cause of sorrow to the missionary whenever his best actions are misunderstood, the helping hand rejected, word and deed scorned. It is so unpleasant to be treated with distrust."

On the one hand, Karo interpretations of the missionaries' motives may be seen as a replication of the accepted pattern of seeking and accumulating wealth in foreign lands—wealth that might be brought home to advance one's local status. On the other, they may also be seen as an astute reading of the situation, given the extent to which the mission's presence supported, and was supported by, the political and economic interests of the planters and the colonial government. This latter view does not seem to have occurred to the missionaries—or at least they were unwilling to acknowledge publicly such a possibility.

Yet they were well aware of the actual contradictions in which the colonial mission was enmeshed. The image of the amoral, materialistic pagan provided a tentative ideological resolution of those contradictions. A reflection of Calvinist views of the essential baseness of human nature as much as it was a mistaken universalization of the meaning of money in a market-dominated society, it served in part as a justification of colonial rule: a fantastic representation of "heathen" society as more oppressive than its oppressors—the woman "bought with gold" being a key image here. At the same time, it also allowed the missionaries to mount an assault on worldly values in a more general sense and, more important, to present, in the guise of "ethnography," a veiled critique of colonial exploitation and of the blatantly self-interested actions of the European planters—upon whom the Karo mission was regrettably dependent for financial support. In Wijngaarden's account, Karo misrecognition of missionary disinterestedness becomes a revelation of the interested motives that guided the other Europeans whom the Karo had encountered, and a mark of the moral distance separating the missionaries not only from their pagan flock but also from their worldly European brethren.

For more than a decade this negative image of the Karo as pure exemplars of the egoistic ethic of the marketplace defined the mission's attitude toward Karo society. But by the second decade of the twentieth century it had entirely disappeared from the mission's public discourse. In its place was a kind of nostalgic reverie over the decline of a traditional way of life, intertwined with a more positive view of Karo "practical materialism" as leading to both moral and material advancement.[71] The Dutch Ethical Policy, the principles of which are reflected in this revised view of Karo materialism, provided a framework that could accommodate the often antagonistic positions of missionaries, colonial administrators, and European entrepreneurs regarding the proper relation between colonial state and colonized peoples. It mediated the encounter between European and native societies in the East Indies, and—from the European side of that encounter—cast both parties in a comprehensible and morally tolerable light by misrepresenting colonial exploitation as a form of social exchange, a permanent reciprocal arrangement beneficial to all. In the colonial marketplace—as Beru Bembem had said of the rather different market that bore her name—conflicts might be resolved and "boundaries of sharpened stakes" forgotten, for (at least in theory) "all will win, all will receive a share."

From the Karo side of this unbalanced exchange, other processes of misrepresentation and misrecognition were also at work. Equating market investment with status display is one example of this, and strategically reinterpreting the abstract equality of market transactions in terms of the fundamental asymmetry of status established between giver and receiver of money (as did the old man in the Berastagi market whose story opened this chapter) is another. Mutual misrecognitions of this sort might, for each partner in exchange, symbolically and satisfactorily transform one's other into a mirrored reflection of oneself, yet—given the actual power of the colonial state to enforce and to "materialize" its particular representation of reality—they ultimately smuggled the colonial marketplace into the heart of the Karo world.

On all sides, then, there were profits to be made and positions to be defended through strategic misrecognitions and self-(mis)representations. This was the lesson of Si Ajar Taki—whose name, not coincidentally, can be translated as "learning-the-tricks."[72] Displayed in Deli as the "handsome Batak king," he gained the means to oust his usurping uncle and become the sibayak of Kuta Buluh. One imagines the delight of the Karo storyteller displaying this tale, with its sly mockery of the gullible lowlanders whose dollars financed Si Ajar Taki's return to power, to the eager young missionary Meint Joustra, representative of the newest source of lowland wealth.

Viewed retrospectively, the situation's ironies multiply, for the Dutch came to fill the narrative positions both of generous lowland audience and of usurping ruler in the history of Karo anticolonialism. And in *this* story the final (and unexpected) outcome of colonial double-edged "benevolence" was the enthusiastic and near-universal Karo commitment to the overthrow of Dutch rule during the Indonesian Revolution. That local resistance movements in Karoland were largely organized through, and financed by, nationalist produce marketing and distribution cooperatives is not without an appropriate element of poetic justice.[73]

Such an ironic upshot to the marketplace encounter between capitalist "benefactors" and Karo "materialists" should alert us to the dangers of predictive history, even when its predictions are made in comfortable retrospect. The assumption of an inevitable and seemingly "natural" growth of universal capitalism on whatever precapitalist soil it may happen to fall is one such misrecognition. The moral representation of market activity as a Hobbesian "war of all against all" is another misrecognition, no less an idealization than the image of the idyllic meeting-place of the people from upstream and downstream for which Beru Bembem sacrificed herself.

These misrecognitions—the triumphal as well as the Hobbesian—derive from the discourse of aggressive individualism and cumulative historical progress underlying what William Reddy (1984:10–11) has labeled the "market culture" permeating Western economic thought and action since the nineteenth century. As such it has supported a remarkable diversity of official and counter-official visions of social reality and practice. The notion of a progressive historical trajectory directed by the self-interested desire for individual gain and resisted by a collective social awareness—an oppositional consciousness variously represented as a static and nonindividuated "primitive mentality"; a retrospective moral economy of traditional, "precapitalist" values; a historical awareness of the shared experience of class oppression (what Marx imagined as the beginning of the end of capitalist "prehistory"); or, like the wishful vision of Karoland's Calvinist missionaries, a spiritual "community of the faithful" oriented toward gain but without desire—has consistently provided the framework for our moral dramas of modernity. Between these imaginary antipodes we chart a familiar Manichaean course, which (depending on our philosophical persuasion or ideological bent) we may label as either the decline or the advance of human society. We should, I think, allow the weight of our moral judgments to rest rather more lightly than that on the complex and uncertain engagements in which people's lives are, for better or worse, in fact lived.

The capitalist market economy in Karoland was fundamentally different, both qualitatively and quantitatively, from precolonial systems of trade and social reproduction. Colonial capitalism introduced new ideas and novel material forces into the Karo world, and these had a profound effect upon individual lives and upon the life of the community. For women in particular the produce market, despite its instability, created new possibilities for economic independence and a certain (partial) freedom from the most extreme forms of masculine control and authority. But these new ideas and forces did not replace a local kinship-based experiential order with some generic replica of the capitalist "society of the marketplace." Rather, they interpolated themselves into the fabric of Karo social life, producing there new, pervasive effects of shadowing and contrast, an alteration in the texture rather than the pattern of Karo experience.

Such indeterminate alterations in the weave of social practice significantly outplay the familiar binarism of "continuity" and "change." Yet it is within these apparently antithetical categories that we have most often attempted to contain and to comprehend historical experience, our own and others'. In the next chapter I shift the scene of colonial engagement from the market of Berastagi to the marvelous terrain of Mount Sibayak. There, the moral dramas take a more fantastic form. On the borderland of official order, stories of spirits, bandits, and outlaws evade the antinomy of continuity and change, and offer us another angle of historical vision, which I call the "fugitive's eye view."

Four

On Mount Sibayak

ON A CLEAR DAY, if you look west across the open rice fields that spread around the outskirts of Padang Bulan, you can see the jagged triple peaks of Mount Sibayak, a soft blue shadow-marker of the final ascent to the highlands. From this distance the dreamy elevation of the volcano's broken cone, the "gateway" to the Karo plateau, seems an appropriate habitation for those powerful and benevolent keramat spirits who form the core of the contemporary pantheon of Agama Pemena.

No one was entirely sure what these keramats were. Some people described them as autochthonous nature spirits; others said that humans directly metamorphosed into spirits could also be so categorized; still others used the term for supernatural sites or the spirits associated with such places; and some referred to any spirit of exceptional power. But there was a general agreement that the keramats were good, though sometimes strict with those who failed to follow their ethical directives. They conveyed the power to cure, to protect against malevolent supernatural forces; most of all, they brought good luck and prosperity to those who honored them. And so on auspicious days crowds would gather at Lau Debuk–Debuk, near the Daulu turnoff where the Berastagi highway begins its final tortuous ascent to the Karo plateau, to give offerings to the spirits, to ask for their blessing, or to request a special boon.

In early colonial accounts of Karoland and its inhabitants, a much less benign image of the mountain appears. There Mount Sibayak is described as the source of fevers and plagues, a bleak and desolate place populated by a "mob" of nature spirits and ghosts, of whom the local people lived "in perpetual anxiety" (Hagen 1882:531; Romer 1910:217; cf. Westenberg 1891:225). The spirits of Mount Sibayak, Dr. Romer (1910:258) remarked facetiously, "do not even stand in awe of Europeans, who have nothing to fear of others of them!" Western travelers in colonial Karoland commented frequently on the reluctance of Karo villagers to enter the wild domain of these spirits. Thus, for example, when the German doctor B. Hagen wished to climb Mount Sibayak, he could find no one to accompany him, for, he writes, "they are very frightened of the Sombaons [a Toba-Batak term roughly equivalent to the Karo *keramat*] that have a homeland there."[1] It was only after he had promised to sacrifice a white

A prayer to the spirits, Lau Debuk-Debuk, 1985.

chicken to the mountain spirits that "a couple of heroes" agreed to join him (ibid.:528; cf. Westenberg 1891:230–32 passim).

But Mount Sibayak's rugged slopes have also provided a refuge for some. The mountain was a haven for outlaws, fugitives, and others who, perhaps, found the companionship of their fellows less congenial than that of the spirits. Richard Tampenawas, a Menadoese Christian who served as a teacher in the mission school located in the Karo dusun village of Pernangenen, recounts the story of one fugitive's escape to Mount Sibayak and his fortunate encounter there with the mountain spirits:

> Once a guru came here who was reputed to be an Acehnese guru. It was said that he was of Acehnese origin, but had then been in the Bataklands for 30 years. According to his own account he had come here with Acehnese [presumably a raiding party]. These were killed; he fled to Mount Si-bayak, and hid himself there for three years. In that time he learned to recognize all sorts of medicinal herbs. In his hiding place were other people, who lived sequestered there. These people could make themselves invisible; they were *omangs* [*sic*]. They taught him all sorts of important things. When he left them, they sent all sorts of medicines along with him. After three years he showed himself again. The Bataks did not recognize him any more so that he could move about freely. He gave himself out for a guru, which actually succeeded. Through the knowledge which he had picked up in solitude he gained a reputation. (Tampenawas 1895:242–43)

Mount Sibayak, where spirits and fugitives meet, is the appropriate terrain for the guru's story. Sitting literally astride the border between the Karo plateau and the piedmont dusun region and not entirely covered by the authority of either, it is a place of refuge and risk. Whether seen from afar, as a soft, distant backdrop against the lowland sky, or as the harsher landscape of earlier times and closer view, the mountain seems distant from the everyday world and the social concerns shaping that world. Yet, as every fugitive must know, places of refuge *and* the need to seek them are defined by the authority of particular social realities, within particular historical moments. Unofficial history takes a "fugitive's eye view" of that social-historical reality.

SPIRITS AND BANDITS

In the days before the Dutch conquest, travel between the Karo highlands and the downstream dusun region was a risky business. That is why long-distance travelers often acquired, or at least aspired to, an aura of supernatural power. The mountains along the rim of the highland plateau and the passes leading through them were particularly dangerous places, for numerous spirits made their homes in these inhospitable wastelands. Among these were the umangs—reclusive, supernatural "wild men" whose resemblance to humans was only contravened by their short stature and backward-turned feet. While umangs occasionally shared their supernatural knowledge with favored humans (like the Acehnese guru described above), more often the mischievous and aggressive side of their personality prevailed, and they were known to pelt intruders with rocks or even throw them down the mountainside. Umangs seem to have had a penchant for human mates as well, and they were said to abduct "nice girls" and "comely youths," whom they might hold captive for years (Westenberg 1891:232).[2]

Other spirits were even more dangerous to cross. Travelers' inadvertent improprieties, such as urinating on or near a spirit-home located in a tree, rock, or stream, might be punished by the offended invisible residents of the spot. Mischievous spirits might lead travelers astray in the wilderness. On the lower slopes of the mountains the ghosts (bégu) of the unpropitiated dead gathered. Lonely, malicious, or simply hungry for offerings, these spirits might attach themselves parasitically to human hosts or, by merely "greeting" a passer-by, cause this unintended victim to suffer the pangs of the bégu's death-throes. More actively malevolent spirits, the *hantu*, inhabited the cliff faces, ravines, and forests; these brought plagues and epidemic diseases, and their hunting dogs, the *sangkar na pitu*, devoured the entrails of living victims.

Entering this spirit-filled world called for a certain fortitude—a fortitude often bolstered by magical knowledge and protective amulets—and a willingness to provide whatever offerings might ward off the attentions of the spirits. Thus there were particular spots along the mountain passes known as *percibalen*, where travelers, and above all those passing through the region for the first time, might leave small gifts to propitiate the spirits of the wild. This, Bartlett writes, is the significance of

> the offerings on little altars which visitors see at the crater rim on the volcanoes Si Nabun and Si Bayak and the *sirih* [betel] leaves placed in cleft wands, which one will find wherever people [including Bartlett's Karo assistants] have been gathering produce in the mountain jungle or otherwise intruding upon the premises of the mountain spirits. (Bartlett 1973:49–50)

Most often these offerings were of *belo cawir*, a "complete" betel leaf with perfectly symmetrical veining and intact stem and tip, or of *belo bujur*, betel prepared for chewing with a bit of lime and a slice of areca nut, folded lengthwise along the stem. The betel was placed in the cleft end of a thin wand, whose other end was then stuck in the ground. Once this was done, a brief prayer asking the spirits' permission to enter their domain was offered. The traveler's face was then marked with spots of red betel-juice, a temporary disfigurement perhaps intended to deflect the spirits' envy or desire.[3] Failure to perform this little ceremony might result in minor or serious accidents, fever, bad luck, or other molestation by the spirits (Hagen 1882:527; Kruijt 1891:331; Romer 1910:227; Westenberg 1891:232).

But spirits were not the only hazard the traveler faced in the mountain passes. C. J. Westenberg, who accompanied the Dutch military expedition of 1904 as titular assistant resident of the independent Batak region, describes this wild borderland between dusun and highlands as an area of "almost complete lawlessness" prior to annexation, where bandits could act with impunity, having little fear of reprisal. Deep ravines, sharp precipices, and dense forest "offered plenty of opportunities for the bodies of victims to disappear" without a trace, and there were "innumerable" incidents in which unwary or unprotected travelers were robbed, murdered, or kidnapped and held for ransom.[4] "In short," Westenberg concludes, "until the expedition of 1904 pretty well only the law of the jungle [vuistrecht] reigned in the passes" (Westenberg 1914:477–78).

This situation may not have been quite the anarchic brigandry that Westenberg took it for. Many of these so-called bandits made their homes in villages adjacent to the passes where they operated, and their activities seem to have been more than tolerated by the local authorities. Westenberg notes, for example, that the villages of Bassem, Kampung Jawa, and Barus Julu along the Cingkem pass, and Rumah Berastagi and Pecerén at the head of the XII Kuta pass were notorious strongholds of banditry (ibid.). Berastagi in particular had a disreputable name in those days, and, as missionary van den Berg rather delicately puts it, "many a deed was done [there] which could not bear the light of day" (van den Berg 1909: 73). Not only were local rulers unwilling, even under pressure from the Dutch, to investigate incidents of banditry within their territories, but— an indication of the collusion, if not downright identity, between village leaders and bandits—captured travelers were often openly brought to their attackers' home villages to be placed in stocks as prisoners of war, with the justification that a state of enmity existed between the villages of captors and captives (Westenberg 1914:478).

If this claim is taken at all seriously, then what appears from the Dutch vantage as simple banditry takes on a rather different coloring. For a village such as Berastagi, which asserted a hereditary right to the resources of Mount Sibayak, unauthorized travel through the XII Kuta pass along the mountain's southeastern flank might appear as a violation of the village's territorial integrity as well as a threat to its trade connections with downstream allies and kinspeople. From Berastagi's perspective, the lawless freebooters of the passes might equally be construed as (arguably) legitimate defenders of village authority and interests.

Seen in this light, the presence of "bandits" in the XII Kuta pass appears not unrelated to that of the troublesome spirits who in a like manner defended their own wild territory there. Just as a ruling lineage's control of village land was based upon its historically constituted relationship to the ancestral and territorial spirits that guarded the village and its environs, so a village's right to natural resources—forest products, game, mineral deposits, and so forth—depended on an established bond between its bangsa taneh and the free spirits of the wild. Berastagi's claim to Sibayak's resources was predicated upon such a connection between its rulers and the chief spirits of Sibayak's peaks—a bond variously represented as a political alliance or as an actual tie of kinship.[5] It was the existence of this bond that justified—again from Berastagi's perspective—at least some of the activities of the bandits in the XII Kuta pass.

Spirits and bandits defended the same geopolitical terrain; the actions of both relied upon and legitimated local lineage claims to political authority and territorial integrity. This double-barreled defense of local authority was dramatically illustrated during the final years of Karo independence, when escalating colonial interventions in the spirit-infested border zone around the XII Kuta pass provoked a predictably angry response from its human and supernatural guardians. In 1899 the datuk of Hamparen Perak, a Muslim Karo functionary of the East Sumatran native government, opened a coffee plantation near Bandar Baru, a military outpost just below the pass, and began collecting sulfur from Sibayak's peak. Around the same time, a government engineer began surveying for a highway through the XII Kuta pass. Interpreting these colonial maneuvers as an overture to annexation, a contingent of armed Karo men from Berastagi confronted the datuk in August 1900, demanding compensation for the intrusions.

Rumors of an impending Karo "invasion" of the lowlands led to government intervention in the dispute, which was temporarily resolved with a good-faith payment and official promises to look into the matter further. In the following year, however, a series of natural disasters—a severe drought, a cholera epidemic, and serious outbreaks of rabies and the epizoötic *bernung*—struck the highlands. These calamities were widely taken as signs of the spirits' extreme displeasure at the continuing foreign encroachments in their territory (Joustra 1902a:55–56, 60; Schadee 1920:23–24). They were also, in a sense, a violent moral valorization of local independence, inscribing the legitimacy of Karo claims in the visible suffering of the community.

This was not, however, the sort of legitimacy that the Dutch could recognize—either politically or, indeed, notionally. After the conquest of the highlands, main force and spirit-derived authority—the two prongs of precolonial Karo political power—were replaced, in an attempt to end the "lack of discipline in the region," by a legally sanctioned system of inheritance of political office (van Rhijn 1936:37). A legal rather than a supernatural basis was established for local rights to land and natural resources, and territorial boundaries were fixed by government fiat. Berastagi's claim to the resources of Mount Sibayak came to be guaranteed by Dutch-inspired adat law rather than by the spirits of the mountain, and traffic through the XII Kuta pass came to be regulated not by the bandits of

Berastagi and Pecerén, but by Dutch troops and Dutch tax stations. The denial of the mountain spirits' role in the constitution of political authority was also a denial of the legitimacy of acts of "banditry" in the passes.

Two different visions of official order thus appear within the literature of colonial Karoland. The first vision, that of the colonial state, is defined by legal institutions and fixed, rational hierarchies of control and authority. Its borders are clear-cut and closed; Mount Sibayak and its inhabitants, human and supernatural, are excluded from this terrain. The spirits and bandits of Mount Sibayak are reduced to simple representations of the disorder and danger that colonial rule is intended to suppress, for the good of the people. The second, Karo vision is defined less by centralized institutional forms than by a complex, flexible network of social relations within which both spirits and bandits could be at least partially incorporated. Obscured but not entirely erased, this latter vision nevertheless retains a marginal place in the colonial texts, in which it appears not as a particular *form* of order, but rather as an *absence* of order: "no democracy, but anarchy," as one colonial official later complained (van Rhijn 1936:38). Creating the fiction that the Karo political order was simply a "failed," and thus a "disorderly," version of the colonial one, these texts rewrite conquest as housekeeping.

There is, however, a third, "unofficial" vision that does not accord entirely with either the rational impulse of these colonial texts or the obscured Karo vision of political order that finds a marginal place within them. It is a personal vision, composed of a multitude of singularities and located in the experiential "here-and-now." Not in itself confrontational, this vision nevertheless contains a potential subversion of all the authoritative, normalizing forms of official discourse. If, within the colonial discourse, Karo images of official order are obscured—"overwritten," one might say—by the rationalizing urge of the colonial observer, so too the sudden, brief flashes of this third vision, which appear in stories of spirit-encounters, find a place in colonial texts primarily in order that they may be denied. Tracing this third vision requires an examination of the narrative strategies of exclusion, containment, and displacement utilized to reduce—or to reverse—its subversive potential.

Marvelous Encounters

In the "literature of the imperial frontier," as Pratt has noted, a common form of "othering" appears, in which

> [t]he people to be othered are homogenized into a collective "they," which is distilled further into an iconic "he" (the standardized adult male specimen). This abstracted "he"/"they" is the subject of verbs in a timeless present tense, which characterizes anything "he" is or does not as a particular

historical event but as an instance of a pregiven custom or trait. . . . "He" is a *sui generis* configuration, often only a list of features set in a temporal order different from that of the perceiving and speaking subject. (Pratt 1986:139–40)

Such a "denial of coevalness," Fabian (1983:25) comments, "almost invariably is made for the purpose of distancing those who are observed from the Time of the observer."

More than temporal distancing is involved in this sort of discursive strategy. The detemporalized other under observation is portrayed as a passive object—a kind of cultural automaton—composed of various essential (and disconnected) traits, customs, and beliefs. These characteristics are often chosen precisely to accentuate both the radical difference (and implicit inferiority) of the native and the "rightness" of colonial domination.[6] The enumeration of supernatural beliefs, and particularly beliefs that reflect the "irrational" dread of personified natural forces and objects to which the native is "naturally" disposed, plays a significant part in colonial strategies of "othering," in which subject peoples are represented as "natural victims" of their own benighted imaginations, adrift in an incomprehensible world and at the mercy of an uncontrollable nature.

Focused on the difference between observer and observed, this discourse leaves little room for differences among those being observed. Where such differences are noted, they tend to appear as a significant lack on the part of one person/group, which appears as an incomplete representation of the generic other. Alternatively, the relation between such others may appear as a replication of the relations of domination and exploitation that obtain between colonial observer and the observed subject, so that colonial intervention is justified by the desire to improve the lot of the "exploited" group within the colonized society. Colonial images of native women are particularly notable in this regard, and the discussion in chapter 3 of the Karo woman "bought with gold" may serve to exemplify the strategies involved in this sort of representation.

The experience of the colonized subject thus becomes deeply problematic for the colonial observer. Accounts of such experience—in the rare instances in which they appear in the colonial literature—are consistently reduced to decorative embellishments on the smooth surface of the text, where their presence serves to underscore and exemplify the truth of the text's collective representation of otherness or to provide the site for a secondary strategy in the production of difference. Events and actions, detached from their "real-time" or "real-world" referents, become components of a neutralized ethnographic portrait from which their practical aims and consequences are deleted.

This process of othering may be illustrated by the following description of Mount Sibayak and its supernatural inhabitants, taken from the account of his travels "among the cannibals of Sumatra" in 1887 by German explorer Baron von Brenner:

> Spirits fill the world, the people meet them everywhere, but there are also isolated places, distinguished by an extraordinary appearance, designated as the residence of one or more specific spirits and then either especially revered or feared to a great extent.
>
> [Mount] Sibayak, which ascends proudly and sends its pale yellow clouds upwards from a mysterious abyss into the blue heavens, must harbor especially numerous evil spirits. For this reason no one ever dares to climb it, and there are marvels to be told of the experiences of those who undertook such a foolhardy venture. (von Brenner 1894:220)

Beginning in a seemingly neutral tone that effaces both his own presence in relation to "the people" (as well as to the spirits), and his own judgments on the matter of the reality of the spirits, von Brenner rapidly moves to undercut the authenticity of the experience he purports to describe. On one hand, he claims, "no one ever dares" to climb Mount Sibayak, for fear of its malevolent spirits. Yet, on the other hand, there are "marvels to be told of the experiences of those who undertook such a foolhardy venture."

This apparently guileless bit of oxymoronic hyperbole, in which Karo appear first in the negative (to demonstrate what they never do) and then at second hand (as agents within the marvelous stories told of experiences that von Brenner has just asserted they never have) prefaces and serves as an ironic disclaimer to one of the few tales of personal encounters with the mountain spirits that appear in the colonial literature. The story, told by von Brenner's guide, recounts an attempt to collect sulfur from Mount Sibayak, and the disastrous results of this endeavor:

> So our guide Sibayak Si Put reported the following event, for the truth of which [he] stood security. "His father, an especially eminent person, once sent people up [Mount Sibayak] to fetch sulfur; but of these only a few returned and, to the terror of those left behind, with heads upside-down and feet turned backwards. Afterwards *of course* a celebrated guru (magician) arrived, who healed them through a magic spell, *otherwise we could see them today!*" (von Brenner 1894:220; emphasis added)

This ironic retelling of Sibayak Si Put's story, disingenuously posed as a simple quotation of the guide's words, reproduces precisely the contradiction with which von Brenner has introduced the tale. Presenting his guide's story as an illustration of the "marvels to be told" of encounters with the mountain spirits, von Brenner at the same time denies (with, for example, his strategically skeptical "of course") the tale's authenticity as a representation of "real" experience. The particular incident recounted by Sibayak Si Put is absorbed into the normalizing discourse of the generic, while, at the same time, the text increases the distance separating the author from the credulous native who vouches for the truth of the patently fantastic tale.

More than the obtrusive presence of human others in the landscape of the colonial text, it is the scandalous possibility of the coevalness of the supernatural "other" posed by these stories that the European observer is at pains to deny. The few reports of spirit-encounters that appear in the colonial literature are dismissed as folly—as von Brenner does here—or fraud. By rejecting in the particular what is accepted in the general, the text locates the spirits in a timeless zone of generic belief rather than in the "here-and-now" of particular historical conjunctures.

Detemporalized, generic statements regarding the spirits stood at some remove from the "real time" of the observer, and thus could be presented as ethnographically factual (as in von Brenner's remark, "Spirits fill the world"). Encounters with spirits in the distant time-world of myth could also be reported in a straightforward manner, for these likewise did not impinge on the observer's present/presence. So, for example, von Brenner's distancing irony may be contrasted to the studied neutrality of another European-reported encounter with the spirits of Mount Sibayak, one located in the "long forgotten times" of myth:

> In long forgotten times a quarrel occurred between Deleng [Mount] Sinaboeng and Deleng Sibajak [Sibayak]. This became so intense that for seven days and seven nights everything was covered in darkness and from afar a wild roaring was audible, like the rumble of thunder, through which heavy human-like voices were heard. It was impossible to see. Sinaboeng fled, followed after by Sibajak, whereupon the latter hewed a piece out of the thigh of Sinaboeng, so that Deleng Seroentang was formed from it. In his turn the crippled Sinaboeng followed after Sibajak and struck his head so hard that it was slung for 10 km. in a southerly direction, which it now lies on the highlands as Deleng Koetoe. This is the reason that Deleng Sibajak no longer has a peak, and Sinaboeng a broken slope. Now that the Sibajak's head was cut off, the weather cleared up. Then the chief of Berastepoe spoke to the chief of Seribakti [Surbakti]: "Come, let us ascend Sinaboeng together and ask the mountain spirits why it has been dark for seven days and seven nights and why such a noise and turbulence have been made." They climbed Sinaboeng and, arriving at the top, they offered the five betel-ingredients and let loose a white chicken. Then they asked the spirits, "How have you made all that noise, for we could not see what you did?" Out of the crater, named Batoe Perbaringbing, spoke a voice, "Hei Pengulu, go back to your kampung, take batu simagorsing (yellow stone, i.e. sulfur), mix this with arang (charcoal) and cindawa (saltpeter) and you will get gunpowder." Then the

pengulus of Berastepoe and Seribakti descended to their kampungs and thus they came to know gunpowder.

The chiefs of Lingga, Berastagi and Gadjah,[7] hearing the explosion of the gunpowder, asked the chiefs of Berastepoe and Seribakti, who would not themselves let out the secret entrusted to them. . . . The three chiefs then climbed their own holy mountain, Sibajak, likewise offered betel and a white chicken, asked the same question and received from the crater of Sibajak (Batu Sinoermala) the same answer as the spirits of Sinaboeng had given. So gunpowder became generally known among the Bataks. (Horsting 1927:91–93)

Stories of personal experience could be detached from their historical moment and subsumed into generic "fact" or dismissed as sheer fantasy; similarly, myth may be—as it is here—detached from its political context, located in "long forgotten times,"[8] and transformed into ethnographic or scientific "evidence." Thus the fantastic battle between the two mountains is presented by Horsting as proof that Sibayak's sulfur was gathered by Karo "in earlier days" (though no longer, since the Dutch had taken over its collection) and that this sulfur had been used to make gunpowder. That it also refers to the pact between local rulers and the mountain spirits, and thus may be linked to the rights of certain ruling lineages to appropriate the sulfur, remains unmentioned.

This is the same erasure of social-political context that occurs in the colonial discourse on the spirits and bandits of the mountain passes. The mythic narrative, which has much to say about the relation between spirits (and, indirectly, bandits) and local authority—not least in that it purports to account for how gunpowder, a prime ingredient in coercive physical power, "became generally known among the Bataks" (ibid.:93) and how, through the intervention of the mountain spirits, certain local rulers gained access to its secret—loses here every connection with the political "here-and-now."[9] Spirits, bandits, and patterns of local authority each appear as unrelated, autonomous cultural items, and their particular social-historical meaning dissolves into a generic listing of such pregiven "facts."

The pact between local rulers and mountain spirits, and the political rights that this pact entailed, forms the equally unmentioned subtext in the story told to von Brenner by his guide, Sibayak Si Put. If the Karo myth of gunpowder loses, in its retelling, its anchorage in everyday experience and in the politics of violence, von Brenner's retelling of Sibayak Si Put's story, in a similarly fragmenting, depoliticizing move, disengages this tale of a marvelous encounter in the everyday world from its anchorage in the mythic, presenting it as an exercise in sheer implausibility and an illustration of incomprehensible otherness. To restore this subtext, we must bring together and particularize these two narratives of marvelous encounters on the mountaintop.

First, there is the name of von Brenner's guide, "Sibayak Si Put." The honorific "sibayak" indicates that the man, and, of course, his father— the man who led the disastrous expedition up the mountain—was a member of the ruling lineage (and probably of the immediate family of the pengulu) of his home village. This village is presumably Lau Cih (or, in the alternative Malay translation, "Sungai Siput"), a Karo village located between Medan and the nearby plantation town of Arnhemia (now Pancur Batu). Lau Cih was closely allied with the highland urung of XII Kuta, through its common bangsa taneh, the Purba subclan, to which, as the title "sibayak" indicates, von Brenner's guide belonged.[10]

In the tale of the battle between the two volcanos, one of the men who climbed Mount Sibayak to speak to the mountain spirits was the pengulu of Berastagi, that notorious stronghold of banditry along the XII Kuta pass. Berastagi was one of the originary (perbapan) villages of Urung XII Kuta; its territory was jointly "owned" by two lineages of the Purba subclan. The Purbas of Berastagi claimed a special bond with the mountain spirits which, as I have argued above, accounted both for their rights to the mountain's resources and for their "toleration" of the acts of banditry committed along their borders. It is to this bond that the "myth of gunpowder" indirectly refers.

Sibayak Si Put's story suggests the everyday political implications, beyond the explanation of features of landscape and of technological innovation, of the mythic narrative. The disaster that befell the men of Lau Cih can be read not as a random occurrence but rather as a supernatural retaliation for a violation of the alliance between the mountain spirits and the Berastagi Purbas by the latter's lowland kin (cf. Middendorp 1929b). The story depicts a "real-time" emergence of the mythic in the everyday world, and its telling grounds mythic reality in the practical authority of personal experience.

Linking the personal, political, and mythic dimensions of Sibayak Siput's story in this way reestablishes its connection to what I have described as the obscured "second vision" of official order as the Karo saw it. Within the colonial literature, as in the colonial reformation of Karo political institutions, this second vision is consistently "de-officialized" by severing the linkages between domains, by establishing, as it were, fixed and impermeable conceptual boundaries between the "natural" (as defined by the colonial observer) and the supernatural, and between the generic and the personal. Spirits, permitted to exist in the imaginary domain of the generic, cannot intrude into the "real world" of human experience, any more than bandits can find a place within any legal order other than the "law of the jungle." And so Sibayak Si Put's story is presented as an authentic representation of generic belief, and, at the same time, as an inauthentic representation of personal experience.

"TRUE STORIES"

This erasure of social-political context, which detached reported encounters with the mountain spirits from the world of social experience and thus allowed for the absorption of the particular into the general, was only one "strategy of containment" (Jameson 1981:53) employed by colonial observers to deny the coevalness of the spirits.[11] An opposite, though related, move was also applied: that is, to particularize and thus, in a sense, to politicize the *telling* of such stories. This strategy—which stresses narrative inauthenticity over generic "truth"—is utilized by Westenberg in describing a woman's claim to have been carried off by umangs, a "foolish story" that Westenberg cites as evidence of Karo willingness to "shrink back from no false explanation" in order to protect the interests of friends and kin:

> I shall never forget the testimony given by an elderly woman, a certain Amei Kata Mehoeli, in a misdemeanor case. It concerned the burning of a drying-shed on the Goenoeng Rintei estate, which misdeed, as appears from a bamboo-letter (poelas or soerat moesoeh berngi[12]) found hanging up at the scene of the fire, seemed to have a connection to an argument between the husband and the former son-in-law of the witness in question. During the days just before and after the fire the woman had been absent from her village without the foreknowledge of her spouse, who had sought her everywhere. When she finally returned and was interrogated by the Controleur concerned, who, correctly or incorrectly, assumed that she could put him on the trail of the arsonists, she answered this official's query [as to] where she had been during the seven or eight days of her absence, as cool as a cucumber, that she had spent this time ... among the hobgoblins (omang)! (Westenberg 1914:540–41; ellipsis in original)

Despite threats and promises, the woman held to her story, and, since she was known as a "clever" and "sharp" woman, there was "not the least doubt of [her] awareness of her falsehood. Though she was made to understand in all possible ways that no one was taken in by her and [that] her story was perfectly unacceptable, she let herself not be led in this way, she had been with the hobgoblins, with the direst oaths would she swear it" (ibid.:541). By focusing on the particular context in which the woman's story was told, and on her motives for telling it, Westenberg casts her claim to have been with the umangs as fraudulent and self-serving untruth, by which "no one was taken in"—least of all Amé Kata Mehueli herself.

A similar desire to reveal the motives behind the telling of such tales, and thus to contain their subversive potential, appears in Joustra's account of one guru who was the proud owner of several old Carolus dollars, which he claimed to have gotten from the spirits:

> Among the dollars were a pair of very old Carolus dollars: one from 1740 with the image of Philip V and one from 1780 with the image of Maria Teresia. The guru said the dollars had been received from the bégus. Previously he had had six [dollars], but he had once changed two at the Bank, and the bégus had punished him for the sacrilege with a crooked arm. The wicked world brought me the news, however, that he had been shot in his arm while stealing a goat. He then took flight. For a few months no one saw him. Then he popped up again and revealed himself as a guru. (Joustra 1902c:7)

Rather curiously, this revelation of the goat-stealing guru's unreliability appears in a footnote to Joustra's description of a major Karo ritual, the *persilihi mbelin*, for which the guru appears to have served as the primary informant. In a move reminiscent of von Brenner's presentation of Sibayak Si Put's story as both fact and fancy simultaneously, Joustra allows the guru's authority in regard to information *about* Karo religious practices, while rejecting that authority *in* practice. Similarly, in Westenberg's account, Amé Kata Mehuli's testimony is allowed as evidence of a generic character trait (dishonesty)—which indeed Westenberg asserts is a universal characteristic of "Eastern" peoples, though he qualifies this by stating that Karo are in fact more honest than most—but not of Amé Kata Mehuli's own particular situation, except insofar as that situation leads her to tell such a "perfectly unacceptable" story. In each case, we find the subordination of personal experience to generic "truth." That is, these tales are not "true stories", but they are true *as* stories.

Each of these colonial accounts displaces the author's skepticism, allowing the other to do the observer's discrediting for him. Von Brenner does this, as I have noted above, by strategically misquoting Sibayak Si Put, presenting his own interpretation of the story as a direct quotation of the guide's words. Likewise, "no one was taken in" by Amé Kata Mehuli's story; even she herself was aware of her "falsehood." It is the "wicked world" that brings Joustra the news of his guru's larcenous activities; that is, his source is, presumably, skeptical Karo villagers who knew the story behind the guru's story, and who offered their own counter-narrative as evidence of his duplicity.

What I am suggesting here is not that this strategic displacement of disbelief is entirely a colonial misrepresentation; quite the contrary. The questioning of the veracity of these tales of marvelous encounters cannot be seen simply as a rational, colonial strategy aimed at denying the co-evalness of the spirits. It is a part of the general movement through which unofficial narrative experience may be incorporated into official discourse. Indeed, while colonial texts provide a particularly visible arena for exposing strategies of officializing and de-officializing—because of the radical difference between European and Karo visions of official order, and also because of our own (somewhat less radical) distance from the ideological productions of colonial discourse—they are by no means the unique site of such strategies, which are in fact generally employed wherever one official order is being supplanted—or represented—by another.

Narratives of personal experience always risk both an absorption into the generic or authoritative forms of official discourse and a particularizing rejection as either aberrant, absurd, or interested. The plausibility of personal experience, retold, must always be qualified, if only because of the lapsed time between experience and telling. There is always a double context to such stories, the situation of the event and the situation of its telling, and each may provoke its own sort of skepticism.

That Europeans were not alone in their distrust of such stories is indicated by the case of the Acehnese guru whose sojourn with the umangs of Mount Sibayak was described at the beginning of this chapter. "Our Acehnese," as Richard Tampenawas—the Menadoese teacher who describes the encounter—calls him, offered to tell fortunes for the small fee of a gambir disc. Nevertheless,

> [t]here were not a few people, who would not let him tell their fortunes, because they knew him from before; they said that he was a liar and for him it only had to do with the payment. . . . I asked him to read my palm. He read in my hand why I had come to the Bataklands; I had had a row with my parents; my first wife was dead (which he naturally already knew from the people); I was hot-tempered, we should get a son (which actually happened, the njora [his wife] had then not yet given birth). In quite a few instances he was off the mark. (Tampenawas 1895:243)

Here it is not primarily the Menadoese observer who casts a suspicious eye on the guru's tale and his reasons for telling it. Tampenawas indeed seems unsure both of the truth of the man's claim to have studied with the umangs and of his ability to foretell the future. Rather, it is the Karo villagers who, knowing him "from before," label the man as a liar whose motives are purely mercenary—the latter accusation, at least, being in Tampenawas' eyes dubious, given the minuscule fee (one gambir disc was approximately equal to one Dutch cent) that the guru was asking for his services.

There is, as this suggests, a certain discredibility inherent in all accounts of personal experience—and not simply those involving encounters with spirits. Although such tales were by no means always "perfectly unacceptable" to a Karo audience, as they may have been to missionaries or colonial administrators, neither were they necessarily accepted without question. If the colonial observer strategically battened onto the skepticism engendered by such narratives in order to (among other things) protect the ethnographic authority of the colonial text, and preserve the veracity of generic statements, this does not mean that this skepticism was not in fact present. Whether Amé Kata Mehuli was in fact "aware" of her "falsehood," or whether the Acehnese guru was lying about his spirit-derived powers, is beside the point. The *possibility* that their stories may indeed have been misleading—or mistaken—is very much the point.

PARTIAL VOICES

As these responses to Karo stories of spirit-encounters suggest, efforts to normalize such narrative "misfits" move in two directions. Officializing strategies aim at regularizing experience by transmuting contingent events ("what happened" in a particular situation) into singular representations of a generic model of "what happens," including them within the scope of an accepted social reality. De-officializing strategies make the opposite move: excluding an event from the generic representation of that social reality, reducing it to mere happenstance, to the expression of private, individual interest, or to the realm of the aberrant or "scandalous."

Official discourse, and especially those concepts and principles within which a social group forms an image of itself, both "sanctions and imposes what it states, tacitly laying down the dividing line between the thinkable and the unthinkable, thus contributing towards the maintenance of the symbolic order from which it draws its authority" (Bourdieu 1977:21). The ability to impose such official definitions upon situations or to eliminate those situations from official consideration is closely linked to political authority; that is, it is associated primarily with those who control or have privileged access to what Marx and Engels (1965:61) labeled the "means of mental production" within a social community. By creating a generic representation of social reality, official language provides, roughly speaking, the rules of the social game, as these are defined by those group members with sufficient "social capital" to make their own particular version of these rules stick.

Yet these generic claims to social propriety or to natural truth— these models of and for social reality—effectively obscure the partial and contingent foundation upon which their claims to truth or virtue are based. This erasure of social positioning within and through the production of an apparently impartial "truth that fits"—what Donna Haraway (1988:581) has termed the "god-trick" of transcendent objectivity, a view seemingly from nowhere—is not simply a feature of Western scientific epistemology or of colonial modes of intellectual domination. Rather, it appears in any universalizing (and thus exclusionary) claim to truth or knowledge.

Within the discursive field constituted by the "subjectless practice" (Bourdieu 1977:35) of an officially represented reality, the social experience of members of subaltern groups as such may appear less apposite or meaningful than that of members of dominant groups. Subaltern experience tends to be particularized from the official side, which defines it as private or anomalous insofar as it does not conform to official standards—indeed often defines it a priori as socially irrelevant, duplicitous, the inappropriate working of a "bad subject." Subaltern groups and individuals may have fewer resources at their disposal for constructing a credibly official or counter-official representation of social reality, and less authority to make their version stick. In this situation, stories of personal experience, while not directly countering or opposing the authority of official representations at the generic level, may offer other routes to narrative plausibility and other avenues for pursuing individual and collective interests. Such stories engage what I call an "unofficial" vision of narrative experience.

These stories are always—and in both senses of the word—partial. That is, they are on one hand explicitly *partisan*, interested accounts, and, on the other, they are *incomplete*, fragmentary. Hence their fundamental indeterminacy: speaking only for themselves, and making no claims to narrative authority over another, they also accept no others' claims over them. The uncertainty they provoke is surely an effect of their (at best) tangential relation to the official interpretive field/s of their reception. Ordinary standards of evaluation do not apply; we don't know where we stand with them. This narrative uncertainty is more than some epiphenomenal residue of official processes of exclusion or incorporation. Rather, it seems to me that this interpretive indeterminacy is the defining feature of an unofficial vision, and that this, more than anything else, is what makes it both subversive and open to official subversion.

And so it is the fugitive on the borderland of official order that I have chosen to represent this peculiar view of the world. The fugitive is one who, like Amé Kata Mehuli, is aware of her exclusion—or, rather, her partial exclusion—from the official world, and who acts on it. The fugitive takes this position seriously, for it may be a matter of life or death. Hoping to return to a restored, or improved, social position, she does not reject official order but subverts it from within the singular, ungeneralized perspective of a radical, accepted alterity. She knows the power of the official; it is the power that labels her as a "fugitive," a "liar," or a "mere individual," the power that defines her experience as "out of order." If Amé Kata Mehuli's "perfectly unacceptable" tale—another unofficial history—claims no authority outside of itself, neither does it accept any authority, except for that of lived experience: of one "true story" among many.

Obtuseness

The stories of marvelous encounters with the mountain spirits that I have presented here comprise the entire corpus of such accounts in the literature of colonial Karoland. Others may, of course, have been absorbed into generic representation, or excluded altogether from the texts. These accounts, it must be stressed, are not the same as the stories themselves; at best, they provide a trace of these stories' presence. Indeed, most of what makes these stories unofficial is left out of the picture here; they have become part of an official discourse, and an alien one at that.

What might these stories, as told, have been like? It is safe to say that they must have been quite different. And that difference, I believe, can be located in the quality of "obuseness"—to borrow a term from Roland Barthes—which permeates any unofficial account of lived experience. And which is, conversely, so significantly absent from official versions of that experience.

In a study of photographic stills from the films of Sergei Eisenstein, Barthes distinguishes three levels of meaning: the first—the informational content of the image—is its "message"; the second, which Barthes calls its "obvious" meaning, refers to its relation to a common symbolic lexicon; and the third is its "obtuse meaning." Both the first and second meanings are "evident in a *closed* sense, participating in a complete system of destination" (Barthes 1985:44). In contrast to these, the third meaning appears excessive, "a supplement my intellection cannot quite absorb, a meaning both persistent and fugitive, apparent and evasive." The obtuse meaning exists in the peculiar and seemingly incongruous elements of the image that jostle (but do not dislodge) its obvious meaning—elements that produce "a kind of blunting of a too evident meaning, a too violent meaning." Explaining his use of the term "obtuse" to denote this third meaning, Barthes writes:

> An obtuse angle is greater than a right angle: *an obtuse angle of* 100°, says the dictionary; the third meaning, too, seems to me greater than the pure perpendicular, the trenchant, legal upright of the narrative. It seems to me to open the field of meaning totally, i.e., infinitely. I even accept, for this obtuse meaning, the word's pejorative connotation: the obtuse meaning seems to extend beyond culture, knowledge, information. Analytically, there is something ridiculous about it; because it opens onto the infinity of language, it can seem limited in the eyes of analytic reason. It belongs to the family of puns, jokes, useless exertions; indifferent to moral or aesthetic categories (the trivial, the futile, the artificial, the parodic), it sides with the carnival aspect of things. *Obtuse* therefore suits my purpose well. (Ibid.)

Similar to Barthes' "third meaning" is what novelist/essayist Walker Percy (1987) has called the "mistaken" aspect of metaphorical language. As a kind of intentional misnaming, Percy argues, metaphor offers more immediate access to being, a fuller knowing of the object so named. The less such naming partakes of informational or obvious symbolic meaning the greater the possibility of its conveying something of the "inscape"—the otherwise ineffable "apprehended nature"—of the thing so named. Percy illustrates with the anecdote of a boyhood hunting trip the process whereby a privately apprehended experience is shared and validated by its obtuse (and, in this case, erroneous) naming. At the woods' edge Percy and his companions see a marvelous, bright bird flying swift and straight then dropping suddenly and disappearing into the woods. It is, their guide tells them, a blue-dollar hawk. Learning later that the "proper" name for the bird is "blue darter," Percy is disappointed by the descriptive nomination, which describes only what the bird does as a rule rather than capturing its inscape—what it is, uniquely, for him at the moment of its apprehension—as the mysterious name "blue-dollar hawk" does.

The presence of this obtuse meaning, even in brief, occasional flashes, transforms the story. It becomes "no longer merely a powerful system (an age-old narrative system), but also and contradictorily a simple space, a field of permanences and permutations" that permits the reader/spectator "to achieve a structuration that leaks from inside" (Barthes 1985:58). The obtuse meaning, discontinuous and indifferent both to the story and to its obvious meaning, is, for Barthes, the epitome of "counter-narrative"; and, if followed, it can establish an altogether different "script" from that of the narrative sequence itself, "an unheard-of script, counterlogical and yet 'true'" (Ibid.:57).

The obtuseness of an image cannot be described, says Barthes, though its site may be designated. As he puts it,

> the obtuse meaning is signifier without signified; whence the difficulty of naming it: my reading remains suspended between the image and its description, between definition and approximation. If we cannot describe the obtuse meaning, this is because, unlike the obvious meaning, it copies nothing: how describe what represents nothing? (Ibid.:55)

The emergence of these obtuse elements in narrative (as well as the possibility of narratives that act more or less obtusely upon the "texts" in which they are embedded) is thus perhaps best shown by illustration, and so I offer the following fragment of unofficial history, the story of an event that occurred around 1935 and its aftermath, as it was told to my companions and me in 1985 by an itinerant tobacco seller living on the outskirts of Medan.

THE TOBACCO SELLER'S STORY

I first met the tobacco seller at a neighborhood curing ritual. He was himself a part-time guru; his wife, who was also present at the ritual, was a spirit medium. I struck up a conversation with his wife, as one does in the dull parts of these ceremonies, and she invited me to visit them at their house on the outskirts of the city.

Wanting to know more about their curing activities, I turned up unannounced on their doorstep one night, accompanied by several friends and the obligatory bag of refreshments. Although his wife was not home, the tobacco seller invited us in, and we settled in to a long conversation, concerned—perhaps because of the opportunity for such reminiscences his wife's absence provided—more with his life and loves than with the specific information that I had had in mind. A skilled raconteur, he managed to fill up most of the night with stories (my companions later complained, sleepily, that he was just spinning yarns for us rather than providing solid ethnographic "data").

He had lived a wild life, he said, though he had now settled down into a relatively calm maturity. As a young man, after the Indonesian Revolution, he had, among other irregular activities, smuggled ganja from the Karo highlands to Medan, bringing his illegal cargo to the city by truck and returning to Karoland with a load of (tax-free) fertilizer each time. During this period he avoided the law by hiding out on Mount Sibayak, where he came into contact with the mountain spirits and, like the Acehnese guru, learned something of their supernatural skills. Because he was under the spirits' protection, he said, he didn't need to fear either the police or his desperado companions. How else could he have pulled off such outrageous exploits, how could he have eluded capture if he hadn't been helped by the mountain spirits?

But this was not his first experience with the keramats of Mount Sibayak. His story, told over cakes, sweet tea, and the crying of neighbors' children, was concerned with this earlier encounter—when, as a boy, he was carried off by the daughters of the umang-king.[13]

In the season of my youth, he began, *I was with them for four and a half years. I'd go back and forth between their place and my home. I was about ten years old.*

The very beginning was like this.

It was the mburo-*time in the village. Chasing the birds from the rice fields. So,* nandé [mother] *and* bapa [father] *went together to chase the birds.*

Well, what should I eat, I thought. I looked at the rice, it was already cooked. But she hadn't fixed anything to eat with it.

Eh, what do I eat with my rice? Mh. That's not edible, I thought. So then, there was a léto, a quail, a léto to use as a lure. I'll catch a léto first, I thought, that'll be good.

I took this léto in its cage, I carried it to somebody's field. Then I was looking for crickets, so I'd have something else to eat too. I was looking for crickets, I saw a lot of money! Silver. All dollars. Yes.

Iih! Who put that money here? There's so much of it, I thought. I looked all around as far as I could see. Yes.

I took that money, four people came up. Yes.

Two policemen, and then one was purely a woman, the other one, her voice was like a woman but you couldn't tell for sure if she was a woman or a man.

Taap! She was really pretty. Her clothes were all in one piece, skirt, waistband, and jacket. Ah.

She started talking right away. Said, We, the reason we've come, I want to be yours. The one who was maybe a woman and maybe a man. So, my friend here is for you too. Our witnesses are these policemen. I'm for you too. She said that, too.

Well, I was still a youngster, I'd love to have just one, here they were offering to give me two of them! Oh, they were pretty, too. Nice legs. You couldn't criticize them. Really pretty! Yes.

So we finished talking, suddenly I didn't see them anymore. Yes.

I don't know where they went.

I'd said yes to them. I didn't think about it at all, I didn't have any doubts. Just normal. Oh, that's a mountain keramat, maybe they'll carry me off far away, off over there. If that's what happens, then that's what'll happen, I thought. I remembered she was a keramat. Then I took the money.

I didn't bother with luring léto. What's the use of catching birds if you've got a lot of money? Ah.

I took the léto back home, then I went straight to Berastagi. Iyah! When I got to Berastagi, I looked for some stylish trousers, like people were wearing then.

Iyah! Where are you coming from, with those new clothes, son, said nandé later.

Well, my bapa, he had a little bit of guru's knowledge. There's a keramat with him now, said bapa. He knew it. Yes. So, to propitiate it [he said], if Sibayak Berastagi isn't the one to do it, then Guru Melas should. Otherwise, Guru Pergendangen. Bapa only mentioned those three.

So, we didn't go to any of those three gurus. Ah.

I was enjoying myself too much. All that time, I had no worries at all. Neither did nandé, neither did bapa. "Here's the money I owe you," someone would say. We hadn't loaned anyone any money! "That's not enough, I'll pay

*the rest later." Said, "When I have some more money. Just don't ask me for it,
and I'll pay the rest later." Nandé didn't dare accept it. Just put it in my betel-
pouch, she'd say. Nowhere had we loaned anyone any money! Yes.*

*So, this went on for four and a half years. Sometimes I was at home, some-
times I was over there, sometimes here, sometimes there. In the keramat-vil-
lage. If they wanted to fetch me, then we'd just meet. Then we'd be there, in
their village. That's where I met their bapa and nandé. I ate there often.*

*Their house was indescribable, it was like a fine house. From there, I
couldn't say which direction was the sunrise, I didn't know where upstream
was, or downstream. If we're there, our thinking isn't like it usually is. We
don't know anything. Ah. We lost our memory.*

*So, it'd been four and a half years. When we were here, our thinking was
still like that.*

*So, the one that you couldn't tell for sure if she was a woman or a man, we
never had a chance to just enjoy talking together. We couldn't even get close.
I'd think, this time let's talk to her. We hadn't said anything yet, but she already knew! She'd make up an excuse. "The other one that was given over to
you," she said, "you can talk to her." But that one, no matter what, we
couldn't get close to each other.*

*So, this happened over and over, I never had a satisfying chat with her.
Couldn't even sit close to her.*

*At that time—we weren't together then—I thought, they've tricked me.
She's a prisoner here, too, the one they've given me. If she was really a kera-
mat, well, it wouldn't be this way, waiting around for four and a half years.
She was a prisoner too. I thought!*

I didn't say it, but my feelings were like that. Ah.

*She's like me too, just a prisoner. She's not really a keramat, it's the other
one who's the authentic keramat. That's what I thought. She got mad! She
knew what I was thinking, and my flesh just disappeared! It was all gone! If
you'd seen me, you'd have said, this fellow, there's nothing left for him to do
but die. Ah.*

*So, my auntie [bibi, FZ] said, my uncle [bengkila, FZH] said, "Well, what
can we do?" they said. Move to another village, to their village! Bunga Baru,
near Berastagi. Well, that's when they called in Sibayak Berastagi. Yes.*

They called Guru Melas.

*I was too far gone, they said. There was nothing they could do. So then, if
you're talking about chickens, I don't know how many dozens of them went
to Sibayak Berastagi. How many dozens for Guru Melas. For offerings. I still
didn't get any better.*

Finally, a man from Deram came. He wasn't a guru.

*He wasn't a guru, he'd been carried off by the keramats once. He was set
free in the middle of the old forest. Finally, someone had pity on him. It was*

a keramat too. But he didn't know it. If you want to go home, father, study this first, the keramat had said to him. He told it to us.

What do I have to study? I said to this friend of mine. "To make a rempu," he said. Is there some sort of rempu that you can teach me about? I said. "There is," he said.

On the mountain, you know, there's ketang [rattan]? He'd taken the ketang, sewed it around his wrist. Sewed it on his wrist, when he was finished making the rempu on his wrist, he found himself in the village, without knowing how he'd gotten there. He hadn't walked there.

So, he said to me, to nandé and bapa, "If I sew this rempu onto his wrist, he'll surely be separated from that keramat. But I'm no guru, so he may die anyway. Other than that, I don't know anything."

Well, he's as good as dead now, if he dies, he dies, they thought. He sewed it on my right hand.

After he was done sewing it on my hand, it was like the forest just collapsed! Deraak! Deross!

Everyone in the village heard it. Not just one or two people, all of them! Men and women heard it.

That's why they all talked about it, village people are like that, their mouths are the strongest part of them.

Well, once the rempu was on my hand, my flesh all came back. It didn't come back immediately, but it was quick, you'd say, my thinking changed immediately. Yes.

I wanted to take a drink. I wanted to eat rice.

So I made a promise [to the spirits]. Because for a long time there'd been a lot of expenses, we made an offering, just a little one, a little sangka, we put in ten coins in my shirt. Yes.

So I wouldn't die.

That's how it was.

So then, every day I ate in Berastagi. Well, didn't I get fat quickly?

Well, how do we finish it off, they said to the one who made the rempu. Said, "Change his name." My name, he meant.

So that's why my name isn't the name I was born with. The name I was born with was Selbang. Selbang Ginting. Now, it's Selam Ginting.

Roving from village to mountain to market and back again, along the blurred lines separating human society from the world of the spirits, Selam Ginting's tale maps his social world with a fugitive's eye. Yet what sort of map is this, of a place where—in a common Karo metaphor for the confusion induced by unrequited love or by madness—upstream and downstream are indistinguishable? Should the story be assigned to the time of the boy Selbang Ginting, or that of Selam Ginting, the tobacco seller and former smuggler of ganja? To the imagination or to the everyday world? Sometimes I was at home, the tobacco seller says, and sometimes I was over there.

Like the puzzled boy in the story, I find it difficult to distinguish the "authentic" elements of the narrative from extraneous objects caught up in the web of its telling—its "prisoners," as it were. Silver dollars, policemen, stylish trousers: In which world are these located? The pretty girl-spirits, with their parents and their indescribable house that is "just like a fine house" defy categorization. They fit none of the patterns I have set out above. If they are not the benevolent and helpful supernatural characters that contemporary Karo meet on the mountainside, neither are they the "evil and terrible" spirits that European accounts describe. They are umangs, the tobacco seller says, but they have "nice legs," rather than the backward-turned feet typical of these wild mountain dwellers.

Nor do these ambiguous spirits have any connection to the "official" side of the mountain through which local authority was constituted. In fact, they significantly reject officialdom and its representative. The unsuccessful guru Sibayak Berastagi, who (despite the "dozens of chickens" given as offerings) could not appease the spirits, was the headman of kesain Rumah Gergeh in the village of Berastagi. He was the one person who, within the Karo order of things, should have been able to negotiate with the mountain spirits. It is instead the mysterious "man from Deram," neither guru nor political figure but rather a former prisoner of the spirits, who teaches the boy to make the rattan bracelet—the rempu—which frees him from the spirits' power.

Like the stories of marvelous encounters with the umangs told by Amé Kata Mehuli and the Acehnese guru, the tobacco seller's story shies away from generic truth and toward the singular, obtuse inscape of the experienced here-and-now. As Barthes says of the "obtuse meaning," there is something in these stories that "outplays meaning—subverts not the content but the whole practice of meaning. A new—rare—practice affirmed against a majority practice (that of signification), obtuse meaning appears necessarily as a luxury, an expenditure with no exchange" (Barthes 1985: 56–57). Surrounded by a master narrative within a colonial text, or indeed within the text I am producing here, much of the obtuseness of these stories is drained away. Just as the story of the man from Deram is naturalized by its location within Selam Ginting's story of *his* experience, so Selam Ginting's story, located within *my* retold experience (that stock figure, the Ethnographer At Work), takes on a new purpose, a new meaning, and a different kind of credibility—whether I wish it to or not.

The fugitive's eye, in Barthes' phrase, "outplays" official reality not by envisioning some alternative generic truth of its own, but by sidestepping the question of meaning altogether. Like the blue-dollar hawk, it opens up "a space between name and thing" such that "the thing [is] both sanctioned and yet allowed freedom to be what it is" (Percy 1987:73). It trumps the official view with the obviousness of the apprehended moment, thereby staking a claim to the truth beyond ideology—which is, to be sure, the site where ideology most fully resides. Yet in so doing it also entertains, with a narrative wink to its audience, the risk of skeptical dismissal: as "mistake," "anomaly," or (most devastatingly) "irrelevance." This uncertain outlook, glancing at once toward and away from the Real, is what we need to learn to recognize, and enjoy, in the vision and revision of stories.

Five

Signs of Habitation

THERE IS a kind of natural magic in landscape. The concrete traces of human experience enliven any terrain marked by human passage, however transient that passage may have been. Place names, paths, signs of habitation; the sense of space as formerly known or occupied (even if the presumed Knower or Occupier is, today, unknown); an awareness, perhaps illusory, of the pulses of life and event that once animated an otherwise vacant terrain—all of these offer a kind of comfort that can perhaps be most clearly recognized in its absence.

This absence of comfort is perfectly captured by Sinik beru Karo in her song-narrative "Exodus in the Physical Revolution of 1947." Images of Karo evacuees fleeing along "roads never traversed by humankind" and in forests "wide as the empty unrippled sea . . . never before trodden by humankind" evoke the terrifying vacuity of uninhabited space. In contrast, there is the intimately known and precisely inventoried space of home: for Sinik, "the lands of Lau Cih, founded by Karo mergana . . . that is, Urung Sepuluh Dua Kuta, the gateway to Medan, the turn-off to Binjei . . . our fields at Kilometer Eleven." And whether or not you and I know where Kilometer Eleven is, we are nevertheless assured by the knowledge that there is such a place, eleven kilometers from somewhere, and that someone once farmed there. This assurance is a part of what I mean by the magic of landscape.

Human experience is literally embodied in the Karo landscape through the magic of spirits and their shrines. Certain remarkable environmental features—most notably large boulders and bodies of water—are said to originate in human metamorphosis, startling responses to often minor social infractions or misunderstandings. One such is Lau Kawar, the large lake locally deemed to be the transubstantiated remains of an old couple who (literally) dissolved into tears of grief when a greedy boy, delegated to deliver their noonday meal, ate the food himself and presented them with a lunch of gnawed chicken bones (Neumann 1927b). Gravesites and shrines may be imbued with the power or personality of the deceased—like the contrary *silan* (village shrine) of Jinabun, aphorized for its backwards, yes-means-no oracular statements[1]—or with the experience of death itself. Drownings, suicide, murder (by "natural" or by sorcerous means), or fatal automobile accidents seem particularly to saturate the environment with terror and rage, producing an affective vortex that can draw in both the unwary and the like-minded. The little fenced offering-gardens known as *nini galuh*, "grandparent banana-tree," which were once a common sight in Karo villages but are now mostly relegated to less conspicious places, contain and domesticate the anger of those who died by violence "in a single day," the unfocused desire of infants dead before their teeth could appear, or the unfulfilled yearning of girls who died unwed.

On the outskirts of the Karo social world are spirit-inhabited sites with no formal link to bounded communities of propitiation such as the perci-balen, places along mountain paths where travelers leave small offerings of betel or cigarettes for the spirits; or those "great residence[s], some-where in the forest or on the mountain" where the "worthies" (D., *de braven*) of the spirit world lead a settled existence (Westenberg 1891: 225). Like the angry scenes of violent death, the influence of these more tranquil spirit-domains—which Westenberg designates as *keramat*, fol-lowing the Malay-Arabic usage—may increase through a sympathetic at-traction of like to like.[2] Such is the case of Lau Debuk-Debuk, the hot springs at the foot of Mount Sibayak where the girl-spirits known as "Beru Karo A-Matched-Pair" (*sada nioga*, literally, "a double ox-yoke") come to bathe. Westenberg's (ibid.) passing reference to them as "the spirits of two sisters, Siberoe Tandang Maria and Siberoe Tandang Karo, daughters of the penawar (great guru) Kandebata, both of whom suc-cumbed to smallpox" and came to reside on the slopes of Mount Sibayak in company with the other young victims of the disease, suggests—partic-ularly if one appreciates the uncharacteristic lack of commemorative rit-ual in the disposition of Karo smallpox victims—a landscape pervaded with the sorrow of neglected souls.[3] Smallpox having been eradicated in the highlands some three generations back, this sorrowful company is nowadays joined by spirits of untended shrines, spirits whose Christian kin no longer provide for them, the vagrant spirits Karo describe as *bégu la rempu*, ownerless ghosts.

A history inscribed in landscape is emplotted less by chronology than by coincidence. As in Karo divinatory practices, which chart temporal events against the cycling of certain emblematic creatures around the eight points of the compass, meaning is generated precisely where, in contradic-tion of the "ancient rule" (Fabian 1983:29) of physics, two bodies simul-taneously occupy the same space. Sympathetic encounters constellate across time, and inspire stories that trace in the pattern of coincidence and conjuncture a moment of encompassing origin which is itself a repetition.

Like living experience, this history is always as it were "read backwards" from a revelatory conclusion constantly under revision. Take Selam Ginting's story of his adolescent adventure with the umang-princesses of Mount Sibayak. Twenty years after his connection with the mountain spirits was brought to a sharp halt by the rattan circle braided onto his wrist, the story of these events would retrospectively be reopened, and enmeshed in another story—which, by a circuitous route, explains how he finally came back to Mount Sibayak as a curer.

Before the boy Selam Ginting ever met the mountain spirits, his older sister had been brutally murdered. She had been left at home alone while the rest of the family attended a ceremony in a nearby village. Her murderer, who had been seeking human organs for a particularly malign form of "made" magic, was himself killed before completing the sorcery; and, like the horse or water buffalo or tiger that causes a person's death, his spirit merged with that of his victim. To keep this doubly potent guardian—she dead "in a single day" and still unwed, he a powerful sorcerer—within the family, a ceremony was held installing the girl's spirit (and thus her murderer's too) as her younger brother's protector, his jinujung. This was about a year before the boy's encounter with the umang-princesses. It was, in fact, the presence of those supernatural guardians that opened the door to the world of the spirits for him, and thus made possible his romantic interlude on Mount Sibayak, which in turn gained him safe refuge there during his smuggling days.

Much later, when Selam Ginting was already a baptized Christian living lawfully on the outskirts of Medan, a family crisis drew him back into the realm of the spirits. His son, suffering from a broken heart, dropped out of school and the family began to fear for the sanity of the lovelorn young man. *So I prayed to the Lord,* he said, *but it wasn't set right, I prayed but it wasn't set right. One whole night I didn't sleep a wink. Around dawn, Oh, there's still my village shrine, I thought. Even if I'm already in the church, what's the harm? So I went up to the highlands.* There he asked the spirits' help—*but not if you're satans,* he qualified his request—which they seem to have granted because by the time he returned home his son had already gotten a job and was beginning to take an interest in life again. Later he learned that these family spirits had curative powers, too, especially the murdered sister, his original jinujung, who was able to help women in childbirth. He began to work as a guru, drawing on the knowledge of medicinal herbs he had gained during his earlier sojourn with the umangs.

Then one day, in an unexpected and ironically repetitive resolution to his wanderings between home and mountain, the shrine spirits told him not to visit them in the village anymore. *No need to seek us here, they said. No, we're not here anymore. We've moved to Mount Sibayak, we're afraid to stay here. Too many people have gone to the church.* Now his clients—some of them, no doubt, Christians—come, one after the other, once or twice a month, maybe three times, asking him for help, asking him to accompany them to Mount Sibayak to seek a favor from the spirits of the mountain.

Well, that's what my dream said, Selam Ginting explained later, when we asked where he had learned the story of how the girl-spirits known as Beru Karo A-Matched-Pair came to stay on Mount Sibayak. *Because I go there a lot. Maybe I'll take someone along, or I just go by myself. . . . So, according to how it was taught, there's still something that I've left out. I really don't understand why. I tell it over and over, but I can never get it right.*

Like Selam Ginting's dream-taught history, the stories people told about the spirits of Mount Sibayak never seemed to come out quite right. Something was always out of place; there was always another turn of events that could have been traced, another narrative trail that could have been followed. Perhaps too many stories intersected there, so that not even the mass-productions of print and public ceremonial could establish a single canonical version, without the interruption of other stories, other inscriptions of the possible and the fantastic, each story providing not a way out of, but only a step further into the narrative entanglement. This is what I mean by natural magic: the sense that there is always another story embedded—slightly askew—just beneath the surface of the story that is being told. Then again, it may all simply be a kind of narrative *trompe l'oeil,* a technique whereby experience stakes its own claims to authenticity, on the edge of exclusion, through the contagious effects of the real.

THE HISTORY OF GURU PENAWAR

You all will be late getting home if I open up this history, Selam Ginting had warned us. It was late already, but almost before our politely noncommittal "That's all right," he launched into the story of Guru Penawar and his daughters Beru Tandang Meriah and Beru Tandang Karo. *Ah! Back in the old days people used to carry goods downstream to sell. They'd come back with salt, fish, oil. Yes.*

This Guru Penawar he was telling us about was a great magician from the highland village of Kandibata. The story was a familiar one; I had already heard many times how the guru and his wife, who was herself a spirit medium, traveled to Aceh during a smallpox epidemic, chasing—so the story goes—yellow gold, clear silver, red copper. Despite his wife's warnings, he left their "matched" daughters, Beru Tandang Meriah and

Beru Tandang Karo, at home. Predictably, the two girls were soon struck by the disease. The guru's kinsmen sent messages to Aceh, but he refused to return, saying: "If they die bury them carefully; as long as a single bone is left, even one no bigger than the tooth of a comb, I can bring them back to life." So the girls died alone and still the guru stayed on, accumulating wealth and sure that he could eventually revive them. And when he finally came home, not a single bone was left: they had all been carried off by the sympathetic umang-king of Mount Sibayak, who pitied these sad little ghosts.

When he learned what had occurred, the guru sought his daughters on the mountainside but he could not recover them. In anger, he threw all his magical ointments and oils, his *pustaka* books of spells, his magic staff, and his amulets, into the pool known as Si Biangsa, on the mid-slope of Mount Sibayak above the village of Daulu.[4] That is why nothing grows there, and even birds flying above it are poisoned by the pool's fumes, which carry the residue of Guru Penawar's magic.

People insisted that all this had really happened, about three generations or so ago. Details added to the story's frame enhanced its plausibility as well as the authority of the teller. Sometimes the girls' "real" names were given as Beru Tandang Kumerlang and Tandang Suasa. Sometimes they had a brother, other times not. Some said that Guru Penawar was actually of the Perangin-angin clan. He came from the village of Kacinambun, but later moved to Kandibata, where the ruling lineage was Karo-Karo Sinulingga. There he became an honorary senina (clanmate) of the village headman; hence his daughters' appellation "Beru Karo." Others, Berastagi Purbas mostly, claimed that the girl-spirits were called "Beru Karo" in honor of Karo-Karo Sinipurba, the local bangsa taneh (that is, themselves). In Kandibata people said Guru Penawar was given a rice field just across the river from the village; you could still see it today. One man there insisted that as a boy he had been the fishing companion of an old man who had himself been Guru Penawar's great friend and heir. My neighbor Darma claimed that his grandfather, the headman of a village some distance from Kandibata and a friendly rival of the famous guru, had inherited Guru Penawar's magical knowledge, which Darma had in turn inherited from him.

With its catchy narrative refrain, "chasing yellow gold, clear silver, red copper," and its edifying conclusion, "people who chase after gold often forget their own children," this tale of greed and family betrayal seemed to strike just the right note with Karo today. Its place in popular memory had been assured by repetitive mass-production. "Reworked" from Karo folk tradition into a sentimental morality tale, the story of Guru Penawar and his daughters first appeared in print in the Karo Cultural Almanac of 1962. In the early 1960s it was performed as a *toneel* (play) by a traveling

Karo drama troupe, and it was recorded as a cassette drama in the late 1970s. In 1981 a nearly verbatim Indonesian translation of the original published Karo text was included (without citation) in a collection of North Sumatran folktales issued by the Indonesian Department of Education and Culture.[5]

The story was also reproduced through less mechanical means. Most of the mediums I knew counted one or the other of the guru's lost daughters among their helping spirits. Whenever these doleful little spirits alit on one of their human perches, you could be sure they would repeat a part of their story before being consoled with kind words and little gifts. Temporarily cheered by this show of human concern, the Beru Karos would powder their faces, fix their hair, and put on the pretty scarves of transparent green or pink or lavender or white that were set aside just for them, and ask the musicians to play their special song, "Odak Odak," a bouncy, upbeat number that sounded like the kind of pop standard it had in fact become.

Mediums told us the story of Guru Penawar's daughters to explain why the keramats that guided them were so good and generous, and why these spirits were so eager to find new "mothers and fathers" to replace their own neglectful parents. Other people used it to illustrate why today's *komersil* mediums were, like the greedy guru, no good. One man said it was about the sin of pride, and why all medicines ultimately had to fail. Guru Penawar's magic could bring the dead back to life, he explained: If we had that power, why would we need God? Selam Ginting told *his* version—which he learned, he said, in a dream—to explain why the herbs that grow around Si Biangsa, where Guru Penawar threw away his magic, only bring bad luck. *They're never any use,* he said. *For traders, the trade stops. Medicine? No. If they were medicine, why would there be all those carcasses? All around that field, as we Karo say, it's all worthless.*[6] And then—to our surprise—he turned the familiar tale inside out, transforming this magical family drama into a story for traders and travelers.

In the old days, there was this Jawi [Malay] who had a shop near Sembahé. It was called Sayum. That's where people used to go. Not to Medan. People usually couldn't make it all the way to Medan. Yes.

Later, they went to Medan too. Yes.

The road, back then, to this Sayum, right at the Daulu turnoff, where the shops are now, from there it went right down the slopes, till you hit Martelu, then toward Mount Barus to Bandar Baru. Or Barangki, which is just below Bandar Baru. You see?

There were these three traders. From the mountains. So they got to the

Daulu turnoff. Back then it was called "Percibalen." It wasn't called the Daulu turnoff. Percibalen, actually.

"Let's make an offering here," said one of those traders. "Go ahead if you want to, friend. We're afraid to make an offering here in these hills," said the other two. "Well, as for me, I'm not scared to make an offering anywhere," said the first one (whom Selam Ginting now decided to call Si Patuh, meaning "respectful" or "proper"). *So they all wanted to make an offering. When they'd done making the offerings they went on down the slope, over behind where the shops are now. Yes.*

They got to Sayum. This Jawi at Sayum, he knew. That's how the history goes. Yes.

So this Jawi, "You made an offering back there at Percibalen, Patuh?" this Jawi said. "Yes, we made an offering, father." "Oh, well then, can I get you to carry a message?" said this Jawi. "Sure, father."

They spent the night in Sayum. Dawn. When it was light, the other two fellows, whatever was the usual price of oil, the usual price of fish, the usual price of salt, that's what the Jawi sold it to them for. Those two fellows. Si Patuh, this Jawi wouldn't let him pay for anything. Whatever he could carry, if it was oil, or even fish, whatever he could carry, he didn't pay anything at all. Yes.

But this Jawi sent something. Yes.

What he sent was, one green coconut. One mandarin orange [rimo keling]. *One fish.* (There were special names for these offerings, too, the Sayum shopkeeper explained to Patuh. The fish was called *piar-piar*. The green coconut was called *kerbo-kerbo*. The mandarin orange was called *gelang-gelang*.)

That's why, till now, all the people who go to Lau Debuk-Debuk, there are some who give offerings of fish. Eh, because of this history. Yes.

So they left going uphill, from the downstream direction, they got to the place. Straightaway Si Patuh cleaned the place up. So there would be a place for the offerings, for the fish, the orange, and the coconut. That's what he did. There at the Daulu turnoff. There in the hills.

The daughters of Guru Penawar came. "Rock-a-bye, little sister, grow up quickly, don't you cry. Here's our uncle [mama, MB], *he's brought your kerbo-kerbo, he's brought your gelang-gelang, he's brought your piar-piar. Those other two fellows were scared! Yes.*

So Patuh, "Please come over here, if your intentions are good, whether you're keramats, or whatever you are, don't stay away. Let's meet here, if you please," he said. The daughters of Guru Penawar came! You see?

Now, when they were with Guru Penawar, they were Si Beru Tandang Meriah and Si Beru Tandang Karo. Now that they were living with Raja Umang, they were called Si Beru Tandang Suasa and Si Beru Tandang Kumerlang. You see?

"Well then, uncle, I'll give you a package. Because I'm really a child of

humankind too. My mother is still alive, my father is still alive, too, my mama [MB] and mami [MBW] too." Said Si Beru Tandang Meriah.

"Iyah, if they're really still alive, what do you want to send them? I can take it to them," said Si Patuh. "I just have this kepel to give you," she said. Yes.

Well, kepel, you'd say, now you'd call it a package, or a letter.

"Iyuh, go ahead and make them up, no matter how many you make, I can deliver them for you," said Si Patuh.

She knotted them up, knotted, knotted, knotted, knotted. Because back then, back in the old days, there weren't any schools. Yes.

You just made knots, then you'd know how to figure things up. Isn't that right?

"Well, this is for mami." One knot. "This is for mama." One knot. "This is for my kaka tengah [middle older brother]." (That was for her mama's son, she didn't have a real brother.) "This is for my kaka nguda [youngest older brother]." That's all of them. She gave some to the other two fellows. But those fellows, they just took their own stuff.

Well, Si Patuh, he put all the rest together. He wrapped them up all neat in a cloth, he tied them up nicely, he put them in his basket. Those other two fellows, they put their things in his basket too. Then they left, going uphill.

When they got to Tongkeh, these two fellows, they felt like there was something alive on their backs. "I think there's something alive in this basket, what do you think?" "I think so, too," said his friend. "Well, let's take a look, how about it?" he said. They opened them up, opened them both. Scorpions, centipedes, snakes inside. They had to throw everything away! These two fellows had nothing. Si Patuh, he felt something alive too. Yes.

"Well, if something's alive in there, as long as my pack doesn't come loose, it doesn't matter. It doesn't even feel heavy. Whatever is going on in there, even if they're romping around, it doesn't seem heavy, not at all. It doesn't hurt at all. It's not even rattling," he thought. Let it stay there. That's what he thought. Yes.

He kept on walking. Soon they got to Kandibata. Si Patuh, he went to see Guru Penawar right away. "Do you have a child that was carried off by Raja Umang?" he said. "Iyuh, I still haven't gotten to the bottom of that, what's the story?" said Guru Penawar.

—Now this Guru Penawar (Selam Ginting explained, digressing), he was so busy curing people that his own two children died. Yes.

Because he went all the way to Aceh, all the way to Singkel, he went everywhere curing people: "If someone's been dead for four days, I can bring them back to life." His wife was like that too. Ah.

So, they told him that Si Beru Tandang Karo and Si Beru Tandang Meriah were sick. "If they die, you bury them. If there's nothing left but a bone I can fix them," said Guru Penawar. Yes.

They buried them. You see?

When he was done curing people, he looked in the grave. Not even their *clothes were there. The only thing left was a bamboo mat. Well now, that couldn't be fixed up, could it? They'd already been carried off by Raja Umang to Mount Sibayak. Ah.*

—*"They said, 'When I was with my mother my name was Si Tandang Meriah and Si Beru Tandang Karo. Now my name is Si Tandang Kumerlang and Si Beru Tandang Suasa,'" said Si Patuh,* said Selam Ginting, returning abruptly to the main trajectory of his story.

"Well, what should we take them?" said Guru Penawar. "Well, take rice and meat, and something to drink, whatever you think would satisfy them, take cakes, this and that," said Si Patuh.

Guru Penawar, if this fellow (meaning Si Patuh, who had finally explained to the astonished guru what had happened to his lost daughters) *said "Sit," he'd sit. Yes.*

If he said "Stand up," then he'd stand up. Someone who'd straightened up this situation, well, wouldn't you be scared of him? "When you've done this, then do that. Go meet them at the Daulu turnoff."

There they ate with Tandang Kumerlang. "Well, let's go home to Kandibata," they said. Guru Penawar said it, and their mama and their mami, everyone said they should go home. "We can only be kin now, mama, we can only be kin, mami, bapa, nandé," she said. Yes.

"We can never go home again."

"Iyuh, we're all here together, that's just not true," he thought. He grabbed her! Well, you can't grab the wind, can you? They were just apparitions. Yes.

So finally, "We can't eat your gifts any more mama, mami, nandé, bapa," she said. "Just try, my child." He was going to pounce on them. "Well, please eat something, my child, try." They hung up a white cloth. That's why until now people carry white cloths to Lau si Debuk. Ah.

They hung up the white cloth. Then she could eat. He pounced on her, white cloth and all! Didn't get her.

"Well, if it's like this, I guess what I have isn't worth anything at all," thought Guru Penawar. He went up above Daulu, there he dumped all of his magic. Ah.

At Si Biangsa? we asked.

Yes! He poured it all out there. All of his knowledge, if it was like they do at the church now, you'd say he burned it all up.[7] That's the history.

LAU DEBUK-DEBUK

The Daulu turnoff, where Si Patuh said his prayer to the mountain spirits, was located on the Berastagi highway just below the series of switchbacks on the final ascent to the Karo plateau. Once an isolated spot in a region of wild spirits and dangerous men, it now sported two large, comfortable

"Dangers! Don't jump here." Lau Debuk-Debuk, 1984.

coffeeshops, where today's travelers—noisy groups of stylish guitar-wielding students from Medan and shabby international tourists (the locals call them *hipis*) on the budget Bali-to-Bangkok circuit—gathered in preparation for the climb to Sibayak's volcanic peak. A narrow gravel road winding off the highway led to a well-tended parking lot and a booth where admission tickets were sold to tourists. Beyond this was a branching footpath. One fork passed the village of Daulu before continuing up the mountainside by Si Biangsa, where Guru Penawar threw away his magic. The other fork led to Lau Debuk-Debuk, the hot springs where the guru's daughters, with their entourage of umangs and other lonely souls, came to bathe.

Screened and half-encircled by sulfur-stunted trees, the hot springs formed two pools, one about two hundred meters in circumference, the other less than a meter across. In front of the pools was a grassy bank and a small shop selling tea, cakes, and ears of roasted or boiled corn. Affixed to a tree overhanging the larger pool was a sign in Indonesian and English: *Dangers! Don't jump here.* On most days the shop's only customers were a few tired climbers enjoying a dip in the warm waters after descending from Sibayak's peak, but on *cukera dudu*, the auspicious thirteenth day of the Karo lunar cycle, it was usually busy serving people who had come to perform the *erpangir ku lau* hairwashing ceremony and to ask favors of the keramats of Lau Debuk-Debuk.

Except during the fasting month of Ramadan, when, in deference to Muslim sensibilities, ritual performances were rarely scheduled, cukera dudu usually drew a dozen or more groups to Lau Debuk-Debuk. Then the parking lot would be filled with gaudy buses and sudakos festooned with fresh herbal bouquets, and the grassy banks would be festive with picnicking groups from all over Karoland. Laughing or grumbling, clusters of men and women in bathing sarongs would be picking damp flower petals, the debris of *lau penguras*, the hairwashing liquid, from their hair or, for youngsters and occasionally their whimsical elders, rinsing them away with a quick leap (despite the warning sign) into the large pool. Blasting from competing cassette players, tinny renditions of gendang music—some home recordings, some tapes produced commercially for the keramat market—called down the spirits to accept their offerings and to settle briefly upon a chosen human perch.

The small pool was the focus of most of this activity. Above it was another sign—this one in Karo—designating it as *ingan ercibal ras erpangir*, the place for offerings and hairwashings. The name "Lau Debuk-Debuk" onomatopoeically referred to the pool's bubbling, which was, I was told, the key to an efficacious hairwashing: you had to wait until a large bubble emerged at the pool's center, then scoop that up to add to the mixture of herbs, flower petals, ground spices, chopped citrus fruits, and cologne for the hairwashing liquid. Sometimes it got so crowded around the pool that the offerings on display would stack up on the low stone wall that encircled it: bowls of scented penguras water for hairwashing; heaps of green-orange mandarin oranges and combs of sweet bananas; *belo bujur*, betel folded and prepared for chewing, with lime and areca nut, or *belo siwah sepulsa*, a packet of twenty (literally, nine-and-eleven) prepared betel leaves; red-and-gold packs of clove cigarettes (filter-tips preferred), with matches; chickens roasted or boiled and sometimes a spicy braised carp for the umangs; steamed cakes of rice flour, coconut, and palm sugar; occasionally a green coconut (*mumbang*), whose sweet juice is the spirits' favored drink, but more often "city coconuts"—bottles of Orange Crush, which Karo jokingly call *mumbang Medan*. There would usually be special gifts for the Beru Karos, too, mostly combs and mirrors (because they were quite vain), cosmetics, and cologne—"Charlie" was a favorite brand at the time—and once I saw a new blue toothbrush included as well.[8]

Beside the small pool was a Chinese offering box advertising Bodrex cold medicine, the contribution of a grateful petitioner who got the son he

Scooping the bubble at Lau Debuk-Debuk, 1985.

wanted. Off to the side was a broken cross memorializing Johnson Iskandar, a pilot whose plane crashed on the mountainside (brought down, some thought, by Si Biangsa's lethal fumes) and who now occasionally received offerings himself. Usually a few white chickens—live offerings to the spirits (*kahul*), soon to be appropriated by daring local boys—wandered about, pecking nervously at the litter of former offerings: scattered flower petals, cleft sticks holding betel or cigarettes, banana leaves on which food had been displayed.

Nandé Randal, the Arisan's senior medium, had grown up in the village of Gurusinga, not far from Mount Sibayak, and so I asked her once if Lau Debuk-Debuk had been this popular in the old days.[9] *Absolutely not!* she snapped. *Back then,* she explained (meaning the 1930s and 1940s of her young adulthood, when she began to work as a medium), *to cure someone, you just did it at home. Not at Lau Debuk-Debuk, no. Back then, no one dared to go to Lau Debuk-Debuk! If you went there, or if you climbed the mountain, if you were pretty, you had to mark up your face so you'd look ugly; otherwise, you wouldn't come back.*

Beru Karo powders her face. Lau Debuk-Debuk, 1985.

Now it was more the other way around. Lau Debuk-Debuk had gotten so crowded that the true keramats were afraid to go there, and just sent their underlings and servants down to meet their devotees. It was too dirty for them. Nandé Randal was not referring to the litter, which was, in any event, kept under control by the local Office of Tourism and by the foraging chickens. She meant the spiritual pollution of disrespectful tourists doing who-knows-what in the bathing pool, the supernatural clutter of misfortunes washed into the water by incompetent gurus, and the residue of black magic deposited there, intentionally or not, by sorcerers.

You could say it had all started with Nandé Randal's mentor Pa Kantur Purba, the Berastagi headman better known by the honorific title Sibayak Berastagi. The guru who hadn't cured the umang-afflicted boy Selam Ginting, he had been more successful in Nandé Randal's case, turning the afflicting spirit sent by her spurned lover into a sympathetic and empowering guardian. His reputation as a curer, ladies' man, raconteur, and chess champion extended well beyond the Berastagi area. He was a skilled courtroom orator (*once he had spoken,* said Nandé Randal, *there was nothing left to say*); in the late 1930s he had played a chess match with then-world master Dr. Eeuwe, which ended in a stalemate. He was also the first person to claim the tutelary spirits of Sibayak's peak as his own jinujungs.

Pa Kantur told a version of Guru Penawar's story around the Berastagi coffeeshops of the 1930s (no one I asked could remember how it went, but they were sure it was quite different from the current version), and he counted among his spirit-guides that tale's key figures, Beru Karo A-Matched-Pair and the king of the umangs. Various other "Beru Karos" and umangs—those located lower on the mountain slopes and farther down the supernatural chain of command—he passed along to his clients and to protegées like Nandé Randal, so they too would have a "friend" on the mountainside. Every year he would climb the mountain to perform his erpangir in the crater-pool at the mountain's peak. Nandé Randal had never accompanied him (you couldn't go if you were pregnant, or if your child's teeth hadn't yet formed, she explained) but she remembered his warning: *If you climb Mount Sibayak, child, only go on cukera dudu or* belah purnama [full moon, the fourteenth day of the lunar cycle]. *On other days, all the wicked things come out. On the good days the King of the Hill has a gendang orchestra, he strikes the small gong* [penganak], *he strikes whatever isn't good. "Don't you come out," he says. That's why you should hear the gendang when you climb Mount Sibayak. Otherwise, it's dangerous.* She remembered, too, hearing the gendang echo from the mountain at precisely nine o'clock on the night in 1948 when he died.

Although Sibayak Berastagi's curing practice doubtless added to the benevolent reputation of Mount Sibayak's keramats, it was not until the late 1960s that, through the ceremonial activities of a Karo cultural organization known as Persadan Merga Si Lima, the Association of the Five Clans, the mountain spirits became the object of widespread popular devotion. Between 1967 and 1973 this organization sponsored a mass erpangir ceremony every year at Lau Debuk-Debuk. At its peak in the early

1970s, there were Merga Si Lima chapters in villages throughout Karoland as well as in Medan and other cities, and the group's former leaders recall "thousands" of devotees attending their annual hairwashings. But it began in 1966 in the Berastagi market, with a hilltop flood and the unlucky dream of Nandé Ngena, Sibayak Berastagi's last patient.

BEGINNINGS

When I met them in 1985, Nandé Ngena and her husband owned a small tree nursery on the outskirts of Berastagi, but at the time of her dream in 1966 they were produce brokers struggling in the wake of Sukarno's 1962 confrontation with Malaysia and the brutal military-led reprisals of 1965–66. A woman of the Rumah Mbelin Purba lineage of Rumah Berastagi, Nandé Ngena had been marginally involved with mediumship since around the time of her marriage in the late 1940s, when she began to suffer spells of erratic behavior. These manifestations of spirit-affliction, which signaled the spirits' desire to follow her, were cured by Sibayak Berastagi. Unfortunately, he died before completing Nandé Ngena's formal initiation as a medium. Because of the spirits' power, no one else dared to finish the rites, and so she finally initiated herself, with the spirits' help.

As the post-Gestapu reprisals drew to an end in 1966, the Karo highlands suffered a season of extremely bad weather. Heavy rains, severe windstorms, hail, and landslides seemed to mirror in nature the violent and uncertain social climate of the times. Ten people died in a landslide near Kampung Keling, a village at the foot of Mount Sibayak; another was killed in a flash flood on Gundaling Hill in Berastagi. Hilltop floods are unusual occurrences, and so this event became a topic of conversation around the Berastagi market. In the Chinese-owned Jénda Kita coffeeshop, the town's traders and produce brokers speculated about the possible implications of these unnatural disasters. Among the shop's market-day habitués were Sibayak Berastagi's son Gok Purba and another local guru, Tabas Karo-Karo. Following customary protocol, they suggested a gathering of the Berastagi Purbas and their anak beru to discuss the situation.

It was around this time that Nandé Ngena had her dream. In it she was climbing Mount Sibayak, where she saw a group of prisoners. Dreams of hostages are considered particularly inauspicious or "entangling" (*gulut*), and usually require some ceremony of purification and redemption to cancel them out. But no one other than Nandé Ngena seems to have taken this particular dream very seriously until after the Gundaling flood, when it began to appear that the dream's message might not be for her alone. Entering into the discussion at the Purba group's meeting, it seemed to confirm an already general suspicion that the unruly weather was a sign of the spirits' displeasure.

This is how Nandé Ngena remembered her dream: *The reason I said that I had a dream that formed Merga Si Lima, I had a dream, it was like I was on Mount Sibayak. On Mount Sibayak, there were two beautiful women, Beru Karo. They were really beautiful, then they said, there are hostages on the mountain. Said, sixty people. So then, why are they being held? I said. Said, because, Merga Si Lima isn't being followed any more. So then, you tell them tomorrow down in the valley, said, tell them to form Merga Si Lima. Said, the eight relationships, the three bonds.*[10] *So then, yes, I said, if that's how it is. When it was light, I woke up. Then, I told those who were like me, you'd say, who believed in keramats. I said, now how about it, here's my dream. If Merga Si Lima isn't formed Mount Sibayak will tumble down, Gundaling Hill, that's what my dream said, I said. No one wanted to do it. So then Mount Sibayak fell in, collapsed, eleven people washed away in Keling, one struck by lightning in Gundaling, so they formed Merga Si Lima.*

Stories of the founding of Merga Si Lima are shaped by sets of images rather than a fixed sequential emplotment. Even within a single narrative, the befores and afters that mark for us the sure pathway of a plausible history seem a kind of afterthought; and indeed they were mostly added in response to my chronologizing inquiries. Like Nandé Ngena's remembered dream, these stories tend to condense a series of events into an emblematic scene displaying the centrality of a single actor (usually, but not always, the narrator) in the association's genesis. To construct a sequential account of Merga Si Lima's rise and fall from these dramatic vignettes is thus not only difficult, it profoundly misrepresents the group's history as it was locally experienced and as it is apprehended today. What Merga Si Lima meant, what it accomplished, how it began and where it went, depends largely on the vantage of the situated observer, which is what these various origin stories are intended to convey. In these stories, origins are everywhere: everyone, in a sense, comes first.

However, in the narrative thickets that have grown up around Merga Si Lima's disputed beginnings there are a few generally acknowledged landmarks. There were the post-Gestapu reprisals, then the landslides that signaled the spirits' dismay, and finally the meeting of the Berastagi Purbas, at which it was determined that they, as the proper intermediaries to the spirits of Mount Sibayak, should hold an offering ceremony to restore the keramats' good will. This ceremony, which featured a mass hairwashing at Lau Debuk-Debuk and a parade through Berastagi to the newly built meeting hall (*jambur*) on the outskirts of town, came to be known as the "gendang jambur," the meeting-hall orchestra.

Nandé Ukat, another of Sibayak Berastagi's former protegées, also attended that first meeting of the Berastagi Purbas. She told a different story of the gendang jambur, and of her own prophetic encounter with the mountain spirits: *Back then, I was trading in Medan. Going home, the bus was late. I didn't go by my usual bus, the Star Line. So then, there was one person on the bus, from Padang Bulan, what they call the New Market, the afternoon market it is. So then, he got in. He was wearing a military uniform. He bumped into me. Oh well, it didn't matter. It's a bus, I thought.* She struck up a conversation with the man, which soon turned to the landslides; Nandé Ukat was afraid the bus might get stuck around Sembahé. But the man said that she could take care of it. Tomorrow, he said, she should go to Kabanjahé, to any government office—say, the Justice Department— and tell them to make an offering to the mountain spirits. *"Iya! If I say that, they won't even answer," I said. "Your words are the gong-words," he said. "What do you mean 'gong-words'?" I said. "Whatever you say, they'll follow straightaway." he said. "The big people there, we'll have a talk with them right off, they'll make use of your words," he said. So then, "I'll tell them," I said. "So you'll know: Do this, no matter what office you go to, they won't contra-dict your words. Whatever you say, they'll say the same," he said.*

When Nandé Ukat looked around—this was near Sembahé, she said— the man had disappeared. He must be one of our ninis, she thought, the warchief of our ninis. *So I told it the next day. To Sibayak Berastagi's son. "Iya, that's not the way to go about it. If it's like you say, to stop it, let's have a meeting [I., rapat]," he said. Iya, let's have a meeting, they gathered to-gether straightaway. . . . Whatever I said, they all agreed. So then, set a date. They set a date, you'd say, at the meeting, to do it as soon as possible. So then, what do we do, they said. "Iya, whatever you want to do," I said. They did it all, everything, they told everyone and straightaway arranged for the cere-mony. It took three meetings, I guess. So then, figure up the rice, figure the musicians, they met about that.*

For Nandé Ukat, this beginning contained in germ what would be Merga Si Lima's ultimate failure. That failure is signaled in her account by Gok Purba's offhand dismissal of her spirit-inspired "gong-words": *that's not the way to go about it . . . let's have a meeting.* It is further specified by her use of the Indonesian word *rapat* to designate the Purba gathering. Other participants consistently referred to these meetings as *arih-arihen*, "deliberations." This Karo term, which figures significantly in Merga Si Lima's rhetoric of unity, connotes a customary etiquette of negotiation, conciliation, and ultimate agreement.[11] *Rapat*, in contrast, suggests an altogether different kind of gathering—a business meeting with an agenda, an organizational hierarchy, and little time for the slow and in-clusive persuasions of formal oratory.

But whether the Purba gatherings started out as occasions for consen-sual deliberation or as business meetings, they soon moved in the latter direction. Once plans for the gendang jambur were underway, the origi-nal group of organizers invited an influential ex-politician, Pa Raja Balé

Purba, to join them. The son of the former pengulu of the Berastagi market, Pa Raja had been a member of the district legislature (Dewan Perwakilan Rakyat) from its founding in 1946 until 1963, when, in the context of a divisive conflict between leftists and moderates in the Nationalist party, he retired from public life. As a legislator Pa Raja had lent his support to Karo cultural organizations, and although he was nominally a Muslim, he took an active interest in organizing the Purba ceremony.[12] According to his advocates as well as his opponents, Pa Raja recognized from the beginning the gendang jambur's potential for mass social mobilization. Under his guidance the group's original plan expanded considerably. Contributions were solicited from the produce brokers, bus owners, and truckers who formed the prosperous core of the Berastagi market community, and guests from all over the Karo area were invited to attend.

The Purba group had planned to take their offerings to Mount Sibayak's peak and, in their capacity as Berastagi's ruling lineage, to perform the erpangir there at the top of the mountain. With Pa Raja's extension of the guest list, however, it soon became clear that an alternative locale would be necessary. At the last minute the organizers shifted the site of the hairwashing to the more convenient and spacious Lau Debuk-Debuk, just off the main highway at the foot of the mountain.

Participants at the gendang jambur remember fifty-eight, sixty, seventy-eight busloads of devotees, coming from all over Karoland. *I guess there were sixty busloads to Lau Debuk-Debuk. It wouldn't hold them all! All the way up the road!* recalled one of Pa Raja's adjutants. *They all performed the hairwashing, everyone wore a white cloth, everything. Really nice, in traditional costume, like that! We all wore new clothes. After the hairwashing we slaughtered an ox up here. The jambur was full! There was a gendang and everything, a day and a night.* The parade to the jambur stretched all the way from the revolutionary monument in the center of town to the town limits. Eleven mediums and one male guru led the way. The spirits came down, they sang the song "Odak Odak," the leitmotiv of Beru Karo A-Matched-Pair. Everyone danced, everyone who wanted to went into trance, and some of the onlookers who had come to harass them saw how enjoyable it was and joined in the celebration. It was all a tremendous success.

A RETURN TO TRADITION

During the discussion and preparation for the gendang jambur, small devotional groups had begun to take shape informally; after the ceremony some of these remained intact and others formed to provide ritual arenas in which to continue the newly instituted conversation with the spirits. The song "Odak Odak," which was to become Merga Si Lima's

Members of Persadan Merga Si Lima march through Berastagi on the first anniversary of the gendang jambur. Mount Sibayak is in the left background.

anthem, was performed so regularly at these gatherings that their members became known as "Perodak-odak."[13] Christians in particular began to use the term as a derogatory appellation for the enthusiastic new devotees of the mountain spirits.

It was not until the first anniversary of the gendang jambur that Persadan Merga Si Lima was officially created to coordinate and unite these devotional groups. Pa Raja's adjutant explained: *So finally, let's form Merga Si Lima, they said, the ones who didn't want to be Christians or Muslims. They formed it in villages. Then, come inaugurate us, they said. So we went to all the villages. All the way to Deli Tua, even to Binjei. So then, after it was formed in the villages, if they had an erpangir, they invited us. That's how Merga Si Lima started.*

Under Pa Raja's leadership, these groups were incorporated within an organizational structure headed by the Berastagi group, with by-laws, regular dues, and elected officials. Local chapters were set up as mutual aid societies; each was expected to have its own set of cooking pots and dishes and floor mats, which members could borrow for ritual performances. Loans from the group's treasury helped defray the costs of ritual sponsorship and group members were expected to attend one another's ceremonies. The organization as a whole sponsored an annual erpangir ceremony to commemorate the first gendang jambur, to which all the local chapters were invited; likewise, the Berastagi leadership attended the smaller hairwashings sponsored by the local chapters.

This was around the time of mass Christian evangelization, when rumors were circulating that persons without an officially recognized religion would be considered Communists. A Muslim politician, a man of the Tarigan clan, had given a speech in Singamanik claiming that 99 percent of the Karo were PKI, members of the Communist party. After PKI "exploded" in 1965, said one of Pa Raja's sons, *no one thought about family anymore, they just wanted to save themselves. "Issues"* [rumors] *sprang up, if you didn't join a religion, they'd cut your throat!* That was why Pa Raja founded Merga Si Lima, he said: *to reunite the five clans, so adat would live on.*

As this suggests, Merga Si Lima's officially stated purpose was to promote and preserve Karo adat, which its members saw as eroding under the political upheavals of the 1960s. But it was also intended to protect the rights of Karo who were "without a religion." Pa Raja's adjutant remarked that the association's pro-adat stance, while in itself completely sincere, also contained an element of strategic ambiguity: *One time an official came, from the Ministry of Religion. "This, what is this?" he said. "What kind of organization is this? What kind of religion are you making?" "Oh, this here is Karo tradition* [tradisi Karo], *sir. Not religion." The government started calling us all the time. "What is this?" they'd say. "It's Karo tradition." They called us to Kabanjahé, to the prosecutor's office, to* [the military administrative center at] *Bukit Kubu, they came from the provincial Department of Religion. They saw we weren't disruptive, they backed off. There wasn't any trouble, anything like that. So then, hairwashings, and house openings. That's not religion, we said. Because with religion you have to be listed.*

For the Karo Protestant Church, this movement by people "without religion" to define themselves as the protectors of Karo custom was a serious concern, especially when—as one Church publication complained— they "spread rumors that Christians had left adat behind" and described "Christianity as a foreign religion and themselves as the original religion [agama pemena]." In the Church's view Merga Si Lima was an organization of "fanatical" pagans led by disenfranchised politicos seeking a new base of popular support (Team Penelitian GBKP 1976:126).

The Church treated us as an enemy, said a Berastagi journalist who described himself as one of the group's early promoters and co-author of its anthem "Odak Odak." Merga Si Lima was not a religious organization, he insisted; anyone could join, regardless of their religious affiliation. Of course (he quickly added), no Christian would have become a member because of the Church's opposition, so Merga Si Lima's constituency was—*this was purely coincidental, you understand*—almost entirely confined to followers of Agama Pemena. After a pause, he continued: *I said we weren't political, and of course we weren't, but!—Pa Raja and I, we were pulling the strings. The others didn't know what our real purposes were.*

It was a time of crisis, he explained. *Karo society was considered 100 percent PKI. So, efforts to remove that 100 percent image were consolidated through Merga Si Lima, in which not a single member was admitted if they were involved in politics or implicated* [in PKI]. *To defend its purity. We wanted to show that not everyone was PKI. Look, we're not PKI. That was our intention, to show who we were. That there were still Karo people who weren't PKI.*

Casting his explanation in the rational idiom of political symbolism, the journalist later elaborated on what he understood to be the religious and political intentions lying behind the nonreligious, nonpolitical stance of Merga Si Lima's leadership. *It was a product of the times,* he said, *so all of this was mixed up with politics a little. Because there, according to how our thinking developed, among the organizers of Merga Si Lima, including me!— this system of trancing was a, what you'd call, acting out a drama at the home of our ninis on Mount Sibayak. The way Karo think about it, keramats are all-knowing. They have authority, and they don't want to do what isn't good. So to straighten out people's thinking, borrow the term keramat. To straighten out things that are considered bent. Merga Si Lima, they looked for members, whoever tranced. Whoever made traditional medicines. Because they were considered the purest. They were still considered simple people, guileless, pure in their manner of thinking. So it flourished, based on—because if it was called political then surely the government would prohibit it, because it wasn't the time for politics. We called it cultural uplift, on a social basis. So, social, that means mutual assistance. The government didn't prohibit that. With that basis Merga Si Lima flourished, a social basis. To offset rumors that Karo couldn't be trusted anymore. To purify again. It was one recipe like Rinso, a cleanser. Also to commemorate a sector of society that we considered guileless, simple, and pure, through our ancestral spirits, which includes the household spirits. It was a manner of physical and spiritual purification through erpangir.*

Odak Odak

Persadan Merga Si Lima remained active for about seven years, although its membership gradually dwindled. Around the time of the 1971 general election it became officially affiliated with Golkar, the umbrella organization of progovernment "functional groups" through which much of the support for the New Order regime is directed. During the election, "Odak Odak," the Merga Si Lima anthem, served as the Golkar theme song for the Karo area, an official recognition that has no doubt contributed to the catchy tune's current popularity as a secular "folksong."[14] Merga Si

Lima's "Golkarization," which some members viewed as "selling" their votes to the government, was the first step toward the group's dissolution. Rumors of shady dealings among the group's officers and internal struggles over chapter leadership also weakened the organization's popular support. By the mid-1970s only a few local chapters were still active. Nevertheless, Merga Si Lima remained officially listed with the Department of Education and Culture as a government-approved "sect." When the Karo branch of Parisada Hindu Dharma was created in 1977, this moribund organization provided the (nominal) institutional framework—and, perhaps more important, the formal association with Golkar—needed to establish Agama Hindu Karo as an officially approved religion.

From an institutional standpoint, Merga Si Lima's history as I have sketched it here follows a familiar movement from charismatic beginning to routinized decline. This particular historical emplotment is of local interest, however, mainly to the small group of (male) organizers and leaders whose intentions guided that particular trajectory. For most of the rest of the movement's participants, the institutional history of Merga Si Lima is significant primarily as an opening onto another kind of history, an infolding of timely personal experience with the timeless, repetitive existence of the mountain spirits. From this perspective, what the organization created for its members was not so much a political shelter from public harassment (which it seems to have generated as much as it protected against), but rather a chance to become the heros of their own enacted stories.

So it is not surprising that my efforts to discover the origin and history of the song "Odak Odak," which (as one man put it) "arose in the midst of Merga Si Lima," were, depending on how you look at it, either not very successful or too successful altogether. Everyone seemed to have a different idea of where the song came from, what it was, and who had created it.

Questions of origin rely on the assumption of a core identity against which historical continuity and change can be measured. But Karo song texts are relatively unfixed; melody and lyrics are both "motivic," improvised around standard sets of themes, associations, and images and often augmented by musical and verbal associations borrowed from other such thematic sets.[15] To complicate matters further, a particular melody may have several different names, or the same name may be given to several (perhaps unrelated) songs. Different parts (percussion, instrumental melody, vocal line) within a single musical performance may be referred to by different "song" names—as, for example, when singers begin a performance by announcing that they are singing the song "Katoneng

Katoneng" to the gendang tune "Simelungun Rayat." Like the beginnings of Merga Si Lima, then, the origin of "Odak Odak" could, depending on how you defined that object of historical investigation, plausibly be located in various moments, and in the enactments of various social actors.

The term "odak odak" itself is the name of a dance figure, a wave-like gliding dip in which the dancer's arms swing gently back to front, imitating the seductive manner of a young woman's walking. Because of the step's coordination of hand and leg movements, it is also a conventional trope of harmony, accord, or unity: *sada pengodak sada pengolé*, one movement one voice, Karo say. "Odak Odak" was thus particularly appropriate, both as the the musical theme of the flirtatious Beru Karos, and as the catchphrase of Merga Si Lima.

Indeed, stories about the founding of Merga Si Lima almost always prominently mentioned "Odak Odak." Most of Merga Si Lima's male organizers credited the song to Pa Sampit, the seruné player at the jambur, whose musical arrangement made the song so nice to dance to. Pa Raja's adjutant, for example, attributed the remarkable spontaneous entrancement—*kontak*, he called it—of participants at the gendang jambur to the music's appeal: *The gendang played, contact! That was the beginning of Odak Odak. Everyone sang it! Everyone danced. It was the song* [the spirits] *liked, it was called Odak Odak. That's the beginning of Odak Odak. The seruné player played it. Contact, everyone! Whoever heard the sound, contact! Everyone danced. The whole jambur was dancing! The spectators danced outside on the ground, everyone was dancing.*

Others made their own claims to the song. Nandé Laga, another of Sibayak Berastagi's former protegées who attended the gendang jambur, insisted it was hers: *It came from me, my child. You see, brrnang brrnang brrnang brr, like that, the gendang was fast, fast, toss Nandé Laga into the center, they said. I went to the center, then I danced. My keramat had come: "Me, all of you sibayaks of Berastagi here, the Karo-Karo clan, the Purba clan, I'll talk a bit, I'll dance to this gendang." Said my jinujung. "Which song do you want, Beru Karo?" they said. "For me, it's our gendang from the top, the song Odak Odak. This will be my song from now on, seruné player. You sit in your chair there, let me sing it, then we can dance," she said. The song sada pengodak sada pengolé. That's what our nini sang. "Ih, that was nice to dance to, Beru Karo," they said to my jinujung. "One speech one agreement, that's Merga Si Lima, really," they said. That's the beginning of the song Sada Pengodak Sada Pengolé. My keramat. I'm the one who sang it first back then.*

Nandé Ngena, whose dream of hostages had initiated plans for the gendang jambur, said that the song had been introduced earlier, at the Purbas' planning meetings; and that, as Beru Karo's perch there, she had been the first to sing it. Nandé Ukat, who encountered the ninis' uniformed warchief on the bus from Medan, agreed that they learned the song at the Purba gatherings, but claimed that it was *her* cowherd-spirit who taught them the song, to entertain the Beru Karos. *It was around the time of the gendang jambur,* Nandé Ukat said. *That Odak Odak, that is, our ninis came, during our meeting. We met, he said he was a herder. That's the one who sang it, who created the gendang Odak Odak. After he sang, they straightaway played it on the flute, put it on tape, or whatever, I don't know. Because I was in trance, if he came through me. During the meeting. Then, get your flute, he said. I want to play the flute, he said. So then, that's it. Straightaway they played it just like that, ndeh ndeh ndeh, like that. So he sang, he made the song Odak Odak, that's it, they all mastered it, up till the end of the gendang jambur. Till today, like that.*

The journalist-promoter who considered himself one of the organization's masterminds thought the song had been popular around Berastagi even before the gendang jambur. But he and another man had composed new inspirational lyrics for the song, appropriate to its incarnation as the Merga Si Lima anthem. That made them, in his opinion, the song's real creators.

A local musician who took a more skeptical view of the whole business agreed that the song had in a sense preceded the gendang jambur. It was actually a version of a very old song, he said, called "Odak Odak Nipé Soré"—*nipé soré* being the name of a harmless light-brown darting snake—only played faster to facilitate trancing. There had been a song by that name, one guru confirmed. It came from the story of a woman named Mangun Soré who had seven husbands. "Odak Odak Nipé Soré" was the song she sang to keep the peace, so they would all get along. Men are so unruly (he added) that they would have killed each other if she hadn't been clever, which is why women since then have only been allowed one husband.

Nandé Randal, the old medium of the Arisan of Simpang Meriah, remembered that song too. It was the one she sang for Sibayak Berastagi, Beru Karo's song, whenever they called down the spirits to cure a client. *So, when we treated people back then at the beginning we used clear water, or penguras water. The same if they were insane, or whatever. I sang a little, they were cured right away.* Except for the repeated phrase *odak odak,* Nandé Randal's song didn't sound to my untrained ear at all like the "Odak Odak" I knew, but on the other hand that phrase (in ritual performance *odak-odak odakken kéna ari turang* or in its pop incarnations *odak-odak odak-odak Lau Biang turang*) is about the only consistent element in the song's narrative composition. Here is a rough translation of Nandé Randal's words, as she sang them for me on one occasion:

Hiya reeled in, nini, come here to the house
come to the house, bringing poison-antidotes
come to the house bringing the world's love magic
come in, in consideration of our patient
strengthen the blood, strengthen the guardianship
hiya reeled in, waving
moving gracefully
the graceful movements of the darting snake
beneath the pandanus-plant of former days
hiya reeled in, place it just so
that's a continuation of the world's love magic
neutralizing too, as you are able
follow this student of yours.[16]

From the Top to the Bottom

Nandé Ukat lived in a neat Dutch-style bungalow with freshly painted green shutters on the outskirts of Berastagi. My companions and I met her there, by appointment, on belah purnama, the day of the full moon, which was the only time the spirits would allow her to speak of them. Five of us sat uncomfortably in the tiny formal parlor filled with naugahyde furniture arranged squarely around a coffee table. The floor was polished and the photographs on the walls recently dusted; a vase of orchids sat on the table. Through the doorway we could see the more familiar lived-in clutter of a Karo home, which we were not invited to enter. Grandchildren crawled underfoot, staring at the strange intruders; Nandé Ukat ignored them, even when their eventual screams made conversation barely audible. But that was after she had gotten caught up in her story.

We had been directed to her by several of the gendang jambur's organizers. That surprised her, but she acknowledged that we were correct in coming to her for information. She was one of Pa Kantur's first protegées, having been called by the spirits some fifty years earlier—before he ever cured Nandé Randal or Nandé Laga, her erstwhile colleagues, and long before his death interrupted Nandé Ngena's initiation. *At the very beginning,* she explained, *I was sick. Sick, you know. Because I'd been everywhere, but I hadn't gotten any better. I'd been to the doctor, everywhere, but I didn't get better. And then bengkila* (Sibayak Berastagi, who was her classificatory HF) *said—he often passed by here, and there was something flashing on top of the house, like lightning flashes. "That means there's a great keramat with this daughter-in-law* [permén] *here," he said. Sibayak Berastagi, our guru. He said it.*

There were, in fact, two keramats with her then. One was the great king at the top of Mount Sibayak—*I don't dare ask his name,* she explained, *he's just like the president. When he descends he has a complete escort. He has an automobile on the top of the mountain.* Her other spirit was from Lau Debuk-Debuk. No, she corrected us, it was not Guru Penawar or his daughters. Guru Penawar was human, after all, but this keramat was not: he was the king who was there before Guru Penawar came in search of his daughters. His place, where she performed her erpangir, was not the bubbling pool where the Beru Karos' devotees gathered, but a small spring just above the swimming pond: *That's the bathing pool of the ninis from up above when they come down to the bottom. At particular times. From the top to the bottom, that's what they say.* Every full moon for seven months she made a kerja for the spirits, four months for the nini at the top and three for the one at the bottom. *There was a gendang for the first ceremony and for the last, and then it was really straightened out, it was all in order.*

It was actually a matter of hurt feelings, she said. *There was a doctor, he was my good friend. He was German. I was trading oranges then, I'd get good ones for him. "Your feelings are hurt, orange-seller," he'd say all the time. We had a good time with that doctor. They said he was the best doctor around.*

See, it was like this back then. Your uncle (bengkila, meaning her husband), *there were three brothers, your uncle was the youngest. Then the middle one died. So, you know, when that happened, after that, my feelings were disturbed. Because his brother was dead, they said she had to come here, to this household. With us, you know, it's like that. Your uncle didn't want to at all. Still, with all that trouble, you feel sort of sad.*

What Nandé Ukat meant was that according to custom her husband was expected to take his brother's widow as a second wife. *"Not me,"* he said. *"If you don't do it her children can't be taken care of," said all our kalimbubu. "And who'll take care of my children?" I asked. Finally she went to the older brother, they have three children now. Because your uncle, the one who comes to this house, didn't want her. But still, it really hurts, doesn't it?*

So that's what happened so that I was a little sick, when the doctor said I was heart-sick. Your feelings are hurt, he said. That's when our ninis made themselves known. All our ninis from up above, they said, "There's nothing to be afraid of. You just arrange a gendang for us. You'll never again have troubled thoughts, not till you're middle-aged will you ever feel tired." And it was just like that, just like I'm telling you. We didn't know why, but there was always something to eat. Money, no. That's how our ninis helped me.

So I was really respectful to them. No matter how unnecessary it seemed, if they said, "Make a gendang," I just did it. The money would be there, I don't know where it came from. "Do it," they said. "Iih!" I said. Then, I didn't know how to trade, it was just rowes, rowes, rowes [the sound of money pouring in]. *The money just seemed to keep doubling itself. And then after there weren't any more gendangs the money just wasn't there any more.*

As a Purba affine and a prominent local medium, Nandé Ukat had been closely involved in the early planning of the gendang jambur. She was (by her own account) the designated spokesperson for the mountain spirits, the speaker of their "gong-words" and the perch of the cowherd spirit who introduced the song "Odak Odak." But for her—and this was why she was surprised we had been referred to her—the gendang jambur was neither the continuation of an ongoing conversation with the spirits nor the beginning of a new one. It was, rather, an encoding of silence in speech. Propelled by nearly twenty years of resentment, her conversation returned, over and over, to the betrayal that the gendang jambur represented to her: *They'd already heard from our ninis at the top, but* they *were the ones who were glorified.*

The original plan, she said, had been to send a small group of people with offerings to the top of the mountain, according to local custom. *If there's to be a meeting with the ninis—*she announced at the first Purba gathering—*we have to do it on the mountain. I'll go to the mountain, I said. Who'll be my companion? I said. So then, it was done. We talked it over. Fifteen people will go to the mountain, I said. "If that's what you say, that's all right," they said.*

Then, after that, they had meetings like I just said, they set a date, they invited all the villages, all of the bus-owners.

So the fifteen of you went to the mountain, auntie, to the top? I interrupted.

Wait a minute, I'll tell you about it. "Yes," they said, "It's all set. You take gifts to the mountain," they said. And then, there was another meeting.

All right, I said. I can arrange everything. You do all that, I'll arrange it with our ninis, I said. We'll make an offering table, get areca nuts, everything, green coconuts, cakes, I said. So then, they did it.

Then it was cancelled. There were maybe five more days, it was cancelled. We won't be going to the top, they said. Why? I said. "Lots of guests have already arrived, I don't know how many have already been invited, tens, how many hundreds, I don't know."

They wanted to fill up the jambur. I don't know how many hundred they said, there can't be too many guests, they said. Oh, if there are a lot of guests, our ninis won't appear, I said. "No," they said, "call them from here. If you call them they'll come, you know," they said. I can call them to wherever you want; our ninis will come, I said.

But because I'd already said I was going to the top, well, I just don't want to do it, I said. I'll not be there. Do it yourselves, I said.

Three of us backed out, one was Si Tabas, whose father was a devotee of Guru Penawar, one was Sibayak Berastagi's son, Gok. Because there was no visit [to the top]. *Because nowadays only the bottom king is glorified. The king at the top isn't glorified. Because only the top ones should be revered. The bottom ones, don't they just wait down there?*

So, I just don't want to anymore, I said. I left them straightaway, I didn't want to do it anymore. They all did the erpangir, I don't know how many tens of buses. To Lau Debuk-Debuk. Our ninis just screamed, they wept.

They wept—I made a ceremony here. I made it complete, here. I made their food, I got five chickens. Complete, you'd say, I made the ceremony here. So then, there was, I got someone with the second sight [dua lapis matana, literally "double-layered eyes"]: *This house of ours was full! Our ninis descended! They came down carrying packages. They came by car! Because they have buses on top, just like some of us here. They came straight here! Five buses stopped out there. All who could see, you know, at the jambur, they were amazed, that our ninis came here, all of them. This one from the top, this one from Lau Debuk-Debuk.*

So as far as the gendang jambur is concerned, I didn't go there, I formed it.

Because I'd already arranged everything. Place the offering table on the upstream side, I said. To receive our ninis. They put it in the middle. I said, you can't put the gendang there. They didn't pay attention to what I said any more.

It seems the spirits didn't really come to the jambur, auntie, I said.

How could they? They were here, in this house! In this very house were all our ninis. Five carloads of them came down. All in this house. Over there at the jambur, it was just their underlings, their servants. The keramats from above, not a one of them came. All of them, there wasn't one that came. So that's why the ones who were doing it over there were furious. That's the history of the gendang jambur, I formed it, my child. I wasn't there.

And I'd already seen the cash they've got up there, lots of cash, I don't know how many sacks full, it should have gone to the ones who sponsored the ceremony. They took it back home. Leaves, those leaves are our ninis' money.

So then, in the jambur, if I'd been there, Iya, nini! I'd have said. Go home! I'd say. Because I, if, suppose I'd been there, I'd have gotten chairs for our ninis, I don't know how many. The chairs would have had a layer of white cloth, all of them. I'd have make them a place to sit.

It wasn't like that! How could it be, they didn't know how it should be. I talk with our ninis all the time, they don't.

At the gendang jambur. Our ninis wept, here they've come, they said on top there, on top.

That's the history of the gendang jambur.

I formed it, my child, I wasn't there.

New People

"We were all new people back then," said Pa Timbang, meaning that he and most of the others who founded Merga Si Lima had been at the time relatively unacquainted with the world of the spirits. "Odak Odak" must have been an old song, he explained, since the spirits knew it, but *they*, the devotees, didn't, and so they took it for something new. Traders like Pa Timbang created through Merga Si Lima a space for the stories they wanted to tell; and they assumed—since the spirits' time ran upstream and downstream at once—that these stories were both uniquely their own and part of a timeless pattern preserved in the spirits' memory, a concord or conspiracy between myth and history, like the retrospective prophecy of Nandé Ngena's dream of hostages.

In Merga Si Lima's revisionist history, the opening of Lau Debuk-Debuk as a zone of storied encounters was not simply the chance outcome of a passing trader's conversation with the spirits, or of a pragmatic politician's opting for convenience over custom in selecting a ceremonial site: it was an unexpected conjuncture of affinity and necessity. The stories of Lau Debuk-Debuk and Guru Penawar's lost daughters, with their intertwined themes of individual greed, family failure, and commercial success, offered Merga Si Lima's "new people" a script for narrative engagement and a field of experiential possibilities encompassing both the mountain and the marketplace. The Beru Karos' song "Odak Odak," with its simultaneous evocations of social harmony and personal enticement, opened a space for yearning and for hope in the new world of commerce and wonder that they shared with the mountain spirits—the spirits who, as Nandé Randal once told me, "care for traders, but for farmers not at all."

Nandé Ukat's counter-narrative stands on this terrain as a negation of such redemptive scriptings of the gendang jambur. Her story is one that *resists*: it has no hope for an independent existence, it can only abide in opposition and thus exercises a kind of complicit mirroring of the official story it denies. The *filling* of the jambur coincides with the *emptying* of the Purbas' words to the mountain spirits, the spirits' *presence* at Nandé Ukat's house signifies the *absence* of their (and her) authorizing attendance at the jambur. Rapat replaces arih-arihen in the history of Merga Si Lima's founding. The bags of leaves/money waiting at the top of the mountain remain unclaimed, while Lau Debuk-Debuk becomes so crowded with devotees that the spirits, the *real* spirits, refuse to descend. Instead they send their supernatural proxies and underlings, whose imitative attentions testify to the simultaneous plenitude and emptiness of the magical landscape they occupy. To interpretations of the gendang jambur as a moment of supernatural reconciliation or a return to "Karo tradition," there is Nandé Ukat's retort: *So, it's not like that, I said. What do you really want to do?*

But there is really no choice, here or elsewhere, between redemption and negation; for to choose either is to read reality in the simple language of loss. What seems to me to be a more productive approach to narrative experience is to recognize in all its framings the necessary tension between complicity and denial: in Nandé Ukat's story of the failure of the gendang jambur as in Nandé Laga's claim to have been the first to sing "Odak Odak," in the journalist-promoter's translation of a discourse of spirits into the rhetoric of political symbolism, or in Selam Ginting's apology for his inability to tell the dream-taught story of Guru Penawar in full. The stories that spin across the face of Mount Sibayak endow it with a complex eventfulness that both denies any possibility of narrative closure and increases the plausibility of every other story told there. They are not accommodated by the structures of nostalgia or of melancholy; they are the uncertain signs of habitation, the traces of passage—at once here and gone—through which a natural landscape comes to be saturated with the ambiguous magic of experience.

Six

Someone Else Speaking

a terror which threatens us all, that of being judged by a power

which wants to hear only the language it lends us.

—ROLAND BARTHES, "Dominici, or

the Triumph of Literature"

WHAT COUNTS as a story? Karo stories, good ones—which means, in Karo terms, mostly the kinds of stories that men tell—begin in a moment of exile or dispossession. They move in rhythmic progression from event to event toward a future unknown but foreordained. Dangers are revealed as opportunities; chance encounters unfold into recognitions of kinship. Intricately threaded around formulaic interludes and embedded dialogue and punctuated occasionally by song, such stories compel their listeners, in ways familiar to us all, to submit to the narrator's artistry, at least for the time of the telling.

The heroes of these stories are most often orphans. Perhaps this is because only they, forcibly excluded from the warm and demanding circles of kinship, can gain the freedom necessary to act heroically. Born paradoxically outside the social world, and literally under a bad sign (*tula erpagi-pagi*, at the dawn of the sixteenth day of the lunar cycle),[1] the heroic orphan in Karo narrative struggles against fate for recognition and incorporation. Like the fugitive, the orphan seeks to return to a restored, or perhaps improved, place within the official order; and although generations may pass before this restoration is complete, the orphan's story usually ends happily, with a proper marriage duly celebrated.

These misfit orphan-heroes are also mostly male, for the man without kin stands a chance of winning his way back into social standing—of finding new "mothers and fathers" in his wanderings, of gaining wife-giving kin through marriage, and of acquiring followers and potential wife-receivers through industry or charisma or luck. The girl without kinsmen, in contrast, has no guardian, no one to speak for her in marriage negotiations or to receive her marriage payment, and thus no value in the system of marital exchange. She cannot be the "conduit of a relationship" (Rubin 1975:174) between men; she is a channel through which nothing flows. It is precisely this absence of value that is faced and corrected by Beru Rengga Kuning, the one exceptional Karo female hero who acts like a man.[2]

Writing of the lives of Western literary women, Carolyn Heilbrun (1988:48) has remarked that for "women who wish to live a quest plot" of the sort that men's stories allow or even encourage, some adventitious event must transform the conventional trajectory of their lives into an eccentric one. For Beru Rengga Kuning, it is the unlikely intervention of a talking magpie that begins her eccentric quest. The bird's mockery reveals that the orphan girl has a full "matched" brother, a ne'er-do-well disowned by his family for squandering the money for his bride price payment.[3] *However bright your silver ear-ornaments*—the magpie taunts her—*however long your golden necklaces, what use are they when your brother is imprisoned in the east, locked up in cingkam-wood stocks.* Later the bird teases her again: *All the boys of the village work-crew, they're no use to you if your brother doesn't dare meet his mama* [MB], *doesn't dare meet his mother, for he's gambled away his mama's gold, gambling in the east.*

Her mother denies the magpie's story: *You're the only one, amé,* she tells her daughter.[4] *So learn well to weave and to braid, amé, so you can gain many brothers, many fathers; when you've cloths and mats of your own making, then you'll have brothers too. If you have none of these, then you'll get no brothers either.* Beru Rengga Kuning decides to take matters into her own hands more directly, literally enacting her mother's unintentionally prophetic words: *You're my only girl-child, my boy-child too.* Offering betel to her father's spirit to ask his blessing, she dresses herself in man's clothing and, with her purple-specked hound (*biang si anggur-anggur*) and Siamese cat as traveling companions, goes to find and redeem her brother.

Disguised as a man, Beru Rengga Kuning travels from one gambling place to another. Because she always wins, her gaming partners, whose ineffective luck-charms are presumably specific to male adversaries, begin to suspect that she is a woman. She is variously tested, and in each case her animal companions trick the suspicious gamblers. When she bathes with the men, their attention is distracted by the antics of the dog and cat; when she demonstrates her throwing-strength, the cat shakes oranges down from the tree struck by her stone; when she marries her opponent's sister it is with the dog's wedding-night help that she convinces her bride that she is a man.[5] And in the end, of course, she finds her brother and redeems his debt. They return home along with Beru Rengga Kuning's "wife," whom she passes along to her brother before herself accepting a

husband ("My wife will be my sister-in-law" she explains, neatening up
a potentially very messy set of affinal relations). "O mother: *You're the
only one, amé,* you said," says Beru Rengga Kuning triumphantly, "but
here I've found my brother and gotten a wife for him. So let the orchestra
play!"

I like to think of Beru Rengga Kuning's story as a subversive message
passed from one generation of women to another, as it was for my friends
Ernalem and Hanna, who learned a version from their maternal grand-
mother. I like to think of it as a story of the arbitrariness of gender dis-
criminations and gender categories, of how one can slip out of the constraining guise of what might have seemed some fundamental identity
and live as someone else, at least for a while. I like especially the story's
gender-bending jokes, which multiply according to the whim and imagination of the teller and open up rich possibilities for envisioning gender as
parodic performance. And I like the potential it seems to offer for Karo
women to "back talk" a world of male privilege and authority, and to
become subjects of their own stories for a change.[6]

But to read resistance thus from (or into) women's folktales or poetry
or ritual performances obscures the fact that such narrative enactments
exist *outside of* everyday experience, and that these stories entertain at
least in part because they do not literally reflect the quotidian world.
However familiar Beru Rengga Kuning's predicament may be to Karo
women, and however it may resonate with the concerns of contemporary
Western feminists, her solution cannot be taken in any sense as a practical
guide for living a Karo woman's life. Whether it should be taken as an
instance of narrative resistance to male hegemony is also uncertain. For
despite the tale's irreverent cross-dressing challenge to masculine prerogatives, it carries the clear—and also familiar—message that to claim a
subject-position, either discursively or socially, one must act, and speak,
as a man.[7]

Power, writes Carolyn Heilbrun (1988:44), "consists to a large extent
in deciding what stories will be told" and what stories will remain unspoken—or indeed unspeakable. When those decisions are made by men,
women may, like Amé Kata Mehuli speaking in the colonial courtroom of
her sojourn with the umangs, find their own stories "perfectly unacceptable" to the official order they confront, or in which they live their lives.
They may learn that speaking for themselves requires that, like Beru
Rengga Kuning, they speak as "someone else." Like the restless natives in
some colonial script, they may find themselves collectively acting the
stock part, filling in the background for someone else's heroic drama. Or
they may discover what Ashis Nandy (1982:198) describes as the ulti-

mate, ironic violence of colonialism—that the terms of resistance have already been set by the discourse against which resistance is directed.

What counts as a story? Much of our ethnographic reportage is shaped by the kinds of events locally deemed worthy of telling as a story, as well as by local conventions of how that telling should be done. But it also depends crucially on what we recognize as a story, and on our own conventions of how ethnographic narratives should be made. What Edwin Ardener (1989a, b) has called the "problem of women"—their simultaneous statistical presence and experiential absence in ethnographic accounts—is an effect of narrative misrecognition and erasure on both sides of the ethnographic divide. Beru Rengga Kuning's tale offers a focal instance against which to measure the misrecognition of women in Karo society and in ethnographic representation; but to respond to the "problem of women" with more than the figure of the eternally silenced subaltern, we need to attend not just to stories told about women, nor only to our own translations and retellings of such stories, but also to the politics and the practices of storytelling—not least of all our own.

We can begin this project by looking at the way that official histories—our own, others'—are narrativized, at how official narrative genres construct and limit men's and women's experiences. We can look beyond the silencing toward the site where silence lapses, toward the "misfit" in the scripts of dominion; and we can look for other ways of telling a woman's story.

Nandé Laga's Dream

Way back in the history of all this, Nandé Laga began—

Way back then, first this spirit came to me. That was in the Dutch times, when Nandé Laga was a young bride, around 1941, which she remembered as the year before Japan came. *It made me crazy, I couldn't think straight anymore.*

It probably didn't matter that we didn't know Nandé Laga well. Traders and spirit mediums—and she was both—were used to dealing with strangers. A former friend and colleague of the Arisan's Nandé Randal, she too had been a protégée of Pa Kantur Purba, the guru better known as Sibayak Berastagi. One of the eleven spirit mediums and gurus chosen to lead the parade to the gendang jambur, Nandé Laga was the one who claimed to have been the first one there to sing "Odak Odak," the song of her spirit-guide Beru Karo.

Trading and curing were, for Nandé Laga and other mediums of her generation, complementary activities. *We can't sell these medicines of ours, our ninis said. The blind are to be strengthened. The weak are to be strengthened. Said, the lame, they are to be strengthened so they can walk. Said, if they're blind, wake them up. Said, they'll open their eyes straightaway. Treat them. I only come to humans to gain mothers and fathers. Said, we don't seek for cash. If cash is what you want, you'll make a profit trading. Said, I'll see to that. They're already sick. If you ask them for cash, well, won't they figure they're as good as dead?*

Nandé Laga had surely made her profits in the market. Now she and her husband owned a two-story house on Berastagi's main street and she rarely worked as a medium, but she still came down to the city regularly, carrying garlic to sell in Medan's huge Central Market. On market days she stayed with her daughter in Padang Bulan, and it was there, during a long conversation one evening in a front room furnished mostly with a few tattered mats, a kerosene lamp, and towering heaps of the garlic bulbs she was sorting, that she told us—"us" being myself, my co-worker Juara Ginting, and Nandé Laga's daughter, who had heard it all before—the story of her encounter with "our ninis," the mountain spirits who taught her to cure.

> *So then the spirit came to me, said: I'll follow you, I will.*
> *Then someone—*
> *I treat them, cured.*
> *This is my patient, cured.*
> *So then, what is the sickness?*
> *For example—*
> *if you tell it to our ninis, this is the cure, they say.*
> *They say it.*
> *Through my throat.*

This is the official version, the culturally appropriate scenario, of a medium's initiation. All the legitimating tokens of Karo mediumship are contained within this detemporalized, minimalist narrative: a spirit chooses its new "alighting place" then reveals its presence and its wishes through the suffering of the one so chosen; a pact is established between the spirit and its new host; patients come and are cured by the spirit; the spirit's knowledge emerges from the medium through the characteristic "throat-speech" (*erkata kerahung*), a whistling sound produced within the throat that Karo say is the twittering, bird-like speech (*déwal*) of the spirits.[8]

This is the story a Karo medium is expected to tell, in which authority is claimed by denying responsibility and authenticity is asserted by denying agency. The spirits' intervention changes her life from the usual story to one conventionally designated as "eccentric." The story is complete, enclosed, self-sufficient: the cure is signified by the spirits' presence; the spirits' presence is signified by the cure.

But closure is less secure in the middle of the everyday world, where everything naturally has something else after it, and the "necessary or

usual consequent" of anything is more or less up for grabs.[9] Over the
course of the evening, Nandé Laga told us five other stories about the
events that led to her becoming a medium. These other tellings didn't elaborate or complete her first, sketchy outline; neither did they contradict it.
Instead, they veered away, resisting my guiding efforts to construct a narrative in properly Aristotelian fashion, moving stepwise chrono-logically
from beginning through middle to end. Nandé Laga's stories continually
shifted the narrative terrain, opening up new ground. Each was, simply,
somewhere else.

And so her second story was about a dream, about the first time the
spirits came to her.

> *The first time they came? Well, I had a dream.*
> *They came in my dream.*
> *There were, I guess, two girls, then after that three men.*
> *Then, who are you? I said.*
> *Said, Beru Karo.*
> *Where are you from, I said to those two girls.*

And we interjected: They were from Mount Sibayak, right?

> *From Mount Sibayak.*
> *How many in your family, I said.*
> *Said, how many, five—*
> *Said, three male, two female.*
> *Said, let's go together.*
> *Said, make medicines, we'll follow.*
> *Oh, in that case, that's fine, I said.*
> *So, I went to the water, the hairwashing ceremony—*

How many times? we asked.

> *Four times.*
> *The first time we got three chickens, we made a three-*
>   *chicken offering.*
> *I bathed in the water, washed my hair.*
> *So then, after that, these three—*

(meaning the chickens)

> *After the water, they—*

(meaning the spirits)

> *came to the house, they ate them.*
> *We'd made their food offering, cakes, or bananas, oranges,*
>   *they ate those too.*
> *After that, say, if anyone was sick, I'd treat them, cured.*

A crazy person, I'd treat them, cured.
That's it.
If someone was bothered by a spirit, I'd fix it up, the spirit
    would come.

Karo women's storytelling was like that: fragmentary and inconclu-
sive, starting often from an authoritative position (the "official version")
and then shifting ground, swooping into uncertainties and narrative
dead-ends only to move the story elsewhere, or—sometimes—repeating a
phrase or image (as Nandé Laga does here, at her story's end) as a kind of
narrative refrain, a brief clinch whereby differing accounts resolve into a
moment of transient, and perhaps illusory, accord. Women's stories
ended only to begin again, in a different key, with a different stress, so
that narrative closure was always postponed, meaning always deferred.
Women's stories were constructed by complicities—of common experience and shared knowledge, unspoken because generally known—complicities that we, outsiders, could only experience as epistemological
gaps.[10] Shaped to long acquaintance rather than transient encounter,
women's stories were patient with the interruptions of everyday life—a
child's demands, a fire to stoke or rice to stir, customers' marketplace
queries, the digressions of another's memories jostled—and attuned to
the cadences of the perpetual open end—the "to be continued" and the
"more to come."[11]

To hear such stories, "[o]ne would have to listen with another ear, as
if hearing *an 'other meaning' always in the process of weaving itself, of*
embracing itself with words, but also of getting rid of words in order not
to become fixed, congealed in them" (Irigaray 1985:29). How, then, can
we understand these "contradictory words," as Irigaray describes them,
"somewhat mad from the standpoint of reason, inaudible for whoever
listens to them with ready-made grids, with a fully elaborated code in
hand"? How can we resist the desire to fill in the narrative gaps and close
the loopholes, to erase the necessary complicities of women's storytelling
practice and to conceal our own difference from those who speak? And
how can we begin to find a place for someone else speaking such words
within the grids and codes of the stories that *we* are expected to tell?

THE PROBLEM OF WOMEN

The glossy, heart-shaped leaves of the pepper vine known as betel—Karo
name them *belo*—serve in Karo social life as a kind of material copula. In
the old histories, a traveler is always offered the courtesy of betel even
before he is asked to identify himself. Today most men prefer cigarettes,

Betel-leaf bundles in a Karo market stall.

but female guests arriving at a ceremony are immediately offered betel as a courtesy; older women, upon meeting, exchange betel pouches as a token of friendship and a stimulant to conversation. Karo mediums, calling down the spirits to alight on them, hold prepared betel leaf between hands pressed together prayer-wise as a mark of deference, and betel-leaf offerings still appear at spirit-shrines and along forest pathways as conveyances of small personal requests to the local keramats. But then again: the betel leaf may also be the vessel of poison, love-magic, or the substances of sorcery.

Every Karo market has its sellers of belo, older women usually, dressed in sarong and tudung. They sit or squat behind tables arranged with rows of neat leaf-bundles, while customers study the freshness of the leaves, inquire into their provenance, or perhaps—regular customers shading easily into friends—sample their flavor while joining the seller in marketplace talk, a rich and distinctively womanly mix of jokes, gossip, and well-worn complaints fractured and punctuated by quick transactions, shouts to passers-by, and the raucous heckling of competitors. Prices vary, depending on buyers' familiarity and bargaining skills as well as on sellers' costs, but unlike other marketplace measures of quantity the betel-leaf bundles (*kepit*) are always the same size: twenty leaves, stacked neatly one atop the other, with stems projecting together to enable an easy count.

Bagi belo la ertangké, Karo say, Like a betel leaf without a stem. I borrow the metaphor here to designate the problem of Karo women: *tied up in the bundle, left out of the count.*[12]

"I leave the women without comment," wrote missionary van den Berg in 1906, "because they form an element that counts for nothing in Batak society and thus her joining [the Church] has only relative worth" (van den Berg 1906:250). Karo women were in fact generally left out of the missionaries' count, and thus out of the historical picture, except where, as part of the Christian campaign against pagan "materialism," they could be invoked normatively as victims of oppressive custom and of Karo men. Tying up the bundle of Christian virtue, Karo worldliness, and the subordination of women, missionary Joustra "gladly exclude[d] the women" from his general assessment of Karo spiritual indifference, adding that "precisely for that reason is it more a shame that they lie strictly out of our reach" (Joustra 1896:242–43).[13]

Joustra describes Karo women as virtual beasts of burden within the household: performing all domestic labor, gardening, and tending the small stock while "her lord and master (except for a few exemplary cases) acts the great lord, or . . . plays nursemaid while mama is working in the fields." To Joustra, women's work as well as women's status was reflected in Karo poetic terms of reference for the wife: *si man bana*, "what belongs to him"; *si rukat nakanna*, "the one who stirs the rice"; the "lowly sounding" *si meré babina*, "the one who feeds the pigs"; or simply *jelmana*, "his person" (from which "something contemptuous shines through"). But the most frequently used Karo term, and the one that the missionaries found most revealing, was *tukur mas*, "bought with gold," from which they concluded that women were no more than commodities circulating in the Karo marriage market (Joustra 1902b:403).[14]

If for the missionaries the worldly pagan represented primal human nature unaware of its own sinfulness, this corrupt nature was most profoundly manifested in the "buying" and "selling" of other human beings.[15] "Toehan Deibata has made people in His image and in His likeness," Richard Tampenawas told his Karo audience, "and for that reason a human being is no commodity" (Wijngaarden 1894b:71). The woman-as-commodity demonstrated the need for moral intervention in the Karo field; beyond that, she was a silent reproach to the social and sexual commodification that, in the Reformed view, pervaded all civil society not guided by Christian moral values—and not least of all the vulgarly commercial "dollar land" of the Deli plantations.[16]

This is a version of the familiar colonialist "discourse of salvation"

(L. Mani 1990:117; cf. Spivak 1988), in which bad (native) men victimize powerless (native) women in the name of "custom" or "religion." It does not produce the silence of Karo women any more than the British in India discursively "invented" sati; rather, it stakes a moral claim to their already absent voices, magnifying their oppression for a foreign audience, expanding its own authority by displaying, repeating, replicating the silence that it pronounces. But whatever ideological purposes might have been served by the missionaries' salvationist critique, and however misplaced their designation of the marriage payment as the source of all the sexual, social, and spiritual oppression of Karo women, their emphasis on the marital trade in women nevertheless cut to the heart of the matter.

In Lévi-Strauss's (1969:115) well-known formulation, the transaction of marriage is a "total relationship of exchange . . . not established between a man and a woman, where each owes and receives something, but between two groups of men." Opening an extended (and often heated) debate over the place of women in this "marital dialogue of men" (ibid.:496), Lévi-Strauss argued that "the woman figures only as one of the objects in the exchange, not as one of the partners between whom the exchanges takes place" (ibid.:115). Feminists have rightly objected to the foundational status of woman-exchange in Lévi-Strauss's cultural paradigm; less attention, however, has been paid to what Strathern (1988:312) identifies as the "unfortunate" commodity idiom of autonomous (male) subjects and passive (female) objects into which his argument is cast, an idiom repeated and indeed reinforced in many cases by his feminist critics.[17] This uncritical appropriation (salvationist or otherwise) of Lévi-Strauss's language of subjects and objects has tended to obscure rather than clarify the nature of this "traffic in women." For this reason the transaction frequently glossed as "wife-giving" and "wife-receiving" should be approached with some care. This is especially true when, as in the Karo case, the objectifying anthropological idiom of woman-exchange imbricates a prior and isomorphic discursive figuration of "woman-as-commodity."

As I have described in chapter 1, marriage ties form and maintain the linkages uniting exogamous patrilineal descent groups in the intricate web of kinship and mutual obligation that constitutes the Karo social world. It is the permanence of these bonds that is betokened by the marriage payment, the initial return for what Karo describe as the unending debt owed to the bride's kin for their gift of generational continuity. *Pace* Lévi-Strauss (1969:60–68), what is "given" in marital exchange is not the bride herself but the patronymic identification of her children. The bride is not what is being transacted by these groups of men.

If the bride is never subject-partner in her marital transaction, being, as Lévi-Strauss (ibid.) notes, "merely the occasion of" a social relationship of reciprocity formed between men, neither is she, strictly speaking, the mere object of masculine transaction. "The woman in marriage"—according to Judith Butler's poststructuralist revision of the woman-exchange problem—"qualifies not as an identity, but only as a relational term that both distinguishes and binds the various clans to a common but internally differentiated patrilineal identity" (Butler 1990:38–39). Within a system of generalized exchange,

> the bride functions as a relational term between groups of men; she does not *have* an identity, and neither does she exchange one identity for another. She *reflects* masculine identity precisely through being the site of its absence. . . . As wives, women not only secure the reproduction of the *name* (the functional purpose), but effect a symbolic intercourse between clans of men. As the site of a patronymic exchange, women are and are not the patronymic sign, excluded from the signifier, the very patronym they bear. (Ibid.)

In Karo terms, a woman is "no buffalo, that can be bought." As daughter, bride, sister, mother, she is always the indeterminate and polyvalent "conduit of a relationship" (Rubin 1975:174) between patronymically identified groups of men, neither social subject nor subject's object.[18]

A Karo woman claims neither "to be" the name of the father nor "to become" the name of the husband. That is, while a man is described as "having" a natal clan-identity (*mergana*), a woman is referred to as a "woman of" (beru) her patronymic group, to which she is attached as a permanent jural minor, the anak beru of her brothers and fathers. Upon marriage a woman becomes the responsibility of—though not a member of—her husband's descent group, and then she may also be referred to as "there with" (*jé*) his clan. She is expected to follow this group's dietary prohibitions, to fulfill her husband's obligations to kin, to "stir his rice" and produce his descendants, and, where religiously appropriate, to propitiate his family spirits rather than those of her own kin.

This positional indeterminacy has immediate and practical consequences for female autonomy both within and outside the household. Women have no independent access to either productive or reproductive resources—rights to land and rights to children being identified with the patronymic group. Divorce—a rare occurrence but a not infrequent threat to unruly wives—or, more commonly, desertion may mean for a woman the loss of her children and of her livelihood, since her access to both depends upon her husband or other male kin. A woman's authority, even within the marital household, is thus limited by her husband's last word in any dispute, the warning (whether spoken or not) that he may "send her home" to her father and brothers.

As ambiguous "outsiders" in both their marital and natal households, Karo women have no official voice in the public spheres of social discourse and collective decision-making in which their lives are transacted. Informally, of course, they participate loudly and actively in community life. Women may gather to talk in social corners, in the market or at the hearth, while washing at the river, in the midst of other activities, in all those places where talk is labeled as "gossip." They may lobby behind the scenes or shout their opinions from the sidelines of a public gathering. But the arenas of narrative production both leisured and formal—from the storytelling sessions in the coffeeshops that comprise a quasi-official locus of male solidarity to the ceremonial oratory of official kin-group negotiations—are prescriptively occupied by men. This was, of course, the point of the magpie's taunt to Beru Rengga Kuning: *However bright your silver ear-ornaments, however long your golden necklaces, what use are they when your brother is imprisoned in the east, locked up in cingkam-wood stocks.* Without men to represent them Karo women cannot be officially represented; they are "left out of the count," they "count for nothing."

This process of representation, as Spivak (1988:279) has argued, must be understood as operating simultaneously in political practice and in the narrative "staging of the world." For Karo women, the problem is thus not simply that they cannot speak on their own behalf in public debate, but rather that public debate constructs a world in which someone else's stories are the ones that count. Karo public discourse is shaped to the measure of male interests, which are officially represented as universal social values; its rules are men's rules, that is, the rules that men conform to when they are playing by the rules (cf. Bourdieu 1977:22). Women's interests, insofar as they diverge from that official measure, are cast along an evaluative scale ranging from unofficial to scandalous to—literally— unimaginable. It is the same with women's experience. Generic standards of narrative authenticity (what counts as a story) and style (how a story should be told) are organized by reference to the social experience of Karo men—as patronymically identified subjects occupying stable positions in a relationally constituted and flexibly hierarchical social field, and as social actors who *do* count for something in public discourse. This is, on both points, precisely the sort of social experience that is structurally unavailable to women, who are thus doubly discounted: first by the literal muting of their voices, which leaves them unpracticed in public debate and unheard in public speech; and second by the discursive limits of narrative plausibility, which require women's stories to be cast in the borrowed phrasings of men's interests and men's experience, if they are to gain an audience.[19]

But however fully hegemonic an official order may appear to be, there always seem to be loopholes in its constraining pattern of structural and discursive exclusions. These may be officially provided, or they may form as if spontaneously around the pattern's flaws or weaknesses. Sites of evasion and indeterminacy, loopholes generate an internal "elsewhere," a built-in plausible deniability that allows them to operate by giving them the appearance of being *nothing of the kind.*[20] Loophole subversions work under the cover of an inability to measure up to official standards of narrative plausibility. This means that they are necessarily subject to official strategies of containment both appropriative and dismissive.

In the Karo order of male discursive authority, one such loophole takes shape around the female spirit medium, or guru si baso. Neither keepers of family shrines nor interlocutors in a political dialogue between the community and its spirit-guardians, women may nevertheless serve as conduits for relationships between the human world and the realm of the spirits. When spirits speak through them, women move into the center of the social world; they gain an audience otherwise unreachable. Yet here the loophole seems to close on them, for what is said in the double-voiced discourse of spirit/medium goes unrecorded, or else bespeaks the language of authority and male privilege, which is the language of the public sphere. The medium's indeterminate voice, as it merges with the intentions of her audience, marks the official limit of women's narrative experience. Stories about mediums do not restore her speech.

STORIES ABOUT MEDIUMS

At the beginning of November a peculiar ceremony took place,

which is called for short "rumah bégu." The meaning is this,

that the bégu (soul) of a dead person visits his rumah (kam-

pung) to communicate, through the mouth of the medium, his

present circumstances. We went in the evening to take a

look. . . . There was more dancing, music and the peculiar

sing-song wailing and lamentation of funeral mourners, until

finally one of the gurus reached a state of ecstacy (inspired by

the soul of the deceased). We could not hold out until then,

however, in the stifling, smoky atmosphere, saturated

with the nauseatingly sweet scent of opium.

And of what was said through the gurus I understood nothing.

—M. JOUSTRA, "Verslag van de zending onder de Karo-Bataks,

over het jaar 1895"

Karo mythic narratives tell of the emergence of the medium's voice at a moment of crisis. One such story hinges on the competition of two brothers for the love of their impal [MBD].[21] Promised in marriage to one cousin, the girl runs away with the other; then, ensorcelled by the spurned fiancé, she secretly kills her lover. Remorseful, she collects the offerings that will henceforth be prescribed for the perumah bégu funeral seance. Various creatures offer to take part in the ceremony: the dancers are a house cat and a wildcat; the drummer is a frog; an earthworm plays the seruné (oboe); the woodpecker and treefrog strike the small and the large gongs. The green wood-pigeon's cooing is the sound of the spirit's voice. And *kuliki si mangki-angki*, the harrier-hawk, whose weeping cries *kulik! kulik!* reveal the murdered man's fate, is the guru si baso.

Sometimes in stories a grieving daughter speaks for the spirits: called back by her mourning, as by their own hunger, the beloved dead return to give advice, to share their sadness, to reveal a truth—and to establish a pathway, which is the woman's body, between their world and that of their living kin. Sometimes, as in the story of the "crock-shrine" (Guci Pajuh-pajuhen) of Namo Cengké, the medium is the vehicle for a super-natural valorization of lineage rule:

> When the older brother of the first sibayak [of Namo Cengké] was born, lightning struck and the child was born lifeless. It had four hands and four feet. It was immediately burnt on the water's edge and all that was not burnt was thrown in the water. Then one day Si Gandil (the uneven, or the mis-shapen) spoke through a medium: "I am not someone who should be burnt, but someone to whom offerings should be made." The bones were then fished from the water and the soul was called up and asked, through a me-dium, what should be done. It said, "Make a place for me upstream from the village, plant there sangké sempilet, besi-besi, arimas, selantam, kalinjuhang [kinds of medicinal herbs associated with spirit-shrines], as a sunshade for my soul. Place a crock with water next to me so that I can see myself reflected there. . . ." All this was done, and it became the village offering-place. (Neumann 1927b:520–21)

These voices speak of social obligation and responsibility, they establish the contours of familial and community authority. Their stories end, as rituals do, with order restored, however tenuously. *Sai mara ku rumah tendi*, the medium says at the ceremony's close: the crisis is ended, the soul returns home. *Sai utang gancih ido*, the debt is paid, turned to credit.

The medium's appearance also marks a moment of crisis in the confi-dent epistemologies of otherness typical of the European literature of co-lonial Karoland. Here the arena of possession is not the site of a reclama-tion of social order; rather it becomes a gendered heart of darkness into which all moral order dissolves. "Not by chance is the possessed body essentially female," Michel de Certeau writes of the demonic exorcisms of medieval Europe: for "behind the scenes a relation between masculine discourse and its feminine alteration is acted out" (1988:245). The same relation is rehearsed in colonial texts, where, "for easily comprehensible reasons"—I borrow Dr. Hagen's offhand explanation of the usual sex of the medium—women are also recruited for the role of Order's alter. As in Hagen's description of mediums' entrancement, there is in these accounts a constant slippage between a carefully maintained clinical detachment and a mythologizing fascination:

> Through various means (dancing, balancing on tiptoe, being smoked with benzoin under a cloth, insistent beating of a metal bowl close in front of both ears) the media [*sic*] are transported to a violent, overexcited condition, such that they often dribble a bloody froth from their mouths; in this condition they are able to give oracles and answers of the spirits called upon. (Hagen 1882:638)

Unlike the smooth, coherent figure of the Karo woman-as-commodity, spirit mediums appear in colonial texts mostly in flamboyant montage, uncanny image-fragments of bodies in bits and pieces: bloody froth (most likely red betel-juice) on lips, black hair loose and flowing, a knife held in a quivering hand, a flaring wild eye, a breast exposed. The possessed woman engenders a kind of narrative excess, a frenzy of adjectival elaboration that to me always seems a cover-up for some epistemological failure of nerve. Here is Baron von Brenner's description of a seance he witnessed in 1886 in the village of Pengambotan:

> [H]er movements . . . became more passionate, so that her black hair came loose and soon fell down over her face and neck, flowing wildly around her head, beneath which a distorted, glowing face with blazing eyes appeared. All grace, all propriety gone, madly racing back and forth, she presented the frightening, repulsive image of a raving witch, a lunatic or one possessed. (von Brenner 1894:76)

In his best colonial Gothic style, von Brenner dwells with fascinated disgust on the details of the scene unfolded before him, slipping from the uncontrolled eroticism of the dancer's "passionate" movements to the horror evoked by the figure of this "raving witch." But in a moment this image of femininity transgressed ("all grace, all propriety gone") dissolves into sheer grotesquerie, and the medium is pictured ludicrously "cowering on the ground, the magic-knife in the thin, convulsively twitching hand," tossing her "wet, tangled hair back and forth," and speaking "with quavering lips of what she saw or pretended to see" (ibid.:77).

This sort of representational overkill typically overlies a refusal to acknowledge the medium's speaking voice. Although he did not know the language, von Brenner could dismiss her speech as "confused, unclear and nonsensical" (ibid.). A decade later Joustra, who did speak the language, said of a seance that he attended: "And of what the mediums said I understood not a word" (Joustra 1896:229–230).

I could recite other, more familiar stories about mediums here. These would tell of such matters as "village strife acted out in trance" (Belo 1960); strategic status enhancement or skirmish in the war between the sexes (Lewis 1989); calcium deficiency syndrome (Kehoe and Giletti 1981); allegorical representation of the "body politic" (Kessler 1977); female role-dissatisfaction and "hysterical predisposition" (Obeyesekere 1970); the "dialectic of culture and nature" embodied by women (Kapferer 1983); the management or transformation of psychic distress (Crapanzano 1977a, b). Some of these seem to me reasonable attempts to comprehend the medium's experience, in our own hypercoherent and evasive way, as a neurophysiological "fact," a sociological phenomenon, or a symbolic drama. What is lost in translation, once again, is the medium's speech.

No loopholes here: and no raving witches, weeping birds, or bloody oracles either. These explanations, for all their elegant coherence, seem to shut down rather than open up grounds for conversation between ourselves and those who speak the indeterminate loophole language of the spirits. For us—for myself, I should say—marvelous encounters and mountain spirits mark the beginning of a disbelief requiring suspension. I cannot move beyond the limits of my own narrative experience, cannot trade stories with Nandé Laga—cannot, in fact, properly understand the plain stories of less than mythic contour told by this woman I knew but not well, in a dim room heaped with garlic bulbs. *What counts as a story?*

LOST ON THE MOUNTAIN

Nandé Laga, beru Ginting she was, grew up in the village of Gurusinga, in the heart of Berastagi's expanding zone of commercial vegetable production. Open land was already scarce there when her father came as a bachelor from Suka, in Ginting territory, to work the rice fields of his anak beru, a man of the Gurusinga ruling lineage who had married his father's sister. Being economically dependent upon those who should properly have considered him their "visible god" may have contributed to the falling out between Nandé Laga's father's and some of his Gurusinga affines; in any event, the rift was serious enough that some years later, when Nandé Laga met and agreed to elope with a young Gurusinga man, she did not even realize that he was her "true" impal.[22] *How could we know?* she said. *Our families didn't even speak to each other!*

The marriage brought a happy ending to the conflict. *Well, of course they were delighted! My father had no land, he got land from them. His father got the child of his kalimbubu!* The marriage payment, said Nandé Laga, was an extravagant *f.*300, and she herself received a gift of *f.* 50, for getting herself properly married.

Nandé Laga was an only child until around the time of her marriage, when her father's second wife produced an heir for him, a half-brother for her. Soon afterward her own son Laga was born. It was 1941, the year before the Japanese came and the Dutch left for the first time—and shortly before her encounters with the spirits began.

These were things that we asked about, expecting answers that could be fitted to one or the other of our explanatory grids and codes. For Nandé Laga none of this touched the curing, the madness, the meetings with the mountain spirits. Her marriage was happy, she said; there were no conflicts.

We asked about Sibayak Berastagi, the guru who performed her hair-washing ceremony. *Around here,* she told us, *he's the one who took every-one to the water for the first time, for spirit-troubles. I was crazy when the grandparents, the ninis, came.*

What was it that made you crazy? we asked, searching for an explanation.

> *I didn't know anything anymore. I'd walk around, I'd*
> *   walk around, I didn't know anything.*
> *So then I—*
> *I'd talk in the middle of the road. I was always wandering.*
> *So they called for Sibayak Berastagi, right away the spirit came.*
> *It was fixed up right away.*
> *Said, Go to the water, the hairwashing ceremony. We want to*
> *   be with her always, said our ninis.*

It was a famous cure, I later discovered. *Oh, she was completely mad!* one woman told me. *She wanted to cook her baby! She called her neigh-bors*—this was in one of the old-style houses, with eight families, four households on either side of a long central aisle—*said "Come on, let's eat! Fried noodles, Mmmh, delicious!" She was going to toss her baby in the pan! Cook it up!*

Nandé Laga didn't tell us this.

Struggling to establish an orderly chronology, we asked if her dream of the spirits had come before or after her madness. She answered, *My dream? I'd already been lost, my child. I was there!*

At the—

The mountain. See, I ran away. Your father—she meant her husband but politely referred to him by my kin relation to him (*bapa*, F, FB, MZH) rather than her own—

> *thought I'd gone to the river. We'd just gotten married. . . .*

And so she told another story of the mountain spirits, this time of her wanderings on Mount Sibayak. There was no dream in this story, and despite its dream-like surreality, Nandé Laga insisted on its real-world locale.

> *I took a white cloth, I ran off.*
> *No one saw me go.*
> *The reason no one saw me is this: the spirits were protecting*
>   *me. Said, don't tread on a single rice stalk and no one will*
>   *know your plan.*
> *Said, no one would see me leave.*
> *No one saw me go. OK?*
> *This going of mine, oh, you'd say, I had one child. Si Laga,*
>   *the oldest. He was about four months old when I got*
>   *carried up.*
> *Said, to meditate.*
> *Said, a time to study.*
> *So I went, I came to the top, I guess.*
> *After I got to the top, there was a man, two men, who came.*
> *There were five old folks too.*
> *Then, when I got to the top, the five old people weren't there!*
> *Iih!*
> *Said, My child, aren't you thirsty?*
> *I wasn't scared, you know?*
> *I wasn't scared, I was happy. On top.*
> *Yes, I'm thirsty, I said.*
> *Said, If you're thirsty, my child, just lick that.*
> *I looked, it was a stone. I licked it. I wasn't thirsty anymore.*

A rock? we asked.

> *A rock. I thought it was a rock. They said it was a rock. On top*
>   *there's no water, just rocks.*
> *I sat down like this, and these kids came out, a whole lot of kids,*
>   *about that tall. Kids everywhere.*
> *These men I was telling you about, I guess there were three of*
>   *them.*
> *Said, You must be hungry. To me.*
> *I didn't dare tell them I was hungry. Oh no, I said.*
> *Then that old woman came and said, Aren't you hungry, my*
>   *child?*
> *She was about as old as I am now.*
> *Well, I am, I'm really hungry, I said.*
> *Call me granny, she said—for it's rude to address someone*
>   without using the proper term of address—

I'm really hungry, nini, I said.
So there was this—
it was about as big as this, like a whetstone.
Said, well, lick that. You won't be hungry anymore.
So I licked it, I wasn't hungry anymore.
Then I'd been on top for one night. When can I go home, nini,
I said.
Said, not yet, girl. You're meditating. When you hear something
like the sound of the gendang orchestra, then you can go
home.
Iih, I've been hearing that already, I said.
Said, not really, my child. Aren't you happy?
Oh, I guess I'm happy, I said.
So all of them who were there came up one after the other. The
sibayak hadn't come, the king there hadn't come yet, you see?
So, you're still just a young girl, aren't you? they asked.
Oh no, I said. When can I go home, I said.
Go home—
I don't—
maybe my baby is crying, I said. I'd remembered my baby.
Oh no, they said. He doesn't even remember you.
Well, it seems like I'll never get back, granny, ah! I said.
Said, Oh no, my child.
Said, when you hear the sound of the gendang
then you can go home.
Two nights passed. This was the next day.
Those kids were all my companions. Kids. The nini said, what
I'd thought were kids, well, they were really umangs—
Those kids were really umangs.
They didn't know how to talk.
Whatever I asked for, hah hah *was all they said.*
Said, hah hah.
They didn't know,
they just kept crowding around.
What could I say, when these kids, not one of these kids knew
how to talk.
So I thought.
Well, wasn't my heart in a tangle?
What did I care how many of these kids there were, if none of
them could talk?
Let's go fishing—in the lake of the volcano's crater—
I said.
I figured there must be lots of buses on top, or something like
that.

So I was there.
I don't know how.
There was something, you'd say, as big as my house,
even now if I think back I can remember it.
Just like coral it was—
that stone, at the top, like a house.
At the top.
Oh, nini, I said.
"What?"
Can I go down? I said. Can I go home right now?
"Just a little while longer, I think . . ."
Brrnang brrnang brrnang brr
I heard it!
There's the sound of the gong, nini, I said.
"Iih! I think you're right, my child."
Said, But the moon hasn't risen yet. When the moon rises, you
    tell us right away.
Said, Get ready.
Brrnang brrnang brr. The gong, you see?
Then there were two of us.
Well, I just fell in love with that man.
He was really good-looking. Even his lips were just like gold. I
    just wanted to laugh when he talked.
"Iya!" he said. Said, "Let's go, OK?"
Iya, let me ask about your clan first. What's your clan then?
    I said.

—because even if he were a spirit, formal avoidance rules would have to
be followed had they been "siblings" of the same clan. But fortunately—

Perangin-angin, he said. Which one would you rather ride, an
    airplane or a horse? he said. To me.
Said, Look, I brought my airplane here.
He'd brought his plane.

Which one did you choose? we asked.

My answer? Well, whichever you want, I said. Whichever you
    want.
Said, If you want to fly, here's the plane.
It landed, too, my child.
Said, If you want us to ride horseback, here's the horse.
He pointed to a white horse.
Whichever you want, I said.
Said, well, let's see, if we ride the horse, you'll have to hang onto
    my shirttail on the way home.

Beru Ginting, he called me.
Said, well, don't you love me?
Yes, indeed! I said.
Said, well then, I want you to hold onto my waistband.
Said, should we ride the horse or not?
If you say ride the horse, well, let's ride the horse, I said.
Nges! *That fellow put me up on the horse, I grabbed his waist-*
    band. Taak! *I tied us together up there with the white cloth.*
    Ah!
So then, the next thing I knew we were back in Gurusinga. I
    don't know which direction we came from. I guess I let go of
    his waistband.
Then I arrived—bllgang bllgang it went—arrived at the house.
Sibayak Berastagi was there at the house.
Calling me. With the orchestra. Because they had been calling
    me from down there.
Said, Play the gendang! He kept going up and down the center
    aisle, waving a white cloth, up and down, up and down,
then raap! *there I was in the house!*
It startled everyone in the house! because no one knew where
    I'd come from.

And they were having an orchestra in the house right then? we asked,
puzzled by the coincidence.

Right. The ones who were waiting. They played it.

"They were calling her," explained Nandé Laga's daughter from the
corner.

Dudu, *that's the Karo word. They were* calling *me.*

Who? The spirits? (We still didn't understand.)

Sibayak Berastagi. He was my guru. Let's play the orchestra so
    she'll come back, he said, said Nandé Laga.

"Because right now"—the daughter added, summarizing the action for
us—"Right now," he said, "she's meditating with the spirits," he said.
Said, "because they called her. So, if she's finished over there, if she's all
ready over there, then if she's called back, she'll come. The spirit will
bring her back to the house."

In the house, straightaway I became entranced. Up and down,
    up and down I went.
So then, because of our longing for one another—
I was the only one—
my mother—

*Taak! "My child!" said my mother. She wanted to grab hold
of me.*
Right away Sibayak Berastagi pushed her aside.
Said, "Don't hold her." Said, "You can't touch her."
*So then no one was allowed to hinder me. I danced to the
orchestra to my heart's content, as far as my strength would
permit, up and down, up and down.*
"So, is it you then, Sibayak?" said the mountain nini

—that is, the spirit who was speaking through Nandé Laga, in trance—

to him, to Uncle.
"It's us indeed, nini," he said.
Said, "Well, hasn't Beru Ginting come home, Sibayak?"
"She has," he said.
Said, "We went to the mountain to meditate and study."
"Well, nini, it's like this, don't take this perch of yours—mean-
ing Nandé Laga—*to the mountain anymore. Can't you med-*
itate here at home?" the sibayak said.
*"The meditation is done." Said, "The studies are completed."
Said, "We can."*
*So I didn't go to the mountain anymore to meditate. I stayed at
home, no more meditation.*
But when I was meditating before, you know—
I'll tell you, OK?
I didn't piss, I didn't pass anything.
That's it.
*I didn't pass anything at all. I didn't eat. I wasn't thirsty. When I
was studying.*
The ninis did that.
Eh. So now you know.
That's how it was with me.

VOICES AND AUDIENCES

On the one hand, we can never know who is speaking or what

is being spoken; on the other, we find a knowledge that tends

to reclassify the alterity that it meets.

—MICHEL DE CERTEAU, "Discourse Disturbed"

In Karo curing rites, offering-ceremonies, and funeral seances, all those
occasions in which spirits are called down to speak to a human audience,
women's bodies most frequently serve as corporeal vehicles for spirit-

pleasure: bodies with which insubstantial entities can eat and drink, engage in dancing and conversation, dress themselves in finery, flirt maybe or play gently ribald pranks, enjoy again the flavor of betel or cigarettes, the odors of cologne and incense. But the spirits' presence leaves little trace: their advice and their pleasures disappear with them; their acts will be repeated, at another time, perhaps through another medium. Like rumors, their uninscribed words are soon forgotten.

The ephemeral voices of spirits speak within a woman's words; their whistling talk sounds in the medium's throat like doves cooing, telling her audience that someone else is speaking. *They say it,* as Nandé Laga said, capturing the referential ambiguity of spirit-talk. *Through my throat.* In Michel de Certeau's (1988:246) paradoxical formulation: " 'There is someone else speaking within me': thus speaks the possessed woman."

Seluk, the Karo term for what we often describe as spirit "possession," ambiguously denotes the intermeshing of awarenesses that occurs when a spirit "alights" on its human host (*peninggeren,* "perch"). As Neumann (1904b:365) notes, *seluk* "actually means to 'put on' something, to 'fit one another,' e.g., to put on a shirt; or: to clasp the hands." To paraphrase Neumann's puzzled conclusion, it is not altogether clear from this usage whether the medium is getting into the spirit or the spirit is getting into the medium.

Conventional wisdom in Karoland as in Western scholarship regularly refers to the "amnesia" that results from the temporary displacement of the medium's everyday self by an invisible, controlling Other. Karo claims to supernatural authority are publicly articulated in this idiom of a distinct and singular someone else who "possesses" the medium's body and speaks in the medium's stead. Privately, though, mediums describe the experience in terms closer to the interhabitational ambiguity of seluk: as a kind of doubled vision, a semidetached awareness at once their own and that of another. Ask a medium directly and she will deny any knowledge of her trance experiences; yet memories of seluk are regularly cited in mediums' conversations, as in (for example) Nandé Laga's story of her return from the mountain. Often there is a blurred identification of medium and spirit: words and experiences that, strictly speaking, should "belong" to the spirit are claimed by the medium as her own; conversely, a spirit may ambiguously identify itself with the experiences and feelings of its human "perch."

Even more than in their own performances, skilled mediums recognize in the practices of their colleagues a fully double-voiced habitation of language. Like a novel told by a narrator or posited author who stands between author and audience, the medium's speech is understood as serving the intentions of two speakers, medium and spirit, simultaneously— with the difference that in the medium's case neither speaker can be said to be "posited" by the other.[23] This double-determined speech is not taken by mediums as a sign of incompetence or duplicity; rather it is an acknowledgment of the inconstancy of the spirits' presence as they skip from one alighting place to another, and of the necessary impact of the conduit medium on the message being transmitted through her.

Nor does the ambiguity of intention end here, for spirit-identities, too, are indeterminate and unstable. Spirits are sometimes merged, at death or thereafter, with another "passenger"-spirit; or they may become attenuated or fragmented in their journey to the human world. Some foreign spirits "bring their own translators" through whom they speak. There are spirit imposters and uninvited guests, hungry and anonymous, looking for a chance to crash someone else's party. Popular spirits like the umangs usually have a number of relatively indistinguishable but inferior doubles (mediums sometimes refer to these as *pesuruh*, "servants") who may pass themselves off to the unaware as the "real thing." The girl-spirits of Nandé Laga's dream, for example, were among many "Beru Karos" who inhabit the lower slopes of Mount Sibayak: the original, "strong" spirits were the two sisters Beru Karo A-Matched-Pair, who died of smallpox and were then carried off by the sympathetic umang-king; the others (Beru Karo Si Rulo, they are called, the multitude of Beru Karos) are their servants and underlings, weak imitators who have absorbed a part of the sisters' experience and enact it as if it were their own, more or less competently. And there may be more dangerous intruders as well: spirits of sorcery, made from fragments of human bodies and deployed by the envious and resentful, who may invisibly haunt a ceremony, hindering entrancement and distorting the messages transmitted through the mediums.

Most of this ambiguity is lost on the medium's audience, who are looking for definitive answers and singular messages. Official interpretations of the medium's words seek a determinate identity for that which speaks through her—a name, a history, a simple, fixed subject-position. Stories about mediums and authorized versions of the medium's experience are told as if such identifications were possible, and any lapse from this clear determination of voice-identity tends to be interpreted by the audience as a sign of either fraud or incompetence on the medium's part.

Mediums do not publicly dispute these monologic accounts; privately, however, they recognize and (as it seemed to me) enjoy this loophole in language, which "open[s] up the possibility of never having to define oneself in language . . . of saying 'I am me' in someone else's language, and in my own language, 'I am other'" (Bakhtin 1981:315). Seluk is not women's empowerment; nor is it a form of resistance to male hegemonic authority. But in its mobile and untranslatable subversion of identity, in the plural voice that speaks through women's throats, there is a chance to escape momentarily from the language of subjects and objects—a language in which women, being neither, are continually left out of the count.

If power consists at least in part in the capacity to define what counts as a story, then the other side of this capacity is the ability to tell a compelling story. Another way of putting this, as Anna Tsing (1990a:122) does with reference to the Meratus Dayaks of Indonesian Borneo, is that "power means . . . the ability to convene an audience." This is not, of course, simply a matter of drawing a crowd, but rather of gaining attentive and comprehending listeners, which requires narrative plausibility as much as strategic self-dramatization. Convening an audience means telling the kind of story that counts for something to those for whom it is intended. It is in this dialogue of plausible voices and convened audiences that narrative experience, ours and others', is constituted.

In this regard there is a story for us within Nandé Laga's story, wedged there between two audiences. The first audience is on the mountaintop: the kids, or umangs, who crowded around but couldn't understand her. *Who cares how many of them there were,* she says, *if they couldn't talk at all?* Nandé Laga's second audience is back at home, where she is allowed to dance to her heart's content, and then is respectfully granted an audience—precisely because it is not she who speaks. These, it seems to me, are the two unsatisfactory poles of women's narrative experience: one may speak for oneself and not be understood, or speak as someone else and convene an audience.

Nowhere in the world are women silent; rarely, I would suspect, have they ever been so. The problem, rather, has been their inability to convene an audience. If we fail to attend to their talking in corners, on the edges, in moments snatched from and cadenced by the demands of everyday labors—and to their speaking at the centers of public discourse, in someone else's words—then we are not simply recording the exclusion of women's voices; we are repeating that exclusion. If we approach women's stories as information-retrieval sites (Spivak 1986:262) in order to reconstruct "women's experience" quite apart from the women whose experience is being appropriated; if we continue to invoke uncritically the universal figure of female subjectivity and to privilege its "authentic" (though perhaps inaccessible) self-inscription in women's artistic or ritual productions; then we will not have resolved the intractable problem of women, but only overwritten its intractability with smooth and coherent images of duplicitous familiarity: woman-as-object, woman-as-commodity, Third World woman.[24]

Like the medium's audience we want to hear stories of autonomous subjects and fixed objects, stories we can comprehend as narratively situated somewhere in particular. Listening for those locatable stories with their independent orphan-heroes and their recognizable beginnings, middles, and ends, we run the risk of missing those which, like Nandé Laga's tellings, are persistently "elsewhere" in our grids and codes. Attending only to the language that we lend her, we fail to apprehend other meanings—mobile, contradictory, "somewhat mad from the standpoint of reason"—in the medium's message. We also fail to note our own complicity in the apparent madness in her narrative method.

The fragmented quality of Nandé Laga's stories may have been as much an effect of my inability to participate fully in the mutual, dialogical construction of shared narrative experience (in that sense we weren't much better than the umang-kids) as of her unfamiliarity with or unwillingness to engage in the kind of coercive storytelling demanded by a quiet and submissive audience. The unease that her stories evoke is almost surely an effect of our own narrative expectations of closure, consistency, and the shaping logic of causal explanation—all of which Nandé Laga's narrative delicately refused to entertain. Part of the apparent disconnectedness of her storytelling may in fact have been produced precisely by our interruptive demands for closure and consistency, our quest for explanation. Other disruptions have been produced in translation, by my need to tell a story compelling to an audience attuned to the language of ethnographic grids and codes.

The questions we have to begin to ask here are thus questions about *our own* voices and audiences. To whom do we, as storytellers, speak? How do we go about constructing a story compelling to that audience? Or, to put it differently, how do we convince our audiences that our stories *are* compelling? More important, we have to begin to reconsider our narrative practice by attending to our own *audiencing practice*. For stories are always shaped, at least in part, to the measure of their audiences, and no storyteller can be entirely free of her audience's intentions and expectations. We need to learn to convene ourselves as someone else's audience, to learn to listen to someone else speaking. And we need to find ways of shaping our stories less to the plausible demands of the ready-made grid and the fully elaborated code and more to the everyday cadences of the perpetual open end.

The "problem of women" thus becomes a problem of what can be lost or found in translation, which is a matter more properly addressed from the relatively modest position of the translator rather than that of the coercive and controlling author. The translator's task, as Walter Benjamin has written, is not simply to convey information to an audience unable to understand the original text. Such an endeavor can only achieve an "inaccurate transmission of an inessential content" while effacing the unfathomable, mysterious "something else" that resides within the text (Benjamin 1969b:70). Perfect linguistic conversion being in any event an impossible goal, a good translation should be shaped literally to the syntax and rhythms of its original despite the interpretive trouble this may cause its audience. This "literalness" has the double effect of producing, in the language of translation, the supplemental "echo" of the original's intended effect, and of rescuing both original and translation from the truth claims of any singular language system. The misshapen and double-voiced language of translation, always "another's speech in another's language" (Bakhtin 1981:324), offers the possibility of critical reflection on our own mode of narrative production.[25]

Western notions of integral selfhood tell us that words, ideas, narrative styles, the texts that we produce and the voices with which we speak, are (or should be) the "private property" of individual consciousness. It is one of the fundamental conventions for coherence in our own narrative practice that the text should appear both as product and as replica of the unified and self-identical "subject"/author. From this perspective the medium's (or translator's) statement, "It is not I who speak/s," is a meaningless proposition.

But we can consider this matter of narrative "possession" from a rather different angle. Like the medium's speech, the word in language, as Bakhtin puts it, is always "half someone else's." Appropriated from another's context and inhabited by one's own intentions, words can become, in speech, one's temporary (and partial) possession—although here too, as in the medium's loophole language, it is not clear in which direction such discursive "possession" operates. Not all words, Bakhtin continues,

> submit equally easily to this appropriation, to this seizure and transformation into private property: many words stubbornly resist, others remain alien, sound foreign in the mouth of the one who appropriated them and who now speaks them; they cannot be assimilated into [this] context and fall out of it; it is as if they put themselves in quotation marks against the will of the speaker. *Language is not a neutral medium that passes freely and easily into the private property of the speaker's intentions; it is populated—over-populated—with the intentions of others.* (Bakhtin 1981:293–94; emphasis added)

If we take the medium's indeterminate message as a guide for moving away from a language of unified subjects and experiential authenticity, we may be able to open up a collaborative loophole within the grids and codes, for a heteroglot multitude of fragmented, mobile, and only dubiously truthful voices—our own included. As mediums recognize, voices are never singular, meaning is always negotiated, and there is room enough in any story for someone else's speaking. Though Nandé Laga's story has been reshaped to the contours of a foreign tongue, and her words to the enduring forms of a printed text, there should remain the trace of her intention, someone else speaking, within my twice-told tales.

A garlic trader tells a compelling story to a pair of strangers with a tape recorder: *Then, when I didn't come home, your uncle searched everywhere, all the fields of our village. He looked in every tree, because maybe she's hung herself, he thought. Two days. Then they went to Berastagi. Said, she's lost, Sibayak. Said, a disaster for Gurusinga. Two nights, after two nights I'd come back, he said. Two nights. Play the gendang-orchestra, he said. So she'll come now. Said, are you sure she'll come, Sibayak? Sure, he said. Don't make a fuss, my child. I'm here. My child, he didn't even cry. For those two nights he didn't cry at all, they said.*

Later those strangers learn that perhaps the story wasn't "true" at all, that Nandé Laga's original spirit helpers may not have been the benevolent and generous keramats of Mount Sibayak but rather the notoriously bad-tempered spirits of nearby Deleng Kutu. Or so another medium insists. Narrative experience is always situated in a complex web of intentions and plausibilities.

But to properly understand Nandé Laga's story (that is, according to *her* intentions rather than someone else's), I would have to shift my attention away from its situated plausibility—how, after all, does one get to the bottom of reported encounters with spirits?—to the indeterminate elsewhere marked, for me, by her voice calling: *I'm here.* Attending to that claim to "count for something," I would be directed not to explanations but to effects, not to what made the story happen but to what the story makes happen—and not to the convening of an audience but rather to the making of a decent living. Moving from a narrative to a material locus of empowerment, I would then call attention to the broader dimensions of women's possession and women's property—and to the autonomy as well as the alienation engendered in the trader's life. And so I would turn, as Nandé Laga does at the very end of her narrative, from the spirits of the mountain to the medium of the marketplace.

> *That's the history, my child*
> *I was lost, I was carried off by the ninis, that's the history.*
> *I came home, Uncle was calling me in the house,*
> *playing the gendang in Gurusinga.*

I came from Mount Sibayak.
Nini brought me on horseback,
I saw it just like that. . . .
That man was really handsome, too—
even now he comes all the time, child.
If that handsome one comes in a rush, the one I call "Tuanku
    Erkuda"—"Milord-on-Horseback"—
I usually make a profit on my trading.
If he's come.
That's the history of how I became a curer, child.

Seven

A Storyteller

SOMETIMES a refuge can be hard to find. Pak Tua found one, for a while, in the town of Bandar Baru, which is actually a strip of the Berastagi road just below the Daulu turnoff. In 1904 Bandar Baru was the scene of one of the few skirmishes between Karo defenders and colonial troops coming from Medan to "pacify" the unruly highlanders, but now it is a roadside fringe of coffeeshops, restaurants, a few small stores—one of which advertises "authentic Batak primitive art"—and a great many pastel-painted tourist cottages, each bearing the sign: Bungalow. Farther along are a string of "barracks"—shabby, anonymous buildings whose residents are the prostitutes who are the source of most of the tourist bungalows' transient business.

Pak Tua was staying in one of these barracks, a green one he had euphemistically described to us as his friend's "workshop." He was there on some business, the precise nature of which he left unspecified but had to do with the opening of another workshop farther up the road. Looking distinguished in a once-white sport coat, he greeted us in his usual warm but slightly formal manner, which was much the same way that he treated the girls playing cards in the back room while they waited for customers. "They're nice girls," he lectured us. "They're polite and considerate of our feelings, so we should be considerate of theirs, and not embarrass them. The matter of their work, that's between them and God."

"Pak Tua," which means "elder uncle," was what the girls called him; it was only one of the many names he was known by. Elsewhere he was called Pa Rango, "Father Dice," or Pa Suling, "Father Flute," which described his usual occupations, gambling and music.[1] He had been a professional singer-dancer, a perkolong-kolong, but now, at sixty-seven, his voice had roughened and anyway, he said, no one wanted to watch an old man dance. "My mother never wanted me to work," he once told me, to which he added thoughtfully, "Maybe she went too far." He showed his hands, which were not the hardened hands of a farmer. "I've never done any honest work in my life. I'm a thief. You say no, but what else do you call a man who's spent his whole life in coffeeshops playing the flute?"

Now he was a guru, and what he was doing in Bandar Baru was selling medicines that his wife, back at home, prepared from the herbs that he gathered.

This particular meeting had been arranged so that we could record one of the old stories that Pak Tua had learned as a child from his father, who had also been a guru. But that, he decided, would have to wait till another time. The atmosphere was not right, what with the interruptions of occasional customers and the merely curious, who would pop in the open door for a moment and stand silently watching, or peer in the window, or, more casually, stroll by with a look of studied disinterest. There was also the distracting roar of buses and trucks along the highway and the snarling back-and-forth passage of the town's motorcycle-riding informal security forces.

What you need most for telling a story, Pak Tua said, is time. You can't rush a story. You have to go back, repeat, detour, go back again. Pak Tua makes a story like a fisherman makes a net—a knot here, twist to the side, follow this line and that, bring them together. There are long digressions: in the story someone drops an axe, and Pak Tua has to tell you how that axe is made, and the proper way to use it, how the cut and the felling of the tree fit into a larger pattern of events and how one reads the future in the tree's falling, how the tree felled becomes a part of a house, how the house becomes a part of the world. Only then can the axe be picked up again.

Stories like this Pak Tua learned from his father, when he was young, the father telling a part of the tale every night, and then the son telling the father, in turn, the same story the next morning, the father correcting his mistakes. These old stories, which are called *turi-turin*, are like intricate webs, tracing the tangled working of fate through generations, as people become caught up in one another's lives and in the lives of the spirits, until, finally, the threads are pulled together and there is a momentary resolution, in which the pattern of fate emerges clearly, if temporarily. They might be called myths, though Karo call them "history."

Karo gloss the term *turi-turin* with the Malay word *sejarah*, "history," rather than *cerita*, the word for "story." But neither comprehensively covers the word's meaning, and turi-turin might better be translated as "an orderly sequential arrangement." The base word *turi* means "order," as in the phrase, *si serbut bagé la kenan turin*, "what's tangled will not be put in order." Weather that does not follow an orderly pattern, when it rains in the dry season or there is drought in the wet season, has no turi-turin; the incoherence of a lunatic's speech is described in the same way. The turi-turin of a ritual is its performative sequence, the arrangement of objects within the temporal frame of the ceremony, and also the narrative that underlies that particular ordering of objects and acts.

A musical suite may also be called a turi-turin. The *Turi-turin lima puluh kurang dua*, the turi-turin of fifty less two, is, as the name indicates, a suite of forty-eight melodic segments. The most complex of the Karo repertoire, this suite was performed by the five-piece gendang orchestra at the opening of a new house. Each segment describes musically a particular phase in the construction and settlement of the house, establishing an atmosphere of ordered sound within which disorderly influences—spirit-inhabitants of the house's materials, conflicts between resident families—become audible. The power of the musical turi-turin lay in its "words"—which are not expressed in speech or song, nor even in the melody of the seruné, but rather comprise the emotional "narrative" that emerges in the seruné-player's heart as he plays.[2]

The turi-turin are the stories that lie beneath the work of the guru; they tell of the beginnings of medicine, of the sources of magical power, of the "order of things." In their telling alone, Pak Tua said, they can cure, and he sometimes used these stories to heal those who were sick, enfolding the patient's experience within the experience of the story, knotting up the here-and-now of the tale's telling with the narrative net of always-and-ever. He told me some of these stories, but the one I want to repeat here is not one of those. Rather, I want to tell a part of Pak Tua's own story, which has to do with the thread that cannot be knotted, the dropped axe that cannot be picked up. It is a story, you might say, about the decline of storytelling.

AUTHENTIC BATAK ART

"Less and less frequently," Walter Benjamin (1969a:83) writes, "do we encounter people with the ability to tell a tale properly." The storytelling situation—that mutual engagement of teller and listener—is vanishing, leaving behind only an uncomfortable reminder of the failure of communication that Benjamin saw as an intrinsic part of modern life. "It is as if something that seemed inalienable to us, the securest among our possessions, were taken from us: the ability to exchange experiences." In the place of the reciprocal experience of the story we have the solitary form of communication that is the novel, and the mass form of communication, which Benjamin describes as "information." "Every morning," he writes, "brings us news of the globe, and yet we are poor in noteworthy stories. This is because no event any longer comes to us without already being shot through with explanation. In other words, by now almost nothing that happens benefits storytelling; almost everything benefits information" (ibid.:89).

Listening and telling are integrally linked in the art of the storyteller.

For Benjamin, the decline of storytelling is the end point of a long process whereby the *hearing* of stories, the relaxed attentiveness necessary to commend another's story to memory and thus to repeat it in turn, becomes impossible. The memorableness of a story, as opposed to the transience of information, is rooted in its lack of explanation:

> Actually, it is half the art of storytelling to keep a story free from explanation as one reproduces it. . . . The most extraordinary things, marvelous things, are related with the greatest accuracy, but the psychological connection of the events is not forced on the reader. It is left up to him to interpret things the way he understands them, and thus the narrative achieves an amplitude that information lacks. (Ibid.)

The mutual engagement of storyteller and audience, that which constitutes the listener as a partner in the story's creation and as a future teller of the tale as well—which is what Pak Tua means when he says that a turi-turin has a healing power of its own—this is what explanation destroys.

It is not, of course, that the dissemination of information in itself has caused the breakdown in storytelling. Rather, information fills the void into which storytelling has disappeared; it responds to, as well as creates, a different kind of attention, a fragmented awareness that is itself a token of the shattering of the reciprocity of experience—and also the gift that seems to make that loss bearable.

Proper listening, thus proper telling, is intimately connected with the long rhythms and cycles of work, in which leisure and labor are inextricably bound together. And it is one of the many ironies of Pak Tua's situation that this man who insisted he had never done an honest day's work in his life could so perfectly evoke that rhythm in all its calm intricacy. More than anything, that was his art, which could enmesh even one (myself) who had probably had even less experience with those complex rhythms than Pak Tua would claim for himself. It was, precisely, an evocation: calling up something that had only an imaginary place in the world, whose place had perhaps never been more than an imaginary one, but which, at least for the time of the telling, seemed so right that one could not doubt its reality. We who listened became, it seemed, a part of that rhythm. Benjamin writes: "The more self-forgetful the listener is, the more deeply is what he listens to impressed on his memory. When the rhythm of work has seized him, he listens to the tales in such a way that the gift of retelling them comes to him all by itself" (ibid.:91). And my friends could sometimes repeat Pak Tua's tales afterwards (he would only allow tape recording in formal storytelling sessions, because conversation, he said, was not meant to be preserved), reproducing even his intonations and turns of phrase, the odd circuitous paths the story followed, the points where the narrative thread was dropped and where it was picked up again.

And when the story ended, we could also feel the absence of that rightness—the rightness of shared experience—in the world around us, where experience has become solitary, fragmented. Pak Tua often talked about that disjuncture between the shared experience of the story and the solitary, unshareable experience of living in a world where there is nothing to listen to anymore, and nothing to tell, a world where the turi-turin is a nostalgic interlude rather than a pattern picked from the fabric of daily life. "The old ways, the old stories," he told us that day in Bandar Baru, "they can't be discarded. But they can't be followed either." Which explains as well as anything does, I suppose, what he was doing peddling remedies in a brothel.

Turi-turin have not lost their value; indeed, their value may have increased, at least for those of us for whom they have the least to say. But what has been lost is their usefulness. Every real story, Benjamin says, contains something useful, which may be practical advice, or moral guidance, or simply an understanding of the way things happen. This is what the turi-turin are about, but their advice, as Pak Tua told us, can no longer be followed. And Benjamin says the same:

> In every case the storyteller is a man who has counsel for his readers. But if today "having counsel" is beginning to have an old-fashioned ring, this is because the communicability of experience is decreasing. In consequence we have no counsel either for ourselves or for others. After all, counsel is less an answer to a question than a proposal concerning the continuation of a story which is just unfolding. To seek this counsel one would first have to be able to tell the story. (Ibid.:86)

Pak Tua's story is precisely concerned with his search for counsel, a search that requires the ability to tell of his experience, in a world where the counsel of the old stories no longer speaks to that experience, where the experience itself is uncertain. But it is not just the communicability of experience that is at issue here. The question is, ultimately, what sort of counsel can be offered, or followed, in such a world.

IDENTIFICATION CARD

"Do you know, I don't have my identification card [I., *Kartu Penduduk*, KTP] yet," Pak Tua said. This was one of his favorite anecdotes, which he told often, laughing at his own recalcitrance. "Why? I'll tell you. I went to get it, you know, to the village head"—who is Pak Tua's wife's brother, a sincere young man who takes his job very seriously—"and I answered all the questions. But there's a place on the card for your religion, you know? 'You have to tell us what religion you follow,' he said. 'I don't know,' I said, 'What are the choices?' 'Islam, Christian, Buddhist, Hindu, Perbégu,' he said. 'Oh. Well. Put me down for all of them,' I said. All of them! 'Oh, we can't do that,' he said, 'We can't do that, you have to choose one. Only one.'

"Well, how could I pick just one? 'I can't do that,' I said. 'They're all the same, I believe in all of them. All religions are good, aren't they?' I said."

(Here Pak Tua was offering a delicate reminder to his brother-in-law—and to us—of the official Indonesian government policy of religious tolerance. The first and second sections of article 29 of the Indonesian constitution state that: "The State shall be based upon belief in the all-embracing God"; and "The State shall guarantee the freedom of the people to profess and exercise their own religion" [cited in Mahadi 1987: 216]. This formulation was a compromise reached between those who favored and those who opposed the establishment of a Muslim state, a compromise that entailed "making Indonesia an expressly religious nation without making any particular faith the religion of the state" [Kipp and Rodgers 1987:16–17].[3] The contradiction implicit in the principle of "religious tolerance"—that no [monotheistic] religion may be officially defined as superior to any other, but that each citizen must believe that one of these is superior to the others—was what Pak Tua was addressing here.)

"All religions are good, I told him. I respect them all. If I'm in a mosque, I pray in the Islamic style, if I'm with Christians, I pray like the Christians do. If I'm in a keramat's place I offer betel. And so on. It's all the same and I can't choose between them. So you just list them all. That's what I said. 'That means you don't have faith in any of them,' he said. 'You figure it out for yourself,' I said. So that's how it is, I have five religions, but I don't have an ID card."

Choosing a religion is a serious matter, said Pak Tua, because how can we know we've made the right choice? If you choose one, then automatically that means that you think it's better than the others. And what if you're wrong? Then you're really in a fix!

What if you're wrong?

Uncertainty seems a natural outgrowth of a time of revolution, though it hardly begins there. For Benjamin, it was upon the battlefields of the

Great War that the process long underway, which he describes as the declining communicability of experience, first became apparent in Europe:

> Was it not noticeable at the end of the war that men returned from the battlefield grown silent—not richer, but poorer in communicable experience? . . . For never has experience been contradicted more thoroughly than strategic experience by tactical warfare, economic experience by inflation, bodily experience by mechanical warfare, moral experience by those in power. (Benjamin 1969a:84)

And so it was too with the Indonesian Revolution. At first there was a sense of freedom, an escape not only from colonial exploitation and Japanese oppression, but from all of the restraints of the past: from the invisible chains of tradition as much as from the more concrete bonds of imperialism. There was the euphoric rhetoric of *Merdeka atau Mati*, freedom or death, and glorious promises for the future: abundance, equality, electricity everywhere, an end to taxation and corvée labor (Surbakti 1977:43–44). There was an exhilarating rush of new possibilities, embodied in new terms, such as *kedaulatan rakyat*, the sovereignty of the people, which came to have a more ominous ring in the coined term *pendaulatan*, a euphemism for vigilante "justice." Place names that "smelled" of feudalism were replaced with properly democratic-sounding ones: the village of Juma Raja, "the fields of the *raja*," became Cinta Rakyat, "love of the people." Even Mount Sibayak was (temporarily) renamed Deleng Rakyat, the People's Mountain.[4] But there was a gap between revolutionary experience and the rhetoric of revolution, and this gap was filled by rumors, information without a source, which explained the experience of others either as victimizing or as victimized, and attributed the failed promises of revolutionary rhetoric—as well as the spread of rumors aimed at confusing and demoralizing the movement—to the efforts of mysterious "enemy agents" at work within the population.[5]

Except for a common commitment to "Merdeka atau Mati," there was little unity in the revolutionary movement in Karoland, or indeed throughout East Sumatra.[6] The initial armed resistance to the reestablishment of colonial rule following the Japanese surrender came from radical urban youth groups, some of which were little more than street gangs, loosely associated through the umbrella organization BPI (Barisan Pemuda Indonesia, the Indonesian Youth Brigade). This unity, tenuous at best, lasted only a few months. When the formation of political parties was legalized by the Proclamation of November 3, 1945, BPI affiliated with the moderate Indonesian Socialist party—then the ruling party of the Western-oriented intellectual elite—and took the new name Pesindo, Socialist Youth of Indonesia (Reid 1974:80; Surbakti 1977:84). Other parties subsequently formed their own militia organizations, and ideological differences, as well as personal and ethnic rivalries, fissured the revolutionary movement. The relative autonomy of these paramilitary units led not only to a lack of coordination of efforts, but also to conflicts among these groups, which were competing for members, political influence, and, above all, weapons.[7]

Pak Tua served during the revolution as a company commander in the Barisan Harimau Liar, the "Wild Tiger Brigade." BHL, an offshoot of the Karo branch of BPI/Pesindo, had been formed in December 1945 after a bitter dispute over BPI leadership. Associated with the grassroots nationalism of the PNI (Partai Nasional Indonesia) rather than the watered-down internationalist Marxism of the pro-Western ruling Socialist party,[8] the BHL drew its support from the most alienated, and least controllable, segment of the Karo population—the rural and semiurban lumpenproletariat. The organization was led by officers trained under the charismatic captain of the Japanese *Kempetei* (secret police), Inoue Tetsuro. These men had been members of Inoue's short-lived *Kenkokutai*, an independent "secret commando corps" formed in the final days of the Japanese occupation in preparation for an expected Allied invasion, and had been indoctrinated in Inoue's particular ideological blend of ultra-nationalism, extreme discipline, commitment to self-sacrifice in the nationalist cause, and an "almost mystical belief" in the peasantry as the spiritual core of society (Reid and Akira 1986:79).[9] Volatile and anti-establishment, BHL was seen—at least by their political opponents—as a disruptive element in the struggle for independence.

Pak Tua admits that the BHL units were difficult to control, but he argues that the fundamental problem between Harimau Liar and the other groups was one of class: "You have to understand what our troops were like. They had no experience with military discipline. In the military, if your commander says, do this, you have to obey immediately without thinking. But our troops would ask, 'Why?' They wanted to know what was going on. You'd say, 'March to Bohorok now,' and they'd say, 'Let's eat first.' These boys were mostly uneducated. Just imagine, their commandant (me!) was illiterate! Those who had some education went into Pesindo,[10] or the better ones into the army. Automatically, they tended to be from the upper classes, and a lot of them were *féodal*."[11]

"Feudalism," another of the incantatory terms of revolutionary rhetoric, broadly defined the hierarchy of power that the revolution was supposed to sweep away. It included the wealthy Malay aristocracy, the Dutch-educated and allegedly pro-Western intellectuals, the local elite whose wealth and political authority had been created and maintained by the colonial state. The rhetoric of Merdeka offered dazzling new possibilities to choose among, a new world to be built, and "feudalism" was whatever limited those possibilities.

The young peasants of BHL, who were at the bottom of this "feudal" hierarchy before the revolution, had little patience with either the "remnants" of the old feudal system that they saw around them or with the new feudal order that seemed to be emerging within the revolutionary movement itself. A. R. Surbakti, one of the early Pesindo leaders, writes of Harimau Liar activities:

> Several of its members, primarily those that were in the villages, acted violently towards those that they considered counterrevolutionaries. The village chiefs that at that time were called "pengulu" and whose office was inherited, were felt to be too slow in their movements in following the rhythm of the revolution, and because of that some of them were suspected and were "pacified" [i.e., murdered] by the youths. (Surbakti:1977:93)

Harimau Liar groups, or members, seem to have been involved in some of the more egregious acts of violence committed against civilians in Karoland during the period, most notably against evacuees from other parts of East Sumatra following the "First Dutch Aggression" of 1947.[12] According to Jamin Gintings, the TNI (Tentera Negara Indonesia, the Indonesian army) regimental commander in Karoland, these "ill-considered actions" against the evacuees were the result of rumors that "intellectuals and aristocrats" within the refugee groups were collaborating with the Dutch (Gintings 1975:38). And the rumors of such "antifeudal" pendaulatan operations and of military reprisals against these created an atmosphere of growing suspicion and fear, a spiral of antagonism and distrust. When, following the Renville Accord of 1948, the army acted to "rationalize" the military by consolidating the various militia groups within the TNI, this move was opposed by all the parties involved. In South Tapanuli, where the BHL troops were then stationed, it led to a virtual civil war (van Langenberg 1976:701–31; Harahap 1986:47–52; Edisaputra 1985:201–11).[13]

These internal tensions did not end with the final settlement of hostilities with the Dutch in 1950. The postrevolutionary struggle was mostly set within the arena of political parties and the peasant unions and squatters' organizations associated with these. The formation of political parties had been legalized in 1945 because, as Vice-President Hatta neatly put it, "with such parties every current of thought which exists in society can be guided into an orderly path" (cited in Reid 1979:172). Party membership was seen as an almost obligatory part of *demokrasi*, even when the politics involved were not all that clear.

Party formation in Karoland represented less an "orderly path" than a continuation of the various conflicts of the revolution, in which personal ties, antipathies and vendettas, intervillage relations, ethnic and religious differences, and class interests all came into play and were fought out.

PNI continued to be the strongest party in Karoland, but its hegemony was seriously challenged by the Communist party, and the political line between the two was often somewhat blurred. The internecine conflicts that had flourished in the revolution continued, though they were largely kept under control by the army until 1965, when, in the wake of the presumed Communist coup attempt of September 30, mass reprisals against suspected PKI members and supporters occurred (*Gestok*). This ended not only the continuing role of the PKI and associated groups, including the left wing of PNI, in Indonesian political life, but indeed of most local involvement in party politics.

As was the case elsewhere in Indonesia, many of the Karo victims of anti-Communist violence were only minimally aware of the larger political issues involved. "We were all in parties," Pak Tua said, "but you know how village people are. The recruiter would come and say, 'Here's a new hoe,' and they'd sign up. That was all they knew. Then came Gestok and they were all *done for*. After that, I didn't want to have anything more to do with political parties.

"And, you see, this is why I don't want to choose a religion. Because if you can get in that much trouble in this world by joining a political party, how much worse is it going to be when you get to the next world and find out that you've made the wrong choice there?"

THE HURT-FEELINGS BRIGADE

Holding fast to the tail end of the revolution, some of the demobilized militia units refused to disband following the "rationalization" of the army. Instead they formed *gerombolan*, bandit bands, robbing travelers along the Berastagi road as part of their continuing struggle against feudalism. These guerillas-turned-bandits were known locally as the *Barisan Sakit Hati*, the "Hurt-Feelings Brigade."[14]

"They weren't just random bandits," said Pak Tua. "Feudalists, profiteers, and secret collaborators, those were the targets, but there were mistakes too. Say you wanted to rob a tax collector—we'll call him Pak A.—who was supposed to be taking a particular bus from Kabanjahé to Medan. If you were in a hurry, which you usually were, you might not have time to figure out which of the passengers was Pak A., so you'd just rob them all.

"Sometimes there were other problems too. For example, suppose this gerombolan boss B. tells C., who is one of his men, to rob the traitor A. He does it. He gets Rp. 30,000, which he gives to his boss. But A., the traitor, tells someone that he was robbed of Rp. 100,000. B. believes this; why would the man make a false claim? So he decides that C. has kept the rest of the money, that he's a traitor, and orders his execution. Then C.'s friends think that B.'s a traitor, and so on."

The gerombolan, with their rather freewheeling approach to "popular sovereignty" and "social justice," certainly contributed to the postrevolutionary atmosphere of uncertainty in Karoland. Personal vendettas and rivalries, local conflicts, resentment, suspicion, and secrecy, all rippled out from their actions, spreading like rumors through the liquid social expanse. But their actions, as Pak Tua's remarks indicate, were also inspired by that sense of uncertainty. Mistaken identity was the order of the day in a time when, to use a Karo metaphor, experience was *like the flight of the pale butterfly, or even the speckled butterfly, above the wide, lonely sea: it's not that there's no room for flying, a landing place is what is lacking.*

By the late 1950s most of the gerombolan had been "pacified" or had, in the rhetoric of the period, "returned willingly to society." One of these "repentant" brigands described, through the medium of the press, the situation in which he and his fellows had found themselves at the conclusion of the revolution:

> Djumpa Tarigan explained that since the Proclamation [of Independence] he had been a member of the popular militia . . . On January 1 1949 he became a member of the TNI [the Indonesian Army] and on 27 December 1949 he was sent home just as he was, in a situation that was lacking everything, so that even his pants were in tatters. Then *since he felt dissatisfied by his reception and direction, because there was none,* he and his friends founded the People's Brigade of the Republic of Indonesia. That organization, as Tiga Sembiring and Ndakar Tarigan also emphasized, was only intended to struggle to improve their fate and absolutely did not have a political background, as had previously been rumored. ("Kembali kemasjarakat karena keinsjafan," *Waspada*, March 25, 1952; emphasis added)

This lack of "reception and direction"—official terminology that might be translated into a simpler phrase: "no jobs"—is the rhetorical mold within which the public image of the gerombolan is given an official shape; it is the constricted landing place offered for their experience. The Returned Fugitive, the tattered and dissatisfied ex-soldier of the Hurt-Feelings Brigade struggling to "improve his fate" and that of his friends, but without any political motives "as had previously been rumored," is a simple figure, and the solution to his plight is also a simple one: to "receive and direct" him to his proper slot in the social order.

> In the meeting yesterday afternoon, the Police Chief of the Province of North Sumatra stated that their reception will be carried out free from all sentiments and feelings of revenge, and expressed the government's joyful accep-

tance of the desire of those who truly wished to return to society. . . . A large number of them wish to return to their villages because they have families, but there are also those who hope to get jobs. *Everything will be decided according to the potential of each respectively.* But nevertheless it all depends on their own wishes, whether they want to become ordinary laborers or become members of the police or army. (Ibid.; emphasis added)

"According to the potential of each": the phrase, embedded in rich rhetoric of the government's "joyful" acceptance of the gerombolan back into society, has all the flat matter-of-factness of an official judgment. And what it says is that those who were on the bottom before the revolution will come out of it still on the bottom—not because of any failure of the dazzling possibilities of Merdeka, but because their own "wishes" and "potential" (or lack thereof) choose that place for them.

It is precisely in this gap between the rhetoric of official "reception and direction" on the one hand and the illusory freedom of individual potential and individual desires on the other that Pak Tua located his postrevolutionary decision to become a gambler, gently revealing in the process the inadequacy of either to define his experience. "When the revolution ended," he said, "we all had to decide what we wanted to do. They asked each of us. Some said, I want to be a *camat* [a subdistrict officer]. Others, police, or military, or whatever. Well, what could I say? That was when they found out I was illiterate. I thought, you can't have a camat who can't read or write. So when they asked me, I said, I'll just be a gambler. I can't do anything else because I can't read. They were amazed. But you're a company commander, they said. I've got adjutants, don't I? They took care of all the paper work, I said. But if I become a gambler, I told them, you can do this for me: don't arrest me. I had lots of friends in high places."

A SCHOOLGIRL'S CHOICE

One's fate is not private property; it is enmeshed in the fate of others, in the wide field of lived social relations. Just as the gerombolan's struggles to "improve their fate" ricochet off and through the lives of other people, so too Pak Tua's decision to become a gambler affects, and is affected by, other lives. There are the "friends in high places" who tolerate his actions; there are his fellow gamblers, winners and losers in their own particular efforts to improve their fate. Above all, there are the members of his family, whose fates depend on his success or failure—as his fate depends on theirs. And all of these people are equally a part of other intricate webworks of intertwined experience, so that one cannot be separated from the others, and none can be separated from the total pattern that, together, they create.

When Pak Tua's wife told Juara Ginting and me of her own experience during the gerombolan time, she also spoke of fate, and of how her fate was produced in a particular conjuncture of events and circumstances. Here, from the perspective of the hearth, the pattern seems different, more prosaic and more confining. There are no dashing brigands or romantic fugitives, no promises of a glorious future, only the everyday dilemmas of a young schoolgirl (and a great beauty, too) in a time of trouble. She too made a decision, to marry Pak Tua, but it was no freer a choice than his decision to become a gambler.

"You may have noticed," she said simply, "that we're not really comparable. He's much older than I am, and of course he doesn't look like much either.

"This is how we happened to marry. I honestly didn't want to marry him. I was still in junior high school when we first met, he was already old and had already been married many times. At that time he was living with my *nandé tengah* [middle FBW]. When we met he was hanging around with my *turang* [classificatory brother], who introduced us. We talked for a bit, till I could politely leave. I had work to do, I said. After I'd left he told my *turang* that I was the girl he'd been looking for and he wanted to marry me. I was just a kid!

"Then he started coming to our house, he'd always bring presents, meat maybe, or whatever. Back then he always had a lot of money. This was in the gerombolan time, and he was friends with all the bandits, and also with the police, so he had plenty of money. He was a singer, and a gambler, so he knew everyone.

"My family was impressed, but I didn't like him. He'd bring us meat and tell me to cook it. 'I don't know how to cook,' I'd say. When he came I'd stay in the kitchen. I had no intention of marrying him. I had a boyfriend at that time, too. Then he started telling everyone that we were married, that I was his wife. I'd meet his friends in the market and they'd call me '*turangku*' (WBW).[15] I was so embarrassed!

"And since everyone thought we were married, no one else wanted to marry me. Nobody's ever going to take me, I thought. What could I do? Finally I decided, better to just marry him than to be stuck in the middle like this. At that time, too, people were scared to go to market. I figured if I was his wife I'd be safe.

"We got married, and then I really hated him! I wanted to leave, but I already had a baby. As soon as this baby is big enough, I'll go home, I thought. But when it was old enough for me to leave there was already another one, then another, and so on. Six in all. Then when they were all grown, I thought, what's the use anymore? We'd already gotten used to one another, and where would I go anyway? It's just my fate, I have to accept it, I decided. But you can see yourself what he's like! He doesn't know how to work! Everything we've got I've earned myself. And he's illiterate. But if your fate's like that, what can you do?

"And the children take after him too. Not one of them is right."

Kindling in a Hearth-Rack

In 1972 Pak Tua "switched to the herb business." His gambling luck had gone bad. With his old friends in high places either dead or retired, he had to worry about being arrested, too. His mind was confused, he said, and there were lots of problems, one stacked on the other like kindling in a hearth-rack: the dry wood is not yet used up, but has to be burned along with the green wood. Pak Tua's friend and colleague Masin put it more simply: "He was ruined, totally ruined. He'd lost everything gambling."

So Pak Tua figured he could put to use what he remembered of his father's teachings. "If my father made medicines he'd have me sit next to him and watch, or help. I learned a lot like that, observing. But it's all sort of half-assed, you see, because finally he didn't teach me the real core of the guru's power." Seeking that core of power, Pak Tua went to Mount Sibayak, to the dead pool known as Si Biangsa, where Guru Penawar threw away all his magic. But, as Guru Penawar also found out, there are some problems that all the power in the world cannot fix.

"There was a time, you see, when my mind was confused, nothing seemed to be going right. There were maybe twenty gurus, I asked them all. One said this, and the other said that, another said something else. None of them seemed right to me. Then there was one old woman, her name was Nandé Pusuh. She was a guru, and her son was a friend of mine. So I met this friend, he said his mother really didn't want to work as a guru anymore, but maybe she would help me anyway.

"We went to see her, I went with her son, and we figured our kinship relations. That's the proper way to do it. I was her [classificatory] kalimbubu, we reckoned. So she said, since it's like that, let's ask about your problem. 'Please, auntie (bibi, FZ), give me your betel pouch,' I said. So I could prepare betel for her jinujung. 'Oh no,' she said, 'You're our kalimbubu, that's not proper. I'll do it for you,' she said. So she prepared the betel and her jinujung came, speaking through her throat. It was Beru Ginting, from Tongging. 'You haven't tended your kalimbubu's family shrine. There is the problem.'

" 'Which kalimbubu?' I said. Because, you see, there are many kalimbubu. 'You have to answer that yourself. But we can make a test. Get a
bundle of betel leaves, a piece of white cloth, and rice. Get the ingredients
for betel-chewing.' She said.

"We got them, me and my friend. We made the preparations and
wrapped the betel in the white cloth. 'Come back in four days,' she said.
'Pay attention to your dreams.'

"Well, there weren't any dreams. I came back in four days, and we
looked at the betel leaves. Two bunches were rotten. Two were rotten,
and one was moist and two more were still fresh. We asked again, like
before. So Beru Ginting came again, and she said the same thing: 'You've
neglected your kalimbubu's shrine.' And she said: 'You have many sins in
your thoughts.'

"I denied it. I'd never done anything to hurt anyone, I said. But I knew
in my heart, even though I didn't say so. I thought, even if I haven't meant
to hurt anyone, what about the children whose fathers I'd ruined with
gambling? Who had lost all their money, or had to sell their land or
house? I didn't say anything, but she still said, 'Ask for their forgiveness.'
How could I do that, when I didn't even know who they were, or where?
'Ask their forgiveness,' she said, 'and also tend to your kalimbubu's
shrine. That's the way to end the trouble.'

"So I went home. I offered to pay her, but she didn't want anything.
'You're my kalimbubu,' she said. 'I can't take your money.'

"I went to meet my kalimbubu. I asked about their shrine; they'd built
a house on top of it. So it couldn't be tended anymore. My other kalimbubu, they were all Christian, so their shrines couldn't be tended either.

"Then I thought: there is one other one. That was my mother's father,
he had been a guru. I went to see his family, to look at his things. He had
been a guru, so he had all sorts of things; a magic staff, a book, all sorts
of things. Now they were just stuck in a closet. I asked if I could borrow
them, to take care of them properly.

"So, I got some *rimo mungkur* [rough-skinned lime, *Citrus hystrix*], I
cleaned them all carefully, I went to sleep beside them. I slept beside them,
but there was still no dream.

"Well, then, after a while I thought, I'm a wanderer, I can't just stay at
home, I have to travel around. So these things, it's better if my brother
keeps them. He was a guru too.

"I started wandering again. My thoughts were still confused. Then finally I went to Mount Sibayak, I meditated for seven days. For seven days
I didn't eat or drink. I cut off all my hair and left it there, in a hole in the
rock, as an offering.

"Well, I looked pretty funny, what with my hair all gone, and not
having eaten anything for a week. There's a village near there, Daulu,

and I stopped there on my way home. They didn't know what I was! They thought I was a keramat, or an umang! 'Only three people have ever stayed there at Si Biangsa,' they said. 'The first was the Guru Pakpak Pitu Perdalanen, the second was Guru Penawar, and you're the third.'

"There was a woman who was sick. I didn't know her at all. They wanted me to treat her. So I thought about it. Well, what should I do? I'm a stranger here, I don't know what their intentions are. I'm not sure what to do.

" 'Ah, don't bother with her,' said her husband. 'If she dies, she dies. I can always get another wife.'

"This family is definitely not right, I thought. If I treat her, maybe the husband will be mad. But what should I do? I thought, better to keep my knowledge to myself. So I just said, 'If I had some *cekala* [a kind of sour fruit], I could treat her with that.' There was none there. 'Or else, I can use marquisa fruit.' None either. Who ever heard of treating someone with cekala? But it works too. That's what I was inspired to say. I don't know why.

" 'We could go to Berastagi and get it,' they said. I didn't really want them to go. 'Or, if you don't have that, even rimo mungkur will do.' Finally they sent to Berastagi and got a rimo mungkur. I sprinkled her with the juice, and she woke up right away!

" 'Oh!' she said. She was surprised that there were so many people there, she didn't know what had happened. So she got right up and made tea for us all.

"So when I got home, my own wife was sick. She was sick a lot back then, the spirits used to bother her all the time. I said, 'Where's my brother? Why hasn't he come to take care of her?' 'He hasn't come,' they said. 'We called him, but he hasn't come yet.' So I had to treat her myself.

"How did I treat her? The spirit that was after her was our kalimbubu, he was from her family. So I was his anak beru. Anak beru are supposed to respect their kalimbubu, right? I sat down by her, I greeted the spirit. I put my cigarettes down beside her. Then, I took one, I lit it, I blew the smoke right in her face! 'Oh, this is so good,' I said. I acted like I really enjoyed that smoke! And I never even offered one to that kalimbubu! You know, if you're with your kalimbubu you should always offer cigarettes, or sirih, or whatever. But I didn't! I just enjoyed my own smoke. Mmmmmh! I acted just as usual, but I didn't give that kalimbubu anything. Well, wasn't he angry? He went straight away! And then she was better.

"My brother never even came to see her when she was sick. What's the matter here, I thought. By rights he should have come to take care of her while I was away. Because, you see, he was a guru.

"One day, another spirit came to her, it spoke through her throat. It was my grandfather, the one whose things I'd gotten and cleaned up. Take back my things, he said. Because, you see, all those things were with my brother now.

"I went to get those things back. I didn't get them. Because, you see, he had already given them to another of our kalimbubu, in the village of Bulan Jahé. They're still there, you can see them if you want.

"This is why I haven't taken them back. The one who has them, there's a guru staying with him. He's also studying with the guru. This guru, he's from Pakpakland, he's not from around here. They say he's a sorcerer, you know, that he uses black magic. So we don't know about the staff or the other things anymore. He may have put something in them. We don't know what it is, so it's dangerous to use. That's why I haven't taken them back."

KEENNESS

Pak Tua's search for an end to his "confused thoughts" leads to the uncertain heart of a world that, like the speech of a lunatic, "has no turi-turin." His kalimbubu have not only neglected their family shrines, they have destroyed them: one by building a house on top of it, the other by the less material, but equally decisive, route of conversion to Christianity. Still another of his kalimbubu may have infected with sorcery the guru's paraphernalia left in his care. Pak Tua's wife has been attacked by the spirit of another of their kalimbubu, and his brother doesn't bother to come and treat his sick sister-in-law, even though he is himself a guru. The husband of the woman in Daulu doesn't care if his wife lives or dies, because she can be replaced. And above all there is Pak Tua himself, who got into this mess in the first place by acting as if he were not a part of others' lives. Even after his visit to Mount Sibayak, where he apparently received the magical power he was seeking, he continues on in the same way, hiding his knowledge from the people of Daulu, inventing a fanciful treatment for the sick woman because he is unsure of their intentions toward him. When his own wife is sick, he "treats" her not by acting as a proper anak beru should but rather by being insufferably rude to the afflicting kalimbubu-spirit.

The oddest thing is that despite all this both of his patients recover. It is all a matter of "keenness," Pak Tua said. If the guru is keen—the term is *mesinteng*, which refers to the hone of a knife or the clarity of vision as well as to the acuity of the guru—then the cure may be successful. Not always, of course: witness Pak Tua's own case, where Nandé Pusuh is certainly keen enough, but the situation she diagnoses is incurable.

This keenness is not simply a matter of the guru's skill and knowledge, nor of the power of the spirits he or she can call upon, for a guru may be keen one day and not the next. It may be fortuitous and inexplicable, as in the case of the woman from Daulu. Keenness is a matter of hitting the mark, of acting at the proper moment, and in the way that is proper for that moment. And both the guru and the one who seeks the guru's counsel are equally involved in the determination of that moment, in the creation of the guru's keenness—or lack of keenness.

There is a Karo saying, *bunga-bungana si kurang gara, nina guru la mesinteng*, "the hibiscus flowers aren't red enough, says the guru who isn't keen." It is the proverbial reply to one who attributes failure to external circumstances rather than acknowledging one's own responsibility, like the guru who finds fault with the offerings prepared for the spirits. The proverb, at least as it is used today, suggests that the unsuccessful guru, like a failed student (or a dissatisfied ex-soldier or ruined gambler), should be expected to bear the blame for what may also be seen as a more general failure.

If we understand experience in this way, as a thing "owned" by a particular individual, something that can be wrenched from the total pattern of living, then there is little indeed that can be communicated, to ourselves or to others, by that experience. Modern life is woven of this sort of alienated experience, and its pattern both creates and is rendered invisible by the seeming autonomy of its threads—the myriad of isolated, experiencing subjects that are its materials as well as its makers. It is against this view that the storyteller's counsel is directed.

Take the matter of the guru's paraphernalia that Pak Tua was tending. He was a wanderer, he said, and so he left the things in the care of his brother, who then passed them along to someone else. Who should bear the blame, then, for the eventual taint of sorcery attached to the borrowed attributes of the guru: Pak Tua, or his brother, or the kalimbubu who kept them, or the guru from Pakpakland who may (or may not) have added a new "content" to them? Like rumors, blame oozes into all the fissures of fragmented experience; information without a source, explanation without a fixed object, it is the new, uncertain content of modern life. And what is sorcery, after all, if not the immaterial embodiment of blame, or of its underside, which is envy?

The redness of the flowers is a part of the guru's keenness. But the same uncertainty that kept Pak Tua from taking back the guru's paraphernalia now infects the hibiscus flower. He said: "I once talked to an old woman, a guru, who said that you must wear a hibiscus flower [K., *bunga-bunga*] in your hair when you call down the spirits. That's the proper way, so that the guru is keen. Gurus nowadays, you rarely see one who does this, or knows why you should. It's not the ordinary hibiscus flower, the proper bunga-bunga is the one with seven petals. That's the one you have to use. You used to see them everywhere, they were planted in every village. You can't find them anymore, or rarely anyway.

"Why aren't they used anymore? Gurus nowadays, you see, they don't understand what it is, so they're afraid to use it. And even if they know how to use it, they can't, because other people don't understand. Say I made an offering of bunga-bunga at Lau Debuk-Debuk, which is really not wrong, you see, but other people there seeing it would run away! Because, you see, it can also be used for evil purposes, for sorcery. And so, if you use it, they think you must be a sorcerer. It can be whatever you want it to be, really, but when people see it, they figure it must be sorcery. That's why it can't be used, because they don't know what it is."

In this world of blame, the guru, and the storyteller, are needed perhaps more than ever. Yet here, where the guru is called upon to cure the incurable, and the storyteller to counsel those who can neither hear nor tell the turi-turin of experience, keenness is also declining. The reciprocal engagement of curer and patient, or of storyteller and listener, has become an uncertain encounter, a game of chance in which winner and loser are inseparable and, indeed, indistinguishable. And the guru wagers on hope against despair, even though the odds are unfavorable, or else turns away from the game.

"Nowadays it's difficult for us gurus," Pak Tua said. "The reason I say it's difficult, you see, is this: you can't go on any longer in the proper way, but you have to go on anyway. Well, that's the situation now.

"That's also the way to make things right. If not, what's broken just becomes more broken. If we follow all the turi-turin of living and the promise of the guru, the old promise, that's to fix whatever is broken. The guru has to go on, to fix up sickness and troubles, even when the time isn't right.

"So here, you see, they often say the guru isn't keen. Often the guru returns home with the sickness not cured, for all his efforts. And sometimes this guru seems really keen, even though the sickness is very, very severe.

"That's why we have to think it over, over and over, always. That's why, as we said before, you have to allow your thoughts to spread far and wide. Why we always return to the thirty days, and to what we call the dead directions and the living directions. Here's where our thoughts fall. If the day is right, according to the nature of the patient, and of the guru, and of the spirits, then the guru may be keen.

"But now even if the day's not right, the good day passed by: 'You're the only one who can fix things so they're right,' says the one who calls you. Sometimes even if it's not right, you agree too, just so the one who calls you is satisfied. So long as he's satisfied, even if the guru isn't keen.

If that's the only way to do it, that's how it's done. Here, now, there are always people who call you, until the guru isn't keen anymore.

"You could refuse, but he says that's the only way it can be fixed. If you do it, the sickness isn't cured, the debt to the guru has to be paid, all that is just so he's satisfied. And that's a kind of healing, too, in the family.

"So even I, you see, find it difficult to do a guru's work. That's why I went back to farming. In the old days I wandered around, and I never left my flute behind."

Pak Tua and Masin Go to Mount Sibayak

Pak Tua's friend Masin looked at all this rather differently. Masin is also a guru, and the son of one of the best-known curers in Karoland, and the two of them, Masin and Pak Tua, had often worked together, sharing advice, learning from each other, helping each other out. But in recent years they had had a falling out, as a result of a trip they took together to Mount Sibayak.

They told us about it one evening when we had gathered at my house in Medan to try again to record one of Pak Tua's turi-turin. Because of the heavy rain pounding on the tin roof and drowning out our voices, the recording session had to be postponed once more. And so the conversation turned to the old disagreement that began that day on the mountaintop.

"He used to go to Si Biangsa," Masin explained. "Not to the top. 'That's wrong,' I told him. 'You have to go to the top.'"

"So we went to the top of the mountain," Pak Tua said. "All the way to the top, we climbed in the early morning. There we made our offerings, there on the top. I made my offering of betel, I placed it in the correct way, I began my prayer. I closed my eyes, and when I opened them the betel was gone!"

"His offering just blew away," laughed Masin. "So I told him, you're not doing it right, that's what I said."

"I began my prayer," Pak Tua continued, "and then the betel blew away! It blew right away, off the top of the mountain. I looked over at him, he was right beside me, I looked at his betel offering. It was still there! Hmmph! I thought. What's going on here, is this some kind of trick?"

"He was doing it all wrong! I told him—"

"My betel was gone, and his was still sitting there. What kind of wind is this, I thought, that blows away just one of them, and not the other? Not doing it right! he said. 'I know how to do this,' I told him. So I made another offering, this time I fixed it so it couldn't blow away. No way. And I said my prayer but I didn't close my eyes this time. I wanted to watch."

"He thought it was a trick, you see," said Masin. "He thought I'd kicked his betel off the mountain. He thought, 'When I had my eyes closed, that guy kicked my offering away.' He thought I did it!"

"I fixed another betel offering," Pak Tua said. "I thought, this time, no matter what, it can't blow away. I'm going to watch what happens, he won't trick me again. I said my prayer. It blew away again!"

"My offering, it just sat there, it didn't even wiggle, and his just blew away," Masin continued. "He was furious! He kicked over my betel there, he was cursing the keramats, everything. Me, I'm respectful to people I can see, let alone the ones I can't—and here he is cursing at the invisible ones!"

"I grabbed up my things! I didn't say another word, and I just went right down that mountain! This place is useless, I thought, here I am trying to do things right, and my offering isn't even any good. I just walked away, I left."

"After that, he didn't even speak to me for two years," Masin said. "Two years, not a single word! He was that mad, and, you see, it was all his own fault. Why? He asked for the wrong thing. That was the problem. I told him what to do, but he wouldn't listen—"

" 'When you go to the mountain,' he said," said Pak Tua disapprovingly, 'You should ask for money.' "

"That's the thing! Ask for money. And you'll get it. That's what I asked for, and my offering was accepted. I'm doing fine. But he wouldn't do it. Do you know what he asked for? 'Oh nini, put an end to my confused thoughts,' he said. Well, that's not right, of course the spirits wouldn't have anything to do with that. Mount Sibayak, well, *sibayak* means 'the rich one,' doesn't it? So when you go there, you should ask for money."

Pak Tua was silent for once.

" 'Put an end to my confused thoughts,' he said," Masin continued. "Well, he got that, too. Nothing bothers him anymore. He can sleep under a table in some coffeeshop, he can wear the same clothes for a week, he's not clean, but it doesn't bother him at all.

"You know," Masin concluded, "I was going to put him in orbit [I., *meng-orbit-kan*, "promote, popularize"] from here. But a lot of my clients are important people, and they'd take one look at him and run! He asked for the wrong thing, you see. He should have asked for money. Then everything would have been fine. I told him to ask for money, but he just wouldn't listen."

Eight

An Uncertain Death

the illegible returns of voices cutting across statements and

moving like strangers through the house of language . . .

—MICHEL DE CERTEAU, "Quotations of Voices"

LIVING WITH VIOLENCE

On the night of September 30, 1965, six men rumored to be members of a shadowy "Council of Generals" were assassinated in Jakarta in what was officially labeled as the prelude to a Communist-inspired coup attempt (Gestapu, the "September 30th Movement") against the Sukarno government.[1] In the months that followed, military and vigilante groups throughout Indonesia, in frenzied reaction, engaged in a bloody, and frequently arbitrary, hunt for suspected Communists and their sympathizers. During this chaotic period of violence the Indonesian Communist party (PKI) was totally destroyed and a New Order of tacit military rule ideologically supported by the intertwined themes of patriotism, development, and stability established.

Official military estimates place the number of victims of the massacres of 1965 and 1966 at about half a million for all of Indonesia; other estimates are twice that (McDonald 1980:53). There is no record of the number of killings in Karoland or elsewhere in the province of North Sumatra.[2] It is not in statistics that Karo memorialize the time of reprisals, but rather in an image and a phrase. The image is of rivers running red with Communist blood, their deep-cut courses clotted with the bodies of the implicated and the merely unlucky. The phrase is *Jaman musuh-dalam-selimut*, the time of the enemy beneath the blanket.

The image and the phrase are memorials to fear. Rumors of hidden conspirators and enemies of the state fed the violence, as they continue to feed the fear. But the blanketed enemy is more familiar, a more present danger, than these unknown, mysterious figures. Tales still emerge of the false accusations and secret betrayals of that time, of words deadly as bullets: a neighbor's malicious gossip or an envious kinsman's whispered allegation translated into a name on a secret list; a listed name translated into another anonymous corpse in a clogged, blood-red river.

These personal betrayals are the work of the enemy beneath the blanket. Their continuing reverberations in Karo society are heightened by state efforts to preserve the shadowy threat of 1965 in public memory: through periodic warnings of the "latent danger" of Communist resurgence; through the occasional "discovery" of individuals with vague links to the PKI who have slipped into government, social, or religious organizations; through lists posted in local government offices of former Communist sympathizers "reformed" in prison and now returned to their home community. The effects of this conjuncture of the idioms of public and private betrayal are the production of terror and the universal distribution of silence. The victims of "Communist" violence—the murdered generals—survive in monumental form at the scene of their assassination, speaking, as James Siegel puts it, "after their deaths in the only form open to them: inscription" (Siegel 1986:280); but for the victims, innocent or otherwise, of the collective violence of the time of the blanketed enemy there is no monument aside from the empty space once occupied by their voices.

This is how violence has become enshrined in memory: by ensuring "that the event would not be forgotten by taking it out of human memory and inscribing it in a sign that did not need individual memory to be read" (ibid.:279). The word invisibly written on that sign is "Betrayal," the ultimate crime, which contains at once the justification for and the threat of violence. It is the signature of the blood-red river and the blanketed enemy, and the foundation of New Order hegemony.

When I arrived in Karoland in 1983 the first advice that I got about doing fieldwork was not to ask questions about Gestapu and its aftermath. Too many people, on one side or the other and in one way or another, had been affected by the killings. Too many people still lived with the memory and the fear that remain the elaborately tended heritage of that violent time. By 1980 most of the Class B detainees—those who had not been brought to trial for lack of clear evidence of complicity—had been "rehabilitated" and returned to society, but this had put an end neither to the memory nor to the fear.

I never did ask those questions, though I listened carefully to stories of the time of reprisals that emerged occasionally in conversation about other matters. More frequent were the narrative lacunae and the hints whose significance I would miss at the time, which my friends would later explain as signaling in one way or another the events of 1965. These silences and conversational detours seemed to me to mark some official limit imposed on social memory, beyond which was only rumor, repetitively inscribing the terrible clichés of violence.

Rumor also had more immediate events to work over. In 1983 a campaign to eliminate urban recidivists (who could be recognized, so popular opinion had it, by certain tattoos) was conducted by "mysterious marksmen" (I., *penembak misterius*), who were generally assumed to come from the army.[3] This was headline news—and the subject of much conversation—in my first months in Medan, where the nightly shootings had recently spread from their original site in Central Java. Each morning one read of so many tattooed bodies discovered on roadsides: the mysterious marksman strikes again. In America, public manifestations of extralegal state violence were—so I then thought—both subtler and less mundane than these blunt and brutal acts, and I was shocked as much by the wink-and-nudge transparency of newspaper accounts ("we don't know who these marksmen are, but we certainly thank them for their good work") as by the fact of the killings themselves. More disturbing still was the extent to which my Karo friends found the killings a reasonable and proper response to the pervasiveness of petty crime. Rule of law might be possible in a wealthy and stable country like America, I was told, but in Indonesia only violence could control the uncontrolled spread of violence.[4]

Over the course of a year, some four thousand to eight thousand persons were killed as the mysterious shootings rippled across Indonesia, outward from urban centers to smaller towns and villages. Fueled by a largely enthusiastic press, popular acclaim for the program was such that the government eventually lowered the marksmen's thin mask of anonymity and took credit for the killings. Culpability, it seemed, rested not with the shooters but with their victims: "If there are killings," explained the head of the national legislature, "that is the result of the presence of crime" (cited in Pemberton n.d.:25).

There is no way of getting around the partnership of terror and reason—what Michael Taussig (1992:115) has called "Stately cultural practice"—here. "[T]here is something frightening," Taussig writes,

> merely in saying that this conjunction of reason and violence exists, not only because it makes violence scary, imbued with the greatest legitimating force there can be, reason itself, and not only because it makes reason scary by indicating how it's snuggled deep into the armpit of terror, but also because we so desperately need to cling to reason—as instituted—as the bulwark against the terrifying anomie and chaos pressing in on all sides. There has to be a reason, and we have to use reason. Yet another part of us welcomes the fact that reason—as instituted—has violence at its disposal, because we feel that very anomie and chaos will respond to naught else.

Violence echoes through the structures of reason; it is in the silences and evasions those structures enclose and in the possibilities they close out, in the everyday acts and refusals of the political subject, in the maze of small talk that conspires with and also against the secrets of power. Living with violence, you learn to misrecognize it.

The other big news when I first arrived in Medan was the story of two American tourists who had disappeared without a trace, apparently while climbing Mount Sibayak. Some thought the men had fallen into a ravine or wandered off into the forest; others dramatically speculated that they had been eaten by a tiger (there *were* tigers around), murdered by bandits, or carried off by the mountain spirits. More conspiratorial scenarios were put forward as well. The local police were under considerable pressure from provincial authorities, who were in turn being pressured by the U.S. embassy on behalf of the families of the missing men to solve the mystery, which they never did.

Some time later I learned that two young Karo men had been detained by the police at the time. Their only contact with the vanished tourists had been to direct them to the path leading up the mountain, and after being brutally "interrogated" by local police intent on finding a plausible suspect they were fortunately let go. A woman we knew told my Karo companions this story, and warned them that they should be careful of traveling in my company: if anything happened to me they could expect the same treatment, or worse. She was quite correct, and this (in trivial conclusion to what was a quite disturbing realization of my actual "place" in Karoland) is why I could never bring myself to climb Mount Sibayak. Even with the best of intentions it is possible to become a transfer-point in the circuitry of international violence.

Traces of violence are etched with microscopic intricacy into the experience of daily life. Image, act, and phrase repeat the memorialized signals of danger; events, storied events, rumors, dreams, and silences echo the names, spoken and unspoken, of enemies and friends. Narrative experience is not a free zone of imaginative resistance, but the space where political subjects come to recognize themselves. This does not mean that there is no possibility of liberation. I have, then, one last story to tell you here.

A DANGEROUS MAN

Setia Aron Ginting may or may not have been dead for nearly twenty years when his wife Nandé Rita, who was about to join the Church, finally decided to call his spirit home. It was not an easy decision. After all, no one was really sure that Setia Aron was dead, or, if he was, what he would have to say to his living kin. Besides, her children were opposed to the idea. But once Nandé Rita became a Christian there would be no other chance to lay his violent soul to rest. The date set for the seance was April 4, 1985.

The month preceding Easter was the preferred time for baptisms, and it was the busiest season of the year for the few remaining mediums who specialized in the perumah bégu funeral seance. Rooted in Dutch Calvinism, the Karo Protestant Church strongly condemned such communication with the dead. Joining the Church meant relinquishing the spirits' guidance and protection; it meant giving up, perhaps eternally, the comfort of occasional conversation in times of difficulty or joy with one's departed, unconverted loved ones. There was no place in heaven for the pagan dead, no possibility of reunion beyond the grave. It was a hard loss and a serious obstacle to conversion for many. So, pragmatically—or perhaps charitably—the Church maintained a tolerant blindness when incoming converts like Nandé Rita wished to say a final farewell to their deceased kin.

In Setia Aron's case, however, the time for such farewells had long passed, and there were few who wished to commemorate either the time or the event of his departure from their lives. A top cadre of the Communist party in Karoland, Setia Aron had vanished during the post-Gestapu reprisals twenty years earlier, an apparent victim of the slaughter. His disappearance, his presumed execution, had gone unmemorialized and probably unmourned, except by his wife and children in private. Dead or alive, he had been a danger to all those who knew him. As indeed he still was.

For Karo who adhere to the old religion of spirit veneration, funeral rituals are intended to separate the deceased from the world of the living and to prevent any excessive attachment between spirits of the dead and their still-living kin. "Greet us no more," the mourners say, "your mouth is filled with thorns." Gifts are given to the dead person with the left hand, as an insult, and the funeral procession follows a circuitous route to the graveyard so that spirits can no longer find their way home unaided. Four days after the burial, a seance should be held in which the newly deceased spirit is called home, along with the spirits of other family members, by a guru si baso. Through the medium, the returning spirit converses with its living kin, each in proper turn—husband or wife, children, brothers and sisters, anak beru and kalimbubu. Advice and comfort are offered and received, family disputes settled, property equitably divided. In token of remembrance, food and drink are shared with the spirits, who, in turn, promise to watch over and protect their living kin (Huender 1930; Rita S. Kipp 1976:212–64).

Spirits of the dead retain the qualities and partialities they have shown in life, but these are overlaid with the experience of death, which defines the spirit's essential nature. The most powerful spirits are those whose lives were incomplete, whose deaths were unnatural: children who die before their teeth have appeared, women who die unmarried or in childbirth, and especially those who die violently or unexpectedly, "in a single day" (*si maté sada wari*), as Setia Aron presumably had. These latter spirits, crystallized in violence at the moment of death, can, if tended properly, become strong protectors of their family and community. Left untended, such a spirit lingers near its former home, unintentionally afflicting the living by its deadly affection or else, resentful and angry, punishing them for this neglect.

Because of the times there had been no funeral for Setia Aron, and no seance either. No one would have come! Who would have dared to be seen at his funeral? And what kind of protection could such a spirit offer to his family, when kinship alone threatened them with implication in his crimes? Besides, no one was really sure that he was actually dead. Many who disappeared during the time of the massacres were imprisoned rather than killed; some were said to have escaped and gone into hiding. But now that most of the political detainees had been released, now that twenty years had passed with no word from Setia Aron, it seemed clear that he had in fact been executed. And if this was indeed the case, then his family's failure to perform the requisite ceremonies of separation was a matter of serious concern. Now that the immediate dangers of implication had lessened—though by no means ended—it was time, finally, to close off this other danger posed by the continuing presence of Setia Aron's unquiet spirit.

Kuta Kepultaken is a pleasant and prosperous-looking village, with a relatively spacious, orderly layout that is the fortunate consequence of its having been burnt to the ground during the revolution. Its wide, graveled streets are lined with well-built houses, a scattering of small shops, and the ubiquitous coffeehouses where Karo men spend their idle time in chess and conversation. Located politely at opposite ends of the village are a fine, solid Protestant church, emblem of local respectability, and a less imposing but equally respectable mosque. On the main cross-street there is a new billiard hall, somewhat disreputable but popular nonetheless with the younger men. Nearby, Nandé Rita's small house stands inconspicuously, its thatch and unpainted boards drab beside the pastel stucco and zinc roofs of its neighbors.

Village streets are usually deserted after dark, but on the night of Nandé Rita's seance—which was cukera dudu, the auspicious thirteenth day of the Karo lunar cycle—there was plenty of activity. A week before its scheduled date, the seance had already become—along with the price of onions and the World Cup soccer playoffs—a main topic of local conversation. A perumah bégu was always good entertainment, and in this case there were the additional enticements of Setia Aron's infamous reputation and his mysterious disappearance. "No one saw his death," one man explained to me enthusiastically. "Now we can find out how he really died." And his friend replied, skeptically: "And what will he say then to all of you good people who've come to watch him die again?" He grimaced dramatically, mimicking Setia Aron's imagined words: "I'll kill you all!"

By 9:30 the medium's song of invocation could already be heard drifting up the moonlit street as I hurried to join the company that had gathered at Nandé Rita's house to witness the spirits' descent.[5] Groups of men, sarong-wrapped against the chill, loitered casually outside the house, chatting and smoking. Children goggled curiously in through the door and windows, occasionally shouted away by their elders when their shrieks of mock terror became too annoying. Squeezing through the child-packed doorway into the crowded room, which was bare of furnishings except for an old wardrobe and several sacks of rice, I invented a space for myself and my tape recorder on the floor in front of the medium.

Small conversations filled the room. A group of elderly women, the "flatterers" (pertami-tami), who would later interrogate the spirits as they arrived, were busy preparing the offerings. Nandé Pajuh, the officiating medium, sat cross-legged on a small white mat at the front of the room, her hand cupped to her ear as she sang. Unlike the other women, she was bare-headed, and a patterned red cloth was knotted around her waist to strengthen her soul. In front of her on the mat were formal spirit-offerings: a single betel-leaf prepared for chewing and a plate of bananas and small leaf-wrapped cakes, arranged symmetrically around a boiled egg. Located conveniently nearby were a tin-can spittoon, a white bowl containing another egg, a woven rice-bag, and a comb of bananas. An old rusty knife blade was placed beneath the mat. This, I later learned, was intended to "cut off" her need to urinate, for she was required to remain seated on her mat for the duration of the night-long ceremony.

Her voice deep and powerful, Nandé Pajuh sang to beraspati nu taneh, the spirit of the earth, to the guardians of the village and its lands, and to the spirits of the hearth, requesting them all to stand aside and allow the dead to descend. Then she named her own personal guardian spirits, her jinujungs, asking for their help and protection. Finally, she called down the last of her jinujungs, the spirit of a young girl whom she addressed as *Si Mada Dalan*, Pathfinder. This was her *perkentas*, the spirit who would act as the medium's go-between in contacting the souls of the dead. "Come quickly, Pathfinder, don't loiter along the way," she sang, the last syllable changing to a jerky, drawn-out moan—*eh eh eh oooohhh*—as the spirit descended. Nandé Pajuh swayed softly for a moment, then abruptly righted herself, calling out in surprise, "*Eeh Nandé*! Oh Mother!"

The flatterers immediately offered betel to the Pathfinder, bantering a bit as they explained what she had to do. Reacting as a young girl would, the spirit announced that she was afraid of Setia Aron. This "uncle" that they want her to find is a big man. He's carrying a stick, what if he wants to hit her with it? The flatterers reassured her: He's just a *bapa-bapa*, a father, they said. The stick is just his walking cane. "Ech! A man!" exclaimed the Pathfinder in disgust. "Don't you get scared later on, OK?" she teased to the crowd. Oh, no, they answered, laughing.

"They caged him up in a chicken coop, you know. They shut him up in it. Isn't that right, aunties?"

"We don't know," the flatterers replied.

The Pathfinder demanded to be fed, and they gave her cakes and bananas, which she shared with the flatterers. Then she blessed them all, singing:

> *I sing to you all, old age fulfilled, your rice fruiting, chickens*
> > *breeding, your children male and female all healthy, auntie*
> *those in school, may their schooling be extensive*
> *those who farm, may their farming be successful*
> *rock-a-bye, uncle, may you all be healthy, male and female,*
> > *may your fathers earn a good living, little brothers and sisters*
> *rock-a-bye, auntie, rock-a-bye*
> *rock-a-bye, I sing to the spirits of those who died in a single day,*
> > *to the spirits of infants, to the spirits who made this ceremony*
> *rock-a-bye, I sing to you all, sit down, all of your brave men and*
> > *women*
> *sit down here, please, uncle, you can't come near here*
> *the path is broken off, you with the big stick*
> *it's your fate, angry uncle*
> *you can't come to the house*
> *the path is broken, don't you grieve . . .*

Holding the white bowl of water in her left hand, with the metal blade beneath it and a prepared betel leaf between blade and bowl, the Path-finder began to call to Setia Aron.

> *it's amazing, uncle, this fate of yours*
> *fix your journey*
> *don't you stumble or trip*
> *don't think about your torn clothing*
> *if that's how it is, that's just how it is*
> *don't you hesitate, uncle.*

The spirit was still far away. Listening hard to catch Setia Aron's replies, the Pathfinder asked him to give his clan name, then checked his answer, Ginting, with the flatterers. "Whose father are you, then, uncle? Just speak from there, I'll understand, even across the ravine I'll understand. 'Bapa Rita,' is that right?"

> *So depart then uncle of the Ginting clan, Rita's father*
> *don't be amazed*
> *this is a sign that you have departed, your fate and destiny, uncle*
> *come on, take your steps*
> *make your move*
> *you've already departed from this land*
> *here I'm holding your wash-water*
> *in this white bowl here*
> *with white silver, and gold coins*
> *also hard iron*
> *wrapped in betel leaf are perfect areca-nut and clear lime*
> *so that you will be perfect and clear talking to your brothers and*
> *   sisters*
> *your mothers and fathers, uncles and aunts, the woman of your*
> *   household, your children male and female*
> *your maternal uncles and aunts, your cousins and sisters-in-law*
> *don't hinder, don't be afraid*
> *come on, uncle of the Ginting clan*
> *depart, uncle, Bapa Rita, of the Ginting clan*
> *don't you weep*
> *because you've departed from this land*
> *what was left unsaid doesn't matter*
> *depart, then . . .*

The Pathfinder paused, then said: "About uncle's visit later, let's talk a bit. Don't you say things to him like, 'Why did you go away,' this and that. The place where he is now, he has friends there, he's happy. We shouldn't make him regretful. Then, there's one more thing. He has a lot of children, doesn't he, auntie?"

"Four girls and one boy. All grown, and he even has a grandchild."

"Aren't his children here, auntie?" No, they replied. Only the son, Tanda, and two of his daughters have come. "Oh, I don't understand this," said the Pathfinder. "If his children aren't here, won't he grieve?"

"Oh, no," they answered. "His children are really far away, Pathfinder."

> *True, uncle,* she sang again, *don't turn your head to left or to*
> *right*
> *don't spill this wash-water*
> *if it spills to the left the woman of your house will be troubled*
> *if it spills to the right your anak beru will be troubled*
> *if it spills backward your kalimbubu will be troubled*
> *if it spills over the rim, to the front, the Pathfinder will be*
> *troubled*
> *prepare yourself to be cleansed, uncle, don't be hasty*
> *Ginting clan, don't be hasty*
> *so that your children will all be healthy*
> *the boy you left at home with the woman of your house*
> *who wasn't allowed to cry*
> *cleanse yourself, Bapa Rita*
> *Don't weep, Ginting clan*
> *over your fate and your destiny.*

"Ugh! He's too far away, aunties," Pathfinder said as she handed the bowl of water to the flatterers and asked for more betel. "I'm bathed in sweat! You know, I'm really tired."

"Come on, you can have some betel later, when this is all done."

"No, auntie. There's too much to do. It's difficult to catch him."

"That's because he's been gone for so long."

"Oh, I'm fucked then," Pathfinder exclaimed rudely. "This is just like climbing a mountain. I should have worn bathing clothes."

"Well, how else could it be? He probably died in a sweat. And didn't he go around shirtless all the time anyway because he was so fat?" one of the flatterers commented.

"Actually," the Pathfinder continued, "you should have made an offering first so it wouldn't be so hard to call him to the house."

"Oh, my!" the flatterers exclaimed. "We didn't know! She [i.e., Nandé Pajuh, the medium] didn't tell us that."

"Well," replied the Pathfinder, annoyed at the inadequacies of her "perch," Nandé Pajuh, "this is one crazy perch I've got here."

It was nearly midnight before Setia Aron's spirit actually descended on the medium, for the *bégu sintua,* the "eldest spirit" of the household, had to be called down first. This was Setia Aron's mother, a garrulous, bad-tempered old woman whom the Pathfinder addressed as "auntie busybody, chatterbox, Old Selfish," drawing an appreciative laugh ("That's just how she was, too") from the flatterers. As soon as the spirit arrived, she began a litany of complaints about her difficulties after the death of her "brave son," and about her inconsiderate daughter-in-law and spoiled grandchildren, who have wilfully gone to live among "people whose language we don't understand." An hour later the cantankerous old bégu departed abruptly, offended that her younger grandchildren had been sent off to bed before speaking to her. She was replaced by the Pathfinder, who almost immediately called down the spirit of Setia Aron.

When a spirit is brought home for the first time its death throes are reenacted as it alights on the medium; this is how the spirit learns that it no longer belongs to the world of the living. It was this moment of arrival that held the most interest for those with a less personal stake in Setia Aron's history, and so, as the Pathfinder again called him to descend, the room was completely packed with attentive spectators. It was an opportunity to resolve the mystery of his disappearance and to witness, uncompromised but at first hand, a death embodying all the shadowy dangers of the time of reprisals.

The Pathfinder began to pray, calling the spirit to descend. She held the bowl of water in her right hand, at chin level. After five minutes she transferred the bowl to her left hand and began to sing again, holding her right hand to her face. She told Setia Aron that it was not necessary to repeat his story, that the people here only wanted to meet with him. The bowl in her hand began to shake, a sign that the spirit was descending. As she placed the bowl down carefully, the room was entirely silent.

This is Setia Aron's death, as we witnessed it that night. His hands were pulled behind his back as if they were tied; his legs were stretched out in front of him. His body twitched several times as if struck by bullets. The death was a slow, gradual one. The onlookers wept.

He cried out: "Mother! Free my hands! Father! Free my hands! Oh Sweetheart, Sweetheart." Then, for a moment, only gasping breaths.

"This isn't true," a skeptical spectator remarked. "It's just her [Nandé Pajuh's] jinujung." But the others disagreed. "No, that's his death, all right."

The spirit spoke briefly and matter-of-factly about his death. He was going by bus to Kabanjahé, the district capital. The bus was stopped—by whom, he didn't say. And then he was taken off to the riverbank, to a spot famous as the site of mass executions. There he was shot.

After this casual recital of the events of his death, Setia Aron began to sing in the conventional style of funeral mourners—a slow, improvised song of grief punctuated by occasional sobs. Addressing her as turang ("sibling," the affectionate term of address used by lovers), he called his wife Nandé Rita to join him. Arms flung wide, bowing deeply in time to the song's rhythm, he continued to sing, telling of the hardships Nandé Rita had undergone and of how he had longed to see her again, of her diligence in raising their children through difficult times. Nandé Rita sat quietly with eyes downcast, weeping.

After a time he called his children. Looking embarrassed, Tanda came forward reticently with his two sisters. They sat in front of their father as Setia Aron continued his song of mourning. Their mother's suffering should not be forgotten, he said. The two young women wept softly as Setia Aron addressed his son, reminding him of his sisters' sacrifices for him, how they had forgone their own schooling in order to send him to college. "Whatever I have done no longer matters," he told Tanda, "for you now have taken my place. Your mother, your sisters, they are your responsibility and you are their hope."

Next Setia Aron asked for his sisters and his father's sisters, his anak beru by birth. There was no response. Eventually two old women seated across the room called out, "Let him talk to us from here." They refused to come any closer, and another woman—in fact one of Setia Aron's ka-limbubu—came forward saying, "Well, I'll be a sister then." Taking their place, she began to mourn, enacting the role of Setia Aron's sister.

After comforting this "sister," Setia Aron called for his wife's brothers. Angrily, he told them: "For two years you wouldn't even speak to your sister, out of fear. Is that the right way to act?" They stared at the floor; one played with a matchstick, drawing designs in the cigarette ashes on the floor.

"The reason that I lost my way," Setia Aron continued, "was that I thought I was clever. 'Come along with us,' they [the Communists] said. And so I followed them. Whatever fate it led me to, this is the path that I chose. I have no regrets for myself, only for the woman at home and the children. Now you have to care for your nieces and nephew that I've left behind. My departure, the way that I was lost, you needn't think about it anymore, for there is someone to take my place."

Next Setia Aron called for his kalimbubu by birth. No one came forward. "If they don't want to come, so be it. I can accept that," he said. Someone went to fetch his maternal uncles, who had left earlier; finally, the three men came in.

"Whatever disputes you've had with Nandé Rita, take care of her," Setia Aron told them.

"Let's talk it over," replied the uncles.

"There's nothing to talk about," Setia Aron responded angrily. "When did you ever want to pray for me?"

After a long silence, one of the men quietly said, "We *did* want to."

At three in the morning, Setia Aron gave his final words to the audience. He acknowledged that his absence was crucial to the family's well-being, for if his history were officially known, surely his children would not have been able to get jobs, his son would not have been admitted to college. With all the supernatural power of one who died by violence in a single day (and one with the added aura of demonic power that the New Order has bestowed upon its spectral Communist Enemy), he has protected them—by erasing the history of his life and his death from public memory. "So you'll know," said Setia Aron, "I'm the one who has closed all this up, so it wouldn't keep you from getting work. Our children all have good jobs. According to my history, that wouldn't be possible. I've shut it all up. If you don't mention me I won't be angry, because this is for *education*. I'll always protect you." And he went on to speak approvingly of his wife's desire to become a Christian. "You say to me: 'Bapa Rita, I'm learning to pray [*ertoto*, the term referring specifically to Christian prayer].' Whichever Sunday you choose for your baptism, it makes no difference to me. You needn't give me offerings, you needn't think of me any longer. Although you leave me behind, I'll continue to follow you."

So ended Setia Aron's conversation with his family. After his departure, other spirits were called down, but with the night's main attraction gone most of the spectators drifted home, or else curled up on the floor for a few hours' sleep. In the morning, the medium asked if Setia Aron should be called down again. No, Nandé Rita told her, there was nothing more to say. Setia Aron's absence would henceforth be his memorial, for he had appropriated the silence that surrounded him, and offered it to his family as a parting gift, a sign of his power.

THE USE OF MEMORY

We die with the dying:

See, they depart, and we go with them.

We are born with the dead:

See, they return, and bring us with them.

—T. S. ELIOT, "Little Gidding"

Certain deaths, Robert Hertz wrote, have no end. Those who die by violence are (in Hertz's words) the "victims of a special malediction," for the excessive sentiment generated by horrific or unexpected death allows no conclusion to the disaster, no final payment on the debt of life. Caught forever in memory in the shattering moment that separates them from human society, these "unquiet and spiteful souls roam the earth for ever," in deadly and insatiable search of an impossible reunion. But there is no reconciliation for them beyond the grave, and they will find a home neither among the living nor the dead. For them, "death will be eternal, because society will always maintain towards these accursed individuals the attitude of exclusion that it adopted from the first" (Hertz 1960:85–86).

Caught up between forgetting and remembrance in the hard grip of an ultimate crime, we the living also die with the dying. Death by violence, as Karo understand it, effects a ghastly spiritual merger of victim and killer, a mutual implication in the murderous event from which neither finally escapes. If there is no end to this violence even beyond the grave, there is yet the chance that its tragic power can still be turned to account. Like Selam Ginting's brutally murdered sister, who in company with her murderer became her brother's guardian spirit and a healer of women in childbirth, these lost and irreconcilable spirits return, lending their power as indiscriminately to those who would harness the horror of their passing to sorcerous purpose as to those who would recognize the humanity dwelling within this horror.

Many more than those who killed and those who were their victims have become entrapped in the frozen moment of mass violence that inaugurated Indonesia's New Order. Every effort to erase this bloody haunting further saturates its environment with the fear and horror that are its lingering traces. Betrayal and blame, and the understandable desire for a secure and comprehensible space for living in a world too often defined as neither, render inaudible and unanswerable any demand for a recognition that might at least offer a kind of mutual comfort—the partial, provisional healing that is the work of the modern guru, in which (as Pak Tua put it) the sickness remains uncured and the debt is still to be paid. These local agonies are seeded and cultivated in national memory, ensuring that they, like the deaths of a single day, will never end.

I had come to Setia Aron's seance hoping to discover a form of disguised political resistance encoded in ritual, a counter-official judgment passed on the national demonology of the New Order. I was disappointed—as, no doubt, were onlookers anticipating a dramatic confrontation with their Communist Foe—when Nandé Pajuh, through her spirit helper Pathfinder, insisted that politics should have no place in the seance. Her insight was of course keener than mine; and I later saw that by so restricting the scene of Setia Aron's return Nandé Pajuh created the possibility for a more profound subversion and the hope of a mutual healing. Bypassing the official language of blame and betrayal, she could open up a loophole in history, creating, for a moment, an unofficial elsewhere beyond the truths of Old and New Orders, where families and neighbors could begin again to converse with one another in the proper Karo manner, as kin.

History is composed of public representations of past experience: monuments built and rumors shared, stories told or retold, profits and losses calculated, records written and displayed, bodies counted and names listed. There are the official histories, generic versions of the past told from an angle of dominance, and the counter-official histories that attempt to displace them by establishing new generic narratives of power and empowerment. These are the monologic versions of the past: spoken from a position of power, they assert the right to speak for all. This authoritative position allows them to absorb and to draw strength from personal experience; to exclude whatever they cannot contain as insignificant, aberrant, criminal; or indeed to silence that which is unspeakable.

The monument unbuilt, the story unspoken, is no more than an invisible inscription along history's silent edge, marking an official limit placed upon the past by the present. But in the shifting borderlands of official history there are other tales to be told. These are the stories that I have called "unofficial"—accounts of personal experience that move against the grain of the official discourses in which they are embedded. Always susceptible to official absorption or exclusion, these histories nevertheless have a certain power of their own, which is the subversive power of partiality, the power of the singular event to confound generic explanation.

Historical ethnography must not only attend to official representations of past experience and their transformation or replacement by other, equally official versions of the past. It must also consider the stories of personal experience that emerge discordantly from the orderly flow of generic representation to suggest other, partial realities, other mappings of the social terrain. What these fragmentary histories offer us is not some more authentic vision—a "truer story"—of their social-historical moment, but rather a way of seeing the differences obscured by generic representation. What they can show us is the partiality that also underlies official representations of social reality.

Following the fugitive thread of marvelous encounters with the spirits of Mount Sibayak, I have tracked here some of the Karo voices that speak against the grain of colonial and postcolonial representation. Nandé Randal, the old medium of Simpang Meriah, who learned that the mountain spirits cared for traders but not for farmers; Amé Kata Mehuli, who confronted the colonial authorities with the story of her visit with the "hobgoblins"; Selam Ginting, the tobacco-seller who changed his name to commemorate his escape from his umang-brides; Nandé Ukat, who founded the gendang jambur, but didn't go there; Nandé Laga, who was brought back from the mountain by the handsome young man on horseback; Pak Tua, who asked the spirits of Mount Sibayak for the wrong thing, and got it: their stories, intended to do no more than describe—though perhaps not without strategic intent—what happened at a particular moment in the teller's life, are also explorations of the tense and ambiguous relation between singular experience and collective, generic representation.

These stories are not simply products of individual imagination; nor are they transparent reports of "what happened" to a certain person at a certain time and place. They exist within socially constituted patterns of domination and subordination, and within culturally defined patterns of meaning. They are structured by Karo narrative conventions as well as by the social context of their telling. Directly or indirectly, they refer to other stories, other experiences, other moments in the teller's life. They partake of shared values and beliefs, shared assumptions about the nature of reality and of experience. But these stories are told not as illustrations of some officially established generic truth. They are told because of their strangeness: because they are partial "misfits" within an official order of things. It is this strangeness within order that we should learn to listen for.

When Amé Kata Mehuli testified in the colonial court that she had "been with the hobgoblins," she countered the discourse of the colonial legal system with a story so "perfectly unacceptable" that it could neither be affirmed nor denied, however much the colonial officials doubted its veracity. Sidestepping the authority of the court and the disbelief of her listeners, she located herself in a realm of marvelous encounters, a place where anything might have happened. Though the tale's telling is enmeshed in a colonial discourse of otherness, therein signifying Duplicity, Amei Kata Mehoeli's escape—like Setia Aron's return—still testifies to the occasionally subversive power of strangeness: of the inappropriate word, the obtuse word, the word spoken out of place.

Listening for strangeness in Setia Aron's seance, we rediscover some of the harsh complexity of Karo social experience, a complexity that is masked by official representations of the Communist Enemy. The traitor who betrays the ideals of the state; the amoral, godless atheist; the one who—as instigator and as victim—unleashes the violent time of the blanketed enemy: Setia Aron's voice, called back from an uncertain death, moves across these images to reveal a singular life and death, one still deeply entangled in the social web of others' lives. Setia Aron returns not with threats to "kill you all," as some had anticipated, but with a word for the other victims of the reprisals—the mother who lost her "brave son"; the kalimbubu who wanted to pray for their anak beru but did not;

the brothers who did not speak to their sister for two years out of fear; the children whose lives might be jeopardized if their father's history were known; and most of all Nandé Rita, who was left to raise her children alone, without the help and comfort of neighbors or kin. For them, and all the others left hanging without a rope in the New Order's Age of Development, remembrance is still shadowed by fear, but forgetfulness is no remedy. The souls of the dead still haunt the banks of the blood-red rivers; unmourned and unpropitiated, they return silently to plague those who, out of fear or out of faith, have failed to acknowledge them.

Notes

Prologue

1. Intended for use in instructional classes for new Karo adherents, the volume (M. Ginting 1978) was published by Parisada Hindu Dharma as a guide to the "basic tenets" of the Hindu religion. It is nevertheless a fairly esoteric text, with little relevance to the everyday religious practices of Karo devotees like Nandé Randal—many of whom are, like her, illiterate.

2. This event is described in detail in Steedly 1988.

Chapter One. Narrative Experience

1. Voorhoeve's praise appears in his introduction to the second edition of *Een Jaar* (Neumann 1949:5). My thanks to Joseph Saunders, who gave me a copy of Neumann's book that he found in a used book store in Medan.

2. The partial bibliography of Neumann's published writings appended to the second edition of *Een Jaar* lists more than one hundred items, including mission reports; scholarly articles on Karo history, myth, and religion; a grammar of the Karo language; a Karo-Dutch dictionary; texts and translations of Karo folktales and poetry; Karo-language school readers; New Testament translations; and a collection of Bible stories still in use today.

3. Danish sculptor Bertel Thorvaldsen [Thorwaldsen] (1768–1844), whose "austere" religious sculptures found particular approval in the Reformed Church. The Christ to which Henk refers was in the Frue Kirke in Copenhagen. Thorvaldsen's biographer Eugene Plon (1874:200) describes the statue as follows: "The Christ of Thorvaldsen is as beautiful as Raphael's, or Leonardo's. . . . The Man-God is standing up, and one wonders to see that gentle head, so pure and so delicate of outline, united to a chest like that of Hercules. The powerful arms of Jesus are stretched out with a loving gesture, as though He called to Him all those who suffer and need relief; but His strong legs hold the Master of the World firmly to the earth, and the beholder asks if this can really be the slender form which glided over the surface of the waters."

4. Versions of this story, variously located in time and place, were still in popular circulation during my stay in Karoland some eighty years later, attesting to continuing Karo efforts to plumb the bottomless discourse of spirits.

5. The "large" gendang is commonly known as the *gendang lima sedalanen*, the "five-together" gendang. The smaller "three-together" ensemble (*gendang telu sedalanen*) consists of a struck bamboo tube zither (*keteng-keteng*), a small porcelain bowl (*mangkok*), and either a flute (*belobat* or *baluat*) or a two-stringed plucked lute (*kulcapi*) as lead instrument. Today, for reasons of discretion as well

as expense, it is most often the small ensemble that plays in possession rituals, especially in the city. As a result it is sometimes pejoratively called the *gendang bégu* (ghost-gendang). On Karo musical instruments, see Kartomi (1985); Sibeth (1991); Simon (1985); and Sitepu (1977). Simon's (1987) recording of Karo music gives examples of both orchestras, including religious performances. Yampolsky (1992) provides several selections of Karo secular music played on the "five-together" ensemble, accompanied by a singer.

6. For critical (though not unsympathetic) assessments of the "new ethnography," see Boon (1990) and Fox (1992); see also hooks (1990a) and Abu-Lughod (1992) for feminist misgivings.

7. Cf. Foucault (1979:159): "The author does not precede the works, he is a certain functional principle by which, in our culture, one limits, excludes, and chooses; in short, by which one impedes the free circulation, the free manipulation, the free composition, decomposition and recomposition of fiction." It is within the context of Foucault's statement that Ermes Marana, the trickster-translator in Italo Calvino's (1981:159) novel *If on a winter's night a traveler*, can ask: "How is it possible to defeat not the authors but the functions of the author, the idea that behind each book there is someone who guarantees a truth in that world of ghosts and inventions by the mere fact of having invested in it his own truth, of having identified himself with that construction of words?"

8. Jackson's (1989) elegant call for a "radical empiricism" begins from a critique of the subject, but then reinstates an apparently subjectless "lived experience" as the pre- (and post-) discursive ground-zero of his approach. This is a rather different argument from the one I am making here. Cf. Feldman (1991:13).

9. Aside from Barthes (1986a), other readings of the "figure in the carpet" include Iser (1978:3–9) and J. H. Miller (1980). The immediate referent is Henry James' (1986 [orig. pub. 1896]) short story, "The Figure in the Carpet."

10. In a sense, one could argue that Faulkner's displacement of the individual subject as the site of narrative anticipates McGann's (1991:64–65) displacement of "Faulkner" the author through a reflection on the editing of *Absalom, Absalom!* Cf. Orgel (1991) and Stallybrass (1992) for a similar editorial displacement of "Shakespeare" as author.

11. A wide range of political and theoretical positions are covered here, from Irigaray's (1985) celebration of female *jouissance* to MacKinnon's (1989) appeal to the experience of victimization. Chodorow's (1978) work on gender and socialization provided the basis for Hartsock's (1983) analysis of the sexual division of labor; both she and Jaggar (1983) argue that women's experience can generate an awareness of oppression and a potential for social transformation. Morgan's (1984) "anthology of the international women's movement" calls for a global feminist solidarity on the grounds of common experience, for which she has been called to task by Mohanty (1984, 1988). A complex notion of experience as "socio-symbolic practice" is set out in the Milan Women's Bookstore Collective (1990). Young (1990) offers a useful overview of some of the major positions in what she calls "gynocentric feminism."

12. This has, not surprisingly, been a central theme in American feminist literary criticism. Some notable instances in the "reading/writing as a (_____)" debate would include Culler (1982); Kamuf (1980); Fuss (1989b); Showalter (1981); N. Miller (1988a); and Scholes (1987).

13. Here the materials are too numerous to do more than cite a few illustrative examples. For some instances of the concerns of American women of color, see hooks (1990b); Christian (1988); Carby (1990); and the collection of essays by radical women of color edited by C. Moraga and G. Anzaldua (1981). The possibility of male feminism is addressed in the essays in Jardine and Smith (1987). For a provocative argument supporting a right-to-life feminism, see Callahan (1986); but also see Harding (1990) and Tsing (1990b) for alternative perspectives. Rich (1979) offers a particularly powerful critique of racism from a lesbian perspective. See King (1986) for a critique of the appropriation of lesbian experience as feminism's "magical sign." Fuss (1989b) examines the question of "identity politics" specifically in a gay/lesbian context, but notes the applicability of her argument to other forms of identity-based social movement. A few examples of postcolonial criticism would include Trinh (1989); Spivak (1987a, 1988, 1989b); and Mani (1990). On class, gender, and experience, see Joan W. Scott (1988, 1991) and Steedman (1986). On intersections of race, class, and gender, see Spelman (1988) and Fox-Genovese (1982). Haraway (1991a) provides a critical overview of "difference" in feminism.

14. From the French text, "Idéology et Appareils Idéologiques d'État" (Althusser 1970:31).

15. This point is made by Roland Barthes (1986c:61): "The work is caught up in a process of filiation. What is postulated are a *determination* of the world (of the race, then of History) over the work, a *consecution* of works among themselves, and an *appropriation* of the work to its author. The author is reputed to be the father and the owner of his work. . . . The Text, on the other hand, is read without the Father's inscription."

16. Faulkner's progenitively obsessed male narrators are continually being tripped up by their astonished discovery of what Patrocinio Schweickart (1991:527), commenting on Malcom X's "startling reading of Mendelian genetics," calls the "most rudimentary fact of human reproduction: whether you start with a black man or a white man, without a woman, you get *nothing*."

17. Michelle Rosaldo (1980:117–18) notes that Ilongot hunting success correlates roughly with age, with young boys and elderly men being least successful. However, the anthropologists' inquiries into "the extreme variation in hunting successes were seen as potentially disruptive; protesting that all men are equal, Ilongots revealed their awareness of difference only in nervous jokes about men who bagged nothing, and complaints that the animals killed by good hunters had been tainted by magical plants." Cf. R. Rosaldo (1980:143–46).

18. Cf. M. Rosaldo (1980:131).

19. On commercialism in urban Karo curing practice, see Steedly (1989c).

20. This sort of anti-initiation story is probably well on its way to becoming as "hackneyed" as Fox (1992:6) claims that stories of "sudden baptisms" into a local community have become. But however commonplace and discredible such tales from the field may be, narratively, I believe they retain considerable power in organizing (at least the early phases of) the experience of fieldwork. Indeed, it could be argued that by highlighting the "accidental initiation" story as a conventional ethnographic genre, critics have made this particular emplotment virtually inescapable for the fieldworker. One is thus impelled to inscribe it in the text ironically, as I have done here.

21. The relatively public nature of these meetings also helped to assure everyone involved, from the mediums down to my neighbors and the families of my student assistants, that we were not gathering secret knowledge (or seeking personal advice) from the curers.

22. Even the one fairly consistent gender distinction that Karo made regarding ritual roles—that only women may act as mediums in the funeral seance—was not absolute. On one occasion that I know of my (male) neighbor Darma officiated as the medium at a seance held in his mother's home.

23. For a general statement on such selective tradition-making strategies, see Williams (1977:115).

CHAPTER TWO. THE KARO SOCIAL WORLD

1. Apparently following the Malay logic, early European writers defined the term as "pork-eater" (Joustra 1902b; Loeb 1972:20; van der Tuuk 1861; Warneck 1977), thus stressing the religious (i.e., non-Muslim) component of Batak cultural identity. Neumann (1951), however, queries this definition; elsewhere (Neumann 1902a) he notes a connection between *Batak* and *dibata*, the term for the higher deities, also commonly used for ancestral spirits. Because of its association with the demographically dominant Toba, as well as its connotations of paganism, backwardness, and cannibalism, the name "Batak" is not preferred by Karo—nor by Mandailing and Angkola, who converted to Islam in the nineteenth century.

2. The term *dusun* was generally translated by the Dutch as "colony"; among Karo it specifically referred to a pioneer settlement founded by migrants from a "parent village" (*perbapan*) and retaining political ties to that originary community. In a more general sense, the term indicated the entire piedmont region that had been settled by Karo migrating "downstream" from the highlands.

3. Karo are the only Sumatran group who engage in *tegalen* (permanent cultivation of dry-field crops) agriculture (Scholz 1983). Because Karo rice fields were more or less fixed, villages were large, permanent settlements, having as many as several thousand inhabitants (de Haan 1870; von Brenner 1894; Singarimbun 1975). Until single-family houses were introduced early in this century, each village was made up of a number of massive eight-family dwellings, of a type still in use today in some parts of the highlands. On Karo house forms, see Huender (1929) and Singarimbun (1975:55–69).

4. On Karo migration, both before and after Indonesian independence, see Richard D. Kipp (1978). Cunningham (1958) discusses the similar migration of Toba Bataks to the Sumatran plantation zone; Pelzer (1982) gives an overview of the politics of resettlement in postwar North Sumatra.

5. On the equation of Karo and Toba clan affiliations in the context of contemporary migrations, see Richard D. Kipp (1978). On the association of Malays with Karo clans, see, for example, Luckman (1971).

6. For a detailed discussion of *ertutur*, see Rita S. Kipp (1984:918–23).

7. There are several institutionalized exceptions to this general rule. Intermarriage between members of the Meliala subclan and other Sembiring subclans

categorized by a prohibition on the eating of dog meat is not considered incestuous; likewise Sebayang subclan members may marry persons of the other Perangin-angin subclans (except for Pinem), but are sometimes said to be prohibited from marrying members of the Karo-Karo Sitepu subclan. Cf. Singarimbun (1975:73–80).

8. Karo frequently say that impal marriages are socially desirable because they reinforce already existing relations between kin groups and families, and that they are personally desirable for one's children because they rearticulate the intense affective bond between brother and sister in a non-incestuous context. Karo young people, however, often dismiss impal marriages as unromantic, though reliable. Cf. Rita S. Kipp (1976, 1986) and Singarimbun (1975).

9. The (untranslatable) Karo terms *kalimbubu* and *anak beru* actually cover a far wider range of social relations than marital exchange. I use the terms "wifegiver" and "wife-receiver" here simply as convenient glosses.

10. I only touch here on the complexity of Karo kinship and ritual organization. There is a considerable body of literature, both ethnographic and analytical, on various aspects of Karo kinship. Aside from secondary analyses such as Needham (1978) and Leach (1961), these works include Bangun (1981) and Rita S. Kipp (1979, 1984, 1985, 1986). For a detailed description of kinship in Karo ritual, see Rita S. Kipp (1976) and Singarimbun (1975).

11. Anthropologists studying other Batak societies have debated the issue of maintaining traditional patterns of kinship and custom in a "modernizing" world. See, for example, Bruner (1961); Rodgers (1979); Sherman (1990); and Viner (1979). For Karo contributions to a discussion of adat and history, see Tamboen (1952) and Sedjarah Kebudayaan Karo (1958).

12. A more detailed examination of the historical production of Karo adat in the context of colonial adversarial relations appears in Steedly (1989a).

13. For historical and archaeological analyses of precolonial political organization in eastern Sumatra, see Edwards MacKinnon (1984); Micsic (1979); Milner (1982); and Milner et al. (1978). Drakard (1990) describes a similar form of symbiotic political organization between "Bataks" and "Malays" in seventeenth-century Barus, on the west coast of Sumatra.

14. The highlanders' anthropophagic reputation was a matter of considerable fascination for early European explorers, although there is little evidence that this reputation was generally deserved or, indeed, that it had any basis at all. Beaulieu's remarks, as well as several other early (and similar) commentaries on Batak society, are cited in William Marsden's *History of Sumatra* (Marsden 1966:390–91 [repr. 1811]). Following up on the accusation of Batak anthropophagy, Marsden devotes a long section in his own account to a rather ghoulish description of a cannibal feast, which, as he admits, he did not witness himself. Marsden (ibid.:394) attributes the lack of eyewitness account to the "commendable discouragement of the practice by our government that occasions its being so rare a sight to Europeans, in a country where there are no travellers from curiosity, and where the servants of the Company having appearances to maintain, cannot by their presence, as idle spectators, give a sanction to proceedings, which it is their duty to discourage, although their influence is not sufficient to prevent them."

15. Anderson's (1971b:242–302 passim) population estimates for the adja-

cent regions are: Serdang, 3,000 Malays and 8,000 Bataks; Langkat, 7,350 Malays and 13,560 Bataks; Sunggal, 20,000 Bataks. Setting the Malay-Karo population ratio for Deli at a similar 1:2, this would give a total estimated population of 72,000 for the "untrodden" plantation zone in 1823. These figures are admittedly rough estimates.

16. Cf. Anderson (1971b); Edwards McKinnon (1984); Micsic (1979); and Milner (1982).

17. Stoler (1992) provides a detailed account of one such attack by a Gayo-Karo raiding party and its repercussions in the local European community.

18. These intermediate rulers—the datuks of Sunggal, Hamparen Perak, Sukapiring, and Patumbak—were Karo headmen who held Malay lineage titles. Although they were occasionally cast in mission reports as henchmen of the sultan (e.g., Joustra 1902a:55–56), the datuks seem to have been relatively independent of Malay hegemony until the autonomous native government was established (and no doubt remained so afterward). See Luckman Sinar (1971:152–60) for a detailed account of the Batak War of 1872 and its aftermath.

19. Except where otherwise noted, my account of the mission's early years derives from Rita S. Kipp (1990). This historical study details the political intrigues that lay behind the coming of the mission to colonial Karoland, attending scrupulously to personal misgivings and doctrinal differences within the small mission community, as well as to the contradictory political interests that set mission, planters, and colonial administration at odds with one another in East Sumatra.

20. The Dutch characteristically considered highland unrest to be the result of the lack of formal governmental institutions. However, it seems that the political disturbances they observed were at least in part caused by the Dutch presence. In 1900 Joustra paid a visit to the highland village of Batu Karang, where he hoped to have an audience with the pengulu, Kiras Bangun (later the leader of Karo resistance to the Dutch annexation of the region). This request was denied, and Joustra writes: "To my further questions, I learned that Si Kiras did not so much have anything against Europeans, but he had observed that precisely those villages which let in the most Tuans [Dutch] were always 'disagreeing among themselves', the immediate proof being [the villages of] Kaban Djahe and Koeta Boeloeh. Batoe Karang had till now been spared such disaster. The village was well-populated; the people lived cheerfully and in peace with each other, etc. He had thus constantly refused, as other chiefs had insisted of him, to attempt by the mediation of the Controleur to obtain rifles and ammunition" (Joustra 1901b: 77–78).

21. My summary of events leading up to the annexation of Karoland draws primarily on Westenberg's (1904a) eyewitness report to the governor-general on the Karo campaign, as well as Rita S. Kipp's (1990) account of the annexation drawn from mission sources. Kozok (1991b) briefly but carefully sketches these events from the viewpoint of Karo opposition leaders. Given the intricate politics of engagement and disengagement enacted by all the parties involved, it is not surprising that there are some discrepancies among these accounts. On van Daalen's brutal Gayo campaign, see Bowen (1991:62–66) and Kempees (1905).

22. Here I rely on a detailed report on the political reorganization of the Karo

highlands by Assistant Resident Westenberg (1904b), who was largely responsible for the arrangement. Westenberg specifically discusses his resurrection of the "forgotten" titles of the "four kings."

23. However, particularly in the early years of colonial rule, decisions regarding claimants to political office were often based upon Dutch judgments of candidates' suitability for office as much as upon the still-vague "hereditary" right of succession. The perceived favoritism in the colonial administration's selection of office-holders was one source of popular dissatisfaction within the new ruling elite, and helped to drive a wedge between the rulers and the ruled.

24. Such cooptation of local political forms was a common feature of colonial rule, especially under systems of indirect rule. For African examples, see Fields (1985) and Ranger (1983).

25. A man's wife came under the protection of his family spirits, rather than those of her natal family. These latter might, in their role as kalimbubu of the woman's marital household, retaliate for inappropriate behavior among their anak beru by causing illness, misfortune, and, most notably, childlessness. But they were not included among the household protectors, for they were the bégu jabu of the wife's brothers.

26. In a few cases, extralocal lineages were connected through the creation of subsidiary ancestral shrines. The clan history of Siwah-Sada-Ginting (a cluster of nine subclans of merga Ginting) tells of such an incident (cf. Neumann 1927a, 1930).

27. Neumann's (1927b) detailed study of Karo offering places is the best source on village spirit-shrines, including descriptions of the community rituals associated with these. See also Joustra (1897); Westenberg (1891); and Pesik (1895).

28. The Singamangarajas were a line of petty rulers of the Bakkara valley on the southwestern margin of Lake Toba. Although these rulers were, in exceptional circumstances, able to collect tribute from a wider part of the Toba region, they were primarily religious functionaries rather than political leaders. Even in the religious sphere their authority was circumscribed; it was only recognized within the Sumba clan-group (one of the several major groupings of clans into which Toba society is divided). In Karoland the Singamangaraja dynasty was accorded neither secular nor spiritual powers, and there is no indication that Si Singamangaraja played any role in Karo religion prior to the Perhudamdam movement. Cf. Castles (1975). Works dealing with Si Singamangaraja XII include Napitupulu (1971); Said (1961); Sibarani (1979); and Sidjabat (1982). In a letter dated July 23, 1853, the linguist H. N. van der Tuuk briefly describes a meeting with Si Singamangaraja and a similarly "spontaneous" religious movement in western Tapanuli (Beekman 1988:134–38). Drawing on the accounts of Neumann (1918) and van den Berg (1920), van der Kroef (1970) describes the Perhudamdam movement in Karoland; however, his analysis is based on social and economic conditions in the Toba area. Other contemporary sources on the Perhudamdam movement in East Sumatra include Tideman (1922) and the anonymous articles reprinted in the *Indische Gids* (1917, 1918). For a description of a present-day Toba Batak social movement centering on Si Singamangaraja, see Cunningham (1989).

29. Once news of the movement reached the controleur of the Barus subdistrict (Tapanuli Residency), troops were ordered into the area, and several of its instigators were exiled. For about a year the movement remained quiescent, but in October 1916 another mass assembly took place in Tangga Batu, in the Toba subdistrict. Again the Dutch intervened, and approximately fifty of the movement's adherents were captured and exiled. Several months later, the movement again surfaced in the village of Rura Parira. On January 2, 1917, the local constable [*civiel gezaghebber*] W. C. Muller arrived on the scene with ten men (and apparently only one revolver between them). Attempting to disperse a crowd of about five hundred people, Muller was killed in the ensuing altercation. A few moments later government troops arrived, but, being outnumbered by the crowd, simply retrieved Muller's body and then retreated. Several days later troops returned to pacify the area, and about twenty Bataks were killed. Within two weeks local disturbances had ended (Lumban Tobing and Gobée 1919:389–93; Joustra 1918a:147).

30. "Blessed are they who are persecuted for righteousness' sake; for theirs is the kingdom of heaven. Blessed are ye, when men shall revile you, and persecute you, and shall say all manner of evil against you falsely, for my sake. Rejoice, and be exceedingly glad; for great is your reward in heaven; for so persecuted they the prophets who were before you."

31. As Neumann writes, "They ask: why have the children of the land been unjustly fined? By which is meant: why have the whites placed taxes and corvée labor on us" (Neumann 1918:185).

32. However, in late July of that year the American botanist H. H. Bartlett (1918) noted in his journal that at least in the Asahan district of East Sumatra the government's suppression of the movement had not had much effect on local belief in the supernatural powers of Si Singamangaraja.

33. On pemuda activities elsewhere in Indonesia, see B. Anderson (1972) and Cribb (1991).

34. The hardship undergone by Karo during the "time of the exodus" (*jaman mengungsi*) is the subject of a number of Karo songs that are still extremely popular. The best-known of these are *katoneng-katoneng* (a genre of improvised song accompanied by the five-piece Karo gendang ensemble) performed by Malem Pagi Ginting and by Sinik beru Karo. These have been recorded on cassette and are available in Karo music shops, the latter recording in bootleg form. In Steedly (1992) I discuss Sinik's song of the exodus; the entire text is transcribed and translated in Sembiring (1987).

35. Surbakti (1979:381–427) gives a detailed account of these events.

36. On the *revolusi sosial* in East Sumatra, see Said (1973) and Reid (1979). The best source on the social revolution in Karoland is Surbakti (1977).

37. This decision was no doubt also influenced by the political climate of the times, for the gendang orchestra had since the revolution been used for propaganda purposes, first by Karo nationalists and later by political parties.

38. Two token parties were subsequently reinstated: the Sukarnoist (and predominantly Christian) Partai Demokrasi Indonesia, and the Muslim Partai Persatuan Pembangunan (the Development Unity party).

39. According to interviews.

40. This category is listed as "Other" (*Lain-lain*). Aside from followers of Agama Pemena, it includes a few (Chinese) Buddhists, (Tamil) Hindus, and Pentecostals, who are not officially considered to be Protestants.

41. Data on the religious affiliation of Karo residing in Kabupaten Karo are taken from *Buku Tahunan 1984 Propinsi Sumatera Utara*. Indonesian census data do not indicate ethnicity, and it is thus impossible to determine the relative numbers of Karo Christians, Muslims, and followers of Agama Pemena in multiethnic urban settings. The same is true of Kabupatens Deli-Serdang and Langkat. Since the time of my fieldwork there appears to have been a gradual increase in numbers of both Christians and Muslims, and a decline in followers of Agama Pemena. A more recent examination of the politics of religion in contemporary Karo society is Rita S. Kipp (1993), a draft of which I received after this book was in press.

42. For an example of the government's monitoring of *aliran kepercayaan*, see Proyek Pembinaan dan Bimbingan Aliran Kepercayaan/Faham Keagamaan (1979). This is a listing of all known "sects" in Indonesia, with information on locations, leaders, number of adherents, basis and form of instruction, connection with an official religion, activities, public attitudes, government attitude, and "excesses."

43. Cultural tourism is big business in certain parts of Indonesia, most notably Bali and Torajaland in Sulawesi. There public rituals, or touristic reenactments of rituals, contribute significantly to regional (and national, in Bali's case) income. Tourism in North Sumatra has tended to focus on nature—wildlife observation, mountain-climbing, trekking, rafting, and the like—not culture. The provincial government has shown some mild interest in promoting cultural tourism, but the only visible effects I saw in 1980s Karoland were the preservation of the "traditional village" of Lingga and the designation of the hot springs of Lau Debuk-Debuk as a "tourist object"—which meant constructing a parking lot, cleaning the springs occasionally, and charging admission to non-Karo visitors. On cultural tourism in Tana Toraja, see Volkman (1990).

44. The early history of the movement that has now become institutionalized as Parisada Hindu Dharma appears in Geertz (1972, 1973a). A brief description of Parisada Hindu Dharma is included in Boon (1977). An account of the "Hinduization" of another indigenous religious system among the Tengger of East Java is given in Hefner (1985). Atkinson (1987) discusses a similar situation among the Wana of Sulawesi.

45. Brahma Putro's *Karo dari Jaman ke Jaman* (Karo from Era to Era) was published in 1981, shortly after the Karo branch of Parisada Hindu Dharma was founded, under the auspices of the organization's (Tamil-dominated) provincial chapter. The author, a Karo man of the Sembiring Berahmana subclan, was at the time employed by a Tamil-run private school in Medan. The establishment of this historical link between Tamil and Karo "Hinduism" was of some importance within the internal politics of the provincial chapter, where the Tamil leadership was being challenged by a small group of politically influential Balinese. Cf. A. Mani (1979).

46. Since the time of my fieldwork this situation may have changed somewhat; several highland villages now have newly built Balinese-style temples for Hindu worship (Rita S. Kipp, p.c.).

47. Spirit offerings are one of the most obvious elements of "belief" that have been eliminated from secular ceremonies. For example, I once had a long discussion with a Karo church official regarding the propriety of including a prepared betel leaf on the plate on which the marriage payment was placed in wedding negotiations. If no actual concern for spirits was intended by the participants, could this be considered a symbolic (and thus acceptable) gesture of respect to adat, or did its original meaning as a spirit-offering make it unacceptable to Christians? It was the latter, he concluded.

48. A similar reduction in the scope of adat has been noted (though different implications are drawn from this) by Rodgers (1979, 1981) for the (predominantly Muslim) Sipirok Angkola and Bruner (1961) for urban (Christian) Toba.

49. For an examination of the concept of gotong royong in Old Order and New Order political rhetoric, see Bowen (1986). Warren (1990) considers the local reappropriation of state rhetoric as a form of resistance to state authority.

CHAPTER THREE. MARKETS AND MONEY

1. Cf. Wijngaarden (1894a:171–73).

2. The entire logic here seems to be based on a misunderstanding of the Karo term *mas*, "gold." In Karoland, where the usual coinage was silver, *mas* referred specifically to the tiny Acehnese gold coins (*deraham*) which served as a token of the marriage's legitimacy, and which comprised a part of the *ulu mas* segment of the marriage payment. Neumann (1939:564) writes that "[f]rom the giving of the *draham* (Atjehnese coin) many Bataks derive the name of the wife—*toekoermas*." It should be noted that the ulu emas is in fact given not to the bride's family but rather to the groom's kalimbubu by birth (MB's), as a sign that the bride has "become" their daughter, thus bringing the marriage into line with the Karo marital ideal. No ulu mas is paid in the case of actual (immediate) cross-cousin marriage.

3. Neumann, at least, was later to call into question the basic assumption that the marriage payment was a simple purchase. He argues that "although a 'purchase price' is spoken of, it is still very much the question whether 'purchase' (*toekoerna*) in the Batak sense is covered by our meaning of purchase. Previously, when there was as yet no money economy, *toekoer* . . . may well have had another meaning or other shadings than the concept of 'purchase', in particular 'acquire/gain'." At any rate, he adds, "[i]n no case is this a purchase in our sense" (Neumann 1939:561).

4. The best example of this occurs in the debate between Menadoese mission teacher Richard Tampenawas and a group of Karo men on the subject of marriage payments. Rebutting the Karo argument that without such payment the bride's parents would suffer a considerable loss on her marriage, Tampenawas replies: " 'Which is worth more, a person or a cow?' 'Certainly a person,' they answered. 'A person or a horse?' 'A person.' 'If one has a fine horse, large, nicely colored,

nicely built, for how much can it be sold?' 'As much as 200 dollars.' 'Now then, if not more than 120 dollars is paid for a girl, how can that be? I think that something isn't square here. . . . A person is as a valuable instrument, that no amount of money can buy' " (Tampenawas 1895:71).

5. For a detailed discussion of Karo marriage payments and their distribution, see Rita S. Kipp (1976:175–97) and Singarimbun (1975:171–78).

6. "Siwah-Sada Ginting" literally means "Nine-One Ginting." This refers to a cluster of nine subclans of merga Ginting that claim descent from a common ancestor.

7. The entire history is given (in Karo and in Dutch translation) in Neumann (1930). The text given here is slightly abridged from the relevant passage in Neumann's text (pp. 18–21). The translation from the Karo is my own; there are a few slight differences from Neumann's Dutch translation. These do not, however, substantially alter the meaning of the text. A very brief English summary also appears in Singarimbun (1975:199–200).

8. Neumann saw the distribution of the tale as an indication of human sacrifice practiced in earlier times at market sites, although he found no further evidence to corroborate his speculation on this point (Neumann 1926:16).

9. Parry and Bloch (1989:23–30) suggestively argue that such a separation of "transactional orders" into a sphere of individual competition and short-term interests and one of long-term social reproduction, is a general pattern of economic organization. Moral evaluations tend not to be passed upon these separate orders as such but rather upon the conversion of gains in one sphere to another. Thus the transfer of short-term profits to the long-term cycle would be positively evaluated; its moral antipode would be the possibility (illustrated here by Si Aji Dibata's demanding his sister's marriage payment) that "grasping individuals will divert the resources of the long-term cycle for their own short-term transactions."

10. These were mostly mountain passes leading to the coastal lowlands. There were seven such passes. Aside from these, there was the "Alas-road" along which Tiga Bembem was located, and by which traders from southern Aceh traveled through Karoland and on to the Malay trade entrepots of the coast (Edwards McKinnon 1984:23–24).

11. The Ginting Suka subclan's access to Toba derived from their conquest of the Ginting Munthe subclan of Ajinembah (not one of the Siwah-Sada Ginting subclan cluster), which migrated to Karoland by way of Simelungun and controlled the port village of Tongging on Lake Toba. It should also be noted that the area of Gurubenua was subsequently conquered by a Sembiring lineage from Urung Sarinembah.

12. It was on account of these kin- and trade-relations that the rulers of Sunggal were able to call upon highland Karo military support in their opposition to the intrusion of European planters in the "Batak War" of 1872 (cf. Luckman Sinar 1971:156–60; Schadee 1918:187–203). At the time John Anderson visited the Sumatran east coast in 1823 he found that the sibayak of Lingga (the chief village of Urung III Kuru) was staying in Sunggal, where he had extensive pepper gardens (J. Anderson 1971b:70).

13. The alliance of Seberaya and Deli Tua is memorialized in the myth of Puteri Hijo, the "green princess." See Middendorp (1929b) for a historical-

symbolic analysis of this myth; and Parlindungan (1964:494–500) and Brahma Putro (1981:214–38) for (rather fanciful) alternative "factual" readings.

14. See Bronson (1977) for a model of coastal-hinterlands trade based upon the Sumatran and Malay peninsular pattern. Although admittedly schematic and tending to overemphasize the hierarchical relations between lowland trade centers and highland producers, as well as the permanence of ties between producers and particular market centers, this model seems to correspond to the precolonial pattern of trade relations between lowland Malays and highland Karo. Micsic (1985) has recently offered a critique of Bronson's model, also drawing on archaeological and historical data from Sumatra, suggesting that Bronson overemphasizes the importance of foreign influence in the development of coast-hinterlands trade patterns.

15. The Kuta Buluh region was known for its gold. The narrative "Sibayak Kuta Buluh" (Joustra 1914) describes the distribution of Kuta Buluh's customary portion of the gold collected in nearby Lau Simomo and Lau Rencak. Joustra, who visited that village in 1900, was hesitant to ask to see where the gold was collected because he feared that the local people "might have attributed bad intentions to me" (Joustra 1901b:81).

16. Kruijt (1891:357–59) provides a more complete inventory of the market of Tiga Belawan, which he visited in 1891.

17. Gambir cakes were also used as small change; Kruijt (1891:360) reports an exchange rate of 250–300 cakes per guilder. Cf. Bloch's (1989:182–83) description of trade and currency in the "peripheral" markets of eighteenth-century Imerina (Madagascar).

18. By 1898, when Joustra visited Tiga Belawan, gambling had been outlawed there. However, a new market had also been established nearby (Tiga Mbaru, literally, "new market") and gambling was permitted, and flourishing, there (Joustra 1899b:135, 143).

19. Kruijt (1891:361–62) gives a description of such a court meeting held at Tiga Belawan in 1891.

20. See Middendorp (1920) on warfare in Karoland.

21. Tiga Deraya, in Urung III Kuru, is the exception to this. However, in this case there were three major villages, each controlled by a different subclan, who were allied in the urung-federation. Tiga Deraya is located approximately equidistantly from the three.

22. This can still be seen in bus routes and trade links between upland and lowland communities. It is also apparent in the asserted kinship linkages between the ruling lineages of highland communities and Malayized Karo rulers of the lowlands with whom these communities had commercial ties.

23. This text, an episode in the clan history of merga Perangin-angin Kuta Buluh, was recorded following Joustra's visit to Kuta Buluh in October 1900 (Joustra 1901a:118). Joustra's host there, the current sibayak, arranged to bring the teller, a man named Si Onan Katana, to the mission post in Buluh Hawar so that the missionary could learn the tale: "He asserted that it was good that the Tuans [the Dutch] heard it all. The Sultan of Langkat would not have wished that these things were made general knowledge, for then it would appear that His Highness himself had appropriated far too many rights. Koeta Boeloeh had very

old rights to a part of the lowland land and thus claimed a considerable part of the hasil taneh [rental fees for plantation land]" (Joustra 1901b:80). Although the Karo text was not published until 1914, a Dutch-language summary appears in Joustra (1903:158–62).

24. From the ubiquity of this theme in bilang-bilang laments, one might suspect that the lowlands were filled with broken-hearted young Karo men. However, as I was told by contemporary counterparts of the luckless Karo troubadours, this was simply a tactical "line" aimed at melting the resistance of a maiden playing hard to get—pity being the shortest route to seduction—and not to be taken entirely at face value. On bilang-bilang, see Neumann (1929, 1933); Joustra (1902d); and Kozok (1991a).

25. The alliance between Britain and the Dutch monarchy during the Napoleonic wars (1794–1816) provided the opportunity for British expansion into the ostensibly Dutch sphere of Sumatra. The rise of the Islamic Paderi movement in West Sumatra and the decline of the kingdom of Siak in the first decades of the nineteenth century disrupted pepper trade throughout these regions and created a political vacuum that allowed for the emergence of the autonomous sultanates of the east coast. For a concise summary of imperial politics and nineteenth-century trade relations between Penang and the Sumatran states, see O'Malley (1977:107–8).

26. This intervillage warfare apparently contributed to the subsequent decline in the local pepper industry. Netscher, the Dutch resident of Riau, noted in 1863 that the East Sumatran pepper gardens were exhausted and had not been replanted because of the lawlessness of the region (Pelzer 1978:33–34). It should be noted, however, that Dutch competition and the Netherlands' expansionist policy in Sumatra were also factors, directly limiting British influence in the region and indirectly adding to the unsettled local conditions.

27. Anderson consistently uses the generic "Batta" (i.e., Batak) to describe the various highland people he encountered. It is usually clear, however, which group he is speaking of, and I have only cited instances where it is evident that the "Battas" being described are Karo.

28. William Marsden had earlier traveled among Batak groups though not, apparently, in Karoland. First published in 1811, his *History of Sumatra* features some lurid (and admittedly secondhand) descriptions of Batak cannibalism (Marsden 1966:390–95). These appear to have had a considerable influence on Anderson, who asked many of the "Battas" whom he met about their penchant for consuming human flesh. His informants, for their part, seem to have encouraged Anderson's curiosity (and his fears) by enthusiastically confirming these stories. Anderson does note, however, that Karo, unlike other Bataks, were never anthropophagists.

29. Anderson probably means here that the men were of the Karo-Karo clan. This would be appropriate, since the rulers of Sunggal were Malayized Karo who claimed descent from the Surbakti subclan of merga Karo-Karo.

30. According to von Brenner, these earrings, which were so heavy that they had to be attached to a woman's tudung headcloth, might contain the silver from as many as sixty-two dollars (von Brenner 1894:274). I saw several sets of these old earrings in local antique shops that weighed more than a pound each.

31. Kruijt comments: "The currency for gambling is the ordinary [Mexican] dollar and its fractions. The 'fine dollar,' that is, the Spanish, is worth 1.20 dollars. These are saved and buried, for whenever a child marries the bridewealth [*bruidschat*] must be paid in these dollars" (Kruijt 1891:360).

32. The Spanish dollars, von Brenner writes, "all travel little by little to the Toba-lake, from where they never return, because they are melted down and used in the manufacture of jewelry" (von Brenner 1894:21). This final destination of the dollars' journey is probably mistaken. Silver was not used to any great extent in Toba jewelry, the preference being for bronze or gold. Silver jewelry was, rather, a Karo fashion, and Karoland was famous for its skilled silversmiths.

33. *Daulat* in the Karo language can be roughly glossed as "charisma." Andaya writes of the Malay concept of daulat: "Inadequately translated as 'sovereignty', it subsumes pre-Hindu, Hindu and Islamic concepts concerning the immutable power of the ruler, the sacredness of his person, the unseen forces which guarded him. To this daulat was attributed the ruler's control over the non-material world. . . . The possession of this daulat was the ruler's by right of birth and position; it could not be taken away and it was through this that he exerted spiritual and temporal authority over his subjects" (Andaya 1975:25–26). It should be noted that in the relatively egalitarian Karo society the implications of the term are far less grand than in the rigidly stratified Malay society.

34. Cf. Parry and Bloch (1989:26).

35. Or, conversely, it was through gifts of land that kin relations were formed. Cf. Rita S. Kipp (1976:46).

36. The population figure is taken from von Brenner's census of 1888 (von Brenner 1894:361). Although von Brenner's figures were rough estimates based on the number of houses in a village, they seem on the whole to be not inaccurate.

37. See Brahma Putro (1981:92–99) for an account of the founding and history of Rumah Kabanjahé.

38. According to Westenberg, in precolonial legal deliberations in Urung XII Kuta, no decision could be reached if the "anti-authoritarian" villages of Berastagi or Gurusinga disagreed with the opinion of their nominal superiors in Rumah Kabanjahé (Westenberg 1914:494).

39. Unlike their kinsmen in Rumah Kabanjahé, who were not only friendly to the Dutch but had been behind the Dutch conquest of the highlands, at least some of the Berastagi Purbas had joined forces with the Karo military forces that opposed the Dutch military expedition of 1904, and they appear to have been among the ringleaders of the 1902 attack on Rumah Kabanjahé that led to missionary Guillaume's expulsion from the village (Westenberg 1904a). I was told by a former pengulu of the village of Pecerén, a descendant of Pa Jendahen Purba, that Pa Jendahen's eldest son was among the guerillas who attacked the invading Dutch forces near Bandar Baru. The boy was captured, and, using him as a hostage, the Dutch forced Pa Jendahen to allow them into the village.

40. An informative comparison could be made between the effects of the introduction of the potato in Karoland and in other colonial situations. The most notable, and disastrous, instance is, of course, Ireland, where, as Salaman (1985:343) notes, "for close on 300 years the potato both stabilized and perpetuated the misery of the Irish masses." One major difference in the Karo case is that

while in Ireland and elsewhere potatoes became an important dietary staple, they have never formed a significant part of the Karo diet and were raised almost entirely for export trade. Nor, after the first few years of potato-growing (and the first experience of potato blight), did Karo have recourse to monocropping. Ortner (1989:158–59) briefly reviews the effects of the colonial introduction of the potato among the Sherpas of Nepal, where subsistence potato-growing generated new possibilities for wage labor and for the capitalization of wage surpluses.

41. Most notably the Rumah Berastagi Purbas' rival, the "enlightened" Pa Pelita of Kabanjahé, who was the first Karo to plant potatoes, in his fields at Katepul, near Rumah Kabanjahé (Joustra 1915:17).

42. Joustra comments that the ceding of this land was a sign of the high regard that the Karo held for Botje, since they were generally adamant about retaining the rights to their land. I would suggest that the rivalry between the Rumah Berastagi and Rumah Kabanjahé Purbas, and the fear that Botje's experimental gardens might be moved to the Rumah Kabanjahé area, probably was also a factor in this decision.

43. On the establishment of *sawah* (wet-rice fields) in the village of Payung, and the effects of this on patterns of land tenure, see Rita S. Kipp (1976:45–47). For a brief note on the similar situation in Batu Karang, see Reid (1979:58).

44. Wijngaarden (1894a:170–71) commented, for example, that it was the fear of becoming a "coolie" that kept many Karo from converting to Christianity. "For the Batak," he writes, "a coolie is the lowest being that exists. To have to work hard, and also to be beaten and kicked occasionally, the Batak has no desire for it. The coolies are looked down on with boundless contempt, they are beasts of burden." This Karo antipathy to all forms of wage labor has continued to the present.

45. Unlike the case in Onderafdeling Simelungun, where Toba migration was promoted in order to encourage the development of wet-rice agriculture, there was only a limited Toba presence in the Karo highlands (Clauss 1982; Cunningham 1958). Middendorp (1922:462) notes that there were some three hundred Toba migrants in the Karo highlands (presumably in 1917, at the end of Middendorp's tenure as controleur). Many of these were agricultural laborers; none were permitted to own land. The most interesting documents of Karo hostility to Toba migrants are in the early mission reports. The NZG had attempted to augment the staff of the Karo mission by employing several Toba Christian teachers. However, the Karo were so generally antagonistic to these men that the plan was aborted and the Toba teachers sent home (Joustra 1901a:113–15; Neumann 1901:134). On colonial concerns regarding "outside agitators," especially in the Berastagi area, see Holleman (1933:79).

46. This generally remains true to the present, although some Karo migrants to the city have hired Javanese laborers to maintain their village lands on a share basis. A more common pattern is for family members (usually sisters) still residing in the village to work the land of urban migrants.

47. For a discussion of the effects of the depression on the East Sumatran economy, see O'Malley (1977:131–43).

48. Obligations to perform corvée labor of from eighteen to forty days a year had previously been in effect; however, as O'Malley (1977:139) notes, the obliga-

tion could be "bought off" for a fairly small amount. But the depression reduced cash income to such an extent that many people were unable to pay even the reduced amount necessary to avoid corvée labor, and were thus compelled to work without pay for the obligatory period.

49. The villages of Berastepu and Gurukinayan at the foot of Mount Sinabun were particularly noted for their orange groves, and, in one of the few such cases in Karoland, a European planter received a land concession of twenty hectares on the slopes of that mountain to establish an experimental station for improving the strains and productivity of local oranges (Holleman 1933:31–32).

50. For a detailed discussion of Karo land rights, see Slaats and Portier (1981) and Tamboen (1952). Steenhoven (1970) presents an interesting account of a legal dispute regarding the conflict between communal and individual rights to a village's empty land.

51. A. M. van Liere, who was controleur of Onderafdeling Karolanden in 1931, notes that by that time a number of villages in the urungs of XII Kuta and III Kuru had no more empty land and in some cases village woodlands had been wholly or in part held in individual usufruct. He saw this "individualization process" as a deterioration of communal land ownership, which had "naturally gone the furthest in the most densely populated and most developed areas" (van Liere 1931:221).

52. These figures are for the Berastagi area. In Kabanjahé, where land was less desirable, the rates were twenty cents per square meter as present taneh and one cent per meter as the annual hasil taneh (van Liere 1931:66).

53. The distribution of the amount between the local rulers and other members of the ruling lineage is not given, and may have been negotiated among the concerned parties rather than fixed by rule.

54. The general discussion of Dutch "Ethical Policy" presented below is drawn from Furnivall (1939:225–39), except where otherwise noted.

55. On the events immediately surrounding Guillaume's expulsion from Kabanjahé, see Guillaume (1903) and Rita S. Kipp (1990:195–222).

56. Westenberg's (1904a) report on the military expedition and his "Notes on the Development of the Previously Independent Karolands" (1904b) give his account of the Karo campaign and his negotiations with the Karo chiefs.

57. Cf. Bloch (1989:187) for the similar effects in Madagascar of the French colonial replacement of old silver coins with French currency in 1895.

58. Marriage payments were limited to ƒ. 120 for children of the five Dutch-appointed sibayaks, ƒ.80 for children of raja urungs, ƒ. 60 for children of pengulus, and ƒ.50 for everyone else. It is worth noting that while a kind of ranking system was created by this scale, it was fixed by the *individual* status of office-holders within the bureaucratic hierarchy rather than by family status. In any event, the policy seems not to have been successfully implemented, for Karo responded to the regulation by dividing the marriage payment into an "official" payment (*unjuken si arah tan raja*) distributed by the pengulu and conforming to the legally established limits, and the *wang tinepet* or "private money" given directly to the father of the bride and thus not subject to government control. The latter amount, according to van Liere (1931:212–13), was as a rule much larger than the amount of the official marriage payment.

59. Other forms of accumulated wealth were also indirectly affected by colonial policies. For example, the ownership of (largely ineffective) rifles had been an alternative form of accumulated wealth, and Dutch gun control regulations limited access to firearms.

60. See, for example, Parry and Bloch (1989:14); Lan (1989:198); and James C. Scott (1976:97–98). In British Africa taxation was seen as an intentional means of labor recruitment among the native population. Thus, as Fields (1985:108) notes for British Central Africa, mission attitudes toward colonial tax policies ambivalently weighed the merits of "this indispensable nudge toward 'self-improvement' " on one hand, and the oppression of tax-driven proletarianization on the other. In a case that resonates significantly with the Karo situation, Terence Ranger (1985:28–48) describes the failure of British colonial taxation to force the Shona of Makoni District, Rhodesia, into the labor market, largely because of their successful "self-peasantization."

61. It is difficult to determine conclusively from available sources the impact of taxation on the local population. Middendorp (1929a:61) notes, for example, that up to 1920 there had been no local objection to the graduated income tax imposed by the government in 1908. While opposition to colonial taxation figured significantly in the rhetoric of the millenarian Perhudamdam movement of 1915–18, Karo seem to have objected more strenuously to corvée labor requirements. James Scott (1976:92–94), arguing that the inflexibility of tax policies in colonial Southeast Asia violated the "moral economy" of peasant farmers, focuses primarily on the injustice of regressive taxation, but he notes also in passing the importance of the novel abstract equality of state extractive measures under colonial rule.

62. With certain exceptions, most specifically the requirement for corvée labor in families of local rulers, and for members of certain professions, such as musicians.

63. This principle, established by a 1901 ruling by Controleur Westenberg, continued to be controversial throughout the colonial period, and indeed is still a sore point among Karo adherents of Agama Pemena. Cf. Neumann (1902b) and Vuurmans (1930). For contemporary views, see Steedly (1988, 1989c). Comaroff (1985:29) briefly discusses the politics of a similar Christian withdrawal from ritual participation among the Tshidi of southern Africa.

64. On the decline of traditional arts in the early colonial period, see Middendorp (1922:463–64). Middendorp, who was the controleur of Onderafdeling Karolanden from 1914 to 1917, was actively involved in the (temporary) revival of Karo gold- and silversmithing during this period.

65. In Tapanuli, the Toba *gondang* orchestra was outlawed at the request of the Rheinische Mission Gesellschaft, apparently because of its "heathen" nature (Korn 1953). It is unclear why the government of Onderafdeling Karolanden outlawed the secular guro-guro aron, although the objections of the missionaries, who found it an incitement to immorality and gambling, may be relevant here. According to an article published in the Karo newspaper *Pusaka Karo* in 1932, the guro-guro aron was outlawed in 1927, at a time when the Dutch were extremely concerned with subversive activities throughout Indonesia, and this concern may well have played a part in the decision (Teraniaja 1932).

66. In this regard, it is worth noting that elsewhere in the Residency, most specifically on the plantations, gambling was more generally ignored, if not openly tolerated. There it served the purpose of keeping the plantation coolies indebted so that they would not return to Java. Hamka's (1982) novel *Merantau ke Deli* provides a vivid description of the gambling dens that sprang up around the plantations on paydays.

67. Cf. Bangun (1981:189–90).

68. Cf. the discussion of "social capital" in Bourdieu (1977:178–81).

69. Reprinted in the *Mededeeling van wege het Nederlandsch Zendelingge- nootschap*, Wijngaarden's article first appeared in the journal of the Netherlands East Indies Mission Society, *De Opwekker*, no. 151 (October 1, 1893).

70. Cf. Comaroff and Comaroff (1991:191–92, 256) on a similar, and simi- larly astute, "misrecognition" of missionary motives by the South African Tswana.

71. Joustra's shifting views on this matter are a case in point. In 1896 he is deeply critical of Karo "practical materialism"; yet by 1915 he is praising this same materialistic spirit as leading to significant economic advancement in the region (Joustra 1896:243; 1915).

72. The Karo word *taki* (or *taki-taki*) is related to the Toba *tahi*, "wisdom, authority," but is generally used more in the sense of political strategy or trickery. Enjoying one of those linguistic coincidences upon which false etymologies are often constructed, Karo usually glossed *taki-taki* for me with the English word "tactic."

73. Cf. Surbakti (1977:19–23) and Reid (1979:154–55) on Poesera, the Cen- ter for the People's Economy, which was founded in 1943 as a rice-distributing agency in Berastagi. Poesera was involved in nationalist propaganda efforts and organized an effective (if short-lived) boycott of the highland produce markets during the Japanese occupation. Following the Japanese surrender the organiza- tion shifted its efforts to opposing the Dutch reentry. According to Surbakti, it was through Poesera that Japanese weapons first came into the hands of Karo guerillas. Reid (ibid.) gives a more heroic account of the incident. On the ongoing market involvement of revolutionary groups in the Karo area, see Surbakti (1979:229–42 passim). Van Langenberg (1976:364, 526) and Stoler (1988:235) discuss the larger-scale export trade carried on by militia groups in the plantation region.

CHAPTER FOUR. ON MOUNT SIBAYAK

1. Hagen's use of the Toba Batak term *sombaon* here is somewhat misleading, and indicates his tendency to blur linguistic and cultural distinctions between the various Batak groups. In a later essay on Karo religious beliefs, Westenberg writes that "[o]f Sombaons and Soemangots, of which Dr. Hagen tells in detail, [I] have never heard in Karoland, and to my inquiries regarding this have never gotten any explanation" (1891:231). The Toba sombaon is a broad class of spirits, including village guardian spirits (K., *sembah-sembahen*) as well as the autochthonous na- ture spirits associated with particular places to which Hagen refers here, and which are today referred to by Karo as keramat.

2. Umangs seem to have fascinated European observers by their resemblance to the dwarves and trolls of their own folk tradition. Neumann (1926, 1927a), in his speculative history of the Karo clan migrations, presents them as original inhabitants of the region, who were conquered and relegated to the wild by the more advanced Karo invaders. Cf. van den Berg and Neumann (1908). Hagen (1882:533) comments that Karo considered the umangs as "humans" rather than spirits, though with the ability to make themselves invisible. This characterization of the umang as a special kind of human (or rather, quasi-human) being is still current among Karo today.

3. Romer (1910:225–27) describes various therapeutic and ritual practices in which the face is marked or spattered with the red betel-juice (*putari*), commenting that this is done in order to "ward off disaster in general." The Menadoese teacher Henderik Pesik (1895:63) observed this at a ritual aimed at protecting the village of Tambunen from smallpox during a year of epidemic. Neumann (1927b:520) likewise notes that this was done at annual propitiation rites for the spirit-shrine of Lau Simberu near the village of Timbang Lawan.

4. It is unclear whether Westenberg is characterizing the cases of banditry as "innumerable" because there were so many of them, or because, as he acknowledges, such incidents were rarely reported to the Dutch authorities.

5. According to Tamboen (1952), the Purba subclan claimed to be descended from the umang-king of Sibayak's peak. He expresses skepticism about this assertion, however, and suggests that it stems from a desire to hide the Purbas' "true" origin as runaway slaves from the Simelungun region (cf. Neumann 1926). Contemporary accounts of the Purba migrations and the founding of Berastagi locate the group's origin in the Simelungun region, but contain no suggestion of descent from umangs (or from slaves). These accounts do mention marriage to the daughter of an autochthonous spirit-ruler. This is a common theme in clan narratives, in which a founding ancestor's claim to village lands is frequently based on such a spirit-marriage.

6. "In contexts of conquest," writes Pratt (1986:139), "descriptions are likely to focus on the Other's amenability to domination and potential as a labor pool." This is to some extent true in the Karo case, but since an even more "amenable" labor pool (composed mostly of imported Javanese and Chinese laborers) was already present in the East Coast Residency, early colonial accounts tend rather to emphasize the "disorderly" and "anarchic" character of Karo social life, which suggested the necessity for subduing (and thus improving) this "wild" population. Yet lest too much weight is put upon the colonial construction of otherness, it should be noted that the Karo indeed resisted (often violently) proletarianization; colonial accounts thus (over-)stress what must have been to them an unpalatable reality rather than invent it out of the whole cloth.

7. The villages of Lingga and Gajah were, along with Surbakti, the perbapan villages of Urung Telu Kuru. Lingga and Gajah are located near the southwestern slopes of Mount Sibayak. Berastagi, as has been noted, is adjacent to the southeastern side of the mountain.

8. Horsting's reference to "long forgotten times" appears to be a gratuitous addition to the text. The Karo text of the myth is unfortunately not given, but the word used was probably *nai* (as indicated by its consistent use in other similar

narratives), which can be translated roughly as "in the not-immediate past". The word has none of the connotations of mythic time embodied, for example, in the fairytale "once upon a time." The distancing effect of this apparently minor emendation should be apparent.

9. Here, as elsewhere, Middendorp is the significant exception to the colonial rule. In his (1929b) essay on Karo narratives, he argues for a political-allegorical reading of the Karo version of the pan-regional story of Puteri Hijau, the "Green Princess," whom he identifies as symbolic of the Portuguese flag. Joustra's brief (1903:162–65) discussion of the Puteri Hijau story, while not necessarily supporting Middendorp's interpretation, does suggest other political dimensions of the tale.

10. There were, in fact, two urungs identified as Sepuluh Dua (XII) Kuta. One was the highland federation to which Berastagi belonged, and the other was the allied lowland cluster of villages that included Lau Cih.

11. A strategy of containment, according to Jameson, is an ideological formulation "which allows what can be thought to seem internally coherent in its own terms, while repressing the unthinkable . . . which lies beyond its boundaries" (Jameson 1981:53).

12. The *pulas* was an "incendiary letter" written on a bamboo internode stating the grievances (usually an unpaid debt) of an offended party and warning of future retribution if these grievances were not redressed. For examples of the texts of such letters, see Westenberg (1891:226; 1914:591–600) and Voorhoeve (1961, 1975).

13. The account that follows is my translation, from the transcript of our tape-recorded conversation. I have edited out several brief interruptions in the narrative flow. Two of these were my requests for clarification on small points: the tobacco seller's age at the time of his encounter with the spirits, and the appearance of the house of the mountain keramats. The third interruption occurred when the tobacco seller stopped to show us an example of the braided rattan bracelet, the rempu, which plays an important part in his story. These interruptions, which are fairly typical of Karo storytelling situations, do not appear to have significantly affected the shape of the tobacco seller's story.

CHAPTER FIVE. SIGNS OF HABITATION

1. Cf. Singarimbun (1960:117): *Balik-baliken bagi silan Jinabun*, "backwards like the *silan* of Jinabun," referring to a person who says the opposite of what he or she thinks.

2. In Malay, as in Westenberg's usage here, *keramat* refers to places of great supernatural power, most notably the graves of Islamic holy men. Karo sometimes use the term in this way but today more commonly apply it to the spirits themselves.

3. "If someone dies of smallpox, he is immediately buried. Scarcely has someone breathed his last when he is brought to his final resting place. For such a death no lamentation may be keened, much less a funeral ceremony held" (Richard Tampenawas, quoted in Wijngaarden 1894b:75).

4. *Si Biangsa* is the name used for certain powerful supernatural sites, and also for a magical preparation activated by the blood of a sacrificed red hound (Neumann 1927b). The pool is also known as Pertekteken.

5. The story ("Bunga Gedjap" 1962) was pseudonymously published under the title "Guru Pertawar Remé" ("The guru with the smallpox-cure"); its author, Ngukumi Barus, privately published a slightly revised version of the text a few years later. According to Barus, his version incorporated elements of several stories that he had learned in 1939 while doing harvest labor in the Sukanalu area of the Karo highlands (Uli Kozok, p.c.). Barus also wrote the script for the cassette drama, which was performed by the Lau Si Umangen Group under the direction of Abdi M. Noor Tarigan. It appeared (probably around 1978) under the title "Drama Klasik Karo Tandang Kumerlang Tandang Suasa" (Mini Hero ST-724) (Philip Yampolsky, p.c.). Cf. Proyek Penerbitan dan Pencatatan Kebudayaan Daerah (1981).

6. Selam Ginting is distinguishing here between the Karo term *keputusen,* "worthless," and its Indonesian cognate *keputusan,* "decision," both of which derive from the same root word *putus,* "to break off."

7. The reference here is to the evangelical prayer meetings that were at the time going on around Medan, which featured bonfires of magical paraphernalia brought in by Christian converts.

8. These offerings were taken home again by their donors, to be re-presented to the spirits in ritual contexts. The food and drink were consumed by the spirits (through their human "perches"), usually that evening; less perishable items—clothing, cosmetics, and the like—were saved and reused whenever the spirits descended.

9. Most of the material quoted here and throughout the remainder of this chapter comes from tape-recorded interviews; a few short comments are taken from my field notes. Because of conversational repetitions and digressions I have in the case of some recorded interviews used below edited a bit more freely than elsewhere in this book.

10. Nandé Ngena is referring here to a formulaic Karo phrase, *merga si lima, tutur si waluh, rakut si telu,* "the five clans, the eight relationships, the three bonds," by which Karo reference their system of kinship.

11. For example, two of the first Berastagi chapters of Merga Si Lima were named *Sada Perarih,* "One Accord," and *Mari Arih Ersada,* "Let's All Agree." (The third was *Balai Pustaka Adat Merga Si Lima,* roughly, the "Five Clans' Hall of Adat Literature," a play on the name of Indonesia's first publishing house, Balai Pustaka.)

12. Pa Raja Balé Purba was, for example, a member of the advisory council and the adat section of the Karo Cultural Consultative Board (Dewan Musyawarah Kebudayaan Karo, DMKK), an elite organization of Karo artists and intellectuals founded in 1961 under the leadership of Karo composer Djaga Depari.

13. In the Karo language, the prefix "per-" as it is used here denotes one who uses, owns, or is associated with something. Thus, for example, *perkedé* refers to a shop (*kedé*) owner, *perkantong samping* to Karo guerillas (in a famous revolutionary song) whose pants were made with unfashionable side pockets (*kantong samping*).

14. A relatively unsystematic survey of Karo cassette recordings at the time of my fieldwork suggests that "Odak Odak" was among the most popularly anthologized of quasi-traditional popular songs. While it was most often performed by a gendang orchestra, it also appeared in such unique forms as a Karo/Betawi (Jakarta) pop duet. The earliest recording of the popular dance version of "Odak Odak" that I have been able to locate is of a performance by perkolong-kolong singers Bengkel Pinem and Salam br. Tarigan on January 28, 1969, at the Berastagi home of Kongsi Purba, one of Merga Si Lima's original organizers.

15. Philip Yampolsky (1992) has used the term *motivic* to describe Karo melodic structure; here, I extend his suggestion to include lyrical improvisation as well.

16. On this particular occasion, Nandé Randal's words were: *hiya terteren nini mari ku rumah/ku rumah kam maba tawar tulbas/ku rumah kam maba dorma donia/é durmé kam dagé tinambaren 'tenda/tambah dareh min dagé tambah dagé ta-tamin/hiya terteren dagé terodak-odak/odak-odakken/odakken odak odak nipé soré/teruh bengkuang kel dagé si enggo ndubé/hiya terteren maka tamandu dagéna/éme kap penerus kel dagé durma donia/tawari kam kal dagé banci kam kel/arak-araken tinajaren kam enda.* Another time she began a slightly different version of the song (*odak odak nipé soré/teruh bengkuang si rulo*), which she described as a *pagar*, a "protection" to repel sorcery.

CHAPTER SIX. SOMEONE ELSE SPEAKING

1. Such an orphan, whose birth "pushes" or "tears away" its parents, is known as an *anak tunda kaïs*, a claw-hammer child. For examples, see Joustra (1904, 1914, 1918c).

2. The story of Beru Rengga Kuning was a popular one that most of my Karo acquaintances were familiar with; on one occasion I attended a medium's initiation in which "Beru Rengga Kuning" was one of the spirits that was claimed by the medium, but this was an unusual occurrence.

3. The account that follows is drawn primarily from Neumann's (1925) Karo-language text. This was published as a "supplement" to another (unrelated) text, and apparently later suppressed as obscene by the mission (cf. Neumann 1930). A very similar, though less risqué, contemporary Karo version appears in Loebis et al. (1979), along with an Indonesian-language "translation" that injects a moralizing tendency not present in (and indeed rather at odds with) the Karo text. A curious summary of Neumann's text appears in Voorhoeve (1927:161–62 [repr. 1977:469–70]), in which the amount of the marriage payment gambled away by her brother is given as a remarkable two thousand gold pieces, information that is not included in Neumann's version of the story.

4. Several readers have been puzzled by the presence of the orphan Beru Rengga Kuning's mother in the story. Because the children of a marriage "belong" to the descent group of the father, it is the death of the father that technically determines the children's status as orphans. See pp. 183–84.

5. In this regard, Beru Rengga Kuning resolves the dilemma of the Wana woman Paintobo, who "becomes" a man but is unable to gain the necessary

attributes of manhood—that is, a wife and a penis (Atkinson 1990). Cf. Rubin (1975:175): "Melpa women . . . can't get wives, they *are* wives, and what they get are husbands, an entirely different matter."

6. For an elaboration of the notion of "back talk," see Stewart (1990); on gender as parodic performance, see Butler (1990); on women as subjects of their own stories, see Heilbrun (1988) and N. Miller (1988a); on the problems of identifying sites of women's "resistance," see Abu-Lughod (1990).

7. This point is dramatically illustrated by the narrative position of Beru Rengga Kuning's "bride," whose wordless transfer from brother to sister to brother serves to confirm the "masculinity" of our female hero.

8. It is from this whistling throat-speech that the alternative term for the spirit medium, *perdéwal-déwal*, is derived.

9. I follow here Le Guin's (1981:188–89) playful reading of Aristotle's *On the Art of Poetry*.

10. To give one example: Nandé Laga's cryptic reference to the "three-chicken offering" shorthanded an entire apparatus of social legitimation, in which each of the three fundamental Karo kin groups provides a chicken of specific color to represent its participation and approval of the proceedings. Saying that they (the spirits) "ate them" (the offered chickens) similarly shorthands a ceremonial legitimation, whereby the spirits, through the vehicle of possessed bodies, consume the offerings and thereby ratify the new medium's initiation.

11. Dorinne Kondo (1990:260) makes a similar point in comparing the "commanding, masterful performance" of Japanese men's accounts of their work histories and those of female part-time workers: women's "narrative productions of work identity—far from single, seamless performance [*sic*] delivered to a rapt audience—were pervaded by a sense of fragmentation, both in the circumstances of the telling and in the narrative line, as the women simply moved from one part-time job to another, without a teleology to satisfy desires for totalizing narrative closure, a ready sense of progress, or some easily discernible way to perceive continuity."

12. The phrase, familiar from Karo love songs, is cited in Singarimbun's (1960) collection of Karo folk metaphors; I owe the leaf-count of the kepit to Philip Yampolsky (p.c.). As a point of information, five kepit make up one *mpedi*.

13. Why Joustra considered Karo women beyond the mission's reach is unclear; aside from certain reciprocally prescribed avoidance (*rebu*) relationships (e.g., HF-SW, BW-ZH) there are few restrictions on social intercourse between men and women. One of the mission's first converts was, in fact, a woman.

14. This material is drawn from a public lecture Joustra delivered to the Medan chapter of the Indische-Bond in 1902 on Karo "life, manners and customs." Although its references to Karo women are brief, it is the fullest colonial ethnographic account of Karo gender relations. It may be worth noting that Joustra's reputation within the Medan expatriate community was of being something of a *Jan hen*, a "house-husband" or domestic busybody, on account of his willingness to help with household chores. This "inappropriate" behavior did not help his poor standing in the local European community or with the Dutch Missionary Society (Rita S. Kipp 1990:186, 189).

15. The Karo lack of a "sense of sin" was a prominent early theme in the

mission literature. Cf. Joustra (1896:243); Neumann (1910:15–16); and Wijngaarden (1894a:174).

16. The plantation region of East Sumatra was notorious as a corrupt and
decadent society, where anything—not excepting women—could be bought. Cf.
Stoler (1989a, b); and the quasi-fictional descriptions in Hamka (1982) and Parlindungan (1964).

17. There is a long and varied history of feminist reaction to and appropriation of Lévi-Strauss's message that women are "the most precious possession of
men," and thus the ultimate gift upon whose exchange the moral order of society
is founded. A few pertinent examples might include de Lauretis (1984); Elshtain
(1981); Irigaray (1985); Leacock (1981); Mitchell (1974); Rubin (1975); and
Sedgwick (1985). Spivak (1987a:150–51) appropriately warns of the theoretical
and political risks inherent in any simple affirmation of the subject-object idiom
of the Lévi-Straussian formulation. See also Boon (1990:208).

18. Similar interpretations have been offered, in rather different social envi-
ronments, by Strathern (1988) for highland New Guinea; Tsing (1990a) and Atkinson (1990) for Indonesian egalitarian groups; and Watson (1986) for China.

19. The notion of narrative plausibility is drawn from N. Miller 1988b.

20. As Bakhtin defines it, a "loophole is the retention for oneself of the possibility for altering the ultimate, final meaning of one's own words. If a word retains
such a loophole this must inevitably be reflected in its structure. This potential
other meaning, that is, the loophole left open, accompanies the word like a
shadow. Judged by its meaning alone, the word with a loophole should be an
ultimate word and does present itself as such, but in fact it is only the penultimate
word and places after itself only a conditional, not a final, period." Chameleon-
like, the word-with-a-loophole is "always ready to change its tone and its ultimate
meaning" (Bakhtin 1984:233–34). Cf. Morson and Emerson (1990) for an extended discussion of the concept of the loophole in Bakhtin's writings.

21. Cf. Joustra (1904:28–84). In another version (Sitepu 1977:1) it is a bum-
blebee flying into the woman's mouth that produces the medium's "throat-
speech."

22. By "true" or "proper" impal, Nandé Laga does not necessarily mean her
actual FZS here; the term *impal* can properly be applied to more distantly related
kin as well. Cf. Singarimbun (1975:154).

23. Cf. Bakhtin (1981:324) on "double-voicing" and the posited narrator in
the novel.

24. Cf. Mohanty (1984) on the production of the "Third World woman"; and
the exchange between Spivak (1988, 1989b) and Parry (1987) on the "silent subaltern."

25. Cf. Haraway 1991b:195–96 on translation as a critical interpretive mode.

CHAPTER SEVEN. A STORYTELLER

1. In Ginting (1991) Pak Tua appears under the further pseudonym "Pa Surdam" (a *surdam* being a kind of end-blown bamboo flute noted for its melancholy
sound).

2. On the "Gendang Lima Puluh Kurang Dua," see Yampolsky and Steedly (forthcoming).

3. For more on the political implications of Indonesian religious policy, see Kipp and Rodgers (1987). In this collection especially relevant essays are by Atkinson and Tsing.

4. On this political transformation of language in revolutionary Indonesia, see B. Anderson (1989, 1990). Entertaining examples of revolutionary language in Karoland appear in the recording "Turi Turin Leto Kabang" by Panji Tarigan (Karo Cassette, n.d.).

5. Rumors as a counter-hegemonic mode of resistance are discussed in Arnold (1988); Guha (1988); James C. Scott (1990); and Spivak (1987b).

6. Reid (1979) gives the best general account of the political situation in East Sumatra in the early years of the revolution. Van Langenberg (1976) offers a more detailed picture of the political intricacies of the period; Surbakti (1977) gives a participant's perspective. Stoler (1988), who approaches the revolutionary movement from the perspective of its impact on the Javanese plantation workers, tends to blur the distinctions among the various militia groups in order to emphasize the difference between these groups and the Javanese workers.

7. On skirmishes between TNI and guerilla groups over weaponry, see Gintings (1975:41–42, 84).

8. "The PS accepted the argument of its leaders that the time was not ripe to implement socialism, that international support was necessary, and that unruly levelling movements from below had to be opposed. As its opponents repeatedly complained, its westernized leaders showed more faith in left-wing forces in the Netherlands than they did in the revolutionary fervour of the Indonesian people" (Reid 1974:83).

9. On Inoue's creation of the Kenkokutai, see Reid (1979:133–34). Reid and Akira (1986:79–110, 191–216) contains two long exerpts from Inoue's memoirs, *Bapa Janggut*. Inoue's earlier role in the suppression of the Karo Aron movement is described in Reid and Shiraishi (1976).

10. Here Pak Tua is referring specifically to the Resimen Halilintar, the "Lightning Regiment," which had originally been affiliated with Pesindo, the Socialist party. Initially BHL had been affiliated with Napindo, the Nationalist party's umbrella organization. In December 1946 Halilintar switched its affiliation to Napindo in order to create a unified command of guerilla forces. Relations between BHL and the groups previously associated with Pesindo remained acrimonious. See Surbakti (1977, 1979) for the Halilintar/Pesindo viewpoint on the conflict.

11. The extent to which literacy served as a class marker, and the importance it assumed in the internecine struggles between militia groups can be seen in the following comment by Major Liberty Malau of the Banteng Negara Brigade, giving the reason for his unit's attack on Harimau Liar (by then TNI Brigade A) units in South Tapanuli: "His answer was very simple, that is, he wanted to clean the Tapanuli area of rulers who were illiterate. Major Malau was hoping for a return of the intellectual class [*kaum intellectuil*], like when the institution of Military Governor Tapanuli/East Sumatra still functioned. He was hoping for Major General Dr. Gindo Siregar to return as leader. The reason was that if the leadership

was illiterate, the Republican side would be defeated in negotiations with the Dutch side, whose leaders were from the educated class [*kaum terpelajar*]" (Harahap 1986:50).

12. See Gintings (1975:37–40); Surbakti (1977:219–24); and Reid (1974: 115–16; 1979:256). Published (and oral) sources are rather at variance over the extent and motivation of this violence. According to Reid, BHL troops were involved in the killing of "thousands" of evacuees in August 1947; he suggests that the prime motive for the killings was the desire for loot. Reid's (p.c.) unpublished sources give estimates ranging from "tens of thousands" to "hundreds" of evacuees killed by BHL units and by village militia units; much of this violence seems to have taken place in Tapanuli and in the Simelungun region of East Sumatra rather than in Karoland. Gintings and Surbakti, both of whom were involved in controlling these "wild actions," downplay the extent of the violence against evacuees in Karoland and suggest that misguided enthusiasm for the nationalist cause, combined with a temporary "vacuum" in local political leadership, was the cause of the killings. Van Langenberg (1976:581) cites Chinese and Dutch reports that one hundred internees were killed in Kampung Merdeka near Berastagi by a BHL unit, and that Dutch-speaking Toba Bataks were also attacked and killed by men affiliated with BHL. Twenty-six Karo members of BHL were arrested and seven sentenced to death for crimes committed against evacuees at that time (ibid.:703–4).

13. See Surbakti (1979:339–49) for an account of the military "rationalization" from the viewpoint of Major Selamat Ginting, the leader of the Resimen Halilintar; Gintings (1975:83–84) describes the military rationalization from the perspective of the local TNI division. The one point that all of these groups seem to have agreed upon was that any effort to consolidate them should be resisted.

14. One traveler of the period reports: "Travelling from Medan to Kabanjahe, and particularly between Pancur Batu and Berastagi was a hazardous procedure in the years 1956–57. There were several groups of bandits or highwaymen (*gerombolan*) that ambushed cars, buses or trucks travelling singly and unescorted through the hill swidden farms and rain forest astride the thin and tortuous asphalt road along the escarpment between Pancur Batu (formerly Arnhemia) and Sibolangit. But despite the sudden and unexpected nature of their attacks, the gerombolan were seldom cut-throat murderers. They were interested basically in extracting loot from travellers, merchants and above all government officials" (Jaspan 1974:47). For a moving commentary on military rationalization, see Selamat Ginting's letter of protest dated November 12, 1948, and reproduced in Surbakti (1979:344–48).

15. Brother-in-law (*silih*, WB, ZH) being the standard reciprocal term of address between male friends.

CHAPTER EIGHT. AN UNCERTAIN DEATH

1. The so-called coup attempt of 1965 is described in greater detail in Nugroho and Saleh (1967); Anderson and McVey (1971); Hughes (1968); McDonald (1980); and Crouch (1978).

2. However, the extent of the violence may be indicated by noting that the province of North Sumatra contained the largest Communist party organization in Indonesia outside of Java. Its membership was mostly composed of Javanese estate workers and Karo peasants, with many leadership positions held by Karo. The role of the PKI and particularly its affiliated labor unions in North Sumatran politics is discussed in detail in Stoler (1985). For a series of recent essays on the massacres in Java and Bali, see Cribb (1990).

3. *Recidivis* was literally the term used by the press to describe the targets of the mysterious marksmen. It was generally understood to mean "gangster" or "habitual criminal."

4. When I wrote this in 1992, the image of Rodney King's brutal beating by Los Angeles police officers was repeatedly playing on the television news, accompanied often enough by the same sort of public rationale that my Karo friends gave for Indonesia's mysterious marksmen. Rereading the passage now (in January 1993) I am still painfully disturbed by the ease with which, a decade ago, I could confirm my friends' distinction between American "rule of law" and Indonesian extralegal state violence.

5. Although I had frequently visited the village I call "Kuta Kepultaken," I had never met Nandé Rita prior to the seance. I was invited to attend and record the event by one of her close kalimbubu, a prominent local citizen who felt that "an anthropologist should know about such things," and by the officiating medium, Nandé Pajuh, with whom I was slightly acquainted. The perumah bégu seance lasted from 9:30 P.M. until 8:00 A.M. the following morning, and the description that follows is necessarily abbreviated. With the family's permission, the entire ceremony was tape-recorded, except for Setia Aron's conversations, during which, at the family's request, the tape recorder was turned off. Thus, my account of this section of the seance is drawn from my written notes.

Glossary

UNLESS otherwise indicated, the terms below are in the Karo language. The following abbreviations are used:

(C.), Chinese   (J.), Japanese
(D.), Dutch   (K.), Karo
(I.), Indonesian   (M.), Malay

adat (M., I.). Custom.

Afdeling (D.). District; colonial territorial division below the residency (province), headed by an assistant resident.

agama (I.). Religion; *Agama Pemena*, the "original religion" of Karo spirit veneration.

anak beru. "Wife-receivers"; literally, "descendants of the [clan/subclan's] woman"; persons or groups related to one's own natal group through marriage to that group's women (daughters or sisters).

aron. Work crew, usually composed of unmarried men and women and traditionally employed for agricultural labor with the promise of a dance festival (*guro-guro aron*) after the harvest.

bangsa taneh. Founding lineage of a village or village ward.

bapa. Father; also FB, MZH.

Barisan Harimau Liar (I.). "Wild Tiger Brigade," Sumatran paramilitary group during the Indonesian Revolution.

Barisan Pemuda Indonesia (I.). Indonesian Youth Brigade, umbrella organization of nationalist youth groups during the Indonesian Revolution.

bégu. Ghost, spirit of a deceased human being; in contemporary usage sometimes refers generally to malevolent spirits. *Bégu jabu*, a family's ancestral spirits; *bégu sintua*, the "eldest" ancestral spirit of a social unit (household, village ward, village).

belah purnama. Full moon, the midpoint (fourteenth day) of the Karo lunar cycle.

belo. Betel leaf (*Piper betle L.*); *belo bujur*, betel prepared for chewing, with lime and a slice of areca nut; *belo cawir*, "complete" betel leaf with its stem and tip intact; *belo siwah sepulsa* (*siwah sepuluh sada*, nine-and-eleven), a packet of twenty betel leaves with ingredients for chewing, usually including lime, areca nut, and shredded tobacco.

beru. Woman of a particular clan or subclan.

BHL. See *Barisan Harimau Liar.*

bibi. Aunt (MZ, FZ, HM), auntie (affectionately).

bicara. Custom; today it generally is used to refer to local variations in what is seen as the universal pattern of Karo adat.

bilang-bilang. Sung lament, often about unrequited love, which may be incised on bamboo for presentation to a young man's lover.

blik (D.). Gasoline tin used as a unit of volume, approximately fifteen kilograms.

bouw (D.). Building, lot; as an areal measure, .71 hectare.

BPI. See *Barisan Pemuda Indonesia.*

bunga-bunga. Red hibiscus flower (*Hibiscus rosa-sinensis L.*).

camat (I.). Head of a regional subdivision, roughly equivalent in Karoland to the Dutch-instituted office of *raja urung.*

cerita (M., I.). Story.

cibal. To set something in place; *cibal-cibalen, percibalen,* situation, position, also the site for making small offerings, usually in isolated locations as on mountainsides or along forest paths.

cukera dudu. Auspicious thirteenth day of the Karo lunar cycle.

daulat (M., K.). Charisma, the quality of sovereignty. (Cf. *kedaulatan rakyat, pendaulatan.*)

Depdikbud (I.). Acronym for *Departemen Pendidikan dan Kebudayaan,* the Indonesian Department of Education and Culture.

deraham (M., K.). Small Acehnese gold coin used in the marriage payment to symbolize the legitimacy of the union.

DGI, *Dewan Gereja Indonesia* (I.). Indonesian Council of Churches.

dibata teridah. "Visible god," a term of respect for the kalimbubu.

dusun (M., K.). Frontier, colony; in East Sumatra the term was used to refer specifically to the area of Karo settlement in the piedmont area of Upper Deli, Serdang, and Langkat.

erkata kerahung. "Throat-speech," the distinctive whistling sounds indicating that a spirit is speaking through the medium's throat.

erpangir ku lau. Hairwashing rite performed as a preliminary step in most Karo rituals; as a cure for misfortune it is also frequently performed by itself.

gambir (M.). Aromatic resin produced by the catechu plant (*Uncaria gambir Roxb.*) often used to flavor betel for chewing.

GBKP. See *Gereja Batak Karo Protestan.*

gendang. Small drum, orchestra; *gendang mbelin, gendang lima sedalanen,* the "large" five-piece orchestra; *gendang telu sedalanen, gendang keteng-keteng,* the three-piece orchestra. *Gendang bégu* or *gendang mistik,* pejorative terms for the three-piece orchestra that is today the ensemble of choice for indoor ceremonies of spirit veneration.

Gereja Batak Karo Protestan. The independent Karo Protestant Church.

gerombolan (I.). Highwayman, gang of bandits.

Gestapu (I.). Acronym for *Gerakan September Tiga Puluh,* the September 30th Movement, the term for the alleged Communist coup attempt of 1965.

Gestok (I.). Term for the military reprisals that followed Gestapu.

Golkar (I.). Acronym for *Golongan Karya,* "functional groups," quasi-party organization associated with the Suharto government.

guro-guro aron. See *aron.*

Guru. Curer; if unspecified, the term usually refers to the trained male curer/magician. *Guru perdéwal-déwal* is the general term for a spirit medium; *guru si baso* specifically refers to a medium who performs the funeral seance.

hantu. Malevolent nature spirit.

hasil taneh (M./K.). Annual fee paid for land rental in the market towns of the Karo highlands under colonial rule.

impal. Cross-cousin (MBD-FZS); also, potential marriage mate.

jambur. Men's house; community center or pavilion for public meetings.

jé. Literally, "there"; a woman's husband's clan.

jinujung. "Something carried on the head"; a spirit officially installed as a person's supernatural protector; a medium's guide or go-between in negotiations with the spirit world.

juma. Unirrigated field.

kaka. Elder sibling; *kaka tua*, eldest sibling.

kalimbubu. Groups or persons to whom one is related through one's mother's natal clan; those whose women go to one's own group in marriage.

kampung (M.). Village.

kedai (M.). Shop.

kedaulatan rakyat (I.). Popular sovereignty.

Kempetei (J.). Secret police.

Kenkokutai (J.). Civil defense organization founded during the Japanese occupation of Indonesia.

kepercayaan (I.). "Belief"; local systems of spiritual devotion not recognized by the Indonesian government.

kepit. Bundle of twenty betel leaves.

keramat (M., K.). Arabic-derived Malay term for a place of great supernatural power, usually the grave of a holy man; used more generally in Karo to refer to powerful benevolent spirits associated with particular geographical locations.

kerja. Ceremony; *kerja nini*, "grandparents' ceremony," a ritual held to entertain the spirits in return for their continued assistance.

kesain. Village subdivision or ward; also the village common where public ceremonies may be held.

keteng-keteng. Struck tube zither made of bamboo and commonly used in the three-piece gendang orchestra.

kinitekan. See *tek*.

Kompeni, Kumpeni (M./D.). "The Company," general term for the Dutch colonial establishment in the East Indies.

Korte Verklaring (D.). "Short Declaration"; treaty signed by selected Karo rulers in 1904 acknowledging their subordination to the colonial state.

Landschap (D.). Region; colonial territorial division below the onderafdeling (subdistrict). In the Karo highlands, the highest level of native government, headed by a sibayak.

mama. Mother's brother; also WF.

mami. Mother's brother's wife; also WM.

mas. Gold (also *emas* [M.]). See also *tukur mas, ulu mas*.

merdeka (I.). Independence, freedom; *Merdeka atau Mati*, "freedom or death," a revolutionary slogan.

merga. Clan, subclan; *mergana*, a man "of the clan" X.

mesinteng. "Keen," the quality of precision in a medium's insight or performance.

nandé. Mother; also FBW; *nandé tengah*, father's middle brother's wife.

Napindo (I.). Umbrella organization of radical guerilla groups associated with the Indonesian Nationalist party (PNI) during the revolution.

nini. Grandparent; also, polite term of address for spirits.

Onderafdeling (D.). Subdistrict; colonial territorial division below the afdeling (district), headed by a controleur.

padung-padung. Large double-coiled silver earrings once worn by Karo women, but now obsolete.

pandé. Craftsman.

pasar (M.,I.). Market; also (in Medan), road.

pendaulatan (I.). Euphemism for revolutionary killing of suspected collaborators or "feudal" elements of the population.

penggual. Drummer.

pengulu. Head of a village or village ward.

peninggeren. "Perch"; the entranced medium who serves as a vehicle for a spirit in a formal context.

perbapan. Originary village of a group of related communities.

perbégu. "Ghost-keeper," a somewhat pejorative term for the followers of Agama Pemena.

percaya (I.). See *kepercayaan.*

percibalen. See *cibal.*

perdéwal-déwal. See *guru.*

perkentas. Go-between; specifically, the spirit who acts as a conduit or contact between a medium and the spirit world.

perkolong-kolong. Professional singer-dancer.

pertami-tami. "Flatterers"; those persons, usually women, who interrogate and tend the spirits that descend during the course of a ritual.

perumah bégu. "Calling the ghost back home"; funeral seance.

Pesindo, Pemuda Sosialis Indonesia (I.). Umbrella organization of nationalist youth groups affiliated with the Indonesian Socialist party during the revolutionary period.

pesuruh. Factotum, servant (literally, "one who is given orders").

pikul (M.). Unit of measure based on the standard double carrying-basket, approximately sixty-two kilograms.

PKI, Partai Komunis Indonesia (I.). Indonesian Communist party.

PNI, Partai Nasionalis Indonesia (I.). Indonesian Nationalist party (Sukarnoist).

present taneh (D./K.). Initial fee paid for land rental in the market towns of the Karo highlands under colonial rule.

pustaka. Book, usually of magical formulas and divinatory designs, made of folded bark and written in an indigenous syllabary script.

rayat (also *rakyat* [M.]). The people, common people.

rebu. Prohibited or avoidance relationship.

rimo mungkur. "Kaffir lime" (*Citrus hystrix*); rough-skinned citron used in purification ceremonies as well as in magical preparations.

rust en orde (D.). Peace and order.

sawah (I.). Irrigated rice field.

sejarah (M.). History.

seluk. Trance, "possession" by a spirit.

sembah-sembahen. Shrine, place of obeisance.

senina. Same-sex clanmate.

seruné. Small double-reed aerophone similar to an oboe, the melody instrument of the five-piece orchestra.

soedara (M.). Brother, kinsman (properly, *saudara*).

taki (or *taki-taki*). Wisdom, strategy, tricks.

taneh kosong. "Empty" or open land, unused fields.

tek. To believe, believe in; *kinitekan*, system of "belief."

tengku (M.). Aristocratic title.

toké (C./I., *tauke*). In standard Indonesian the term refers specifically to a Chinese shopkeeper, but also may be used informally to refer to an employer or boss; Karo use the term in the latter sense to refer to any mid-range entrepreneur. Thus the owner of a fleet of buses would be described as a *toké motor*, rather than a *permotor* (the owner/operator of a single vehicle).

tongkat. Staff, walking stick; specifically, the carved staff that was an important part of the paraphernalia of a male guru.

tudung. Flat, pillow-shaped turban characteristically worn by Karo women.

tukur mas (toekoermas). "Bought with gold," polite term for a man's wife.

tula. Usually inauspicious fifteenth day of the Karo lunar cycle.

turang. Opposite-sex sibling; also (poetically), sweetheart.

turangku. WBW, HZH; an avoidance relationship.

turi-turin. Story, history, sequence.

ulu mas. Portion of a marriage payment given to the groom's kalimbubu by birth (i.e., his mother's brothers).

umang. Supernatural wild men, distinguished by backward-turned feet, who inhabit wild regions of forest and mountainside.

unjuken. Portion of a marriage payment distributed among the bride's agnates.

urung. Colonial territorial division below the landschap (region); based on putative Karo federations of related villages, headed by a raja urung.

Bibliography

Abu-Lughod, L.

1990   "The Romance of Resistance: Tracing Transformations of Power through Bedouin Women." *American Ethnologist* 17(1):41–55.

1992   "Writing against Culture." In R. Fox, ed., *Recapturing Anthropology*, pp. 137–62. Santa Fe: School of American Research Press.

Althusser, L.

1970   "Idéologie et Appareils Idéologiques d'État (Notes pour une Recherche)." *La Pensée* 151:3–38.

1971   "Ideology and Ideological State Apparatuses (Notes towards an Investigation)." In L. Althusser, *Lenin and Philosophy and Other Essays*, trans. Ben Brewster, pp. 127–86. New York: Monthly Review Press.

Andaya, B. W.

1975   "The Nature of the State in Eighteenth Century Perak." In A. Reid and L. Castles, eds., *Pre-Colonial State Systems in Southeast Asia*, pp. 22–35. Kuala Lumpur: Malaysian Branch of the Royal Asiatic Society.

Anderson, B.

1972   *Java in a Time of Revolution*. Ithaca: Cornell University Press.

1989   "Reading 'Revenge' by Pramoedya Ananta Toer (1978–1982)." In A. L. Becker, ed., *Writing on the Tongue*. Michigan Papers on South and Southeast Asia. Ann Arbor: Center for South and Southeast Asian Studies, University of Michigan.

1990   *Language and Power: Exploring Political Cultures in Indonesia*. Ithaca: Cornell University Press.

Anderson, B., and R. McVey

1971   "A Preliminary Analysis of the 1 October 1965 Coup in Indonesia." Interim Report Series, Modern Indonesian Project, Cornell University.

Anderson, J.

1971a   *Acheen and the Ports on the North and East Coasts of Sumatra*. Singapore: Oxford University Press.

1971b   *Mission to the East Coast of Sumatra in 1823*. Singapore: Oxford University Press.

Anon.

1917   "De Perhoedamdam-Beweging." *Indische Gids* 39:676–77.

1918   "De Perhoedamdam-Beweging." *Indische Gids* 40:624–25.

Ardener, E.

1989a   "Belief and the Problem of Women." In E. Ardener, *The Voice of Prophecy and Other Essays*, pp. 72–85. London: Basil Blackwood.

1989b   "The 'Problem' Revisited." In Ardener, *Voice of Prophecy*, pp. 127–33.

Arnold, D.

1988   "Touching the Body: Perspectives on the Indian Plague, 1868–1900." In R. Guha and G. Spivak, eds., *Selected Subaltern Studies*, pp. 391–427. New York: Oxford University Press.

Atkinson, J.

1987   "Religions in Dialogue: The Construction of an Indonesian Minority Religion." In R. S. Kipp and S. Rodgers, eds., *Indonesian Religions in Transition*, pp. 171–86. Tucson: University of Arizona Press.

1990   "How Gender Makes a Difference in Wana Society." In J. Atkinson and S. Errington, eds., *Power and Difference*, pp. 127–52. Stanford: Stanford University Press.

Bakhtin, M.

1981   "Discourse in the Novel." In M. Bakhtin, *The Dialogic Imagination*, pp. 259–422. Austin: University of Texas Press.

1984   *Problems of Dostoevsky's Poetics*. Minneapolis: University of Minnesota Press.

Bangun, P.

1981   "Pelapisan Sosial di Kabanjahe." Ph.D. dissertation, Universitas Indonesia, Jakarta.

Barthes, R.

1972   "Dominici, or the Triumph of Literature." In R. Barthes, *Mythologies*, pp. 43–46. New York: Hill and Wang.

1985   "The Third Meaning." In R. Barthes, *The Responsibility of Forms*, trans. R. Howard, pp. 41–62. New York: Farrar Strauss and Giroux.

1986a "The Death of the Author." In R. Barthes, *The Rustle of Language*, trans. R. Howard, pp. 49–55. New York: Farrar Strauss and Giroux.

1986b "The Reality Effect." In Barthes, *Rustle of Language*, pp. 141–48.

1986c "From Work to Text." In Barthes, *Rustle of Language*, pp. 56–64.

Bartlett, H. H.

1918   1918 Sumatra Journal. Bartlett Collection, Bentley Historical Library, University of Michigan, Box 11.

1973   *The Labors of the Datoe*. Michigan Papers on South and Southeast Asia 5. Ann Arbor: Center for South and Southeast Asian Studies, University of Michigan.

Beekman, E. (ed.)

1988   *Fugitive Dreams: An Anthology of Dutch Colonial Literature.* Amherst: University of Massachusetts Press.

Belo, J.

1960   *Trance in Bali*. New York: Columbia University Press.

Benjamin, W.

1969a "The Storyteller." In W. Benjamin, *Illuminations*, pp. 83–110. New York: Schocken Books.

1969b "The Task of the Translator." In Benjamin, *Illuminations*, pp. 69–82.

1969c "Theses on the Philosophy of History." In Benjamin, *Illuminations*, pp. 253–64.

Berg, E. J. van den

1905   "Verwachtingen aangaande de Hoogvlakte. 30 December 1904." *Mededeelingen van wege het Nederlandsch Zendelinggenootschap* [subsequently: *MNZ*] 49:383–85.

1906   "Jaarverslag over 1905, van den Arbeid op de Hoogvlakte, Zendingsressort Kaban-djahe." *MNZ* 50:246–55.

1909   "Jaarverslag over de Zending op de Hoogvlakte in 1908." *MNZ* 53:71–81.

1920   "De Parhoedamdambeweging." *MNZ* 64:22–38.

Berg, E. J. van den, and J. H. Neumann

1908   "De Batoe Kemang, nabij Medan." *Bijdragen tot de Taal-, Land- en Volkenkunde* [subsequently: *Bijd.*] 60:89–92.

Bhabha, H.

1984   "Of Mimicry and Man: The Ambivalence of Colonial Discourse." *October* 28:125–33.

Bloch, M.

1989   "The Symbolism of Money in Imerina." In J. Parry and M. Bloch, eds., *Money and the Morality of Exchange*, pp. 165–90. Cambridge: Cambridge University Press.

Bodaan, L.

1915   "De Werkkring Serdang." *MNZ* 59:113–23.

Bohannan, P., and G. Dalton

1962   *Markets in Africa*. Chicago: Northwestern University Press.

Boon, J.

1977   *The Anthropological Romance of Bali*. Cambridge: Cambridge University Press.

1990   *Affinities and Extremes*. Chicago: University of Chicago Press.

Bourdieu, P.

1977   *Outline of a Theory of Practice*. Cambridge: Cambridge University Press.

Bowen, J.

1986   "On the Political Construction of Tradition: Gotong Royong in Indonesia." *Journal of Asian Studies* 45:545–61.

1991   *Sumatran Politics and Poetics*. New Haven: Yale University Press.

Brahma Putro

1981   *Karo dari Jaman ke Jaman*. Medan: Yayasan Massa.

Brenner, J. F. von

1894   *Besuch bei den Kannibalen Sumatras*. Wurzburg: Leo Woerl.

Bronson, B.

1977   "Exchange at the Upstream and Downstream Ends: Notes toward a Functional Model of the Coastal State in Southeast Asia." In K. Hutterer, ed., *Economic Exchange and Social Interaction in Southeast Asia*, pp. 39–52. Michigan Papers on South and Southeast Asia 13. Ann Arbor: Center for South and Southeast Asian Studies, University of Michigan.

Brooks, P.

1984   *Reading for the Plot: Design and Intention in Narrative*. New York: Vintage.

Bruner, E.

1961   "Urbanization and Ethnic Identity in North Sumatra." *American Anthropologist* 63:508–21.

Buku Tahunan 1984 Propinsi Sumatera Utara

1985   Medan: P. T. Saguna Karya.

"Bunga Gedjap" (pseud. Ng. Barus)

 1962 "Guru Pertawar Reme." *Almanak Kebudayaan Karo*, pp. 51–62. Kabanjahé: Badan Musjawarah Kebudayaan Karo.

Butler, J.

 1990 *Gender Trouble*. New York: Routledge.

Callahan, S.

 1986 "A Case for Pro-Life Feminism: Abortion and the Sexual Agenda." *Commonweal*, Apr. 25, pp. 232–38.

Calvino, I.

 1981 *If on a winter's night a traveler*. New York: Harcourt Brace Jovanovich.

Carby, H.

 1990 "The Politics of Difference." *Ms: The World of Women*, Sept.–Oct., pp. 84–85.

Castles, L.

 1975 "Statelessness and Stateforming Tendencies among the Bataks before Colonial Rule." In A. Reid and L. Castles, eds., *Pre-Colonial State Systems in Southeast Asia*, pp. 67–76. Kuala Lumpur: Malaysian Branch of the Royal Asiatic Society.

Chodorow, N.

 1978 *The Reproduction of Mothering: Psychoanalysis and the Sociology of Gender*. Los Angeles: University of California Press.

Christian, B.

 1988 "The Race for Theory. *Feminist Studies* 14(1):67–80.

Clauss, W.

 1982 *Economic and Social Change among the Simalungun Batak of North Sumatra*. Bieleferder Studien zur Entwicklungssoziologie. Band 15. Saarbrucken: Verlag Breitenbach.

Clifford, J.

 1988 "On Ethnographic Authority." In J. Clifford, *The Predicament of Culture*, pp. 21–54. Cambridge: Harvard University Press.

Comaroff, Jean

 1985 *Body of Power, Spirit of Resistance*. Chicago: University of Chicago Press.

Comaroff, Jean, and John Comaroff

 1991 *Of Revelation and Revolution*. Vol. 1. Chicago: University of Chicago Press.

Crapanzano, V.

 1977a "Introduction." In V. Crapanzano and V. Garrison, eds., *Case Studies in Spirit Possession*, pp. 1–40. New York: John Wiley and Sons.

 1977b "Mohammed and Dawia." In Crapanzano and Garrison, *Case Studies in Spirit Possession*, pp. 141–76.

Cribb, R.

 1991 *Gangsters and Revolutionaries: The Jakarta People's Militia and the Indonesian Revolution, 1945–1949*. Honolulu: University of Hawaii Press.

Cribb, R. (ed.)

 1990   *The Indonesian Killings: Studies from Java and Bali*. Monash Papers on
         Southeast Asia 21. Centre of Southeast Asian Studies, Monash Univer-
         sity.

Crouch, H.

 1978   *The Army and Politics in Indonesia*. Ithaca: Cornell University Press.

Culler, J.

 1982   *On Deconstruction*. Ithaca: Cornell University Press.

Cunningham, C.

 1958   *The Postwar Migration of the Toba-Bataks to East Sumatra*. Cultural
         Report Series 5. New Haven: Yale University.

 1989   "Celebrating a Toba Batak National Hero: An Indonesian Rite of Iden-
         tity." In S. Russell and C. Cunningham, eds., *Changing Rites, Changing
         Lives*, pp. 167–200. Michigan Studies of South and Southeast Asia 1.
         Ann Arbor: Center for South and Southeast Asian Studies, University of
         Michigan.

de Certeau, M.

 1984   *The Practice of Everyday Life*. Berkeley: University of California Press.

 1988   "Discourse Disturbed: The Sorcerer's Speech." In M. de Certeau, *The
         Writing of History*, pp. 244–68. New York: Columbia University Press.

de Lauretis, T.

 1984   *Alice Doesn't*. Bloomington: Indiana University Press.

 1986   "Feminist Studies/Critical Studies: Issues, Terms, and Contexts." In
         T. de Lauretis, ed., *Feminist Studies/Critical Studies*, pp. 1–19. Bloom-
         ington: Indiana University Press.

de Man, P.

 1983   *Blindness and Insight*. 2d rev. ed. Minneapolis: University of Minne-
         sota Press.

Dirks, N.

 1990   "History as a Sign of the Modern." *Public Culture* 2(2):25–32.

Drakard, J.

 1990   *A Malay Frontier: Unity and Duality in a Sumatran Kingdom*. Studies
         on Southeast Asia. Ithaca: Cornell University Southeast Asia Program.

Edisaputra

 1985   *Bedjo Harimau Sumatera Dalam Perang Kemerdekaan*. Jakarta:
         Yayasan Bina Satria '45.

 1987   *Sumatera dalam Perang Kemerdekaan*. Jakarta: Yayasan Bina Satria
         '45.

Edwards McKinnon, E.

 1984   "Kota Cina: Its Context and Meaning in the Trade of Southeast Asia in
         the Twelfth to Fourteenth Centuries." Ph.D. dissertation, Cornell Uni-
         versity.

Eliot, T. S.

 1943   *Four Quartets*. New York: Harcourt Brace Jovanovich.

Elshtain, E.

 1981   *Public Man, Private Woman*. Princeton: Princeton University Press.

Ezerman, H.

1926 "Memorie van Overgave van de Afdeling Simeloengoen- en Karolanden." Microfilm. Zug: IDC.

Fabian, J.

1983 *Time and the Other*. New York: Columbia University Press.

Faulkner, W.

1986 *Absalom, Absalom!* New York: Vintage. [repr. 1936]

Feldman, A.

1991 *Formations of Violence*. Chicago: University of Chicago Press.

Fields, K. E.

1985 *Revival and Rebellion in Colonial Central Africa: Revisions to the Theory of Indirect Rule*. Princeton: Princeton University Press.

Foucault, M.

1979 "What Is an Author?" In J. Harari, ed., *Textual Strategies: Perspectives in Post-Structuralist Criticism*, pp. 141–60. Ithaca: Cornell University Press.

1982 "The Subject and Power." *Critical Inquiry* 8(4):777–96.

Fox, R.

1992 "Introduction: Working in the Present." In R. Fox, ed., *Recapturing Anthropology*, pp. 1–16. Santa Fe: School of American Research Press.

Fox-Genovese, E.

1982 "Placing Women's History in History." *New Left Review* 133:5–29.

Furnivall, J. S.

1939 *Netherlands India*. Cambridge: Cambridge University Press.

Fuss, D.

1989a "Lesbian and Gay Theory: The Question of Identity Politics." In D. Fuss, *Essentially Speaking: Feminism, Nature and Difference*, pp. 97–112. New York: Routledge.

1989b "Writing as a Feminist." In Fuss, *Essentially Speaking*, pp. 23–38.

Geertz, C.

1972 "Religious Change and Social Order in Soeharto's Indonesia." *Asia* 27:62–84.

1973a " 'Internal conversion' in Contemporary Bali." In C. Geertz, *The Interpretation of Cultures*, pp. 170–92. New York: Basic Books.

1973b "Ritual and Social Change: A Javanese Example." In Geertz, *Interpretation of Cultures*, pp. 142–69.

1973c "Thick Description: Toward an Interpretive Theory of Culture." In Geertz, *Interpretation of Cultures*, pp. 3–30.

1988 *Works and Lives: The Anthropologist as Author*. Stanford: Stanford University Press.

Ginting, J.

1986 "Pandangan tentang Gangguan Jiwa dan Penanggulangannya secara Tradisional pada Masyarakat Karo." Drs. thesis, Universitas Sumatera Utara.

1991 "Pa Surdam, a Karo Batak *Guru*." In A. Sibeth, *The Batak: Peoples of the Island of Sumatra*, pp. 85–98. New York: Thames and Hudson.

Gintings, J.
1968   *Bukit Kadir*. Medan: C. V. Umum.
1975   *Titi Bambu*. Medan: C. V. Umum.
Gintings, M., trans.
1978   *Upadeça: Tentang Ajaran-Ajaran Agama Hindu (Bahasa Karo)*. [Denpasar?]: Parisada Hindu Dharma.
Guha, R.
1988   "The Prose of Counter-insurgency." In R. Guha and G. Spivak, eds., *Selected Subaltern Studies*, pp. 45–85. New York: Oxford University Press.
Guillaume, H.
1901   "Karo-Batak Zending. Jaarverslag aangaande het Zendingsressort Boekoem." *MNZ* 45:120–28.
1903   "Jaarverslag over het Ressort Boekoem." *MNZ* 47:230–40.
Haan, C. de
1870   "Verslag van eene Reis in de Battaklanden." *Verhandelingen Batavia Genootschap* [subsequently: VBG] 38:1–57.
Hagen, B.
1882   "Beitrage zur Kenntniss der Battareligion." *Tijdschrift voor Indische Taal-, Land en Volkenkunde* [subsequently: *Tijd.*] 28:498–545.
Hamka [Haji Abdul Malik Karim Amrullah]
1982   *Merantau ke Deli*. 8th ed. Jakarta: Pustaka Panjimas.
Harahap, H. M. D.
1986   *Perang Gerilya Tapanuli Selatan Front Sipirok*. Jakarta: P. T. Azanmahani.
Haraway, D.
1988   "Situated Knowledges: The Science Question in Feminism and the Privilege of Partial Perspective." *Feminist Studies* 14(3):575–600.
1991a " 'Gender' for a Marxist Dictionary: The Sexual Politics of a Word." In D. Haraway, *Simians, Cyborgs and Women: The Reinvention of Nature*, pp. 127–48. New York: Routledge.
1991b "Reading Buchi Emecheta: Contests for 'Women's Experience' in Women's Studies." In Haraway, *Simians, Cyborgs and Women*, pp. 109–26.
Harding, S.
1990   "If I Should Die before I Wake: Jerry Falwell's Pro-Life Gospel." In F. Ginsburg and A. Tsing, eds., *Uncertain Terms*, pp. 76–97. Boston: Beacon.
Hartsock, N.
1983   *Money, Sex, and Power*. New York: Longman.
Hefner, R. W.
1985   *Hindu Javanese: Tengger Tradition and Islam*. Princeton: Princeton University Press.
Heilbrun, C.
1988   *Writing a Woman's Life*. New York: Ballantine.
Hertz, R.
1960   "The Collective Representation of Death." In R. Hertz, *Death and the*

Right Hand, trans. R. Needham and C. Needham. Glencoe, Ill.: Free Press.

Herzfeld, M.

1991   "Silence, Submission, and Subversion: Toward a Poetics of Womanhood." In P. Loizos and E. Papataxiarchis, eds., *Contested Identities: Gender and Kinship in Modern Greece*, pp. 79–97. Princeton: Princeton University Press.

Hofman, P.

1933   "Across Sumatra." *Nederlandsch Indië Oud en Nieuw* 18:209–218.

Holleman, F. D.

1933   "Memorie van Overgave van de Onderafdeling Karolanden." Microfilm. Zug: IDC.

Horsting, L. H. C.

1927   "De vulkaan Sibajak." *Nederlandsch Indië Oud en Nieuw* 12:85–94.

hooks, b.

1990a   "Culture to Culture: Ethnography and Cultural Studies as Critical Intervention." In b. hooks, *Yearning: Race, Gender and Cultural Politics*, pp. 123–34. Boston: South End Press.

1990b   "Third World Diva Girls: Politics of Feminist Solidarity." In hooks, *Yearning*, pp. 89–102.

Huender, W.

1929   "Het Karo-Bataksche Huis." *Bijd.* 85:511–23.

1930   "Peroemah Begoe." *Koloniaal Tijdschrift* 19:14–20.

Hughes, J.

1968   *The End of Sukarno*. London: Angus and Robertson.

Intisari Adat-Istiadat Karo.

n.d.   2 vols. Medan: C. V. Ulih Saber.

Irigaray, L.

1985   *This Sex Which Is Not One*. Ithaca: Cornell University Press.

Iser, W.

1978   *The Act of Reading*. Baltimore: Johns Hopkins University Press.

Jackson, M.

1989   *Paths toward a Clearing: Radical Empiricism and Ethnographic Inquiry*. Bloomington: Indiana University Press.

Jaggar, A.

1983   *Feminist Politics and Human Nature*. Sussex: Harvester Press.

James, H.

1986   "The Figure in the Carpet." In H. James, *The Figure in the Carpet and Other Stories*, pp. 357–400. London: Penguin.

Jameson, F.

1981   *The Political Unconscious*. Ithaca: Cornell University Press.

Jardine, A., and P. Smith (eds.)

1987   *Men in Feminism*. London: Methuen.

Jaspan, M. A.

1974   "Karo-land and Its People in 1955–1959: Some Personal Reminiscences." *Sumatra Research Bulletin* 3:46–52.

Joustra, M.
1896 "Verslag van de Zending onder de Karo-Bataks, over het jaar 1895."
MNZ 40:220–44.
1897 "De Zending over de Karo-Batak's: Jaarverslag over 1896." *MNZ*
41:141–62.
1899a "Verslag aangaande de Delizending over 1898." *MNZ* 43:325–38.
1899b "Verslag van een Bezoek aan het Onafhankelijk Karo-Batak-Gebied."
MNZ 43:123–51.
1901a "Een en ander uit de Litteratuur der Karo-Bataks." *MNZ* 45:91–101.
1901b "Iets over Bataksche Litteratuur (vervolg.1)." *MNZ* 45:165–85.
1901c "Karo-Batak Zending. Jaarverslag over 1900." *MNZ* 45:109–19.
1901d "Naar het Landschap Goenoeng2. 15–22 October 1900." *MNZ*
45:69–90.
1901e "Verslag van de Zending onder de Karo-Bataks over 1899." *MNZ*
45:1–17.
1902a "Het Jaar 1901 onder de Karo-Bataks." *MNZ* 46:50–62.
1902b "Het Leven, de Zeden en Gewoonten der Bataks." *MNZ* 46:385–426.
1902c "Het Persilihi Mbelin." *MNZ* 46:1–22.
1902d "Iets over Bataksche Litteratuur (vervolg.)." *MNZ* 46:357–72.
1903 "Iets over Bataksche Litteratuur (vervolg.). *MNZ* 47:140–72.
1904 "Karo-Bataksche Vertellingen." *VBG* 56:1–123.
1905 "Referaat Gehouden op de Jaarvergadering van het Ned. Zend. Gen.
Woensday 12 Juli 1905." *MNZ* 49:355–69.
1910 *Batakspiegel*. Uitgaven van het Bataksch Instituut 3. Leiden: S. C. van
Doesburgh.
1914 *Turi-Turin Karo*. Vol. 1. Uitgaven van het Bataksch Instituut 10. Leiden: S. C. van Doesburgh.
1915 *Van Medan naar Padang en Terug*. Uitgaven van het Bataksch Instituut
11. Leiden: S. C. van Doesburgh.
1918a "De Bataks IV. Godsdienstige Stroomingen." *Indië* 2:147, 163, 179,
195.
1918b *Kroniek 1913–1917*. Uitgaven van het Bataksch Instituut 15. Leiden:
S. C. van Doesburgh.
1918c *Turi-Turin Karo*. Vol. 2. Uitgaven van het Bataksch Instituut 14. Leiden: S. C. van Doesburgh.
Kahin, G. Mc.T.
1952 *Nationalism and Revolution in Indonesia*. Ithaca: Cornell University
Press.
Kamuf, P.
1980 "Writing like a Woman." In S. McConnell-Ginet, R. Boerker, and
N. Furman, eds., *Women and Language in Literature and Society*, pp.
284–99. New York: Praeger.
Kapferer, B.
1983 *A Celebration of Demons*. Bloomington: Indiana University Press.
Kartomi, M.
1985 *Musical Instruments of Indonesia: An Introductory Handbook*. Mel-
bourne: Indonesian Arts Society.

Kehoe, A., and D. Giletti
  1981　"Women's Preponderance in Possession Cults: The Calcium-deficiency Hypothesis Extended." *American Anthropologist* 83:549–61.
"Kembali kemasyarakat karena keinsjafan."
  1952　*Waspada*, Mar. 25, p. 1.
Kempees, J. C. J.
  1905　*De Tocht van Overste Van Daalen door de Gajo-, Alas- en Bataklanden.* Amsterdam: J. C. Dalmiejer.
Kessler, C.
  1977　"Conflict and Sovereignty in a Malay Spirit Seance." In Crapanzano and Garrison, *Case Studies in Spirit Possession*, pp. 295–332.
Kilson, M.
  1966　*Political Change in a West African State: A Study in the Modernization Process.* Cambridge: Harvard University Press.
King, K.
  1986　"The Situation of Lesbianism as Feminism's Magical Sign: Contests for Meaning and the U.S. Women's Movement, 1968–72." *Communication* 9(1):65–91.
Kipp, Richard D.
  1978　"The Social Organization of Karo Batak Rural Migration." Ph.D. dissertation, University of Pittsburgh.
Kipp, Rita S.
  1976　"The Ideology of Kinship in Karo Batak Ritual." Ph.D. dissertation, University of Pittsburgh.
  1979　"The Thread of Three Colors: The Ideology of Kinship in Karo Batak Funerals." In E. Bruner and J. Becker, eds., *Art, Ritual and Society in Indonesia.* Papers in International Studies Southeast Asia Series 53:62–94. Athens: Ohio University Center for International Studies Southeast Asia Program.
  1984　"Terms for Kith and Kin." *American Anthropologist* 86:905–24.
  1985　"Karo Batak Rice Rituals Then and Now." In R. Carle, ed., *Cultures and Societies of North Sumatra*, pp. 253–73. Berlin: Dietrich Reimer Verlag.
  1986　"Terms of Endearment: Karo Batak Lovers as Siblings." *American Ethnologist* 13(4):632–45.
  1990　*The Early Years of a Dutch Colonial Mission: The Karo Field.* Ann Arbor: University of Michigan Press.
  1993　*Dissociated Identities: Ethnicity, Religion, and Class in an Indonesian Society.* Ann Arbor: University of Michigan Press.
Kipp, Rita S., and S. Rodgers (eds.)
  1987　*Indonesian Religions in Transition.* Tucson: University of Arizona Press.
Kondo, D.
  1990　*Crafting Selves.* Chicago: University of Chicago Press.
Korn, V. E.
  1953　"Batakse offerande." *Bijd.* 109:32–51.
Kozok, U.
  1991a　"Historical Survey: The Northern Batak Lands." In A. Sibeth, *The*

Batak: Peoples of the Island of Sumatra, pp. 26–30. New York: Thames and Hudson.

1991b "Batak Script and Literature. In Sibeth, *Batak*, pp. 100–114.

Kroef, J. M. van der

    1970 "Messianic Movements in the Celebes, Sumatra and Borneo." In Sylvia L. Thrupp, ed., *Millennial Dreams in Action*, pp. 80–121. New York: Schocken Books.

Kruijt, H. C.

    1891 "Bezoekreis op het Plateau van Deli (Karo-land)." *MNZ* 35:309–411.

Lan, D.

    1989 "Resistance to the Present by the Past: Mediums and Money in Zimbabwe." In J. Parry and M. Bloch, *Money and the Morality of Exchange*, pp. 191–208. Cambridge: Cambridge University Press.

Langenberg, M. van

    1976 "National Revolution in North Sumatra. Sumatra Timur and Tapanuli 1942–1950." Ph.D. dissertation, University of Sydney.

    1986 "Analysing Indonesia's New Order State: A Keywords Approach." *Review of Indonesian and Malaysian Affairs* 20:1–47.

Lanting, P. A.

    1937 "Vervolgmemorie van Overgave van de Onderafdeling Karolanden." Microfilm. Zug: IDC.

Leach, E.

    1961 *Rethinking Anthropology*. London: Athlone Press.

Leacock, E.

    1981 *Myths of Male Dominance*. New York: Monthly Review Press.

Le Guin, U.

    1981 "It Was a Dark and Stormy Night; or, Why Are We Huddling about the Campfire?" In W. J. T. Mitchell, ed., *On Narrative*, pp. 187–96. Chicago: University of Chicago Press.

Lekkerkerker, C.

    1916 *Land en Volk van Sumatra*. Leiden: E. J. Brill.

Lévi-Strauss, C.

    1969 *The Elementary Structures of Kinship*. Boston: Beacon.

Lewis, I. M.

    1989 *Ecstatic Religion*. 2d ed. London: Routledge.

Liere, A. M. van

    1931 "Vervolgmemorie van Overgave van de Onderafdeling Karolanden." Microfilm. Zug: IDC.

Loeb, E. M.

    1972 *Sumatra: Its History and People*. Kuala Lumpur: Oxford University Press [repr. 1935].

Loebis, R., et al.

    1979 *Peranan Cerita Rakyat Daerah Karo Sebagai Sarana Pendidikan*. Medan: Mahasiswa Fakultas Sastra USU.

Luckman Sinar

    1971 *Sari Sejarah Serdang*. Medan: n.p.

Lumban Tobing, N. S., and E. Gobée

    1919 "Dari Hal Parsihoedamdam." *Koloniaal Tijdschrift* 8:389–96.

MacKinnon, K.

1989   *Toward a Feminist Theory of the State*. Cambridge: Harvard University Press.

Mahadi

1987   "Islam and Law in Indonesia." In R. S. Kipp and S. Rodgers, eds., *Indonesian Religions in Transition*, pp. 211–20. Tucson: University of Arizona Press.

Mani, A.

1979   *Indian Settlement and Religious Accommodation in North Sumatra: A Reconnaissance*. Wisconsin Papers on Southeast Asia 5. Madison: Center for Southeast Asian Studies, University of Wisconsin.

Mani, L.

1990   "Contentious Traditions: The Debate on *sati* in Colonial India." In K. Sangari and S. Vaid, eds., *Recasting Women*, pp. 88–126. New Brunswick: Rutgers University Press.

1992   "Cultural Theory, Colonial Texts: Reading Eyewitness Accounts of Widow Burning." In P. Grossberg, C. Nelson, and P. Treichler, eds., *Cultural Studies*, pp. 392–405. New York: Routledge.

Marsden, W.

1966   *History of Sumatra*. London: Oxford University Press [repr. 1811].

Marx, K.

1967   *Capital*. New York: International Publishers.

1970   *A Contribution to the Critique of Political Economy*. New York: New World.

Marx, K., and F. Engels

1965   *The German Ideology*. London: Lawrence and Wishart.

Mauss, M.

1967   *The Gift*. Trans. Ian Cunnison. New York: Norton.

McDonald, H.

1980   *Suharto's Indonesia*. Honolulu: University of Hawaii Press.

McGann, J.

1991   *The Textual Condition*. Princeton: Princeton University Press.

Meindersma, G. W.

1938   "Memorie van Overgave van de Afdeling Simelungun- en Karolanden." Microfilm. Zug: IDC.

Micsic, J. N.

1979   "Archaeology, Trade and Society in Northeast Sumatra." Ph.D. dissertation, Cornell University.

1985   "Traditional Sumatran Trade." *Bulletin de l'Ecole Francaise d'Extreme-Orient* 74:423–67.

Middendorp, W.

1920   "Het recht van den sterkste of de onafhankelijke Karo hoogvlakte." *Verslagen van het Indisch Genootschap, vergadering van 5/11/1920*, pp. 125–51. Den Haag.

1922   "Het inwerken van Westersche krachten op een Indonesisch volk (de Karo Bataks)." *Socialistische Gids* 7:329–465.

1929a "The Administration of the Outer Provinces of the Netherlands Indies." In B. Schrieke, ed., *The Effect of Western Influence on Native Civilisations in the Malay Archipelago*, pp. 34–70. Batavia: G. Kolff.

1929b "Oude verhalen: Een nieuwe geschiedbron." *Feestbundel* II, Koninklijke Bataviaasch Genootschap van Kunsten en Wetenschappen, pp. 158–77. Batavia: Albrecht.

Milan Women's Bookstore Collective

1990 *Sexual Difference: A Theory of Social-Symbolic Practice*. Bloomington: University of Indiana Press.

Miller, J. H.

1980 "The Figure in the Carpet." *Poetics Today* 1(3):107–18.

Miller, N.

1988a "Changing the Subject: Authorship, Writing, and the Reader." In N. Miller, *Subject to Change*, pp. 102–22. New York: Columbia University Press.

1988b "Emphasis Added: Plots and Plausibilities in Women's Fiction." In Miller, *Subject to Change*, pp. 25–46.

Milner, A. C.

1982 *Kerajaan: Malay Political Culture on the Eve of Colonial Rule*. Tucson: University of Arizona Press.

Milner, A. C., E. Edwards McKinnon, and Luckman Sinar

1978 "A Note on Aru and Kota Cina." *Indonesia* 26:1–42.

Mitchell, J.

1974 *Psychoanalysis and Feminism*. New York: Pantheon.

Mohanty, Chandra

1984 "Under Western Eyes: Feminist Scholarship and Colonial Discourse." *Boundary* 2/3:333–58.

1988 "Feminist Encounters: Locating the Politics of Experience." *Copyright* 1:30–44.

Moore, W. R.

1930 "Among the Hill Tribes of Sumatra." *National Geographic* 57:186–221.

Moraga, C., and G. Anzaldua (eds.)

1981 *This Bridge Called My Back: Writings by Radical Women of Color*. Watertown: Persephone.

Morgan, R. (ed.)

1984 *Sisterhood Is Global*. Garden City, N.Y.: Anchor/Doubleday.

Morson, G., and C. Emerson

1990 *Mikhail Bakhtin: Creation of a Prosaics*. Stanford: Stanford University Press.

Nandy, A.

1983 *The Intimate Enemy*. Delhi: Oxford University Press.

Napitupulu, O. L.

1971 *Perang Batak Perang Sisingamangaradja*. Jakarta: Jajasan Pahlawan Nasional Sisingamangaradja.

Needham, R.

1978 "Classification and Alliance among the Karo: An Appreciation." *Bijd.* 134:116–48.

Neumann, J. H.
  1901   "Karo-Batak Zending.—Verslag aangaande het Zendingressort Boe-
         loeh-Awar." *MNZ* 45:129–38.
  1902a "De Begoe in de Godsdienstige Begrippen der Karo-Bataks in de
         Doesoen." *MNZ* 46:23–39.
  1902b "Verslag aangaande den Toestand der Zendingswerkzaamheden en der
         Gemeente in het Ressort Sibolangit over het Jaar 1901." *MNZ* 46:63–
         74.
  1904a "De Tendi in verband met Si Dajang." *MNZ* 48:101–45.
  1904b "Een en Ander aangaande de Karo-Bataks." *MNZ* 48:361–76.
  1910   "De Bataksche Goeroe." *MNZ* 54:1–18.
  1915   "Het 25-Jarig Bestaan der Deli-Zending." *MNZ* 59:107–10.
  1918   "De Perhoedamdam in Deli." *MNZ* 62:185–90.
  1922   *Schets der Karo Bataksche Spraakkunst. VBG* 63:4de stuk.
  1925   *Si Beru Rengga Koening ras Poestaka Ginting.* Kabanjahe: n.p.
  1926   "Bijdrage tot de Geschiedenis der Karo-Batakstammen" (pt. 1). *Bijd.*
         82:1–36.
  1927a "Bijdrage tot de Geschiedenis der Karo-Batakstammen" (pt. 2). *Bijd.*
         83:162–80.
  1927b "Karo-Bataksche Offerplaatsen." *Bijd.* 83:514–51.
  1929   "De Bilang-Bilang (1)." *Feestbundel,* Koninklijke Bataviaasch Ge-
         nootschap voor Kunsten en Wettenschappen, pp. 215–222.
  1930   "Poestaka Ginting." *Tijd.* 70:1–51.
  1933   "De Bilang-Bilang (2)." *Tijd.* 73:185–215.
  1939   "Aantekeningen over de Karo-Bataks." *Tijd.* 79:529–71.
  1949   *Een Jaar onder de Karo Bataks.* 2d ed. Medan: V. H. Varekamp.
  1951   *Karo-Bataks-Nederlands Woordenboek.* Medan: V. H. Varekamp
         (Lembaga Kebudayaan Indonesia).
Nugroho, N., and I. Saleh
  1967   *The Coup Attempt of the "30 September Movement" in Indonesia.*
         Jakarta: Pembimbing Massa.
Obeyesekere, G.
  1970   "The Idiom of Demonic Possession: A Case Study." *Social Science and
         Medicine* 4:97–111.
O'Hanlon, R.
  1988   "Recovering the Subject: *Subaltern Studies* and Histories of Resistance
         in Colonial South Asia." *Modern Asian Studies* 22(1):189–224.
O'Malley, W. J.
  1977   "Indonesia in the Great Depression: A Study of East Sumatra and Jog-
         jakarta in the 1930's." Ph.D. dissertation, Cornell University.
Orgel, S.
  1991   "What Is a Text?" In D. Kastan and P. Stallybrass, eds., *Staging the
         Renaissance,* pp. 83–87. New York: Routledge.
Ortner, S.
  1989   *High Religion: A Cultural and Political History of Sherpa Buddhism.*
         Princeton: Princeton University Press.

Parlindungan, M. O.
  1964   *Tuanku Rao.* Jakarta: Tanjung Pengharapan.
Parry, B.
  1987   "Problems in Current Theories of Colonial Discourse." *Oxford Literary Review* 9(1):17–58.
Parry, J., and M. Bloch
  1989   Introduction. In J. Parry and M. Bloch, eds., *Money and the Morality of Exchange*, pp. 1–32. Cambridge: Cambridge University Press.
Pedersen, P.
  1970   *Batak Blood and Protestant Soul.* Grand Rapids, Mich.: William B. Eerdmans.
Pelzer, K.
  1978   *Planter and Peasant.* Verhandelingen van het Koninklijk Instituut voor Taal-, Land-, en Volkenkunde 84. 'S-Gravenhage: Martinus Nijhoff.
  1982   *Planters against Peasants.* Verhandelingen van het Koningklijk Instituut voor Taal-, Land-, en Volkenkunde 97. 'S-Gravenhage: Martinus Nijhoff.
Pemberton, J.
  n.d.   "The State of Culture." Unpublished ms.
Percy, W.
  1987   "Metaphor as Mistake." In W. Percy, *The Message in the Bottle*, pp. 64–82. New York: Farrar, Straus and Giroux.
Pesik, H.
  1895   "Iets uit de Aanteekeningen van den Onderwijzer te Tanjoeng Beringin." *MNZ* 39:58–76.
Plon, E.
  1874   *Thorvaldsen: His Life and Works.* London: Richard Bentley and Son.
Polanyi, K.
  1944   *The Great Transformation.* Boston: Beacon.
Pratt, M. L.
  1986   "Scratches on the Face of the Country; or, What Mr. Barrow Saw in the Land of the Bushmen." In H. L. Gates, Jr., ed., *"Race," Writing and Difference*, pp. 138–62. Chicago: University of Chicago Press.
Proyek Pembinaan dan Bimbingan Aliran Kepercayaan/Faham Keagamaan
  1979   *Monograph Keagamaan/Kepercayaan terhadap Tuhan Yang Maha Esa, menurut Propinsi dan Kabupaten/Kotamadya seluruh Indonesia.* Jakarta: Departemen Agama.
Proyek Penerbitan dan Pencatatan Kebudayaan Daerah
  1981   *Cerita Rakyat Sumatra Utara.* Jakarta: Proyek Penerbitan Buku Sastra Indonesia dan Daerah, Department Pendidikan dan Kebudayaan.
Ranger, T.
  1983   "The Invention of Tradition in Colonial Africa." In E. Hobsbawm and T. Ranger, eds., *The Invention of Tradition*, pp. 211–62. Cambridge: Cambridge University Press.
  1985   *Peasant Consciousness and Guerilla War in Zimbabwe.* Berkeley: University of California Press.

Reddy, W.

   1984   *The Rise of Market Culture*. Cambridge: Cambridge University Press.

Reid, A.

   1974   *The Indonesian National Revolution 1945–1950*. Hawthorn, Australia: Longman.

   1979   *The Blood of the People*. Kuala Lumpur: Oxford University Press.

Reid, A., and Akira Oki (eds.)

   1986   *The Japanese Experience in Indonesia: Selected Memoirs of 1942–1945*. Papers in International Studies Southeast Asia Series 72. Athens: Ohio University Center for International Studies.

Reid, A., and Shiraishi Saya

   1976   "Rural Unrest in Sumatra, 1942: A Japanese Report." *Indonesia* 21:115–33.

Rhijn, M. van

   1936   "Memorie van Overgave van de Afdeling Simeloengoen- en Karolanden." Microfilm. Zug: IDC.

Rich, A.

   1979   "Foreword: On History, Illiteracy, Passivity, Violence, and Women's Culture." In A. Rich, *On Lies, Secrets, and Silence*, pp. 9–18. New York: Norton.

Rodgers Siregar, S.

   1979   "A Modern Batak Horja: Innovation in Sipirok Adat Ceremonial." *Indonesia* 27:102–28.

   1981   *Adat, Islam and Christianity in a Batak Homeland*. Papers in International Studies Southeast Asia Series 57. Athens: Ohio University Center for International Studies.

Romer, R.

   1910   "Bijdrage tot de Geneeskunst der Karo-Batak's." *Tijd.* 50(afl.3):205–87.

Rosaldo, M.

   1980   *Knowledge and Passion*. Cambridge: Cambridge University Press.

Rosaldo, R.

   1980   *Ilongot Headhunting, 1883–1974*. Stanford: Stanford University Press.

   1986   "Ilongot Hunting as Story and Experience." In V. Turner and E. Bruner, eds., *The Anthropology of Experience*, pp. 97–138. Urbana: University of Illinois Press.

Rubin, G.

   1975   "The Traffic in Women: Notes on the 'Political Economy' of Sex." In R. Reiter, ed., *Toward an Anthropology of Women*, pp. 157–210. New York: Monthly Review Press.

Said, M.

   1961   *Singamangaradja XII*. Medan: Waspada.

   1973   "What Was the 'Social Revolution of 1946' in East Sumatra?" *Indonesia* 15:145–86, Trans. B. Anderson and T. Siagian.

Salaman, R.

   1985   *The History and Social Influence of the Potato*. Cambridge: Cambridge University Press.

Schadee, W. H. M.
1918   *Geschiedenis van Sumatra's Oostkust.* Vol. 1. Uitgave van het Oostkust van Sumatra-Instituut, Mededeeling 2. Amsterdam: B. van Mantgem.
1920   *De Uitbreiding van Ons Gezag in de Bataklanden.* Uitgaven van het Bataksch Instituut 19. Leiden: S. C. Van Doesburgh.

Scholes, R.
1987   "Reading 'Like a Man.' " In A. Jardine and P. Smith, eds., *Men in Feminism,* pp. 204–18. London: Methuen.

Scholz, U.
1983   *The Natural Regions of Sumatra and Their Agricultural Production Pattern.* Vol. 1. Bogor: Central Research Institute for Food Crops, Ministry of Agriculture, Republic of Indonesia.

Schor, N.
1989   *Reading in Detail: Aesthetics and the Feminine.* New York: Routledge.

Schreiner, Lothar
1972   *Adat und Evangelium.* Missionswissenschaftliche Forschungen, Deutschen Gesellschaft fur Missionswissenschaft. Band 7.

Schweickart, P.
1991   "Reading Ourselves: Toward a Feminist Theory of Reading." In R. Warhol and D. Herndl, eds., *Feminisms: An Anthology of Literary Theory and Criticism,* pp. 525–50. New Brunswick: Rutgers University Press.

Scott, James C.
1976   *The Moral Economy of the Peasant.* New Haven: Yale University Press.
1985   *Weapons of the Weak.* New Haven: Yale University Press.
1990   *Domination and the Arts of Resistance.* New Haven: Yale University Press.

Scott, Joan W.
1988   *Gender and the Politics of History.* New York: Columbia University Press.
1991   "The Evidence of Experience." *Critical Inquiry* 17:773–97.

Sedgwick, E.
1985   *Between Men: English Literature and Male Homosocial Desire.* New York: Columbia University Press.

Sedjarah Kebudajaan Karo: Isi Dari Kongres Tahun 1958
[n.d.]   Kabandjahe: Toko Bukit Mbelin Gunana.

Sembiring, T.
1987   "Lagu 'Mengungsi.' Sada Lagu Perjuangan Kemerdekaan Indonesia." In R. Carle, ed., *Cultures and Societies of North Sumatra.* Berlin: Dietrich Reimer Verlag.

Sherman, G.
1990   *Rice, Rupees, and Ritual.* Stanford: Stanford University Press.

Showalter, E.
1981   "Feminist Criticism in the Wilderness." *Critical Inquiry* 8(2):179–206.

Sibarani, A.
1979   *Perjuangan Pahlawan Nasional Sisingamangaraja XII.* Jakarta: P. T. Bona Torajaya.

Sibeth, A.

1991 *The Batak: Peoples of the Island of Sumatra.* New York: Thames and Hudson.

Sidjabat, W. B.

1982 *Ahu Si Singamangaraja: Arti Historis, Politis, Ekonomis dan Religius Si Singamangaraja XII.* Jakarta: Penerbit Sinar Harapan.

Siegel, J.

1986 *Solo in the New Order.* Princeton: Princeton University Press.

Simon, A.

1985 "The Terminology of Batak Instrumental Music in Northern Sumatra." *Yearbook for Traditional Music* 17:113–45.

1987 *Gendang Karo* (2 LP records). Museum Collection Berlin (West) 13. Berlin: Museum für Völkerkunde.

Singarimbun, M.

1960 *1000 Perumpaman Karo.* Medan: C. V. "Ulih Saber."

1975 *Kinship, Descent and Alliance among the Karo Bataks.* Berkeley: University of California Press.

Sitepu, P.

1977 *Buku Kesenian Kebudayaan Tradisionil Karo.* Medan: n.p.

Slaats, H., and M. K. Portier

1981 *Grondenrecht en zun verwerkeluking in de Karo Batakse Dorpssamenleving.* Nijmegen: Publikaties over Volksrecht 9. Katholieke Universiteit.

Spelman, E.

1988 *Inessential Woman: Problems of Exclusion in Feminist Thought.* Boston: Beacon.

Spivak, G.

1986 "Three Women's Texts and a Critique of Imperialism." In H. L. Gates, ed., *"Race," Writing and Difference,* pp. 262–80.

1987a "French Feminism in an International Frame." In G. Spivak, *In Other Worlds,* pp. 134–53. New York: Methuen.

1987b "Subaltern Studies: Deconstructing Historiography." In Spivak, *In Other Worlds,* pp. 197–221.

1988 "Can the Subaltern Speak?" In C. Nelson and L. Grossberg, eds., *Marxism and the Interpretation of Culture,* pp. 271–315. Urbana: University of Illinois Press.

1989a "In a Word." Interview (with Ellen Rooney). *Differences* 1(2):124–56.

1989b "Naming Gayatri Spivak." *Stanford Humanities Review* 1(1):84–97.

Stallybrass, P.

1992 "Shakespeare, the Individual and the Text." In L. Grossberg, C. Nelson, and P. Treichler, *Cultural Studies,* pp. 593–610. New York: Routledge.

Steedly, M.

1988 "Severing the Bonds of Love: A Case Study in Soul Loss." *Social Science and Medicine* 27(8):841–56.

1989a "Hanging Without a Rope: The Politics of Representation in Colonial and Post-colonial Karoland." Ph.D. dissertation, University of Michigan, Ann Arbor.

1989b "Innocence as Authority: Shifting Gender Roles in Karo Curing Ritual." In S. Russell and C. Cunningham, eds., *Changing Lives, Changing Rites: Ritual and Social Dynamics in Philippine and Indonesian Uplands*, pp. 133–66. Michigan Studies of South and Southeast Asia 1. Ann Arbor: Center for South and Southeast Asian Studies, University of Michigan.

1989c "Modern Travellers: Curing and Commodification in Contemporary Karo Society." Unpublished ms.

1992 "Exodus and Alienation: A Karo Woman's Song of Revolutionary Exile." Paper presented at the annual meeting of the Association for Asian Studies.

Steedman, C.
1986 *Landscape for a Good Woman*. New Brunswick: Rutgers University Press.

van den Steenhoven, G.
1970 *The Land of Kerenda: Background, Procedure and Settlement of Case 43/S/1969 in the State Court at Kabandjahe (Karo-Land, North Sumatra)*. Publicaties over Adatrecht 5, Katholieke Universiteit, Nijmegen.

Stewart, K.
1990 "Backtalking the Wilderness: 'Appalachian' En-genderings." In F. Ginsburg and A. Tsing, eds., *Uncertain Terms*, pp. 43–56. Boston: Beacon.

1992 "On the Politics of Cultural Theory: A Case for 'Contaminated' Cultural Critique." *Social Research* 58(2):395–412.

Stoler, A.
1985 *Capitalism and Confrontation in Sumatra's Plantation Belt*. New Haven: Yale University Press.

1988 "Working the Revolution: Plantation Laborers and the People's Militia in North Sumatra." *Journal of Asian Studies* 47:227–48.

1989a "Making Empire Respectable: The Politics of Race and Sexual Morality in 20th-century Colonial Cultures." *American Ethnologist* 16(4):634–60.

1989b "Rethinking Colonial Categories: European Communities and the Boundaries of Rule." *Comparative Studies in Society and History* 31:134–61.

1992 " 'In Cold Blood': Hierarchies of Credibility and the Politics of Colonial Narratives." *Representations* 37:151–89.

Strathern, M.
1988 *The Gender of the Gift*. Berkeley: University of California Press.

Surbakti, Ar.
1977 *Perang Kemerdekaan di Karo Area*. Vol. 1. Medan: Pro Patria.

1979 *Perang Kemerdekaan di Karo Area*. Vol. 2. Medan: Pro Patria.

Talens, J. P.
1915 "De Karo-Hoogvlakte." *MNZ* 59:124–34.

Tamboen, P.

1952   *Adat-Istiadat Karo.* Jakarta: Balai Pustaka.

Tampenawas, R.

1895   "Een en Ander uit de Aanteekeningen van R. Tampenawas, te Pernangenen." *MNZ* 39:227–46.

Tarigan, P.

n.d.   *Turi Turin Leto Kabang.* Kabanjahe: Karo Cassette.

Taussig, M.

1992   "Maleficium: State Fetishism." In M. Taussig, *The Nervous System*, pp. 111–40. New York: Routledge.

Team Penelitian GBKP

1976   *Benih yang Tumbuh 4. Suatu Survey Mengenai: Gereja Batak Karo Protestan.* Jakarta: Lembaga Penelitian dan Studi Dewan Gereja-gereja di Indonesia.

Teraniaja

1932   "Adat Poesaka Karo atawa Goero2 Aroon Membawa Kemadjoean Tanah Karo Dimasa Doeloe." *Poesaka Karo*, Feb. 2, 1932, p. 1; Feb. 19, 1932, p. 1.

Tideman, J.

1922   *Simeloengoen.* Leiden: Van Doesburgh.

Trinh, Minh-ha T.

1989   *Woman, Native, Other.* Bloomington: University of Indiana Press.

Tsing, A.

1987   "A Rhetoric of Centers in a Religion of the Periphery." In R. S. Kipp and S. Rodgers, eds., *Indonesian Religions in Transition*, pp. 197–210. Tucson: University of Arizona Press.

1990a   "Gender and Performance in Meratus Dispute Settlement." In Atkinson and Errington, *Power and Difference*, pp. 95–126. Stanford: Stanford University Press.

1990b   "Monster Stories: Women Charged with Perinatal Endangerment." In F. Ginsburg and A. Tsing, eds., *Uncertain Terms*, pp. 282–99. Boston: Beacon.

Tuuk, H. N. van der

1861   *Bataksch-Nederduitsch Woordenboek.* Amsterdam: Frederik Muller.

Ukur, F., and F. Cooley

1979   *Jerih dan Juang: Laporan Nasional Survai Menyeluruh Gereja di Indonesia.* Jakarta: Lembaga Penelitian dan Studi—DGI.

Viner, A. C.

1979   "The Changing Batak." *Journal of the Malay Branch of the Royal Asiatic Society* 52(2):84–112.

Volker, T.

1928   *From Primeval Forest to Cultivation*, trans. A. North. Medan: Deli Planters' Association.

Volkman, T.

1990   "Visions and Revisions: Toraja Culture and the Tourist Gaze." *American Ethnologist* 17(1):91–110.

Voorhoeve, P.
1927 "Overzicht van volksverhalen der Bataks." Ph.D. dissertation, Rijks-
universiteit, Leiden [reprinted in P. Voorhoeve, *Codices Batacici*].
1955 *Critical Survey of Studies on the Languages of Sumatra*. 'S-Gravenhage:
Martinus Nijhoff.
1961 *The Chester Beatty Library: A Catalogue of the Batak Manuscripts*.
Dublin: Hodges Figgis.
1975 *The Royal Library, Copenhagen: Catalogue of Indonesian Manuscripts*. Part 1. Batak Manuscripts. Copenhagen: Royal Library.
1977 *Codices Batacici*. Leiden: Universitaire Pers.
Vuurmans, H.
1930 "De pers in het Karo-Batakland." *MNZ* 1930:328–45.
Warneck, Joh.
1977 *Toba-Batak-Deutsches Worterbuch*. Den Haag: Martinus Nijhoff.
Warren, C.
1990 "Rhetoric and Resistance: Popular Political Culture in Bali." *Anthropological Forum* 6(2):191–206.
Watson, R.
1986 "The Named and the Nameless: Gender and Person in Chinese Society." *American Ethnologist* 13(4):619–31.
Westenberg, C. J.
1891 "Aanteekeningen omtrent de Godsdienstige Begrippen der Karo-Bataks."
Bijd. 5(7):208–53.
1904a "Nota omtrent eene Militaire Excursie naar de Karolanden in September 1904." Appendix to G. Schaap, Gewestelijk Bestuur, Residentie
Oostkust van Sumatra No. 4903/4. Mimeograph copy in the Wasson
Collection, Cornell University.
1904b "Nota omtrent de Onderwerping der tot Nu toe Onafhankelijke Karolanden, alsmeed omtrent de Beginselen, Volgens Welke de Bataklanden
in 't Algemeen en de Karolanden in 't Bijzonder 't Best Bestuurd Zullen
Kunnen Worden." Appendix to G. Schaap, Gewestelijk Bestuur, Residentie Oostkust van Sumatra No. 4903/4. Mimeograph copy in the
Wasson Collection, Cornell University.
1914 "Adatrechtspraak en Adatrechtspleging der Karo-Bataks." *Bijd.* 69:
455–600.
Wijngaarden, J. K.
1893 "De Zending onder de Karau-Bataks." *MNZ* 37:397–407. [Reprinted
from *De Opwekker* 151, Oct. 1, 1893. Commentary added.]
1894a "Verslag omtrent de Zending onder de Karau-Bataks over 1893."
MNZ 38:133–85.
1894b "De Zending onder de Karau-Bataks (Deli). Een en Ander uit de Aanteekeningen der Minahassische Onderwijzers." *MNZ* 38:62–85.
Williams, R.
1977 *Marxism and Literature*. Oxford: Oxford University Press.
Yampolsky, P. (ed.)
1992 *Music of Nias and North Sumatra: Hoho, Gendang Karo, Gondang*

Toba. Music of Indonesia 4. Smithsonian/Folkways Recordings (SF-40420).

Yampolsky, P., and M. Steedly
  forthcoming *Gendang Lima Puluh Kurang Dua*. Surakarta: Masyarakat Seni Pertunjukan Indonesia.

Young, I. M.
  1990   "Humanism, Gynocentrism, and Feminist Politics." In I. Young, *Throwing Like a Girl and Other Essays in Feminist Philosophy and Social Theory*, pp. 73–91. Bloomington: Indiana University Press.

Index